A Dictionary
of
Sociolinguistics

A Dictionary
of
Sociolinguistics

Joan Swann, Ana Deumert,
Theresa Lillis and Rajend Mesthrie

Edinburgh University Press

© Joan Swann, Ana Deumert, Theresa Lillis and Rajend Mesthrie, 2004

Edinburgh University Press Ltd
22 George Square, Edinburgh

Typeset in Ehrhardt
by Hewer Text Ltd, Edinburgh and
printed and bound in Great Britain by
Creative Print and Design, Ebbw Vale

A CIP record for this book is available
from the British Library

ISBN 0 7486 1690 X (hardback)
ISBN 0 7486 1691 8 (paperback)

Contents

Acknowledgements   vi

Preliminaries: A Note to Readers   vii

A–Z of entries   1

Bibliography   337

Acknowledgements

We are grateful to the following undergraduate, post-graduate and research students, each of whom worked through a sample of entries and provided invaluable feedback and suggestions on the coverage of the dictionary and the wording of individual entries: Diana Costaras, Eliza Metherall, Amanda Fitzgerald, Andrew Burrows, Helen Swann, Ginnie Kerfoot, Sarah Johnson, Lucy Rai, Paul Bond.

We would also like to express our appreciation to colleagues who advised on particular academic areas, often reading through large numbers of entries and providing detailed and helpful comments: Paul Baker (Lancaster University); Iain Garner (Sheffield Hallam University); Mary Jane Curry, Martyn Hammersley, Ann Hewings, Janet Maybin, Sarah North, Kieran O'Halloran and Will Swann (Open University).

Pam Burns from the Open University helped with formatting and the administration of the project – we would like to thank Pam for her support. Thanks are also due to Sarah Johnson, who acted as administrative assistant at the University of Cape Town.

Preliminaries: A Note to Readers

A Dictionary of Sociolinguistics is intended as a useful resource for students, teachers and researchers in sociolinguistics, or any area of language study that takes a socially-oriented approach (e.g. communication studies, language and gender, language and power, critical discourse analysis). The dictionary is also relevant to the study of related areas that sometimes focus on language, texts or discourse, such as anthropology, psychology and sociology. We hope that, in addition, it will interest people with an 'applied' interest in language, such as educationists and policy-makers.

Sociolinguistics is an exciting and academically vibrant area, marked by increasing diversity. A glance through the programme of any contemporary conference in the subject will reveal a wide range of topics and analytical approaches, informed by divergent, and sometimes conflicting, paradigms and perspectives. This is reflected in dictionary entries, where *velar* rubs shoulders with *ventriloquation*, *post-vocalic /r/* with *poststructuralism* and *substrate* with *subjectivity*. This is not just a matter of discrete research traditions: the same researcher may be engaged with technical linguistic description whilst grappling with contemporary theories about the nature of language, personhood and the self. On a practical level, this means that students of sociolinguistics are faced with a proliferation of terms and concepts – sometimes a minefield, with the same term used to different effect or different terms used to characterise broadly similar phenomena within different fields of enquiry. In explaining sociolinguistic terminology, the dictionary will also map out the traditions and approaches that comprise sociolinguistics and thus help to locate and contextualise terms and concepts.

Academic Coverage

The dictionary covers contemporary sociolinguistics as this has developed since the 1960s. It also covers some earlier work in areas such as dialectology and anthropological linguistics/linguistic anthropology that are relevant to contemporary sociolinguistics. In terms of contemporary approaches, the dictionary adopts a broad coverage. It includes various approaches to the study of language variation and change; language contact phenomena, including bilingual language use; language in interaction; the socially oriented analysis of text and discourse; critical language study; specific topics such as language and gender, literacy, intercultural communication and international/global languages; applied areas such as language policy and planning, and language in education.

Where appropriate, entries indicate changes and differences in the use of terms, and locate these within particular traditions of enquiry. Entries try to provide an 'insider' perspective whilst also adopting a broadly critical approach to the discussion of linguistic ideas and concepts: an overall aim of the dictionary is to support critical engagement and dialogue with the discipline.

The dictionary includes technical terms that we think have some currency in sociolinguistics, and that readers are likely to encounter in academic texts. It does not include terms that are highly specific (i.e. that have limited currency) or that seem unlikely to 'bed down' within the discipline. Nor does it include terms that are also found with the same meanings in everyday language use (e.g. *alphabet*). But it does include terms that are given a particular inflection within sociolinguistics, or that are used differently from their more everyday sense (e.g. *accent*, *dialect*, *style*). We have paid particular attention to terms that are used differently within different traditions (e.g. *discourse*, *text*, *voice*).

We include a small number of names of people who might be regarded as foundational within sociolinguistics (e.g. Labov, Hymes) or whose theories are increasingly being drawn on in sociolinguistic study (e.g. Bakhtin, Foucault). These are restricted to people who have more or less 'adjectival' status within the discipline, and who might be referred to in sociolinguistic texts with limited explanation, on the assumption that their main ideas are known. Because of the way this (and other) academic disciplines have developed, the names include a preponderance of white Anglophone (or European) male academics: a situation likely to change over the next few years. For a fuller list of key sociolinguistic figures, see Rajend Mesthrie's (2001) *Concise Encyclopaedia of Sociolinguistics*.

We faced a problem in deciding which terms to include from linguistic description and analysis. Since, in principle, sociolinguists may study any aspect of language, we ran the risk of reproducing other excellent reference works such as David Crystal's (2002) *Dictionary of Linguistics and Phonetics*. We decided eventually not to include terms students of sociolinguistics might be expected to have as part of their general knowledge about language (e.g. *noun*, *verb*, *adjective*); nor have we included more specialist terms unlikely to occur in the sociolinguistics literature (e.g. *adjunct*). This gives us a bias towards certain types of language description: e.g. common descriptors for sounds, which frequently occur as variables in sociolinguistic analyses of language variation and change; to a lesser extent, some grammatical terms found in variationist research; descriptive terms likely to occur in sociolinguistic analyses of text, discourse or conversation. Crystal probably remains the most comprehensive and concise source for general linguistic terminology.

How entries are organised

Entries may contain minimal information with a reference to other more relevant entries. However, we have tried to make most entries complete in themselves. This produces occasional overlaps in entries for related terms: we have preferred this to extensive reliance on cross-referencing, which would make individual entries harder to read. Nevertheless, entries do include cross-referencing, which should help readers track related terms and perhaps gain a fuller understanding of a set of concepts. Where relevant, entries include examples; many entries include references to further reading (examples of studies, discussion of a topic etc.) for those who wish to follow up a particular idea. Within entries, we have tried to describe terms in a non-technical way.

On specific conventions adopted in entries, see below.

Entries adopt the following conventions:

- **bold type** is used for terms explained in the entry that have no separate entry of their own;
- SMALL CAPITALS are used for terms explained in separate entries, but we adopt this convention only where it may be useful to cross-refer to such entries;
- *italics* are used for examples of linguistic items; where these are explained the gloss may be in quotation marks (e.g. *lune de miel*, meaning 'honeymoon');
- where a term has quite different uses, or where it is helpful to separate out related uses, each definition is separately numbered; however, where uses are closely related we have sometimes found it easier to deal with these together;
- for the representation of speech sounds, we have sometimes used INTERNATIONAL PHONETIC ALPHABET symbols. PHONETIC symbols are enclosed within square brackets (e.g. [b]); PHONEMES are enclosed within slashes (e.g. /b/); LINGUISTIC VARIABLES used in sociolinguistic studies are enclosed within curved brackets (e.g. (ng) for the final sound in *running*). We have given examples of speech sounds, usually from English (RP) as a commonly-used reference point likely to be familiar to many readers. The International Phonetic Association web site includes a full set of phonetic symbols: see http://www.arts.gla.ac.uk/IPA/ipachart.html (last accessed October 2003).
- the asterisk * is used as a syntactic convention to mark a sentence or utterance regarded as ungrammatical (i.e. not used in a particular dialect).

A

a posteriori language   See ARTIFICIAL LANGUAGE.

a priori language   See ARTIFICIAL LANGUAGE.

abnormal transmission   See NORMAL TRANSMISSION, ABNORMAL TRANS-
MISSION.

abrupt creolisation   Term coined by Sarah Grey Thomason and
Thomas Kaufman (1988) for a CREOLE that developed rapidly, within
a generation or two, without the prior existence of a stable PIDGIN.
Such Creoles are called RADICAL CREOLES. Abrupt creolisation contrasts with other types of creolisation in which a stable pidgin or an
expanded pidgin develops into a Creole relatively gradually. It also
contrasts with most cases of LANGUAGE SHIFT in which a pre-existing
TARGET language gradually replaces another language in a community.

Abstand, Ausbau (languages)   Introduced by the German linguist
Heinz Kloss (1967) in the context of LANGUAGE PLANNING. **Abstand**
('distance') refers to the linguistic differences which exist between
two or more language varieties. Abstand languages can be distinguished on linguistic grounds; they are recognised as languages
because of their distance from other languages. Thus German and
English, although relatively closely related (both belong to the West-
Germanic group of languages), are sufficiently different to be
classified as two languages. **Ausbau** ('elaboration') languages, on
the other hand, are varieties which are perceived as different
languages not because of their linguistic distance, but because of
the functions they fulfil in society. Language-planning activities are
typically directed at gradually increasing the linguistic differences
between related varieties and at creating separate STANDARD norms.
Often these are used as a symbolic marker of political and cultural
separateness. For example, ethnic varieties of Serbo-Croatian, such
as Serbian, Croatian and also Bosnian, are perceived by their
speakers as constituting different languages, although they are
linguistically very similar and show MUTUAL INTELLIGIBILITY. See also
AUTONOMY, HETERONOMY.

academic literacy (-ies)   Used principally in three ways, although there is slippage across these uses.

1. The singular 'academic literacy' is often used in a general way to refer to the writing and reading in which students and academics engage in higher education: most obviously this is a type of language use which is more formal and impersonal than many everyday uses of language.

2. The plural 'academic literacies' is sometimes used to refer to the range of TEXT TYPES that are used in higher education, such as the essay, the report, the journal article or the differences between these text types in different disciplines. For example, the structure and style of an argument in an essay in history may be different from an essay in psychology.

3. 'Academic literacies' is also used to refer to an approach to student writing which draws on understandings from NEW LITERACY STUDIES, whereby academic text production is studied as a specific social and cultural practice embedded in relations of power (see Lea and Street, 1998; Jones, Turner and Street, 1999). In this approach the social relations and processes surrounding the production of knowledge are as much of interest as the nature of written academic texts themselves. See also ESSAYIST LITERACY.

accent

1. A variety of speech differing from other varieties in terms of pronunciation (including intonation), and which identifies a speaker in terms of regional origin, social standing and, possibly, ETHNICITY – thus a 'Northern accent', a 'broad accent', 'Scottish accent', etc. In this sociolinguistic sense, all speakers have an accent: the term is not restricted to low-status varieties but includes prestige varieties such as (in British English) RECEIVED PRONUNCIATION: for an argument along these lines, see e.g. Esling (1998). As a term, accent is restricted to features of pronunciation; grammar and vocabulary variation mark differences of DIALECT.

2. Accent in BAKHTIN's work is used in a much broader sense, to refer not just to the sounds of language but to the ways in which all UTTERANCES carry with them the 'accents', that is, the meanings and perspectives, of previous speakers.

In this latter sense, see also ADDRESSIVITY; DIALOGIC.

acceptance The adoption of LANGUAGE PLANNING decisions by the SPEECH COMMUNITY. In order to achieve acceptance language planners need to be aware of the social and symbolic context of language use as well as of speakers' ATTITUDES towards different language varieties.

accommodation The notion of accommodation developed from the work of Howard Giles and his associates. It refers to the phenomenon whereby speakers change the way they are speaking depending on who they are talking to. Speakers may CONVERGE (i.e. become more similar in certain respects) or DIVERGE (become more dissimilar). **Speech Accommodation Theory** (also termed more broadly **Communication Accommodation Theory**) seeks to explain this phenomenon. The traditional interpretation has been that speakers converge in order to express SOLIDARITY or reduce social distance, and diverge in order to emphasise their distinctiveness or increase social distance. More recent models recognise that there are likely to be several different motivations for accommodation, depending on the particular speakers involved, the purposes for which they are interacting, the CONTEXT in which the interaction takes place etc. For instance, a speaker could converge with another sarcastically, rather than to reduce social distance – see e.g. Giles, Coupland and Coupland (1991). See also AUDIENCE DESIGN.

acquisition (of language) See LANGUAGE ACQUISITION.

acquisition planning Introduced by Robert Cooper (1989) to describe LANGUAGE PLANNING efforts directed at increasing the number of users of a given language or language variety. Acquisition planning is sometimes seen as an aspect of LANGUAGE SPREAD, although strictly speaking (planned) language spread involves both an increase in the number of users and in the number of uses or functions. Language teaching (including second-language teaching) is a central part of acquisition planning. See CORPUS PLANNING, STATUS PLANNING; PRESTIGE PLANNING.

acrolang See BASILANG, MESOLANG, ACROLANG.

acrolect See BASILECT, MESOLECT, ACROLECT.

act May be used as a functional unit of analysis, referring to an action carried out by an utterance – e.g. requesting information, warning, threatening. See SPEECH ACT.

act sequence   See SPEAKING.

active   See VOICE (2); PASSIVISATION.

activity theory   An approach to the study of human behaviour and communication which places human activity at the centre of analysis. Any activity, or **activity system**, is made up of three basic elements: the subject (that is the person/people engaging in the activity); the object (that is the aim of the activity); and the tools or 'mediational means' (that is the material or REPRESENTATIONAL RESOURCES that are used as part of the activity). Within this approach language and communication are just one, albeit important, focus of study (see e.g. Russell, 1997). See also GENRE.

acts of identity   A term used originally by Robert Le Page and Andrée Tabouret-Keller (1985) to explain individual speakers' variable language use. Le Page and Tabouret-Keller suggested that speakers draw on features from different languages, or language varieties, to express aspects of their IDENTITY: in particular, speakers create patterns of linguistic behaviour so as to resemble, or distinguish themselves from certain social groups. While these ideas derive from research on multilingual communities in the Caribbean, they have also been applied to speakers' stylistic choices in monolingual communities. See also ACCOMMODATION; AUDIENCE DESIGN; CODE–SWITCHING; FOCUSING, DIFFUSION; INTRA–SPEAKER VARIATION; STYLISTIC VARIATION.

actualisation   See REALISATION.

actuation   The beginning or origin of a linguistic change. Linguists have suggested that new linguistic forms emerge as a result of, for example, accidental mispronunciations or mishearings, leading to the unintentional simplification of complex structures (e.g. CONSONANT CLUSTER SIMPLIFICATION or syntactic ellipsis) and to the formation of novel variants. However, to isolate the precise origin or beginning of a specific change is probably impossible as we cannot know precisely when (and why) a new variant was first uttered by a speaker. For a discussion of actuation, see Milroy (1992). See also LANGUAGE CHANGE; SPEAKER INNOVATION.

additive bilingualism   Refers to a process or educational programme whereby a language is added to an individual's existing linguistic repertoire. This stands in contrast to SUBTRACTIVE BILINGUALISM, where a second or new language replaces the first language. For example the English/French BILINGUAL programmes for English-speaking Canadians are intended to give children a second language, not to replace English or restrict the contexts of its use.

address (terms)   Sociolinguists have studied **terms of address** or **address systems** as interactional phenomena that indicate the relative STATUS of speakers, the degree of intimacy or social distance that is being conveyed, POLITENESS and other social or cultural values. Such terms include, in English, the choice between first name (*Margaret*); title plus surname (*Ms Anderson*); alternative titles (*Dr/Ms/Mrs Anderson*); KINSHIP terms (*Aunt Margaret*); professional terms (*doctor*); terms of ENDEARMENT (*honey, love*). In other languages PRONOUN CHOICE is important (e.g. in French, the choice between *tu* and *vous*, the 'familiar' and 'polite' forms of the second-person pronoun 'you'); or there may be broader linguistic differences involving choices between a range of words or word forms (as in Japanese, Korean or Javanese). See also POWER; SOLIDARITY; T AND V PRONOUNS.

addressee   The person addressed by a speaker or writer. The addressee will affect the forms of language used by the speaker/writer (e.g. a speaker is likely to speak differently to close friends and to a boss at work). Sometimes 'addressee' is used with a more specific meaning, e.g. (in Allan Bell's theory of AUDIENCE DESIGN it refers to the primary person addressed in an interaction – someone whose presence is known and ratified by the speaker, and who is also directly addressed). Bell distinguishes this from other categories such as an 'auditor', who is known and ratified but not directly addressed; and an 'overhearer', who is known to be present but is not a ratified participant in the interaction. Theories such as audience design recognise the need to take into account the roles of different types of participant in a speech event. See also AUDIENCE; INTERLOCUTOR; PARTICIPANT.

addressivity   A key notion in BAKHTIN's theory of language which refers to the ways in which the meanings of specific UTTERANCES are shaped both by the addressor and ADDRESSEE in any given context. An obvious example is the way in which an interviewee (as addressor) will speak in a particular way because of the presence of a particular kind of addressee, the interviewer. Immediate addressivity – between speaker and listener, reader and writer in any given context – is part of a larger historical and cultural 'chain of speech communication' (Bakhtin [1953] 1986: 91). Thus interviewer and interviewee communicating in one specific instance are taking part in a well-established and historically situated type of communication. Addressivity not only refers to the way in which 'real' addressors and addressees influence language use and meaning making, but it also encapsulates the more abstract notion that uses of language are always made, implicitly or explicitly, in response to another person, question or comment. See also DIALOGIC.

adjacency pair   Used within CONVERSATION ANALYSIS to refer to a pair of utterances in which the first part of the pair anticipates a particular second part (or set of possible second parts). For example in English an initial greeting is usually followed by a return greeting; a question by an answer; an invitation by an acceptance or a rejection; a farewell by a return farewell. Adjacency pairs play an important role in CONVERSATION MANAGEMENT (e.g. in negotiating the opening or closing of a conversation).

adolescence (adolescent)   Adolescence – sometimes referred to by anthropologists as 'emerging adulthood' – is conventionally defined as the time located between childhood and adulthood. **Adolescents** typically explore aspects of adult identity and engage in activities which are seen as adult prerogatives (e.g. in Western contexts, smoking, make-up, drinking and staying out late, dating, etc.). In many societies this time is characterised by an increasing awareness of the norms of the STANDARD variety of language (which is taught at school) as well as the playful and sometimes subversive use of NON-STANDARD variants within the PEER GROUP. The extensive use of obscenities and profanity is another (frequently noted) linguistic practice of adolescent peer groups. YOUTH LANGUAGE research attempts to document such adolescent-specific linguistic practices. Sociolinguists interested in LANGUAGE CHANGE have paid particular attention to the language used by adolescents, and in APPARENT TIME studies adolescents have been found to lead CHANGES FROM BELOW. For further discussion, see Eckert (1997) and Chambers (1995). See also AGE-GRADING; JOCKS AND BURNOUTS.

adstrate (adstratum)   Terms for a relation observed in LANGUAGE CONTACT studies when two (or more) languages co-exist and influence each other by mutual BORROWING, without one language being socially and linguistically dominant. Each language is sometimes described as an adstrate (or adstratum) of the other.

Contrast SUBSTRATE; SUPERSTRATE.

affordance(s) See REPRESENTATIONAL RESOURCES.

affricate A term used in the description and classification of CONSONANTS, relating to their MANNER OF ARTICULATION. Affricates are produced when the air stream is blocked and then released (as in a PLOSIVE), but the release is accompanied by friction (as in a FRICATIVE). Examples in English are: [tʃ] and [dʒ] (the initial sounds in *choke* and *joke* respectively). See also INTERNATIONAL PHONETIC ALPHABET; PHONETICS .

African American Vernacular English Formerly also called **Black English Vernacular**, abbreviated **BEV**: a cover term for a variety of English which is learned as a first language by African Americans, and which is used by the majority of African American adults when conversing in informal settings. AAVE developed in the context of social and residential segregation and differs systematically from Standard American English in terms of phonology, syntax and morphology. Well-documented features of AAVE are COPULA DELETION (as in *she clever*); the absence of third-person-singular inflection -*s* (*she read*) and word-final -T/-D DELETION. The term is sometimes replaced by **African American English** as the concept of VERNACULAR is seen as reflecting negative connotations of non-standardness. See also ANN ARBOR TRIAL; EBONICS; VARIABLE RULE.

age Has been found to be a salient SOCIAL VARIABLE in the study of LANGUAGE VARIATION and LANGUAGE CHANGE. Age can be measured either as a continuous variable (in months and/or years) or can be conceptualised in terms of life stages (e.g. childhood, adolescence, adulthood and old age). See also ADOLESCENCE.

age-grading Describes the observation that certain linguistic forms are more frequently used by younger than by older speakers, and that younger speakers change their linguistic practices as they grow older. An often-cited example is the extensive use of slang by adolescents when compared to adults (their parents and grandparents). This contrasts with age differences resulting from a language CHANGE IN PROGRESS: see APPARENT TIME. See also ADOLESCENCE; YOUTH LANGUAGE.

agency Term used by sociologists to refer to the human capacity to act (see Giddens 1979); used to contrast the individual with wider social and political structures (see SOCIAL STRUCTURE). It is understood that individuals are formed by social structures and at the same time, through their actions, contribute to the forming of these structures. This DIALECTICAL tension is prominent in critical and poststructuralist approaches to the study of language: see CRITICAL DISCOURSE ANALYSIS; POSTSTRUCTURALISM; SUBJECTIVITY.

aggravation (aggravate(d))   Involves increasing the force of an utterance. For example, of the following two DIRECTIVES: 'Could you close the door?', and 'Just close the door!' the second would be more **aggravated**. Aggravation may be signalled by a range of linguistic and other means (e.g. certain syntactic structures, intonation, voice quality). Aggravation is usually contrasted with MITIGATION, when the force of an utterance is reduced. Whereas mitigation would be a form of POLITENESS, aggravation would usually be impolite.

allophone   See PHONEME.

alternation   General term for the relationship between alternative forms for a linguistic unit. Thus alternants of the plural of nouns in English are spelt *-s, -es, -en* and 'zero' (as in *cats, churches, oxen* and *sheep*). The term occurs especially in PHONOLOGY for the variation in pronunciation of a particular sound, usually determined by adjacent sounds or syllables. Thus the word *electric* ends with the consonant [k]; but when the suffix *-ity* is added (*electricity*) the consonant is pronounced [s]. There is said to be an alternation between [k] and [s] here (and in many other pairs like *public – publicity*).

For **language alternation** and **code alternation**, see CODE-SWITCHING.

alveolar   A term used in the description and classification of CONSONANTS, relating to their PLACE OF ARTICULATION. Alveolar sounds are produced when the tongue comes into contact with the alveolar ridge, behind the teeth. Examples from English include: [t], [d], [n], [s], [z], [ɹ]. See also INTERNATIONAL PHONETIC ALPHABET; PHONETICS.

ambilingual   Synonym for BALANCED BILINGUAL.

amelioration   An aspect of semantic change in language: amelioration refers to instances when, over time, words lose negative meanings. *Sophisticated*, for instance, once had meanings such as 'adulterated', 'artificial' or 'falsified' (applied to inanimate objects – e.g. wine could be sophisticated in this negative sense). Dick Leith (1997) relates such changes to the social history of English – e.g. in this case gradual shifts in meaning as the word became used in a widening range of contexts by different groups of speakers. *Sophisticated* in its contemporary sense (of 'refined') was applied first to people in the nineteenth century and, Leith argues, re-applied to objects to denote things that appeal to people of taste and refinement. It then came, by extension, to mean 'technically advanced' (e.g. of cameras etc.).

Contrast PEJORATION.

analogy   A type of LANGUAGE CHANGE in which speakers change the form of an existing word or words according to some other pattern evident in their language. In earlier stages of English, some words such as *shoe*, *eye* or *cow* formed irregular plurals (e.g. the plural of *cow* was *kine*). These were gradually changed 'by analogy with' the larger number of regular nouns which formed the plural with -*s*. Analogy, however, does not occur systematically. This can be seen in the persistence of the irregular plural form *children*. Moreover, analogy does not always lead to regularisation: American English has innovated *dove* as the past tense of *dive* by analogy with *ride-rode* and *drive-drove*, whereas the regular form (*dived*) is maintained in British English. Analogy also occurs in LANGUAGE ACQUISITION where transitional forms such as *goed* (instead of *went*) or *speaked* (instead of *spoke*) are the result of the **over-extension** of the past-tense rule for regular verbs. In SECOND LANGUAGE ACQUISITION studies the term **overgeneralisation** is also found.

analysis of variance (ANOVA)   A statistical test which can be used to compare the language use of different groups of speakers or the language used in different text types. ANOVA compares the mean scores (numerical averages) of two or more groups in a SAMPLE, and allows the researcher to assess whether the observed differences between groups are statistically significant (i.e. would be expected to occur in the POPULATION from which the sample was drawn – see SIGNIFICANCE TESTING). ANOVA was used by Lesley Milroy (1987a) in her study of the influence of SOCIAL NETWORKS on language use in Belfast. Milroy compared the language use of those who were closely integrated into local networks with those who were only loosely integrated. She found that markers of Belfast speech were used more frequently by those who occupied a central position in the community.

ANOVA is similar to the T-TEST. However, the t-test cannot be used to test differences between more than two groups.

anaphoric (reference)   Grammatical term used to describe a linguistic feature which refers to a previously mentioned element in any given TEXT. In the case of the following two sentences, for example: 'The water system is failing because of old pipes and a shortage of qualified technicians to repair them. *These* are the reasons why change is necessary', *These* has an anaphoric function, referring back to the reasons given in the preceding part of the text. Anaphoric reference stands in contrast to CATAPHORIC reference, which refers forwards to something expressed in a later part of the text. See also COHESION; ENDOPHORIC; EXOPHORIC; REFERENCE (2).

androcentric generics   See GENERIC MASCULINE.

androcentrism (in language)   See SEXISM.

androgyny   Refers to people seen as possessing both 'feminine' and 'masculine' characteristics. In some 1970s and 1980s social psychological studies of gender identity, androgyny was part of a four-way classification system that also included the categories 'feminine', 'masculine' or 'undifferentiated' (neither feminine nor masculine). All these categories applied both to women and men. This model was used in some studies of language EVALUATION, where the voices of speakers assessed (by forms of self-evaluation) as representing these different categories were rated by listeners. To some extent, listeners' ratings of speakers' FEMININITY or MASCULINITY corresponded with speakers' self-evaluations (see e.g. Smith, 1985).

Ann Arbor trial   A court case held in 1979 in Ann Arbor, Michigan, at which the central issue was the relationship between AFRICAN AMERICAN VERNACULAR ENGLISH (AAVE) and STANDARD American English in the classroom. The plaintiffs were parents and community activists who brought suit in the Federal District Court against the Martin Luther King Jnr Elementary School, the Ann Arbor District and the State of Michigan Board of Education. The plaintiffs charged that the educational opportunities provided to African American children at the school did not address cultural, social and economic factors, which limited their educational experiences at school. Students were fluent in a variety of English, they argued, that was a different system from the standard English of the classroom, not a defective version of it. Several sociolinguists provided expert testimony at the trial, especially William LABOV and Geneva Smitherman (see Labov, 1982).

The presiding judge decided in favour of the plaintiffs that the children's home language was not in itself a barrier but became one when teachers did not take it into account in teaching standard English. He directed the Ann Arbor School Board to use the students' fluency in AAVE as a foundation for developing standard English skills. Training programmes aimed to put this into practice did not, however, succeed. See also EBONICS; FORENSIC LINGUISTICS; NON-STANDARD (LANGUAGE, VARIETY).

ANOVA   See ANALYSIS OF VARIANCE.

anthropology, anthropological linguistics   See LINGUISTIC ANTHROPOLOGY.

anti-language   Used to refer to a type of language used by social SUBCULTURES, such as prisoners, youth gang members, members of counter-cultural movements, such as 'hippies' or 'Rastas' (see Halliday, 1978). Linguistic features of anti-languages include (a) 'relexicalisation', that is giving a new meaning to existing words such as *lift* meaning someone who steals a package and *marker* for someone who is handed a package and (b) 'overlexicalisation', where many words are used to refer to one thing, such as the twenty-one words for *bomb* identified by Malik (1972). Anti-languages are viewed as examples of resistance to standard powerful language(s). See also ARGOT; LEXICALISATION; SECRET LANGUAGE.

anti-sexist (language)   See SEXISM.

apparent time   An approach to the study of LANGUAGE CHANGE that interprets generational differences in language use as an indicator of a linguistic CHANGE IN PROGRESS. The study of linguistic change in apparent time requires the systematic comparison of the speech of older and younger speakers. Based on the assumption that younger speakers are further advanced in their use of new linguistic forms than older speakers, inferences are made about the direction of language change. William LABOV (1972a) described such generational differences in his study of sociolinguistic variation in New York: the incidence of POST-VOCALIC /r/ (the pronunciation of /r/ in words such as *cart* and *car*) was highest among young speakers, who were thus seen as leading a linguistic change towards the more frequent use of this pronunciation in the New York speech community. In interpreting such patterns it is important to establish that one is not dealing with an example of stable generational differences, or AGE-GRADING. Compare REAL TIME.

applied linguistics   Linguistics is said to be applied when its theories, research methods and research findings are drawn on to elucidate and help resolve practical issues and concerns to do with language and language use. In practice, however, applied linguistics tends not to be restricted to linguistic theories and methods: it is usually interdisciplinary, drawing also on related areas such as psychology and educational theory. Applied linguistics has been particularly concerned with the teaching and learning of English and other languages as foreign or additional languages, and sometimes it is used almost as a synonym for this area of study. However, linguistics may be applied in several other contexts (e.g. in relation to language and the law – see FORENSIC LINGUISTICS; in LANGUAGE POLICY and LANGUAGE PLANNING) and the term is sometimes used more broadly to cover this wider range of applications. In this broader sense, applied linguistics often has a strong critical component (e.g. drawing on CRITICAL DISCOURSE ANALYSIS and CRITICAL LANGUAGE AWARENESS). Applied linguistics also overlaps with aspects of sociolinguistics. The term **applied sociolinguistics** is sometimes found for the application of sociolinguistic theories and methods within education, forensic linguistics, language policy and planning, and similar areas. See also EDUCATIONAL LINGUISTICS; TEACHING ENGLISH TO SPEAKERS OF OTHER LANGUAGES (TESOL).

apposition   A grammatical relation in which an element is juxtaposed to another element of the same type, with both elements referring to the same semantic entity. In *Jill Smith*, *the dancer*, *made an appearance*, the underlined NOUN PHRASES refer to the same person and are said to be in apposition. Likewise, relative clauses and pronouns may be used appositionally: in *Jill Smith*, *who is a dancer*, *supports the new party*, and *My uncle – he's ever so smart*, the relative clause *who is a dancer* and the pronoun *he* are used in apposition to the respective preceding noun phrases.

apprenticeship   The notion of apprenticeship is drawn on in social and SOCIOCULTURAL approaches to language and literacy to describe and explain how people become members of a specific DISCOURSE COMMUNITY or COMMUNITY OF PRACTICE. 'Newcomers' or 'outsiders' learn to participate successfully in communities through a process of apprenticeship, whereby they gradually learn the conventions governing particular ways of using language, communicating and behaving from those more 'expert', that is more experienced in the practices of the community. Some accounts focus more closely on apprenticeship in relation to TEXTS or DISCOURSE (e.g. Swales, 1990), whereas others focus more broadly on the activities, including communication, associated with particular communities (e.g. Lave and Wenger, 1991).

appropriateness (appropriate, adj.)   A term used in contrast to PRESCRIPTIVE notions of CORRECTNESS: for instance, whereas non-standard forms of English such as *we wasn't* would probably be considered incorrect by prescriptivists, it would be more usual within sociolinguistics to consider the extent to which their use was **appropriate** in a specific CONTEXT. This is said to be consistent with a DESCRIPTIVE (rather than a prescriptive) approach to language. The notion of appropriateness has been influential within education. It suggests that children should be given access to powerful language varieties because their use is appropriate in a wide range of contexts. However, children's home language varieties, where different, should be respected and seen as appropriate in certain other contexts. This idea has been challenged by those who take a more CRITICAL approach to language, on the grounds that it implies patterns of language use, and associated norms of usage, are clear-cut and agreed (i.e. ignoring the existence of divergent language practices and uncertainty or disagreement about what counts as appropriate). The concept itself is also seen as ideological: not simply as descriptive but as promoting certain types of language use, which serve the interests of socially dominant groups (see e.g. Fairclough, 1992c).

appropriation (appropriate, vb.)   A term used in a general sense to refer to the ways in which different aspects of language are taken up and used by individuals and groups: for example, the learning and use of specific technical vocabulary by student engineers. It is also used more specifically within SOCIOCULTURAL theories of learning, to refer to the ways in which individuals **appropriate**, or take meaning from, the contexts they inhabit, through participation in socially and culturally specific activities or PRACTICES (see Leont'ev, 1981; Newman et al., 1989). See also APPRENTICESHIP; ZONE OF PROXIMAL DEVELOPMENT.

approximant   A term used in the description and classification of speech sounds, relating to their MANNER OF ARTICULATION. Approximants are produced when the articulators come close together but do not touch, so that the air stream is not blocked or impeded to create friction. English approximants include [w], [ɹ], [l] and [j] (the initial sound in *yet*). See also INTERNATIONAL PHONETIC ALPHABET; PHONETICS.

area(l)   In the sense of 'geographical', see LINGUISTIC GEOGRAPHY. For **areal linguistics**, see LINGUISTIC AREA; SOCIOLINGUISTIC AREA.

argot   A set of words and phrases used by a particular social group, usually for reasons of secrecy. Argots are often associated with criminals, street gangs or other subcultural groups who need to protect themselves from outsiders. They may include invented words, or involve various manipulations of word forms or meanings (e.g. BACK SLANG, RHYMING SLANG, metaphor). Argots are not complete vocabularies, and may be subject to 'overlexicalisation' in certain areas (i.e. contain a large number of words for similar concepts related to the group's interests and activities (see LEXICALISATION)). They tend to change rapidly and, like other similar varieties, they may serve to maintain group boundaries. Related terms include ANTI-LANGUAGE; CANT; JARGON; SECRET LANGUAGE; SLANG.

argument
1. In broad terms 'argument' is often used to refer to the taking up and justifying of a particular position with a view to persuading the listener/reader of the validity of this position. An example of everyday argument is 'We should not go to war because too many people will die.'
2. Specific types of argument involve particular sets of procedures and conventions, for example academic argument involves advancing a position by referring to existing evidence and research in a specific field. Frameworks for analysing the elements of argument, such as Toulmin's model have been used to analyse and also teach students how to write academic argument (Toulmin, 1958; Toulmin et al., 1984).

3. 'Argument' is also used in linguistics in a less familiar way where it refers to particular elements required by the verb in a sentence. Thus *ran* requires a single argument (a subject like *Mary* in *Mary ran*), whilst *saw* requires two arguments (a subject and object as in *Mary saw Abdullah*). *Put* is one of the few verbs in English that requires three arguments: *Mary put the car in the garage.*

articulatory setting   Habitual muscular configurations in the vocal tract as people speak: these may differ between speakers even while they are producing the 'same' speech sound, and lend an overall quality to a speaker's voice (e.g. a voice may characteristically sound 'harsh' or 'metallic'); accents and dialects may also be characterised to some extent by particular articulatory settings (see VOICE QUALITY).

artificial language   A language that has been consciously created by an individual or by a language society or language committee. Several hundred artificial languages have been constructed since the late seventeenth century. Initially, the motivation for the development of artificial languages was based on the idea that it would be possible to create a perfect language that did not show the redundancies, irregularities and ambiguities of natural languages, and that would facilitate logical thinking. Detailed symbolic systems were developed by Gottfried Wilhelm Leibniz, John Wilkins, George Dalgarno and others. These early artificial languages were not based on natural language material but found their inspiration in scientific classifications and formal logic. They were therefore called *a priori* **languages**. In the nineteenth century a new interest in artificial languages emerged, but this time the motivation was to facilitate international communication. The linguistic structures of nineteenth-century artificial languages were derived from existing natural languages. They are therefore called *a posteriori* **languages**. However, these constructed languages differed from their linguistic sources (e.g. Spanish, German, English) by their complete grammatical regularity. Esperanto, which was created by the Polish doctor L. L. Zamenhof between 1872 and 1885, is probably the best-known and most successful *a posteriori* language. According to the ETHNO-LOGUE (2002), Esperanto has today between 200 and 2,000 first-language users, and two million second-language users in over one hundred countries (mostly Central and Eastern Europe, China and eastern Asia, South America and South-West Asia). However, compared with English, which is spoken by over 500 million speakers, Esperanto has not achieved its intended status as an international language. While Esperanto was developed by an individual, Interlingua was developed by the International Auxiliary Language Association in 1951. It is today used as a second language by some speakers but no speaker estimate is available as yet. For further details, see Eco (1995). The term AUXILIARY LANGUAGE is also found. See also BASIC ENGLISH.

aspect   A grammatical term for a verb category that specifies information about the duration, completion, repeatedness and so on of the action expressed by the verb. For example, in English the main aspectual categories are PROGRESSIVE versus non-progressive and PERFECTIVE versus imperfective. The progressive/non-progressive distinction indicates whether an action is continuous/on-going or not (independent of the tense of the main verb). Thus while *I go* is non-progressive, *I am going* is progressive, signifying that the activity is of continuous duration. The perfective/imperfective distinction denotes whether an action has been completed or not and whether it has relevance to the present time. Thus *I have eaten* is present perfect.

Other types of aspect include **habitual** (*I used to go*), and in languages other than English **iterative** for repeated action, **inchoative** for the beginning of an action and so on. Aspect is of interest to sociolinguistics since dialects may utilise aspectual distinctions differently. For example, Irish English makes a distinction termed the 'hot-news perfect' for an event that occurs just before the moment of speaking, as in: *She's after eating her dinner.* See also TENSE–MODALITY–ASPECT.

aspiration   Used in PHONETICS to refer to a puff of air accompanying the articulation of certain sounds, and represented in phonetic TRANSCRIPTION by a superscript 'h'. PLOSIVES may be pronounced with aspiration in certain languages or language varieties, and in certain linguistic environments. For instance in many varieties of English /p/ would be realised as [pʰ] at the beginning of words such as *pin*, but not when preceded by /s/ (as in the word *spin*).

aspirers   See INTERLOPERS, INSIDERS, OUTSIDERS, ASPIRERS.

assimilation
  1. In relation to sounds, a process whereby neighbouring sounds in an utterance influence one another and become more similar in terms of their articulation: e.g. the alveolar nasal /n/ in *Banbury*

may be realised as a bilabial [m], influenced by the following bilabial sound [b].

2. In relation to languages, **linguistic assimilation** refers to instances when speakers of a MINORITY LANGUAGE adopt the MAJORITY LANGUAGE; assimilation is encouraged in some forms of LANGUAGE PLANNING: see LANGUAGE DIVERSITY.

asymmetrical (talk)   Asymmetry in talk or interaction is seen when there is some degree of inequality between speakers; this may be associated with factors such as POWER, STATUS or GENDER. For instance, some early studies suggested that talk between female and male speakers was asymmetrical in that male speakers talked more than female speakers, interrupted female speakers more often than vice versa and gave less interactional support. Such straightforward distinctions have since been contested – see LANGUAGE AND GENDER.

atlas (of languages, dialects)   See LINGUISTIC ATLAS.

attention (paid to speech)   William LABOV (1972a) distinguished FORMAL and informal (or casual) linguistic styles in terms of the amount of attention (or **self-monitoring**) that speakers direct towards their speech. In informal, relaxed styles minimal attention is paid to monitoring language use. The more formal the situation, the more attention speakers will pay to their speech, and they will consciously try to avoid the use of NON-STANDARD or low-PRESTIGE features. However, an increase in attention to speech can also be observed in some informal contexts. Native speakers of the STANDARD variety of a language, for example, may deliberately and consciously shift into a non-standard variety of which they have only limited knowledge in order to signal the informality of a situation to their conversation partners. See also CHANNEL CUES; MONITORED SPEECH; STYLISTIC CONTINUUM; VERNACULAR.

attitudes (towards language)   The views and opinions people have about language and language variation. These may be directed at evaluating the relationship between a STANDARD language and NON-STANDARD varieties. However, Leonard Bloomfield's (1964) discussion of opinions about 'good' and 'bad' language use in the oral culture of the Menomini Indians (of Northern Minnesota, USA) suggests that linguistic value judgements are a widespread phenomenon and do not require the presence of a written, codified standard language. Attitudes towards language have been studied as an aspect of SOCIAL PSYCHOLOGY (see EVALUATION) and under various other headings – see for instance FOLK LINGUISTICS; LANGUAGE IDEOLOGY; PERCEPTUAL DIALECTOLOGY; STANDARD LANGUAGE IDEOLOGY.

attrition
1. Loss of, or changes to, grammatical, lexical, or phonetic features of a language on account of declining use by its speakers as they shift to another language. In such a situation there might be simplification in, for example, the tense system or in certain properties of subordinate clauses; some vocabulary items might fall into disuse and phonetic features may be simplified.
2. In studies of language loss in individuals, due to factors like brain impairment in stroke victims, the term is used for similar (or more drastic) reduction in grammar, vocabulary, phonetic features, etc.

audience   Refers conventionally to hearers or listeners, both those directly addressed by a speaker and others present at a speech event who may affect the language produced (see e.g. AUDIENCE DESIGN). However, this notion of audience assumes a relatively straightforward distinction between 'speaker' and 'audience', a notion that has been challenged within some areas of sociolinguistics (e.g. INTERACTIONAL SOCIOLINGUISTICS; LINGUISTIC ANTHROPOLOGY). Within these traditions, audiences are seen as active participants in the creation of meaning: they affect what may be said; their responses will affect how an utterance is interpreted; in many contexts propositions are produced across speaking turns and across speakers; listeners bring their own understandings to bear on the interpretation of an utterance, rather than simply 'reading off' a speaker's intentions. These and similar phenomena have given rise to the notion of the audience as 'co-author' (see Duranti and Brenneis, 1986).

audience design   A concept introduced and developed within sociolinguistics by Allan Bell (1984, 2002) in an attempt to explain variation in the language of an individual speaker (INTRA-SPEAKER VARIATION – for instance, CODE-SWITCHING, style shifting or STYLISTIC VARIATION). Individual speaking STYLE is seen essentially as a speaker's response to an audience: in most cases of style shifting, speakers change some aspect of their speech in order to orient towards the speech of an ADDRESSEE (their main interlocutor) or sometimes another participant. In addition to such 'responsive' style shifts, speakers may also make 'initiative' style shifts, i.e. shifts that initiate a change in the situation rather than responding to this. Initiative shifts primarily involve orienting towards an external reference group, termed **referee design**. Shifting into a more formal style to talk about employment or education (as speakers might to employers or teachers), or adopting the style of their (absent) in-group when talking to outsiders, would be examples of referee design. Within this framework, speakers are seen as constantly designing their speech in relation to their present audience and other reference groups. See the related concept of ACCOMMODATION; also ACTS OF IDENTITY.

audio-recording   Technical developments in audio technology had important consequences for the development of sociolinguistic research. The tape recorder made it possible to record large samples of spontaneous speech and soon replaced the word lists (see INTERVIEW; ELICITATION) of traditional DIALECTOLOGY. Today, mini-disk recorders and radio microphones constitute ever less conspicuous recording equipment. Speakers are increasingly familiar with these devices and thus less self-conscious in interviews when compared to the 1960s and 1970s. See also FIELDWORK.

Ausbau   See ABSTAND, AUSBAU.

Australian Questioning Intonation (AQI)   See HIGH RISING TONE.

authenticity   A term used in SECOND LANGUAGE ACQUISITION and language-teaching research to describe learning interactions and contexts which are culturally and socially meaningful to the students. Much interaction in second-language classrooms is artificial, and 'pretend' conversational routines are common. Teacher–student exchanges in particular often involve highly ritualistic and predictable question–answer sequences. Simulated dialogues (booking a room in a hotel, exchanging greetings, making a phone call, ordering a meal, etc.) are also a typical feature of many language classrooms and teaching materials. Authenticity, by contrast, refers to students' active and creative engagement with the foreign language, and their use of the language in socially and culturally meaningful interactions. Authenticity is also used to describe a quality of teaching materials: authentic texts are those which are not designed specifically for language students (e.g. recordings of TV and radio programmes, newspaper articles, etc.). For further discussion, see Kramsch (1993) and van Lier (1996).

author   Refers commonly to the originator of ideas, usually as expressed in written texts. However, the relationship between author, text and reader is theorised in a number of ways, including (a) *author as invisible or insignificant*: in some traditions, the actual authorship of texts (particularly religious texts, such as the Bible or the Quran) is seen as less significant than the text itself. Here the real originator may be viewed as divine and the actual writers simply as being charged with bringing divinely inspired meanings into existence. (b) *Author as originator of ideas which the reader must retrieve from the text*: the ideas expressed in the text are often understood to reflect the views of the real author. This is a commonsense approach to authorship and readers in many Western societies. (c) *Author as real versus author as implied in the text*: this is an approach prominent within literary criticism, where the real author is distinguished from the author implied in the text. The focus is on analysing the authorial voice as constructed in the text, instead of viewing the text as expressing the real author's views or ideas. (d) *Author or authorial voice as constructed predominantly by the reader*: Roland Barthes (1977) famously talked of 'the death of the author', arguing that it is the reader, through her reading (rather than the author through her writing), who constructs meanings, and thus creates a text. This approach to authorship emphasises the multiple possible meanings of any text (see also DECONSTRUCTION, and contemporary understandings of AUDIENCE). (e) *Authoring as the orchestration of* VOICES: as illustrated by the work of BAKHTIN, this often involves an emphasis on exploring relations across texts through a focus on INTERTEXTUALITY. (For an overview see Burke, 1995.)

authoritative discourse   Used by BAKHTIN to indicate a particular kind of relationship between the individual and language. The authoritative word 'demands that we acknowledge it, that we make it our own' (Bakhtin, [1935] 1981: 343), thus authoritative discourse often refers to ways of meaning and using language which the individual reproduces unquestioningly or feels obliged to use. Authoritative discourses stand in contrast to 'internally persuasive discourses', which are ways of meaning with which the individual has dialogically engaged, that is, by questioning, exploring, connecting, in order to develop new ways of meaning ([1935] 1981: 346). See also DIALOGIC.

authority   Term often used to refer to the language of institutions and professions and the ways in which the use of institutional language bestows legitimacy and POWER on members. Examples of such institutions are medicine, law, education and the church, all of which according to BOURDIEU wield considerable SYMBOLIC POWER (see Bourdieu, 1991). Much research within sociolinguistics has focused on the encounters between professionals and their clients – for example, doctors and patients – and particularly the asymmetry in interactions. Studies focus on the amount of talk, the distribution of speaking turns and forms of address. A specific interest is in how the authority of professionals influences the interaction and is sustained or challenged (see e.g. Sarangi and Roberts, 1999). See also INTERACTIONAL SOCIOLINGUISTICS.

autonomous (model of language study)   Term used in various ways:
1. To denote that linguistics – **autonomous linguistics** – is an independent science in its own terms.
2. To refer to an approach to linguistics which focuses on the internal system and structure of language in contrast to social approaches such as SOCIOLINGUISTICS.
3. In NEW LITERACY STUDIES, to contrast an **autonomous model** with an **ideological model** of literacy.

The latter two usages are often used critically to indicate approaches to language and literacy that ignore the importance of social context.

autonomy, heteronomy   Terms used by Peter Trudgill and J. K. Chambers 1980 to characterise relations of dependence/independence between varieties that are linguistically and historically related, especially in the context of a DIALECT CONTINUUM. **Autonomy** signals a relation of independence – e.g. written standard Dutch and standard German are autonomous with respect to each other, since they have a separate status, identity and different linguistic and orthographic norms. At the spoken level, however, there is a continuum between dialects of Dutch and dialects of German as one proceeds from the Dutch coast to the German interior. On linguistic grounds it is not possible to specify where Dutch ceases to be spoken and where German begins: the border dialects have more in common with each other than with dialects at the extremities of the continuum. Speakers themselves identify their dialects as 'Dutch' or 'German' on the basis of political boundaries and the respective standard language of each country, not the actual linguistic characteristics of their speech. Trudgill and Chambers would characterise this situation as one of **heteronomy**, or dependence: the dialects labelled Dutch are heteronomous with (i.e.

dependent upon) the standard Dutch language, and dialects labelled German are heteronomous with standard German. The autonomy/ heteronomy distinction in British dialectology is similar to the distinction between Abstand and Ausbau languages in the German language planning tradition (see ABSTAND, AUSBAU). The term ÜBERDACHUNG also occurs for the heteronomous relation between standard language and dialect.

auxiliary

1. **Auxiliary language**: an additional language used for wider communication in a community or across communities, not the native language of community members. English and Swahili fulfill this function in many African countries. Speakers often have limited proficiency in the auxiliary language, and the language may also be functionally restricted (e.g. a trade language). The term may also refer to a constructed language such as Esperanto: in this sense, see ARTIFICIAL LANGUAGE. See also LINGUA FRANCA.

2. **Auxiliary verb**: traditionally known as 'helping verb' insofar as it 'accompanies' other verbs and provides specific information relating to their TENSE, MOOD, VOICE, etc. In *I can dance*, the auxiliary *can* modifies the main verb *dance* (also known as a lexical or **full** verb (see LEXIS)). Auxiliaries have special properties that mark them off from full verbs. They do not occur on their own, unless a full verb is 'understood' – for example, *I may* is only appropriate in the context of a preceding question involving a full verb (such as *Will you do it?*). In English, auxiliaries 'attract' negative forms like *not* or *n't*, whereas full verbs cannot: thus *I might not go* or *I mightn't go* versus the ungrammatical **I eat not* or **I eatn't*. Auxiliaries are of interest in sociolinguistics since they may vary according to dialect: for example, US English *Did you eat?* for UK English *Have you eaten?*, or the acceptability of *ain't* as negative auxiliary in some dialects. See also ASPECT; COPULA; MOOD; TENSE; TENSE–MODALITY–ASPECT.

avoidance   Certain languages are said to contain an avoidance style of speaking. This may be used in front of, for example relatives with whom there are restrictions on speaking. Avoidance styles are associated particularly with Australian languages such as Dyirbal and Yidiny. In these cases, a man and his mother-in-law, or a woman and her son-in-law are meant to adopt avoidance styles in one another's presence (they are also meant to avoid direct eye contact).

Avoidance styles do not differ in grammar from everyday speaking styles, but contain special vocabulary items. The term **mother-in-law** vocabulary is also found for such usages. Related practices occur elsewhere. For instance, *hlonipha* is a traditional language practice among speakers of Xhosa and some other southern African languages. Hlonipha refers to the avoidance, by married women, of syllables that occur in the names of their in-laws (women use a range of linguistic devices to avoid uttering such syllables). Hlonipha is meant to show respect, but it is also associated with women's relatively powerless social position. See also TABOO.

axiom of categoricity   Used by J. K. Chambers (1995) to refer to the assumptions about language which inform the generative linguistic tradition established by Noam Chomsky in the 1960s (see LINGUISTICS). An axiom in this sense is a proposition which is accepted without further proof or evidence as a starting point for future research. Chomskyan linguistics has been criticised by sociolinguistics for ignoring linguistic variability and for abstracting language use from its real-world contexts. Chomsky's (1965) notion of the 'ideal speaker-listener in a homogenous speech-community' is a frequently cited example of a categorical and non-variationist approach to language.

B

baby talk   A term used by Bloomfield (1933) for the simplified type of language used by adults of some societies to converse with very young children. Baby talk consists of simplifications of adult grammar and some systematic changes like the addition of diminutives (*doggie* for *dog*). CHILD-DIRECTED SPEECH (CDS) is a more general term used for any form of language used by adults towards children (irrespective of the extent of simplification). The language of young children themselves is termed CHILD LANGUAGE, which shows systematic patterns of development and certain differences from adult language.

back (-ed, -ing)   A descriptive term for sounds: back sounds are produced at the back of the mouth, and/or by the back of the tongue. In the description and classification of VOWELS, back vowels form part of a three-way classification, contrasting with FRONT and

CENTRAL vowels. Examples from English (RP) include [u] (the vowel sound in *boot*) and [ɑ] (the vowel sound in *part*). **Backing** refers to instances when vowels are pronounced further back relative to a particular reference point (e.g. a previous pronunciation in the case of a SOUND CHANGE). See also INTERNATIONAL PHONETIC ALPHABET; PHONETICS.

back channel Back channels, or **back channel responses**, are a form of listener behaviour associated with conversational support – they may include MINIMAL RESPONSES such as *mmh*, *yeah*, *that's right*, the repetition of a speaker's utterance, etc. NON-VERBAL COMMUNICATION such as nodding may also function as back-channel support. Back channels are often distinguished from SPEAKING TURNS – i.e. they are seen as support for another's turn rather than a speaking turn in their own right. See also CONVERSATION MANAGEMENT; TURN-TAKING.

back slang The practice of inverting elements in words, usually based on spelling but sometimes on sound. For example, the French variety Verlan (an inversion of *(à) l'envers*, or 'back to front', 'the wrong way round') inverts syllables, to give *féca* for *café* and *tromé* for *métro*. The British gay language Polari includes some words that are spelt backwards – *ecaf* for *face*, *riah* for *hair*. This is often done to create a SECRET LANGUAGE, but is also a form of LANGUAGE PLAY.

backsliding In second-language acquisition backsliding refers to the reappearance of erroneous or 'developmental' features of a learner's FIRST LANGUAGE which were thought to have been eradicated. Typically, speakers who have mastered a feature of pronunciation or grammar of the TARGET language may revert to an earlier form (usually an error) in situations which are stressful or if the learner's attention is focused on some other part of the grammar. If the INTERLANGUAGE stabilises as a second-language variety, backsliding may become adapted as a feature of STYLISTIC VARIATION or LECTAL SHIFTING.

Bakhtin, Mikhail (1895–1975) A Russian literary theorist and philosopher of language working in conjunction with a group of intellectuals, often currently referred to as the 'Bakhtin circle'. Through translation, his work on language, meaning and authoring began to make an impact in the West in the 1970s mainly in the field of literature. In more recent times key notions such as DIALOGIC or 'dialogism', ADDRESSIVITY, CARNIVAL, INTERTEXTUALITY have been used in linguistics, sociolinguistics and education. There is dispute over the authorship of some of the works published by members of the Bakhtin circle and the extent to which early works can be attributed to Bakhtin or to his colleagues Valentin VOLOSHINOV and Pavel Medvedev.

balance hypothesis   A hypothesis formulated in the 1960s that BILINGUALISM has a detrimental effect on linguistic skills. Human beings are claimed to have a certain neural potential for language learning. Learning an additional language implied fewer skills in a speaker's first language, compared to monolingual speakers. Originally hypothesised as 'a balance effect' by John Macnamara (1966) using the metaphor of a weighing scale. Using Spanish-English bilinguals in Texas as an example, Macnamara asked whether 'the more Spanish a child uses, the poorer his knowledge of English and vice versa' (1966: 15). The hypothesis has not stood up to scrutiny. Successful acquisition of more than one language is achievable given the right social circumstances, and is commonplace in multilingual societies. See also SEMI-LINGUALISM; STABLE BILINGUALISM.

balanced bilingual   A BILINGUAL speaker who has complete fluency in two languages. In theory, such a speaker functions equally well in all domains of activity, and without any influences from one language upon the other. The term differentiates such bilingual speakers from those who may be considered bilingual, but are clearly dominant in their FIRST LANGUAGE. The synonyms **ambilingual** and **equilingual** are also found. See also CLINE.

BASIC English   A reduced version of standard English developed by C. K. Odgen (1938) to facilitate international communication. BASIC is an acronym for 'British American Scientific International Commercial' – a name that outlines the linguistic basis and anticipated functions of this linguistic form. Basic English, as proposed by Odgen, consists of a minimal vocabulary of 850 words and a small set of grammatical rules. See also ARTIFICIAL LANGUAGE.

basilang, mesolang, acrolang   Terms used by John Schumann (1974) for types of INTERLANGUAGE or forms of a second language still being developed by a learner or group of learners. **Basilang** is related to BASILECT in CREOLE linguistics, denoting the 'deep' form of a Creole which shows the greatest difference from the original language it derived from (or from which at least its vocabulary was derived – see LEXIFIER LANGUAGE). However, whereas a basilect is a stable first language, a basilang is typically an unstable, rudimentary second language. Similarly, the terms **mesolang** and **acrolang** are formed by analogy with 'mesolect' and 'acrolect'. Acrolang denotes an advanced interlanguage, close to the TARGET language being learned, that is nevertheless recognisable as a second-language version of it. Mesolang is a loose cover term for interlanguage varieties intermediate between basilang and acrolang.

basilect, mesolect, acrolect   **Basilect** was first used by William Stewart (1965) for the form of a CREOLE language that shows the greatest difference from the original language it derived from (or from which the main part of its vocabulary was derived – see LEXIFIER LANGUAGE). Such a **basilectal Creole** (e.g. forms of Jamaican Creole English) exhibits a totally different structure from its lexifier (English) and the two varieties are mutually unintelligible. A basilect is nevertheless a system in its own right, and serves as a VERNACULAR language. Under certain conditions other varieties arise that are intermediate between a basilectal Creole and its lexifier language. The variety within this CREOLE CONTINUUM that is closest to the lexifier but which is distinguished from it in matters of accent and some minor aspects of grammar is termed the **acrolect**. **Mesolect** is a cover term for a spectrum of varieties intermediate in form between basilect and acrolect.

Bernstein, Basil (1924–2000)   A British sociolinguist who has had a major impact on sociology, education and linguistics. He is best known for his four-volumed *Class, Codes and Control* (1971) in which the distinction between ELABORATED and restricted codes was enunciated and explored (see also CODE). Bernstein focused on the differences in socialisation between working-class and middle-class children in Britain, seeing language as a significant source and cause of disparity in success in educational institutions, which had the same 'orientation' as that of the elaborated codes of the middle classes. Bernstein came under strong attack from sociolinguists, who took him to endorse a DEFICIT rather than DIFFERENCE view of languages and dialects. Nevertheless, he remains an important figure in the field of language in education.

Bickerton, Derek (1926–)   Derek Bickerton propounded the BIOPRO-GRAMME theory of the origins of CREOLES, in which he emphasised the universal mental capacity for language among humans in characterising the features of Creole grammars, rather than socio-historical explanations based on LANGUAGE CONTACT. The adjective **Bickertonian** is found for these ideas. Bickerton was born in Cheshire, UK, and had a distinguished career as novelist, journalist and EFL professor. He is best known for his work on Guyanese Creole English and Hawaiian Creole English. His ideas expressed in *Roots of Language* (1981) have been debated outside linguistics.

bidialectal Refers to the use of two or more dialects. The term **bidialectalism** is also found. In education, usually refers to approaches that seek to teach a standard variety while also valuing children's home or community dialects rather than eradicating these. Such approaches tend to be based on the notion of APPROPRIATENESS: home/community dialects are appropriate in certain (local) contexts but children need also to learn the standard as a means of wider communication. See e.g. Trudgill (2000) for a discussion of this position. On the use of dialects in education more generally, see Wolfram, Christian and Adger (1999); see also Smitherman (2000) on AFRICAN AMERICAN VERNACULAR ENGLISH (AAVE). Dialects, and the relationship between standard and non-standard forms, may be a focus of LANGUAGE AWARENESS programmes. However, bidialectal approaches based on appropriateness may be criticised on the grounds that they ignore differences in power between standard and non-standard varieties: contrast CRITICAL LANGUAGE AWARENESS.

bilabial A term used in the description and classification of CONSONANTS, relating to their PLACE OF ARTICULATION. Bilabial sounds are produced by the lips. Examples from English include: [b], [p] and [m]. See also INTERNATIONAL PHONETIC ALPHABET; PHONETICS.

bilingual (-ism) Bilingualism is the use of two or more languages (the latter is sometimes also called MULTILINGUALISM) by an individual or by a speech community. A distinction is sometimes made between **individual bilingualism** (i.e. individuals who speak more than one language, but who do not necessarily live in a bi- or multilingual community) and **societal bilingualism** (i.e. societies in which several languages are spoken, although not all members of the society are necessarily proficient in more than one language). Although many countries take great pride in the fact that they have a single national language, no modern society is actually MONOLINGUAL (i.e. where only one language is used by the population of the country). Even a highly homogeneous SPEECH COMMUNITY such as, for example, Iceland will include migrants who bring their languages with them, and often English is used by local professionals in international communication (e.g. e-mails, transnational collaborations, etc.). Many countries are highly multilingual, such as Namibia, where over twenty different languages are spoken by a population of just over one million people.

The term **bilinguality** is sometimes found as an alternative to bilingualism. See also BILINGUAL EDUCATION.

bilingual education   Used to refer to education programmes which involve two or more languages. In some national contexts, bilingual education programmes are common, such as in Brunei, where education takes place in standard Malay and English. However, in many contexts bilingual programmes are experienced by only a limited number of students. The stated purposes of bilingual programmes vary but include the following: (a) linguistic and cultural enrichment (often associated with MAJORITY LANGUAGE speakers, such as English-speaking Canadians studying through a bilingual French/ English programme); (b) language maintenance (often associated with MINORITY LANGUAGE speakers, such as Turkish speakers in the UK); (c) language revival (such as Welsh/ English and Irish/English bilingual programmes in Wales and Ireland respectively) – see also RE-NATIVISATION. Outcomes vary depending on the goals, resources and ideology of the programmes in question. Thus enrichment programmes are more likely to lead to ADDITIVE BILINGUALISM, whereas maintenance programmes (with an emphasis on transition from the minority to the majority language) often lead to SUBTRACTIVE BILINGUALISM. Much controversy surrounds bilingual education in relation to minority language speakers, who are typically in a less powerful social position than majority language speakers. (For an overview see Brisk, 1998; Skutnabb-Kangas, 1995.)

bilingual mixed language   See MIXED CODE.

bioprogramme   A theory concerning the origins of CREOLE languages propounded by Derek BICKERTON. Bickerton argued that Creoles were very special languages insofar as they arose in societies in which no language was readily available as a model for the first generation of children. In early slave-holding societies of the Caribbean, for example, neither the European colonial language (see LEXIFIER LANGUAGE) nor the diversity of African languages was readily available to children; the only readily available variety was the rudimentary PIDGIN, which was inadequate as a suitable model for a first language. Under these circumstances, Bickerton argued, the bioprogramme, or human beings' genetic propensity for language, came into play, enabling children to develop a 'full' language having a grammar of its own, while drawing on the vocabulary of the languages of the environment, especially that of the pidgin. This theory of human beings 'creating their own language' when adequate INPUT was absent from the previous generations has attracted a great deal of attention outside sociolinguistics. Within sociolinguistics, however, it is hotly contested and cast into doubt as more socio-historical research unfolds. See also CREATIONISM; GRADUALISM.

Black English Vernacular (BEV)   A term used in the 1960s and 1970s to refer to AFRICAN AMERICAN VERNACULAR ENGLISH.

body language   See NON-VERBAL COMMUNICATION.

border crossing   Used by Norman Fairclough to refer to the ways in which the borders between DISCOURSES are constantly restructured or 'crossed' in language use. Examples include the increasing use of CONVERSATIONALISATION in public domains; and the way in which public service discourse in contemporary job advertisements borrows from the discourse of advertising (an aspect of a process termed MARKETISATION); see Fairclough (1996). Border crossing is often used to refer to questions of inter/intra-ethnic IDENTITY and group solidarity. Studies in the phenomenon of crossing echo and often explicitly draw on Bakhtin's notions of POLYPHONY, DOUBLE VOICING and INTERTEXTUALITY.

border dialect   A dialect spoken in a geographical region which is located along or near a linguistic border separating two well-defined dialect areas (see TRANSITION AREA). According to Chambers and Trudgill (1998) two different types of border dialects can be distinguished: mixed and fudged dialects. In **mixed dialects** speakers alternate in their use of the linguistic forms which are characteristic of the adjacent dialect regions. For example, speakers of the Cologne dialect in Germany show variation between two pronunciations of the verb 'to make': *machen* (pronounced with a [χ] sound between the two vowels) and *maken* (pronounced with a [k] sound); north of Cologne, dialect speakers only use the form *maken*, whereas south of Cologne the form *machen* is used. In the case of **fudged dialects**, instead of variation between forms one finds intermediate forms. For example, in the north of England the word *cup* is pronounced with a [ʊ] and in the south with a [ʌ]. In the transition area between north and south, speakers use a phonetically 'fudged' form: [ɤ].

borrowing   Borrowing occurs when a vocabulary item from one language enters the vocabulary of another, as in English *garage* from French; or French *le weekend* or *lifter* from English (one meaning of the latter is to give someone a face-lift and, by extension, to renovate or rejuvenate). As a noun, 'borrowing' may refer to the process of borrowing or to the borrowed item; a borrowed word is also known as a LOANWORD. The language that receives the borrowed item may be termed the HOST LANGUAGE, and the language that provides the item the SOURCE LANGUAGE.

Borrowing may involve different degrees of integration into the host language: in the case of *le weekend*, *weekend* has been assigned a grammatical GENDER (masculine) but retains its MORPHOLOGY, meaning, spelling and at least approximate pronunciation. *Lifter* has been integrated into the French verb system (it takes French verb inflections), it has French pronunciation and its meaning and use have changed (the English verb *lift* is not used in the same way). Sometimes words or expressions are translated into another language, as in French *lune de miel* meaning 'honeymoon' (*lune* means 'moon' in French and *miel*, 'honey'). This type of borrowing is known as a CALQUE (itself borrowed from French!), or a **loan translation**. Grammatical structures may also be borrowed.

A distinction has sometimes been drawn between an established borrowing and a **nonce borrowing**, with the latter characterised as a less-frequently-used item, restricted to bilingual speakers, and not integrated into the host language (Weinreich, [1953] 1968; Poplack, Sankoff and Miller, 1988). The distinction between nonce borrowing and CODE-SWITCHING involving a single vocabulary item is by no means straightforward (see Myers-Scotton, 1993a).

Borrowing has been the subject of LANGUAGE PLANNING (e.g. borrowing from an internationally powerful language such as English may be resisted, and attempts made to generate new vocabulary items from the existing resources of the host language). See also BILINGUAL(ISM); LANGUAGE CONTACT.

bottom–up   In relation to linguistic analysis, 'bottom–up' refers to approaches that begin with smaller units (e.g. words) and work up to larger units (e.g. TEXTS). In relation to LANGUAGE PLANNING, the term refers to planning activity that takes place in close consultation with the SPEECH COMMUNITY. Bottom–up language planning shows direct community participation and draws directly on existing community practices and attitudes. Contrast TOP–DOWN.

Bourdieu, Pierre (1930–2002)   A French social theorist whose works have focused on power and domination across a range of social practices, including language, education, and aesthetic taste. His work has made significant impact on socially oriented approaches to the study of language, particularly the areas of CRITICAL LINGUISTICS and CRITICAL DISCOURSE ANALYSIS. Key notions drawn on in studies of language and communication are HABITUS and SYMBOLIC POWER.

broad (transcription)   See TRANSCRIPT (TRANSCRIPTION).

Cafeteria Principle   Term coined by J. L. Dillard (1970) expressing scepticism over the alleged heterogeneous origins of different features of PIDGIN and (especially) CREOLE grammars. The analogy is based on an individual choosing food from a cafeteria on an idiosyncratic and eclectic basis. Dillard argued that speakers in a LANGUAGE CONTACT situation do not stand in line picking an item from one variety and another from another (and so on) at will or at random. Dillard's original principle was meant as a critique of those tracing features of English Creoles of the Caribbean and USA solely, or mainly, to various regional dialects of Britain. It was later applied by those critiquing the position that all or most features of these Creoles were obtained from different African languages more or less at random. In both cases the term is used to plead for more careful accounts of the origins of specific features of a pidgin or Creole, making reference to factors relating to demographics (the number of speakers of a language present during PIDGINISATION or creolisation), prominence and/or accessibility of the language and its speakers, and to the specifics of the grammatical feature present.

calque   A type of BORROWING in which words or expressions are translated from one language into another, as in French *lune de miel* meaning 'honeymoon' (*lune* means 'moon' in French and *miel*, 'honey'); or *tasse de thé* (from the English 'cup of tea') as in *Ce n'est pas ma tasse de thé* ('It's not my cup of tea'). This type of borrowing is also known as a **loan translation**.

cant   A set of special words and phrases associated with a particular social group – usually a subcultural group which needs to maintain secrecy from outsiders (see SUBCULTURE). This is distinct from the alternative everyday meaning of 'insincere language'. See also ARGOT.

cardinal vowels   Cardinal vowels are reference points devised to aid the description and classification of VOWEL sounds in a language. Figure 1 below shows the eight primary cardinal vowels. In Figure 1, [i, a ɑ, u] represent extreme points of articulation – e.g. [i] is the vowel sound produced when the front of the tongue is in the highest position it can attain without causing friction in the air stream; [a] is the vowel sound produced when the front of the tongue is in its lowest possible position. [e, ɛ, ɔ, o] represent mid-points, in terms of tongue height, between these extremes. There are additional cardinal vowels to represent a full set of vowels produced with and without lip ROUNDING, and to include vowels in the centre of the chart. Linguists need to learn these cardinal vowel sounds, and can then map actual pronunciations against them.

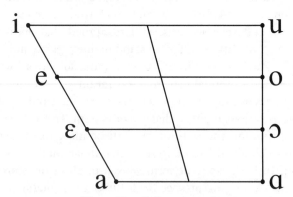

Figure 1   Primary cardinal vowels

careful speech   A MONITORED SPEECH style (i.e. a style in which speakers pay ATTENTION to the way they sound), which William LABOV described as characteristic of formal conversations. Careful speech forms part of a STYLISTIC CONTINUUM and is elicited at the beginning of the Labovian sociolinguistic INTERVIEW when the inhibiting effects of recording and observation (see OBSERVER'S PARADOX) are most noticeable. Contrasts with CASUAL SPEECH.

care-giver speech   See CHILD-DIRECTED SPEECH.

carnival(isation)   A key concept in BAKHTIN's study of literary GENRES and his theory of language. This notion draws on rituals of medieval carnival where conventional power structures and social values were challenged, often through parody of prominent local political or church leaders, and which are exemplified in medieval literature such as works by the French writer Rabelais. For Bakhtin carnival captures the tension that exists between official and unofficial DISCOURSES and is one of the more obvious indications of the DIALOGIC nature of language (see Bakhtin, [1965] 1984b). See also HETEROGLOSSIA.

CARS   CARS is an acronym which stands for Create a Research Space and indicates the MOVES that are conventionally made in introductions to academic research articles (Swales, 1981, 1990). The identification of CARS illustrates a prominent aim of work in TEACHING ENGLISH TO SPEAKERS OF OTHER LANGUAGES (TESOL), that is, to describe key features of academic texts for teaching purposes (see ACADEMIC LITERACY).

caste   Caste refers to a social system in which a person's STATUS and ROLE are determined by birth. Typically, the caste and subcaste a person is born into are identified with specific occupations and marriage is restricted to the subcaste. Such a rigid limitation on SOCIAL NETWORKS gives rise to differentiation within a language, with social DIALECTS becoming associated with specific castes (hence called **caste dialects**). Since castes are hierarchically organised in terms of status, caste dialects show relatively rigid social STRATIFICATION. Among the caste dialects that have been claimed to have distinct characteristics are those of Brahmins (the highest caste of priests and their families) as opposed to non-Brahmin speech in most parts of India (Bright and Ramanujan, 1964), and the dialects of fishermen in coastal areas like Kanyakumari (Pillai, 1968).

casual speech   An unmonitored, informal speech style which is systematically elicited in the type of sociolinguistic INTERVIEW developed by William LABOV, using triggers such as the DANGER OF DEATH question. Casual speech forms part of the STYLISTIC CONTINUUM where it contrasts with CAREFUL SPEECH. See also VERNACULAR.

cataphoric (reference)   Grammatical term used to describe a linguistic feature which refers forward to another element in any given TEXT. For example, in the sentence '*Here* are two examples of fossil fuels:

coal and wood', the word *here* has a cataphoric function. Cataphoric reference, stands in contrast to ANAPHORIC reference which refers to something that has previously been mentioned. See also COHESION; ENDOPHORIC; EXOPHORIC; REFERENCE.

CDA   See CRITICAL DISCOURSE ANALYSIS.

census   Comprehensive demographic data typically collected at the national level using QUESTIONNAIRES. Census data may include information on language use, for example, number of speakers of particular languages, degree of BILINGUALISM, generational and regional distribution of speakers, etc. Census data on language need to be interpreted carefully. Census information elicits a speakers' subjective perceptions and beliefs about language use, and is not necessarily an accurate reflection of their actual linguistic practices. Nevertheless, census data are an important source for the QUANTITATIVE investigation of language use in a country. Unlike SURVEY data, census data is not based on a SAMPLE but provides information on all people in a given country, area or city.

central (-ise(d))   A descriptive term for sounds, used particularly in the description and classification of VOWELS: central vowels are produced when the highest point of the tongue is central in the mouth. These may be contrasted with FRONT and BACK vowels. An example from English is the sound [ə], often termed **schwa**, and heard in unstressed syllables – e.g. the first vowel sound in *about* and the second in *matter*. Sounds are said to be **centralised** when they are produced more centrally (e.g. in certain linguistic environments or as a result of LANGUAGE CHANGE). See also INTERNATIONAL PHONETIC ALPHABET; PHONETICS.

centre, periphery   Influenced by the work of the social theorist Immanuel Wallerstein and his work on world systems (Wallerstein, 1974, 1991), these terms are used to describe relations between the economically and politically powerful Western, highly industrialised countries (**centre**) and the developing, poorer countries (**periphery**). The periphery is understood as being made dependent on the centre in numerous ways – economic, political, cultural – which ensure its peripheral status. The relevance of the centre/periphery relationship to issues of language, literacy and communication has been explored in several ways. For example, centre/periphery relations are critically examined in work focusing on NEW ENGLISHES, and

English as a GLOBAL LANGUAGE (see Kachru, 1992; Phillipson, 1992). Centre/periphery relations are also examined in work focusing on ACADEMIC LITERACY in a global context, particularly the impact of differential material conditions on academic knowledge production (see Canagarajah, 2002). See also LINGUISTIC IMPERIALISM; THREE CIRCLES OF ENGLISH; WORLD ENGLISH(ES).

centrifugual   See HETEROGLOSSIA.

centripetal   See HETEROGLOSSIA.

chain shift   A type of SOUND CHANGE involving a series of closely interconnected changes. Typically, a PHONEME (A) will acquire the phonetic characteristics of another phoneme (B), which as a result will move into the phonetic space occupied by a different phoneme (C). In the SOUTHERN HEMISPHERE SHIFT (Lass and Wright, 1986), which is in progress in South Africa and also New Zealand, the vowel in *bat* has been RAISED and sounds similar to RP *bet*. As a result, the vowel in *bet* has been raised further and now sounds similar to RP *bit*, and the vowel in *bit* has been CENTRALISED to [ï]. Other examples are the NORTHERN CITIES SHIFT, which has been studied by William LABOV and his associates, and the GREAT VOWEL SHIFT. Although chain shifts typically involve vowels, they have also been described for consonants (Campell, 1997).

change (in language)   See LANGUAGE CHANGE.

change from above   Introduced by William LABOV (1972a) to describe linguistic changes of which speakers are consciously aware (the linguistic forms involved in the change are said to be 'above' the level of social awareness). Changes from above support the spread of linguistic forms which carry social PRESTIGE (i.e. forms that are characteristic of the speech of the dominant or most influential social class). Speakers adopt these prestigious variants first in formal speech styles and only later in informal, casual styles. The increase of POST-VOCALIC /r/ in New York, studied by Labov, is an example of a change from above. Linguistic BORROWING is also often motivated by prestige (e.g. borrowing from French in Europe in the eighteenth century, or borrowing from English in many languages today), and speakers are usually aware of their use of foreign language material. Contrasts with CHANGE FROM BELOW. See also CROSS-OVER PATTERN.

change from below   Linguistic changes of which speakers are not consciously aware (the linguistic forms involved are said to be 'below' the level of social awareness). Changes from below typically involve the adoption and spread of linguistic forms characteristic of low-PRESTIGE social varieties. Changes from below affect informal and formal speech styles simultaneously. The SOUTHERN HEMISPHERE SHIFT and the NORTHERN CITIES SHIFT are both examples of changes from below. Contrasts with CHANGE FROM ABOVE. See also CURVILINEAR PATTERN.

change in progress   A not yet completed LANGUAGE CHANGE which only affects certain groups in a speech community or certain linguistic styles or DOMAINS. William LABOV (1972a) has shown in his research that it is possible to describe a linguistic change in progress if one carefully studies patterns of language use across different social groups (defined according to sociological criteria such as social class, gender, age or ethnicity), and across different linguistic styles (CAREFUL SPEECH and CASUAL SPEECH, reading styles, etc.; see STYLISTIC CONTINUUM). In a change in progress not all social groups will use new linguistic forms to the same degree: some groups will use the new form frequently, while others will use it only rarely or never. Moreover, the new forms will not be used immediately in all linguistic styles. The spread of a linguistic change across groups and linguistic styles is usually gradual. See also CHANGE FROM ABOVE; CHANGE FROM BELOW.

channel   In a narrow sense, 'channel' refers to the physical material via which a message is transmitted (e.g. sound waves in the case of speech). However, channel is also found in a similar sense to MEDIUM (2) or MODE, in which case speech and writing might be referred to as channels. See also CHANNEL CUES.

channel cues   PARALINGUISTIC features which signal a shift in the INTERVIEW situation. In Labovian sociolinguistics (see LABOV) particular attention has been paid to channel cues, which are interpreted as markers of informality, and which are believed to co-occur with the use of CASUAL SPEECH. Examples of channel cues are increases in speech rate, volume and pitch range, laughter and rate of breathing. However, paralinguistic features are often ambiguous. Laughter, for example, can also be an indicator of nervousness and might thus appear in the more formal parts of the interview. Increases in speech rate and volume are also characteristic of some CAREFUL SPEECH styles, for example, in the linguistic performances of Hip-Hop musicians or orators (such as preachers).

chi-square   A statistical test which allows one to assess the statistical significance (see SIGNIFICANCE TESTING) of observed differences in the behaviour of two or more groups on a linguistic or attitudinal variable. The chi-square test measures this by comparing the difference between the actual (observed) data distribution and the expected (hypothetical) distribution.

For example, one might be interested in whether students at a university consider their foreign-language classes adequate for their needs. Of a total population of 1,000 students, a SAMPLE of 100 male students and 100 female students is asked a question about this in an interview. Of the male students, assume that 20 indicate that they find the classes inadequate, and of the female students 60 find the classes inadequate. If male and female students were to react similarly to the language instruction provided, one would expect no major differences in their response rate (i.e. more or less the same percentage of male and female students would be dissatisfied with the language instruction). One could now use the chi-square test to determine whether the observed differences in response are indeed significantly different (i.e. are likely to occur also in the population from which the research sample was drawn), and are not the result of a sampling error.

child-directed speech (CDS)   Any form of language used by adults towards children. This cover term includes special REGISTERS like BABY TALK (i.e. simplified language used by adults in some societies when addressing children). Whereas baby talk has negative overtones and involves some degree of 'talking down' to very young children, other forms of CDS like 'motherese', 'fatherese' or more generally 'caregiver speech' may or may not include a degree of baby talk. The original term 'motherese' assumed that mothers were the primary caregivers. 'Fatherese' was coined to make up for the sexism inherent in this assumption, and also allowed for the possibility that mothers and fathers might speak to children differently (see Barton and Tomasello, 1994). 'Caregiver speech' bypasses these gender nuances and acknowledges that a wider range of people may play a role in bringing up children. These registers are of special interest as forms of INPUT (by, respectively, mothers, fathers or other caregivers) in studies of CHILD LANGUAGE, especially in the light of Chomsky's theory of language acquisition, which assigns a minor role to input

in triggering the child's linguistic COMPETENCE. Sociolinguists like
HALLIDAY stress, rather, the emerging interactional nature of language evident in child–adult (and even child-child) encounters. On
cross-cultural and cross–linguistic differences in language addressed
to children, see, for instance, Lieven (1994).

child language   The language of young children, at the stage(s) at
which it is recognisably different from that of older children and
adults. Child language differs from adult language largely in grammar and less so in matters of pronunciation and vocabulary. In
grammar, children go through a 'one-word' stage when a single word
is used HOLOPHRASTICally (i.e. to express what would be a sentence in
adult language). Thus *doggie* supplemented by a gesture could mean
'The dog is approaching.' Child language evolves through regular
stages, with the grammar of the language being mastered largely by
the age of five. Roger Brown's *A First Language: The Early Stages*
(1973) remains one of the key studies in this area. Whereas studies of
child language frequently involve a developmental or longitudinal
perspective, the terms **children's language** and YOUTH LANGUAGE
imply the study of interaction among children or young people with
less emphasis on grammatical stages. See also ADOLESCENCE; BABY
TALK; CHILD-DIRECTED SPEECH (CDS); LANGUAGE ACQUISITION.

citation form
1. In sociolinguistics, the pronunciation of a word or phrase in
   isolation, rather than in CONNECTED SPEECH. Citation forms usually
   produce more careful or formal pronunciations than connected
   speech, in which PHONOLOGICAL processes such as ASSIMILATION
   occur.
2. In lexicography, the form in which a dictionary entry for a word
   occurs. In French a verb is referred to by the infinitive form:
   savoir 'to know'. In Zulu dictionaries the infinitive prefix *uku-* is
   usually omitted, to avoid placing all verbs under 'u' in the
   alphabetical listing: hence *-funda* rather than *uku-funda* 'to learn'
   is listed.

class   See SOCIAL CLASS; for **class dialect**, see DIALECT.

clause   Term in common usage across a range of grammatical approaches to refer to a unit of syntactic analysis (see SYNTAX). In
some grammars, such as Quirk et al. (1985), a clause is described as
a unit smaller than a sentence and larger than a phrase. Thus in the

sentence, *Spring is in the air and the days are getting longer* there are two clauses connected by *and*. These clauses are made up of a number of phrases; for example NOUN PHRASES, such as *the air, the days* and VERB PHRASES, such as *are getting* (see Graddol et al., 1994). However, usages vary in different grammars. In SYSTEMIC FUNCTIONAL LINGUISTICS, the term **clause complex** is used for 'sentence'; GROUP is also sometimes used for 'phrase'.

cline   Refers to a situation in which a linguistic phenomenon has a range or gradient or continuum of possibilities or occurrences. Hence a **cline of bilingualism** is a graded continuum of bilingualism. At one extreme are people who are marginally bilingual, showing minimal fluency in a SECOND LANGUAGE. At the other end are BALANCED BILINGUALS: individuals with full command of two languages. Most bilingual speakers are located somewhere between these extremes.

close (vowel)   A term used in the description and classification of VOWELS: close vowels are produced when the tongue is high in the mouth (the term HIGH VOWEL is also found). This is part of a four-way classification of vowels depending on tongue height: close – **half close** – half open – OPEN. Examples of close vowels from English include [i] (the vowel in *beat*) and [u] (the vowel in *boot*). A half-close vowel would be [e], as in French *thé* ('tea'). The nearest example in English would be the vowel in *date* with a northern English pronunciation. Some forms of SOUND CHANGE result in vowels becoming closer, a phenomenon known as RAISING. See also INTERNATIONAL PHONETIC ALPHABET; PHONETICS.

closed (word class)   See OPEN (2).

closing   In CONVERSATION ANALYSIS, closings are the means by which speakers bring a conversation to a close. This is not as straightforward as it seems – silence is rare in conversation and when one speaker stops talking another usually begins, or at least provides a MINIMAL RESPONSE. In a now classic paper, Schegloff and Sacks (1973) discuss how speakers coordinate their activity to provide an 'opening for a close' that may bring about a closing sequence: see also SEQUENTIAL ORGANISATION.

cluster analysis   A type of multi-variate DESCRIPTIVE STATISTICS which groups cases (e.g. members of a SPEECH COMMUNITY or text SAMPLES) on the basis of similarity. Cluster analysis was used in the sociolinguistic survey of multilingual communities in Belize and St Lucia carried out by Robert Le Page and Andrée Tabouret-Keller (1985), in order to identify groups of speakers based on similarities in their linguistic behaviour. This approach contrasts with the LABOVian tradition, which investigates the language use of speakers assigned to pre-established social groups (e.g. MIDDLE CLASS; WORKING CLASS).

coda   See NARRATIVE.

code
1. May be used to refer to any SIGN system, including human language. Within sociolinguistics, 'code' is sometimes used as a neutral term to refer to a language or language variety, seeking to avoid the subjective nuances associated with terms like DIALECT. The term lays emphasis upon the linguistic system as an abstract code, comprising meaning-bearing elements that may be realised differently in different STYLES or REGISTERS or by different SOCIAL GROUPS. (See also CODE-SWITCHING; MIXED CODE).
2. Also used by Basil BERNSTEIN to refer to particular types of orientation to language use which were differentiated along SOCIAL CLASS lines: see ELABORATED, RESTRICTED (CODES). In more recent work, Bernstein focused on **pedagogic codes**, that is the underlying rules governing professionals' use of language in pedagogic contexts, most obviously in schools (see Bernstein, 1996).

code alternation   See CODE-SWITCHING.

code choice   See LANGUAGE CHOICE.

code-mixing   See CODE-SWITCHING.

code-switching   Refers to instances when speakers switch between CODES (languages, or language varieties) in the course of a conversation. Switches may involve different amounts of speech and different linguistic units – from several consecutive utterances to individual words and morphemes, as in the example below:

Lakini ni-ko *sure* ukienda *after two days* utaipata 'Uchumi' *supermarket* kwa wingi. ('But I'm sure if you go after two days you will get it [Omo detergent] at "Uchumi" supermarket in abundance.')

(Speaker in Kenya switching between Swahili (plain text) and English (italics), adapted from Myers-Scotton, 1993a: 4)

A formal distinction is sometimes made between **intra-sentential code-switching**, where switches occur within a sentence as in the example above; and **inter-sentential code-switching**, where a switch occurs at the end of a sentence. A plethora of terms exists for this form of language behaviour, and these are not always used consistently between studies. **Code-mixing** is found, particularly for intra-sentential switching. Other terms include **language/ dialect switching, language/dialect mixing, code alternation** and **language alternation**.

'Code-switching' may also be found in a narrower or more specific sense: for example, Auer has distinguished **transfer**, or later **insertion**: the insertion of a particular structure (word, phrase etc.) from another language variety; from code-switching into another variety at a particular point in the conversation. Language or code alternation is used as the generic term (see e.g. Auer, 1984, 1998).

Researchers have been interested in the social motivations for code-switching, how this contributes to CONVERSATION MANAGEMENT; and how it relates to the grammar of each language. See also BORROWING; DISCOURSE-RELATED, PREFERENCE-RELATED (CODE-SWITCHING); LANGUAGE CONTACT; LANGUAGE CHOICE; MIXED CODE; SITUATIONAL, METAPHORICAL (CODE-SWITCHING); 'WE' AND 'THEY' CODES.

codification   An aspect of LANGUAGE PLANNING and language STANDARDISATION. Codification involves activities directed at establishing prescriptive norms of the linguistic CODE (i.e. the language system) through the publication of GRAMMARS, spelling rules, style manuals or DICTIONARIES. See also CORPUS PLANNING, STATUS PLANNING.

cognitive frame   See FRAME.

coherence   Term used to refer to the ways in which TEXTS make sense to readers and listeners. It involves a focus on readers'/listeners' extra-linguistic assumptions and understandings, that is the kind of knowledge they bring to a particular text rather than on what is explicitly stated in a text. For example, the following text: *Bremner was offside. The referee blew his whistle. Several Leeds players complained.* is coherent to those who share an understanding of football and even more specific knowledge about who plays for which team.

Whilst a distinction is often made between coherence and COHE-SION — with coherence relating to extra-linguistic knowledge and cohesion relating to textual devices — there is often some confusion and slippage between actual uses of these terms.

cohesion   Used to refer to the way in which TEXTS function as cohesive units. Smaller linguistic units — such as words, phrases, clauses — are bound together through cohesive devices to construct a larger unit or text. **Cohesive devices** may take a number of forms, for example, pronouns, nouns, conjunctions. For instance in the following two clauses: *Dr. Garcia examined the patient. She began by checking his temperature, she* in clause 2 refers back to *Dr Garcia*, and *his* refers back to *the patient.* Clauses 1 and 2 do not stand alone but are bound together through the use of particular cohesive devices, which in this example are pronouns. This is an example of a particular type of cohesion known as REFERENCE (for full discussion, see Halliday and Hasan, 1976, 1985). See also COHERENCE.

collocation   Used to refer to the patterns of co-occurrences of particular words. For example, in English the word *rancid* usually collocates with *butter*, and *spick* with *span*. The systematic study of collocation patterns has been made more possible by the development of computer software tools such as CONCORDANCE programmes (see also CORPUS). Identifying common collocation patterns contributes to the study of meaning, incorporating evidence from instances of language use rather than relying on linguists' or speakers' intuitions; it also has practical benefits, for example in the writing of dictionaries (e.g. Sinclair, 1987). A predilection for unusual collocations makes poetry a special GENRE, as in for example, 'Earth in *forgetful snow*' from 'The wasteland' by T. S. Eliot, 1922 (Eliot, 1972), or '*Mechanical agony* guided her step' from 'In the city of Boston' by Mary Dorcey (1991): see POETIC.

colloquial language   See VERNACULAR.

colonial lag   In history and sociology the idea that colonial societies did not keep up with fashions of the mother country, and, in addition, held on to customs that were being shed in the mother country. The linguist Manfred Görlach (1987, 1991) investigated whether, in matters of vocabulary, colonial varieties of English (in Australia, India, etc.) could be described as 'not up-to-date and not conversant with modern metropolitan varieties'. Görlach argues that despite some archaisms like *wireless* for 'radio' and *bioscope* for 'cinema' in places like India and South Africa, on the whole linguistic examples are rather meagre. He, therefore, dismisses colonial lag in matters of vocabulary as a myth. The concept may, however, have ramifications for studies of 'colonial' accents and grammatical features. See also HETERONYM.

commodification   Refers to the process of turning language into a commodity. Language is most obviously **commodified** in advertisements: decisions about which kinds of language to use, how these should be represented, in terms of colour, size, shape, and the images against which language should be juxtaposed indicate that language is an important product or commodity rather than simply a mode of transmitting information (see discussions in Chouliaraki and Fairclough, 1999). See also MARKETISATION; REFLEXIVITY.

Communication Accommodation Theory   See ACCOMMODATION.

communicative competence   A term devised by Dell HYMES and based on the linguistic notion of **competence**. Noam Chomsky, for instance, distinguished between competence and PERFORMANCE. Competence refers to speaker-listeners' knowledge of the grammatical system of a language, their ability to produce grammatically-correct sentences and recognise ungrammatical sentences. This is an idealised concept, which Chomsky contrasted with performance: the actual UTTERANCEs produced by speakers, with all their hesitations, disfluencies etc. (e.g. Chomsky, 1957). While Chomsky was concerned with the knowledge of an ideal speaker-listener, Hymes, as a sociolinguist, was concerned with the study of contextualised speech: he famously declared that a child who produced any sentence without due regard to the social and linguistic context would be 'a social monster' (1974: 75). Communicative competence, therefore, refers to what a speaker needs to know, and what a child needs to learn, to be able to use language appropriately in specific social/cultural settings. See also APPROPRIATENESS.

communicative language teaching   Also sometimes called the **communicative approach**. Refers to an approach to the teaching of language(s) which is aimed at developing students' COMMUNICATIVE COMPETENCE in the TARGET language(s). Whilst it encompasses a wide range of classroom practices, emphasis is on teaching through meaningful tasks, often interactive, in an attempt to promote authentic communication in the target language. Language is often analysed in terms of functions rather than formal or grammatical categories. See also AUTHENTICITY.

community language See HERITAGE LANGUAGE.

community of practice An analytical concept derived from the work of Lave and Wenger (e.g. Lave and Wenger, 1991) that is increasingly drawn on in sociolinguistic research, e.g. in relation to LANGUAGE AND GENDER. A community of practice is 'an aggregate of people who come together around mutual engagement in some common endeavour' (Eckert and McConnell-Ginet, 1992: 490). This might include colleagues at work, members of a religious group, friends who meet regularly. The idea is based on the premise that ways of speaking derive from activities or practices engaged in jointly by members. Individual speakers are likely to be members of several communities of practice, and to take on different roles within these. Communities of practice, therefore, provide a means of accounting for the articulation of diverse aspects of speakers' identities. They are compatible with a view of IDENTITY not as a social attribute but as a set of contextualised practices. See also APPRENTICESHIP; DISCOURSE COMMUNITY; SPEECH COMMUNITY.

competence See COMMUNICATIVE COMPETENCE; PERFORMANCE.

complaint (tradition) Used by James Milroy and Lesley Milroy to refer to linguistic complaints – i.e. complaints about aspects of language use. Milroy and Milroy (1999) document a long tradition of complaints about the English language. They argue that linguistic complaints are of interest because they can tell us something about the current status of a language and about language change and attitudes towards this. For instance, a sixteenth-century complaint about the continued use of Latin (rather than English) for writing about medicine is indicative of the gradual increase in the status of English in England and the ELABORATION of its vocabulary to cope with a wider range of functions (as an aspect of STANDARDISATION); complaints that became prevalent from the beginning of the eighteenth-century about 'incorrect' pronunciation and grammar in English are part of a struggle to impose uniformity on the language. See also CORRECTNESS; FOLK LINGUISTICS; LANGUAGE IDEOLOGY; STANDARD LANGUAGE IDEOLOGY.

compound bilingualism A type of individual BILINGUALISM in which a person learns two languages in the same context and uses them in an interdependent way, suggesting that their meaning systems exist in one fused form in the brain. A compound bilingual therefore uses synonyms from each language as if they were exactly equivalent. Thus a compound bilingual in Arabic and English would use both *kitab* (Arabic for 'book') and *book* in the appropriate language, but have one common meaning for them (even though there are subtle differences in their use in the two languages, as spoken by monolinguals). This contrasts with CO-ORDINATE BILINGUALISM, in which two languages exist independently. However, many scholars do not accept this distinction.

computer-mediated communication (CMC) Computer-mediated communication or CMC – the language used in e-mails, computer conferencing, internet relay chat, home pages and other internet texts – has become a topic of increasing interest within sociolinguistics and various areas of DISCOURSE analysis. Researchers are interested in several aspects of CMC, including:

- the status of different languages used on the internet: the current global dominance of English, the extent to which this dominance will be challenged;
- the characteristics of CMC: the extent to which this is more spoken- or written-like; specific features such as vocabulary items (*netiquette, flaming, spam, cyber-*), abbreviations and acronyms (*f2f* for 'face to face', *IRL* for 'in real life'), emoticons such as :-) to indicate a smile;
- CMC and LANGUAGE PLAY;
- whether CMC constitutes a distinctive variety (or set of varieties) of English; CMC and LANGUAGE CHANGE;
- CMC as a form of interaction: e.g. how participants manage multiparty interactions in computer conferencing;
- on-line IDENTITY: how identities are expressed and relationships negotiated in the absence of cues found in face-to-face interactions; whether identities become more fluid and shifting; the extent to which POWER, GENDER etc. remain important factors in CMC.

The term **electronic communication** is sometimes found as an alternative to CMC. For a general introduction to language and the internet, see Crystal (2001); on researching CMC, see the brief introduction in Yates (2001); for examples of specific studies addressing linguistic and cultural issues, see Herring (1996).

conative   A term in psychology meaning 'voluntary action', based on the Latin for 'to try'. Two related usages occur in linguistics.

1. Roman Jakobson used the term to denote a function of language that occurs when a speaker desires a particular action or 'readiness for action' from the ADDRESSEE (person being addressed). Conative language often uses the vocative form of address (*Hey, you!*) and/ or the imperative verb form (*Drink up!*). A more transparent synonym for conative is DIRECTIVE.

2. In studies of language ATTITUDES it is seen as one of three components of 'attitude' (i.e. a 'readiness for action'). In this sense it contrasts with cognitive (reasoning) and affective (emotional) components, which are concerned with the formation of attitudes rather than with action. Conative responses are plans of action based on, and interacting with, the other two components: for instance, a person with a favourable attitude to bilingualism might provide the conative response of enrolling in an adult-education language class.

concord   Grammatical term for relationship in which the form of one particular word determines that of another, also known as **agreement**. Thus in English a singular subject requires (or 'takes') an -*s* ending on a third-person, singular, present-tense verb (*Mary sings*), while a plural subject requires a 'zero-ending' (*The girls sing*). In some languages there is a close phonetic resemblance between the inflections or prefixes that mark concord. In Zulu, for example, different classes of nouns have different prefixes, which then determine the concordial prefix of the verb, any adjectives and relative clauses. Thus in <u>um</u>-*fana* <u>u</u>*dlala* 'the boy plays' the singular noun prefix -*um* shows concord with the phonetically similar verb prefix -*u*. In the plural <u>aba</u>-*fana* <u>ba</u>*dlala* 'the boys play' the plural noun prefix -*aba* concords with the similar verb prefix -*ba*. **Negative concord** refers to the grammatical form of negative constructions in some languages and dialects where a negative realisation of one element like a noun or AUXILIARY verb requires a negative form for all related elements in the clause. Thus in AFRICAN AMERICAN VERNACULAR ENGLISH a standard English sentence like *There is no doubt in anyone's mind* is often phrased as *There ain't no doubt in no one's mind*; see also MULTIPLE NEGATION.

concordance   A computer software tool which enables analysts to find out which words occur alongside, or in the near proximity of other words, usually referred to as COLLOCATION (for a brief overview of corpora databases and computer tools for carrying out analyses, see Hockey, 1998).

conflict (model of society)   See CONSENSUS, CONFLICT (MODELS OF SOCIETY).

connected speech   Term used in linguistics and phonetics for continuous speech as opposed to CITATION forms – words read out in isolation. There are significant differences between the two modes, with a greater degree of phonetic ASSIMILATION and deletion in fast speech. For example, whereas in isolation a speaker might say *half-past-two*, in fast speech it is often *ha' pas' two* [hʌpɑːstuː]. Connected speech may also be referred to as **fast speech** in some contexts.

connotation   An aspect of meaning, referring to the associations that words and expressions have for us (in contrast to their REFERENTIAL meaning or denotation). Thus, for instance, *dog* may connote friendliness, fidelity and trust, or ferocity and danger, or being unclean. Connotations vary between specific contexts, between individuals and between cultures. **Connotative meaning** is particularly important in persuasive discourses such as advertising, political speeches etc.

consensus, conflict (models of society)   In social theory a distinction is often made between consensus and conflict models of society (see Collins, 1975; Waters, 1991). **Consensus** models are based on the functionalist sociology of Talcott Parsons. They describe society as a relatively harmonious and integrated 'organism' governed by an overarching consensus of values across social groups and classes. **Conflict** models (most prominently Marxist class analysis) focus on the schisms in society and the divergence of interests and values between different groups. William LABOV's conception of the SPEECH COMMUNITY and his work on language variation in New York and Philadelphia are based on a broad consensus view of society. A conflict model was used by John Rickford (1986) in his discussion of sociolinguistic variation in Guyana, and by James and Lesley Milroy (1992) in their explanation of the persistence of non-standard varieties in industrial societies. See also FUNCTIONALISM; MARXISM; SOCIAL CLASS; STATUS.

conservative   In discussion of LANGUAGE MAINTENANCE and LANGUAGE CHANGE, conservative speakers are those who maintain features of the language variety current in their SPEECH COMMUNITY rather than adopting new or incoming features (contrast INNOVATOR). Studies have identified certain groups of speakers (men, older speakers, rural speakers) as tending to be more conservative. However, it is likely to be aspects of speakers' lifestyles and the SOCIAL NETWORKS they form part of, rather than simply their SOCIAL GROUP, that lead them to be linguistically conservative or innovative.

consonant   Speech sounds are often categorised as consonants or VOWELS. In terms of their articulation, many consonants are produced when the air stream is impeded in some way: in the case of PLOSIVES such as [b], [d] and [g] the air stream is blocked completely and then released; in the case of FRICATIVES such as [v], [s] and [z] the air stream is constricted, but not completely blocked. Not all sounds that function as consonants involve blocking or constricting the air stream: sounds such as [l] or [w] are said to be more vowel-like in character and are sometimes termed 'semi-vowels'. Consonants are often classified, or distinguished from one another in articulatory terms, that is according to whether they are VOICED or voiceless (produced with or without vocal cord vibration – contrast [b] (voiced) and [p] (voiceless)); their PLACE OF ARTICULATION; and their MANNER OF ARTICULATION. For instance the [p] sound at the beginning of the word *pan* in English would be classified as a 'voiceless bilabial plosive' (produced without voicing, articulated by contact between the lips and produced by the lips blocking the air stream and then releasing this.

Consonants are frequently used as LINGUISTIC VARIABLES in QUANTITATIVE studies of LANGUAGE VARIATION and LANGUAGE CHANGE. They tend to be regarded as discrete variables (e.g. studies would identify the variable use of two or more forms, such as the presence or absence of POST-VOCALIC /r/). While pronunciations are usually identified by ear, acoustic measurement may also be used – see Milroy and Gordon (2003) for a discussion of relevant aspects of methodology.

consonant cluster simplification   The simplification of consonant sequences in conversational speech through the deletion of certain phonetic elements. For example, the deletion of the consonant /t/ in the words *cyclists* or *aspects*, or the conversational pronunciation of *nothing stands still* as [nʌθɪŋstænstɪl] instead of [nʌθɪŋstændzstɪl] (Spencer, 1996). See also -T/-D DELETION.

constative (utterances)   In SPEECH ACT theory, constative utterances are statements of fact that may be either true or false, for example *She came round here again last night*. Constatives were initially distinguished from PERFORMATIVES, which carried out some sort of action rather than being statements of fact. This straightforward distinction was, however, subsequently abandoned.

constraints   Used in the sense of constraints (or limitations) on LANGUAGE VARIATION and LANGUAGE CHANGE. The study of constraints aims to identify general principles which guide the historical development of languages, for example the nature of the vocal tract which limits the kinds of sounds we can produce, or our cognitive and perceptual make-up which might support certain language change processes such as ANALOGY.

consultant   See INFORMANT.

contact (between languages)   See LANGUAGE CONTACT.

contact language   A stable language that arises under certain conditions when two or more languages come into contact with each other (see LANGUAGE CONTACT). The prototypical contact languages are PIDGINS, CREOLES and bilingual mixed-languages (see MIXED CODE), which have a separate status, identity and structure from the original languages in contact. Some linguists also accept stable SECOND-LANGUAGE varieties which show extensive influence from speakers' first languages as contact languages (see BASILANG, MESOLANG, ACROLANG).

content word   See LEXICAL WORD.

context   Conventionally seen as linguistic and non-linguistic phenomena that surround a particular linguistic feature or utterance. Context in this sense has been of interest to sociolinguists because of its potential effects on the forms of language produced by speakers, or writers; the intended meanings of utterances; and how these are interpreted by listeners or readers. Linguists who emphasise the importance of context tend to be distancing themselves from approaches to the study of language that focus on linguistic systems (e.g. GRAMMAR, PHONOLOGY, SEMANTICS) in a relatively abstract or 'decontextualised' way.

In practice, different aspects of context tend to be prioritised in different studies. The analysis of an UTTERANCE in an interaction, for instance, might take into account some of the following: the immediate linguistic context (previous and following utterances – also termed CO-TEXT); utterances from other contexts that are seen as relevant in some way (e.g. previous interactions between the same participants); the particular GENRE that the utterance forms part of (e.g. an informal conversation among friends, a discussion between work colleagues); the topic under discussion; the particular SETTING in which the interaction takes place; certain characteristics of PARTICIPANTS, and the relationship assumed to hold between participants (e.g. their SOCIAL CLASS, or GENDER; specific roles such as close friends, or a boss and subordinate at work); participants' interactional goals (these may differ between participants); the broader social or cultural context of which the interaction forms part. Many studies recognise that the relationship between context and language is not unidirectional: studies of CODE-SWITCHING, for instance, have found that a change in language may bring about a change in context – e.g. signalling a shift in relations between participants.

There has been debate about the identification of context, and about the viability of a straightforward distinction between context and language. For instance, it is participants' understandings of context that are particularly relevant, but analysts can only gain access to these indirectly. Some types of analysis limit their interpretations to what is demonstrably relevant in the text of the interaction itself (e.g. CONVERSATION ANALYSIS); others take greater account of broader social and political phenomena (e.g. CRITICAL DISCOURSE ANALYSIS); some consult participants in making interpretations (e.g. studies by GUMPERZ and others adopting INTERPRETIVE or ethnographic approaches – see ETHNOGRAPHY). Focusing on the relationship between context and language implies at least an analytical separation between the two, but certain sociolinguistic concepts – for example, SPEECH EVENTS and PRACTICES – seem to challenge such a binary distinction, seeing language as part of a more general communicative activity. See also CONTEXTUAL VARIATION; INTEGRATIONAL LINGUISTICS; INTERTEXTUALITY; SPEAKING.

context of culture   Term introduced by Bronislaw MALINOWSKI to emphasise that in order to understand the meaning of any utterance it is important to understand the cultural CONTEXT in which this occurs (1923, 1935). Unlike another concept from Malinowski, the CONTEXT OF SITUATION, the context of culture is not easily observable and is thus theorised in a number of ways which can be distinguished broadly in terms of whether they orient more towards linguistic or social theory. An example of the former is SYSTEMIC FUNCTIONAL LINGUISTICS, where the context of culture is theorised in terms of GENRE, for example 'culture [...] can be defined as a set of generically interpretable activities' (Martin, 2001: 156). An example of a social theory orientation is the work of Norman FAIRCLOUGH, who draws on neo-Marxist and poststructuralist writers to theorise the ways in which texts are influenced by, and contribute to, the context of culture. See also CRITICAL DISCOURSE ANALYSIS; CULTURE.

context of situation   First used by the anthropologist Bronislaw MAL-INOWKSI to emphasise that in order to understand the meaning of any particular utterance it is necessary to understand the CONTEXT in which it takes place (1923, 1935). Context of situation refers to the immediate and observable aspects of context in which an utterance occurs, such as the SETTING, PARTICIPANTS, activities engaged in. Malinowski distinguished this from the broader concept of CONTEXT OF CULTURE. Context of situation is also used, following the work of the linguist James FIRTH, in a more abstract way to analyse how a particular 'type' of situation accounts for the specific features of language used, referred to in SYSTEMIC FUNCTIONAL LINGUISTICS as REGISTER. M. A. K. HALLIDAY, for instance, suggests: 'the context of situation of any text is an instance of a generalised social context or situation type' (1978: 39).

contextual variation   How language use varies in different linguistic, physical or social contexts. Contextual variation may refer to the influence of the linguistic environment on a particular feature (for instance, the variable pronunciation of speech sounds in different linguistic environments, as in the slightly different pro-nunciations of /k/ in the words *cool* and *keep*, influenced by the following vowel sounds). In a broader sense, contextual variation may refer to any aspect of the physical or social environment mentioned under CONTEXT above: the influence of PARTICIPANTS, SETTING, topic etc. on speakers' and writers' language use. The term STYLISTIC VARIATION is more commonly found in sociolinguistic studies of LANGUAGE VARIATION. See also CODE-SWITCHING; contrast SOCIAL VARIATION.

contextualisation (cue)   In the work of John GUMPERZ, **contextual-isation** refers to the process whereby people understand what kind of activity is taking place during an interaction, and therefore how an utterance is to be interpreted (given that an utterance may have several different potential meanings). **Contextualisation cues** are certain verbal or non-verbal features that highlight or play down some aspect of CONTEXT and thus point towards a particular inter-pretation. For instance, the adoption of a certain tone of voice, or a switch to a different language variety, may indicate that a comment is to be taken ironically, or playfully. (See Gumperz, 1982.)

contrastive rhetoric   Contrastive rhetoric (CR) involves studies of RHETORIC, or what might be broadly referred to as the representation of meaning, in writing in different languages. Much work in CR focuses on academic texts, such as student essays and academic journal articles. It also includes research in second-language (L2) writing. In contrastive rhetoric, language and writing are considered to be cultural phenomena; written texts are seen as following different rhetorical conventions according to the cultural contexts in which they are produced. See also ACADEMIC LITERACY.

control group   See EXPERIMENT.

conventional implicature   See CONVERSATIONAL IMPLICATURE.

converge (-ence)
1. In studies of speech ACCOMMODATION, **convergence** refers to the process whereby a speaker uses language in a similar way to the person they are talking to. Speakers may converge along a number of dimensions – for example, CODE-SWITCHING (in bilingual con-texts), ACCENT, DIALECT, speech rate and other vocal characteristics. Convergence is said, traditionally, to be a means of expressing SOLIDARITY or decreasing social distance, but more recent studies acknowledge a wider range of potential motivations: e.g. it is possible to converge with another speaker sarcastically (see Giles et al., 1991).
2. In HISTORICAL LINGUISTICS and studies of LANGUAGE CHANGE the term convergence refers to a process by which language varieties that have co-existed within a community or a geographical area become structurally more similar to one another – see LINGUISTIC AREA. Convergence is a LANGUAGE CONTACT phenomenon and results from the mutual linguistic borrowing of sounds, words and

grammatical constructions. Prerequisites for convergence are (a) that there are no major prestige differences between the languages or dialects in contact, and (b) that communication between speakers of different languages or dialects is intensive and regular. In South Africa, for example, widespread English-Afrikaans bilingualism has led to both languages using words in common (e.g. *bakkie* for 'light pick-up truck', *bergie*, pronounced with a velar fricative, for 'vagrant') and also grammatical overlaps (e.g. reduplication of adverbs for intensity, *quick-quick* for 'quickly'). DIALECT LEVELLING is a special type of convergence between closely related linguistic varieties: forms which are common to all varieties will be maintained, while forms which are present only in few of the varieties will be lost.

Convergence has also been discussed in relation to contact between the supra-regional standard norm and the regional dialects in some European countries, where it has supported the formation of so-called REGIONAL STANDARDS (i.e. non-local varieties which show standard as well as regional features and which are used in semi-formal situations).

In both cases, contrast DIVERGENCE.

conversation   Refers to any spoken interaction, not just relatively informal talk. Sociolinguists, particularly those working within INTERACTIONAL SOCIOLINGUISTICS, have been interested in several aspects of conversation, including its formal properties; social, cultural and contextual differences in conversational styles or the use of specific conversational features; the negotiation of relations between participants in conversation (see e.g. CODE-SWITCHING; INTERCULTURAL COMMUNICATION; LANGUAGE AND GENDER). See also CONVERSATION ANALYSIS; CONVERSATION MANAGEMENT; SEQUENTIAL ORGANISATION; TURN-TAKING.

Conversation Analysis (CA)   A tradition of enquiry concerned with the empirical study of naturally occurring spoken interaction (and not just informal conversation as the name may imply). CA grew out of ETHNOMETHODOLOGY, an area of sociology developed during the 1960s and 1970s with a primary interest in people's everyday behaviour. CA itself derives from work carried out by Harvey Sacks with his colleagues Emanuel Schegloff and Gail Jefferson (a classic early study is Sacks et al. 1974).

In CA speech is viewed as a form of activity, and analysts investigate how participants 'get things done' interactionally (e.g.

how they open and close conversations, manage the smooth exchange of speaking turns, and carry out activities such as giving and accepting or rejecting an invitation). Conversation analysts are interested in the overall structure of conversation, its SEQUENTIAL ORGANISATION, and how this is co-operatively managed by participants. Classically, conversation analysts restrict their investigations to what is demonstrably relevant to participants, i.e. what can be inferred directly from the interaction: they have been critical of socially or politically motivated research (such as CRITICAL DISCOURSE ANALYSIS) that, they would argue, interprets data in the light of analysts' concerns rather than participants' own orientations (see e.g. Schegloff, 1997). A counter-argument would be that analysts cannot approach data without any preconceptions and necessarily bring their own interests to bear on interpretations. Some researchers have tried to combine aspects of CA methodology with a more critical interest in interaction. See also CONVERSATION MANAGEMENT; MEMBERSHIP CATEGORISATION; TURN-TAKING.

conversation management   Refers to the process whereby participants jointly organise or construct a conversation. Studies of conversation management have looked at, for instance, the management of conversational openings and CLOSINGS, and TURN-TAKING between participants. Of particular interest within sociolinguistics is the way conversation-management strategies may differ in different social, cultural or language groups. See also CONVERSATION ANALYSIS; INTERCULTURAL COMMUNICATION; SPEAKING TURN.

conversational historic present (CHP)   See HISTORIC PRESENT.

conversational implicature   The philosopher H. P. Grice (see Grice, 1975) distinguished between **conventional implicature** (the implications in an utterance that derive from the conventional meaning of words and expressions) and conversational implicature. To understand something that is conversationally implicated, a listener must be aware not only of the literal meaning of an utterance but also of relevant contextual factors, and of general principles governing the conduct of conversation (termed CONVERSATIONAL MAXIMS). For instance, if speaker A says to B: 'Do you fancy going out tonight?' and B replies: 'It's Jim's quiz night,' A would probably assume B's reply was relevant (Grice's 'relation', or relevance maxim). What is actually implicated by B's reply would depend upon the context, A and B's joint knowledge etc.; for example, it may be that Jim is B's partner, the couple have young children who cannot be left alone so if Jim is going out B will be unable to do so.

conversational maxims   Derived from the work of the philosopher H. P. Grice (see Grice, 1975), these are principles that are said to underlie conversation and that allow listeners to make an interpretation of utterances. Grice identified four maxims:

> *quantity*: make your contribution as informative as is required for current purposes (i.e. do not provide too much or too little information);
>
> *quality*: try to make your contribution one that is true (i.e. not false, and not something for which you do not have enough evidence);
>
> *relation*: be relevant;
>
> *manner*: be perspicuous (i.e. be clear, avoid ambiguity, be brief and orderly).

Together, these derive from a general CO-OPERATIVE PRINCIPLE. A speaker may violate one or more of these maxims (e.g. in telling a lie), but Grice's argument was that, in general, speakers followed the maxims and listeners also assumed the maxims applied. For instance, if a car driver tells a passer-by that her car has run out of petrol, and the passer-by replies that there is a garage round the corner, it is reasonable to assume that the passer-by believes the garage is open, has a supply of petrol etc. If this were not the case, the passer-by would be flouting the relation maxim. Grice suggested that where a maxim was apparently flouted, a listener could make certain inferences to explain this (e.g. if someone says something that they clearly do not believe, a listener may interpret this as ironic). See also CONVERSATIONAL IMPLICATURE.

conversational turn-taking   See TURN-TAKING.

conversationalisation   A process identified by Norman FAIRCLOUGH (1995), which he suggests has been a feature of public discourse since the 1960s. Conversationalisation refers to the use of informal types of language in public domains (e.g. informal conversational styles in formal interviews; use of first names rather than more formal titles). While this may be seen as an 'opening up' of public discourse to practices that a wider range of people may attain, it is also viewed more critically as potentially manipulative: for example, it may be used to simulate a friendly relationship that does not in fact exist. Fairclough sees this as part of a broader process of **informalisation**. See also BORDER CROSSING; CRITICAL DISCOURSE ANALYSIS; MARKETISATION.

co-operative principle   Derives from the work of the philosopher H. P. Grice (see Grice, 1975). Grice was concerned with language use and, in particular, with how people engaged efficiently and co-operatively in conversation. He suggested that conversation was underpinned by a general co-operative principle: make your contribution such as is required, at the stage at which it occurs, by the accepted purpose or direction of the talk. As part of this general principle, speakers needed to adhere to four more specific principles, or CONVERSATIONAL MAXIMS: to provide an appropriate amount of information, be truthful, relevant and clear. While not all conversation observes these principles, Grice's argument was that they are oriented to by speakers and listeners: listeners would therefore make certain inferences to try to explain apparent deviations. See also CONVERSATIONAL IMPLICATURE.

co-ordinate bilingualism   A type of individual BILINGUALISM in which a person learns two languages in separate environments and uses them independently of each other, suggesting that their meaning systems exist separately in the brain. A co-ordinate bilingual keeps the words of each language separate. Synonyms from each language are not treated as if they were exactly equivalent. Thus a co-ordinate bilingual in Arabic and English would not use *kitab* (Arabic for 'book') and *book* in exactly the same ways, but would pay heed to the different nuances these words have in each language. This contrasts with COMPOUND BILINGUALISM, in which a bilingual speaker's languages are believed to have an interdependent relation. Many scholars, however, do not accept this distinction.

copula   'Copula' (adjective **copular**) is a term in logic denoting membership of a set (the symbol ε in x ε A, meaning 'x is a member of the set A'). In linguistics the term is used to denote a similar 'equational' or 'linking' relation between two nouns in a sentence (represented as the verb *is* in *Mary is my granny*); or between a noun and an adjective (the verb *is* in *Mary is sick*). The term **linking verb** is also found for this usage. In languages such as English this relation is expressed by the verb *be*; in languages like Zulu, it is expressed by a prefix to the noun or adjective; in languages like Russian, the copula is expressed in the past tense, but not in the present, in which case one may speak of **copula absence**. See also COPULA DELETION.

copula deletion   Refers to a situation where the COPULA is present in some contexts but is variable or deleted in others. Copula deletion is a feature of many varieties of English, including AFRICAN AMERICAN VERNACULAR ENGLISH (AAVE). William LABOV has shown that, in AAVE, variation in the use of the copula is not random; rather, it is the result of a series of grammatical and phonological rules that are parallel to those of colloquial contraction in standard English (see Labov's 1969 paper on copula contraction and deletion, in Labov, 1972c). Generally speaking, where standard English allows the copula to be contracted (as in *she's sick*), AAVE allows it to be deleted (*she sick*). On the other hand, where standard English disallows contraction (**here she's*), AAVE disallows deletion (**here she*). Labov's interpretation has since been modified by Baugh (1980), who showed that unlike standard English, AAVE favours deletion of the copula in adjective environments.

    Copula deletion is also a typical feature of PIDGIN and CREOLE languages (e.g. Bickerton, 1981). Copula use is typically re-introduced to the linguistic system in the mesolectal varieties of the CREOLE CONTINUUM, i.e. while BASILECTal Creoles show very high frequencies of copula deletion, mesolectal varieties show a gradual increase in the use of the copula (Bickerton, 1972).

co-researcher   See INFORMANT.

corpus   'Corpus' (plural **corpora**) means 'a body' and 'corpus analysis' thus refers to the analysis of a body of language data. A corpus can be small (e.g. one speech or article) or large (several million words of naturally occurring spoken or written language). A great deal of contemporary research makes use of computer tools in the analytic process. For example, CONCORDANCE programmes can pick out particular words selected by the researcher and show where they occur in texts and the words they habitually co-occur or collocate with (see COLLOCATION). Analyses of large corpora of spoken and written English have shown the frequency of occurrence, and patterns of co-occurrence of many different lexical (vocabulary) and grammatical items (see e.g. Biber, 1998). Research may also involve making comparisons between texts, or text types (e.g. comparing the use of vocabulary, grammatical structures etc. in 'literary' and 'non-literary' texts). Whilst much work in **corpus linguistics** tends to focus on textual features alone, recent approaches attempt to take account of broader contextual dimensions: see, for example, the work of Michael Stubbs, who integrates corpus linguistic approaches with CRITICAL DISCOURSE ANALYSIS (CDA) (Stubbs, 1996).

corpus design   The composition or structure of a CORPUS of language data. Corpus design involves questions of sampling, i.e. what kinds of texts and how many should be included to achieve representativeness (Biber et al., 1998) – see SAMPLE.

corpus planning, status planning   Corpus and status planning are aspects of LANGUAGE PLANNING. The distinction was introduced by the German linguist Heinz Kloss in the 1960s (cf. Kloss, 1969) to describe the main activities in which language planners engage. **Corpus planning** refers to activities directed at the language system and includes the creation of new words (or lexical MODERNISATION), the development of a WRITING SYSTEM or orthography as well as the production of normative texts which define the norms of the STANDARD (i.e. grammars, dictionaries). **Status planning** describes efforts aimed at changing the use and function of a linguistic variety within a speech community. This includes, for example, its promotion as an OFFICIAL LANGUAGE, MEDIUM OF INSTRUCTION, NATIONAL LANGUAGE as well as the RE-NATIVISATION of HERITAGE LANGUAGES, such as, for example, Navajo in the United States (Leap, 1983). Jernudd (1973) used the terms LANGUAGE DETERMINATION and LANGUAGE DEVELOPMENT as synonyms for status and corpus planning respectively.

correctness   The idea that certain linguistic items (words, grammatical structures, pronunciations) are 'correct' or 'incorrect'. Frequently, NON-STANDARD forms of language (e.g. *she go* in English) are considered incorrect and STANDARD forms (*she goes*) correct. This is associated with PRESCRIPTIVE ideas about language. Such ideas are commonly critiqued by sociolinguists, who prefer the notion of APPROPRIATENESS (i.e. that forms of language are appropriate, or inappropriate, in certain contexts). Correctness has also been an object of study within sociolinguistics. For instance, James Milroy and Lesley Milroy (1999) have documented a COMPLAINT tradition in English focusing on the notion of correctness, and note that the beginnings of this tradition in Britain in the early eighteenth century were consistent with the development of a substantial body of work to codify English in GRAMMARS and DICTIONARIES. The term **doctrine of correctness** (after Leonard, [1929] 1962) is sometimes used to characterise such eighteenth-century developments. See also LANGUAGE IDEOLOGY; STANDARD LANGUAGE IDEOLOGY; VERBAL HYGIENE.

correlation   A statistical measure used to describe the strength of the relationship between (or interdependence of) two variables. Socio-linguists have observed stable and regular relationships (correlations) between SOCIAL GROUP membership (SOCIAL VARIABLES) and language use (LINGUISTIC VARIABLES). In his study of variation in the speech of New York City, William LABOV (1972a) found strong correlations between SOCIAL CLASS membership and the pronunciations of certain sounds: for instance the variable (th) (the initial sound in *thing* or *thick*) occurred as an interdental fricative [θ] as a prestige variant but was also regularly pronounced as an affricate [tθ] by upper-middle- and middle-class speakers and as a plosive [t] by working-class speakers. A number of statistical methods (such as **Spearman Rank Order Correlation**) are used to calculate the strength of a relationship between variables. Correlations may be positive or negative. In a positive correlation, as one variable increases, so does the other. In a negative correlation as one variable increases, the other decreases. Correlations are measured in the range from 1 (complete positive correlation) through 0 (no correlation) to -1 (complete negative correlation).

cost–benefit analysis (CBA)   In LANGUAGE PLANNING, a term that refers to the assessment of the anticipated costs and benefits of language-planning decisions (see Thornburn, 1971). For example, the introduction of an additional foreign language into the school system would create certain costs (teacher training, production of teaching materials, etc.) but could also generate benefits (improved transnational communication and better business opportunities, possibly better employment opportunities for school-leavers, etc.). However, the application of CBA is problematical as the long time-frame of many language-planning activities makes it difficult to assess costs and benefits accurately. More importantly, the more general political or social implications of the planning decisions (e.g. political unity, cross-national communication, or conflicts between linguistic groups) cannot be assessed straightforwardly in terms of costs and benefits. See also RATIONAL CHOICE.

co-text   Used by some analysts to refer to the linguistic environment or CONTEXT of an utterance or feature under study: for instance, the text that follows or precedes a particular word, and that may affect how it is interpreted. In this case, co-text would be distinguished from non-linguistic aspects of context.

counter-elite   See ELITE.

covert prestige   See PRESTIGE.

creationism   In PIDGIN and CREOLE studies 'creationism' refers to theories that view pidgins and (especially) Creoles as systems in their own right rather than as restructured versions of existing languages. Two approaches have been labelled **creationist**: the BIOPROGRAMME theory of Derek BICKERTON (1981) and the gradualist accounts of, *inter alia*, Philip Baker (1995); see GRADUALISM. Ironically, these two approaches are in opposition to each other. Bickerton views creolisation as an instantaneous creation of a new language by first-generation children in situations where a PIDGIN has been the main LINGUA FRANCA. Baker, on the other hand, stresses the gradual evolution of a Creole with considerable overlaps with earlier pidgin stages. See also ABRUPT CREOLISATION.

creativity   In linguistics, 'creativity' conventionally refers to a speaker-listener's ability to produce or understand a (potentially) infinite number of sentences they have not previously encountered. In STYLISTICS, the term may be found in a sense similar to its more usual meaning: to refer to originality as a property of LITERARY LANGUAGE. Of particular interest in sociolinguistics is the extension of this second sense to encompass 'literariness' or 'verbal art' in everyday language use. Recent research suggests that 'everyday' linguistic creativity is pervasive. Often, it takes the form of LANGUAGE PLAY, as speakers use puns, rhymes etc. for a range of interactional purposes (to 'oil the wheels' of communication, establish SOLIDARITY with co-participants, reproduce POWER relations etc.). Ronald Carter (2004), Guy Cook (2000) and David Crystal (1998) provide evidence of the pervasiveness of such creativity and argue that this plays an important part in human development and cognition.

Creole (creolisation)   A Creole, on traditional accounts going back to Robert A. Hall (1966), has been defined as a new first language of a community which had previously had to rely on a PIDGIN as its LINGUA FRANCA. The Creole was believed to be a considerably developed version arising from the transformation of a pidgin (a rudimentary second language) into a first language without an available TARGET. This language process, termed **creolisation**, was argued by Derek BICKERTON to be driven by children lacking access to a suitable model for language acquisition (see BIOPROGRAMME). Creolisation typically arose out of enforced movements of people from different language backgrounds for labour purposes in the colonial era. Creole languages tend to draw their vocabulary from the sociopolitically dominant language in a community (see SUPERSTRATE), which was frequently a European language. Hence linguists use labels like Creole English, Creole French, Creole Portuguese, etc. The grammatical structure of such Creoles is drawn from a number of sources, including the languages of the labour force (see SUBSTRATE).

Current research questions the traditional accounts of creolisation. First, many linguists now accept that a Creole can be formed abruptly (see ABRUPT CREOLISATION) without the existence of a preceding pidgin: they cite the fact that despite considerable historical research no trace of a pidgin stage of any Caribbean Creole has been found. Second, where pidgins have existed and are undergoing creolisation, as with Tok Pisin in Papua New Guinea and West African Pidgin English, there appear to be no qualitative differences between an 'expanded pidgin' and a Creole. Furthermore, adults are active participants in the process of the creolisation of Tok Pisin and West African Pidgin English, contrary to Bickerton's bioprogramme formulation. It is therefore becoming common to use the term **pidgin/Creole language** for such varieties.

Pidgins and Creoles are studied as a subfield of SOCIOLINGUISTICS, under the banner of **Pidgin and Creole Linguistics**, or **creolistics** for short. The field is to some extent an independent one, with researchers also interested in oral and written Creole literatures, and more narrow structural, acquisitional and historical studies than is usual in sociolinguistics (Arends et al. 1995). There is also considerable interest in the relationships between a Creole and its superstrate, which give rise to new varieties of the Creole long after the initial period of creolisation – see CREOLE CONTINUUM. See also CREATIONISM; GRADUALISM; NATIVISATION.

Creole continuum   In societies in which a CREOLE originates as a first language a wide range of varieties may subsequently develop between the Creole on one hand and the dominant colonial language (or

SUPERSTRATE) on the other. This 'Creole continuum' develops when the colonial language is accessible to Creole speakers and there is social mobility and education which make it a desired target. Under these conditions, **decreolisation** occurs – resulting in varieties that are intermediate between the original Creole and the superstrate. The Creole continuum is segmented by linguists into three significant sections – the BASILECT (or deep Creole), acrolect (a variety closest to the superstrate) and the mesolect (a set of intermediate varieties between these endpoints). Individual speakers may be described as basilectal, mesolectal or acrolectal on the basis of their casual speech. However, many speakers master a slice of the continuum and make adjustments to their speech moving 'upwards' towards a more acrolectal variety in formal styles and 'downwards' towards a more basilectal variety in casual speech (see LECTAL SHIFTING). The term 'Creole continuum' is preferred to the earlier term **post-Creole continuum**, since the latter misleadingly suggests the demise of the Creole.

creoloid   A term coined by J. T. Platt (1975) for a second-language variety that bears resemblance to a CREOLE language, insofar as it involves significant restructuring of the TARGET language and is used for communication between speakers from originally different language backgrounds. Platt's example was Singapore English, which arose under British colonialism among speakers of Malay, Chinese and Indian languages. Although introduced largely via the educational system (making it historically different from a Creole), Singapore English evinced a range of varieties reminiscent of the CREOLE CONTINUUM. BASILECTal Singapore English shows COPULA DELETION, few verb inflections for person, number or tense and other features that Platt argued were Creole-like. Although some linguists are unconvinced by the analogy, the term 'creoloid' is a useful one that draws attention to the systematic restructuring of a target language, usually in a multilingual context by subordinate groups of people who use this INTERLANGUAGE with each other as a relatively neutral LINGUA FRANCA, which may then develop into a durable second language and even a permanent first language.

critical   Term used to refer to an orientation to the study of language which emphasises issues of POWER and IDEOLOGY and which has an emancipatory aim. An example of a sociolinguistic question about power at an interactional level is who dominates in conversation and how is such interactional DOMINANCE achieved? An example of a question about power at an institutional level is who determines language policies and whose interests do these serve? A key aim in many critical approaches is to make visible the relationship between language and social emancipation, that is, the part language may play in freeing individuals from discriminatory social structures and conditions.

Critical approaches usually involve drawing on Marxist or neo-Marxist theories and include feminist as well as some poststructuralist approaches (see MARXISM; FEMINISM; POSTSTRUCTURALISM).

critical age (of acquisition) There is substantial evidence that LANGUAGE ACQUISITION is affected by the passage of time, and that there is a critical age after which language learners rarely achieve native-like competence (see NATIVE speaker). This is well documented in studies of SECOND LANGUAGE acquisition: adult learners typically retain a foreign ACCENT and also show incomplete mastery of GRAMMAR and PRAGMATICS. The idea that there is an age limit to full-language acquisition is further supported by evidence from delayed first language acquisition: DEAF children of hearing parents who acquire SIGN LANGUAGE only late in life, as well as so-called 'feral' or 'wild' children who grow up without social interaction and regular exposure to language. Both groups of children show impaired language acquisition and use. 'Genie', for example, was imprisoned by her father shortly after birth and grew up in complete social isolation until the age of thirteen. 'Genie' never learned to produce more than telegraphic speech: *Apple sauce buy store* or *I like elephant eat peanut* (see Curtiss, 1977; Newton, 2003).

Studies of second language acquisition and SECOND DIALECT ACQUISITION have shown that phonological attainment in particular is strongly conditioned by the age of the learner, and most studies indicate age six as a rough cut-off point for achieving native-like ability on this level. The term **critical period** is also found for this phenomenon.

Critical Discourse Analysis (CDA) Researchers working within Critical Discourse Analysis are interested in the ways in which DISCOURSE PRACTICES reproduce and/or transform power relations within society. There is a wide range of approaches, drawing on linguistics, psychology and sociology. For example, Teun van Dijk (1993) uses sociocognitive approaches; Ruth Wodak uses socio-historical methods (Wodak, 1996; Reisgl and Wodak, 2000); and Norman Fairclough (1992a, 1995, 2001) draws on HALLIDAY's work in SYSTEMIC FUNCTIONAL LINGUISTICS. Fairclough's approach has been particularly influential. He aims to explore the relationship between the micro study of texts, focusing on the details of how texts work, and the macro politics of society. His framework is three-dimensional, involving a focus on TEXT, DISCURSIVE PRACTICE and social PRACTICE.

Approaches in CDA are influenced by a range of social theorists, including Marx, Gramsci, FOUCAULT and Habermas. Notions from the work of such theorists, including IDEOLOGY, HEGEMONY and DISCOURSE, are used to explore the relationship between language and power relations within society. Recent work by Chouliaraki and Fairclough (1999) draws on work in CRITICAL REALISM to explore the nature of discourse in late modernity (see MODERNITY).

Considerable debate surrounds work in CDA and criticisms have included the over-emphasis on a conflict model of society, a deterministic approach to individual language use (i.e. the limited options available to individuals) and biased interpretations of texts (see e.g. Hammersley, 1996; Widdowson, 1996; Stubbs, 1997).

See also CONSENSUS, CONFLICT (MODELS OF SOCIETY); CRITICAL LINGUISTICS.

Critical Language Awareness   An approach to teaching about language which is influenced by work on CRITICAL LITERACY and CRITICAL DISCOURSE ANALYSIS. Critical language awareness (in contrast to other forms of LANGUAGE AWARENESS) focuses explicitly on the ways in which language is used to construct particular worldviews or ideologies in order to maintain particular power relations within society (Clark et al., 1991; Clark and Ivanic, 1999). Critical language awareness has been advocated for use particularly within schools and has been significantly developed in terms both of pedagogy and research in South Africa, notably by Hilary Janks as way of challenging the ideology of apartheid (Janks, 1993, 2000).

critical linguistics   A type of text analysis developed in the 1970s which draws on some aspects of social theory in order to identify the hidden meanings or ideology of texts (see Fowler et al., 1979; Hodge and Kress, 1993). The tools of SYSTEMIC FUNCTIONAL LINGUISTICS are often used in order to analyse the ways in which specific linguistic features serve to represent particular worldviews. For example, a focus on TRANSITIVITY in texts shows how participants are represented in clauses. Thus the clause *Demonstrators are shot* represents a different worldview from *Police shoot demonstrators*: in the former case the perpetrators of the shooting are made invisible, in contrast to the latter where they are clearly marked.

Critical linguistics is often considered a precursor to CRITICAL DISCOURSE ANALSYIS. But it is also seen as one particular approach within Critical Discourse Analysis.

The term **critical sociolinguistics** is also used to refer to an approach to sociolinguistics which emphasises issues of POWER, participation and access (Kress, 2001).

See also CRITICAL LANGUAGE AWARENESS.

critical literacy   Critical literacy is strongly associated with the work of Paulo FREIRE, a Brazilian educationalist who advocated an approach to literacy which involved 'reading the world' rather than simply 'reading the word' (Freire, 1972; Freire and Macedo, 1987). The aim of critical literacy is *conscientazacão*, 'conscientisation', which encompasses the aim of raising awareness about the social, cultural and political conditions in which people live and the potential for action in the world against oppressive elements of reality. Freire's work has been influential in diverse educational contexts – for example, adult literacy campaigns in Nicaragua, mainstream schooling in the USA. Luke and Walton draw on Freire's work to talk of a 'critical social literacy' which 'entails the analysis and evaluation of textual ideologies and cultural messages, and an understanding of the linguistic and discursive techniques with which texts represent social reality, relations, and identity' (1994: 1194). This latter strand of critical literacy involves an explicit focus on the linguistic features of a text and the ways in which these construct a particular world view or ideology. See also CRITICAL DISCOURSE ANALYSIS; CRITICAL LANGUAGE AWARENESS; CRITICAL LINGUISTICS; CRITICAL PEDAGOGY.

critical pedagogy   Strongly associated with the work of Paulo FREIRE, who contrasted a 'banking' approach to teaching and learning, where the teacher transmits information to the learner, with a dialogical approach, whereby teachers and learners together generate the focus and direction of instruction. Critical thinking is an essential aspect of this dialogic pedagogy and the means by which both teacher and learners move towards a greater understanding of reality. Critical thinking involves an explicit articulation of the power relations at work in any given social and historical context, and thus the language used to describe and define reality is an important focus in critical pedagogy. Compare CRITICAL LANGUAGE AWARENESS; CRITICAL LITERACY.

critical realism　Critical realism is an approach to knowledge which starts from the premise that that there is no simple correspondence between the real world – physical or social – and our understanding or consciousness of it. Rather, any understandings of the world are said to be mediated, that is apprehended via, for example, cognition or language. Critical realism stands in contrast to **realism,** or what is sometimes termed **naïve realism** where a correspondence between the world and how we apprehend it is usually accepted. A key notion within more recent approaches in critical realism is that the social world is an 'open system', whose internal structures or mechanisms interact with each other in complex ways. Thus predictability and knowability – what we can know and predict – are far from straightforward. This openness also means that the social world is not fixed or determined: it may be transformed by human action and thus social emancipation is possible (see Bhaskar, 1979).

Critical realism is being used in some socially oriented approaches to the study of language, for example in more recent work in CRITICAL DISCOURSE ANALYSIS (see Chouliaraki and Fairclough, 1999).

critical sociolinguistics　See CRITICAL LINGUISTICS.

critical theory
1. Used in a general way to refer to those theoretical approaches which adopt a CRITICAL orientation to the study of society.
2. Used more specifically to refer to a philosophy developed by the **Frankfurt School,** notable members of which are Max Horkheimer, Theodor Adorno and Herbert Marcuse. Drawing on the work of Hegel and Marx (see MARXISM), this is a 'praxis', or action-oriented philosophy, which focuses on the emancipatory possibilities facilitated by the progressive use of reason (for overview, see Wiggershaus, 1994). Critical social theory is drawn on in many areas of sociolinguistics, notably CRITICAL DISCOURSE ANALYSIS.

cross-cultural communication　See INTERCULTURAL COMMUNICATION.

crossing　See BORDER CROSSING; LANGUAGE CROSSING.

cross-over pattern　A pattern of language use which has been reported in several studies of linguistic variation, and which is indicative of CHANGE FROM ABOVE. The term refers to the cross-over of lines found in graphs which summarise quantitative differences in the linguistic behaviour of SOCIAL GROUPS (see Figure 2).

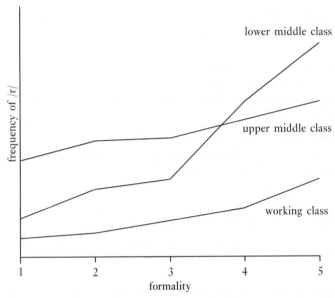

*Figure 2   Schematic representation of cross-over pattern
(as reported in Labov, 1972a)*

Note: 1 = casual speech; 2 = careful speech; 3 = reading style;
4 = word list; 5 = minimal pairs

The pattern was first described by William LABOV (1972a) for New York. The cross-over pattern relates to the sociolinguistic phenomenon of HYPERCORRECTION, that is the desire of individuals belonging to social groups of intermediate status to sound more like those belonging to higher-status (i.e. more prestigious) social groups. However, when consciously trying to reproduce the PRESTIGE norms in formal styles, speakers belonging to intermediate-status groups actually overshoot the mark and use prestige forms more frequently than speakers belonging to the highest social group. Thus, in New York City (see Figure 2) only speakers belonging to the upper middle class use high frequencies of POST-VOCALIC /r/ (pronouncing the /r/ in words such as *car*) in informal speech styles. In more formal styles, lower-middle-class speakers attempt to emulate the prestige norms set by the upper middle class, and in doing so use post-vocalic /r/ more frequently than upper-middle-class speakers. Labov suggested that hypercorrect behaviour supports the spread of prestige variants and thus leads to an acceleration of LANGUAGE CHANGE (Labov, 1972a: 141).

cross-sectional study   A study based on observations of a number of individuals at a single point in time. Contrasts with LONGITUDINAL STUDY.

cultivation   From the German *Sprachpflege* (lit. 'language care'). A near synonym of LANGUAGE PLANNING.

cultural capital   Term introduced by the sociologist Pierre BOURDIEU as part of his economics-based theoretical model of cultural reproduction (Bourdieu, 1977, 1984). Cultural capital refers to the different forms of knowledge, values, language and meanings that individuals come to possess through their everyday living in specific social contexts. Bourdieu argues that different kinds of cultural capital have a differentiated social value, akin to economic value within society. Language is a key aspect of cultural capital, with certain types of language being more highly valued than others. The kind of cultural capital that individuals possess helps to account for the ways in which their life trajectories become structured. See also SYMBOLIC POWER.

cultural literacy   Term which has been used to describe, and advocate the teaching of, a particular set of cultural values, as in the US literary academic E. D. Hirsch's *Cultural Literacy: What Every American Needs to Know* (1987). Controversially, Hirsch provides a detailed list of the kind of cultural knowledge – dates, literature, historical figures – that he argues that every literate American should know.

culture   As used in SOCIOLINGUISTICS, LINGUISTIC ANTHROPOLOGY and related areas, 'culture' refers to a set of everyday practices and associated beliefs, ideas and values that characterise a particular community or group, contribute to that community's sense of identity and need to be learnt by younger or newer community members. The term implies appropriate and accepted beliefs, practices etc. This is a broader meaning than the more restricted sense of culture as art, literature or other forms of 'high culture'. In this broader sense, language and its associated NORMS of usage constitute part of culture.

This broader meaning also incorporates a view of culture not just as something that people have but also as what they do: i.e. culture is seen as being actively reproduced, or perhaps challenged, in everyday activity. Such activity may include certain WAYS OF SPEAKING (evident in everything from formal religious ceremony to greetings, games and gossip) and researchers have studied these in a range of **cultural groups**. INTERCULTURAL COMMUNICATION (or cross-cultural communication) has been concerned with communication between different cultural groups, often identified broadly in terms of ETHNICITY or language background, e.g. communication between NATIVE and non-native speakers of English; see also INTERETHNIC COMMUNICATION. See CONTEXT OF CULTURE.

curvilinear pattern   As used by William LABOV (2001), a pattern of language use in society where usage does not increase or decrease gradually across the social hierarchy (i.e. from lower- to higher-status social groups). Instead, the highest frequencies of usage are found in groups that are located in the middle of the social hierarchy. Labov (2001: 32–3, 460) formulated the **curvilinear principle** or **curvilinear hypothesis** on the basis of a comparison of studies. He suggests that in the case of CHANGE FROM BELOW the use of novel linguistic forms shows a curvilinear pattern with regard to social group membership (highest frequencies of usage in the (lower) middle class, low frequencies in the upper middle class and working class). As the change progresses, frequencies will increase for speakers who are in the middle of the social hierarchy, while upper-class speakers will often reduce their usage of these forms initially (see Figure 3). With regard to age, however, there is a gradual increase, i.e. highest frequencies of novel forms occur in the youngest age group.

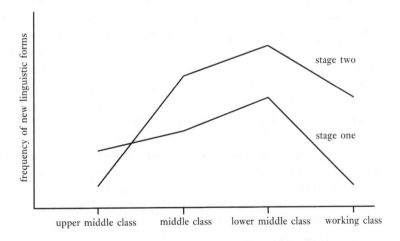

Figure 3   Schematic representation of the curvilinear pattern in the distribution of novel linguistic forms across social class groups at two different points in time (as reported in Labov, 2001: 32)

D

danger of death (interview question)   A strategy used by William LABOV (see Labov 1972b) in his sociolinguistic INTERVIEWS. The aim was to divert the speakers' ATTENTION from monitoring their language use and to elicit samples of informal, casual speech. The interviewer would ask the speaker: 'Have you ever been in a situation where you were in serious danger of getting killed, where you thought to yourself, *this is it?*' Typically, speakers would get involved in narrating their story and forget about the FORMALITY of the interview situation. Their speech would thus shift towards their VERNACULAR norm. Questions about childhood games, dating and courtship, religion and ghosts are also used strategically in interviews to achieve a shift in level of formality and to encourage informal, casual speech. See also STYLISTIC CONTINUUM.

Deaf   The adjective 'Deaf' with a capital letter is used to emphasise the fact that the Deaf community is not a group whose members can be identified by their medical condition alone. The Deaf community constitutes a cultural and linguistic group defined by a common culture, beliefs, experiences, rules of behaviour and, most importantly, the use of SIGN LANGUAGE. The use of a capital letter is in line with the orthographic conventions of English when referring to speech communities (the Italian speech community, the English speech community, etc.). The capital letter is not used when referring to an individual's audiological status.

declarative   A sentence type whose primary role is in making statements, for example, *The car has arrived* is a declarative, in contrast to questions (*Has the car arrived?*), or imperatives (*Run!*). Some sentences with declarative form may have hidden imperative force: *It's a bit cold in here* may be intended as a polite request that a window be closed (see SPEECH ACT).

deconstruction
1. An approach to written texts, associated with POSTSTRUCTURALISM and in particular the writings of Jacques Derrida (1978). Deconstructing a TEXT starts from the premise that there is no one deep, clear meaning to be recovered from a text, but rather that many,

indeed endless, meanings are possible. A key focus in deconstruction is to question the dichotomies or binary contrasts which commonly structure our view of the world, for example good/bad; feminine/masculine; logic/emotion. This is a prominent approach in feminist writings (see FEMINISM); see discussion in Cameron (1992).

2. Deconstruction is also used more broadly to refer to approaches that aim to uncover hidden or masked meanings in texts, such as in CRITICAL DISCOURSE ANALYSIS. See also INTERTEXTUALITY, HETEROGLOSSIA, POLYPHONY.

decreolisation See CREOLE CONTINUUM.

deductive See INDUCTIVE, DEDUCTIVE (METHODS).

deficit (hypothesis)
1. The **deficit hypothesis** (sometimes also termed **deficit theory**) was formulated in the mid-1960s. Supporters of the hypothesis argued that the communicative strategies used by middle-class parents supported the development of abstract and logical thinking. The working-class environment, on the other hand, was believed to lead to the formation of highly context-dependent discourse strategies and restricted verbal skills. The high rate of school failure among working-class children was thus explained as a consequence of their limited linguistic abilities. Subsequent research has shown the inadequacies of this theory. Researchers found that the apparent 'silence' of working-class children in the classroom environment was not a result of linguistic inability but a response to the structures of the education system, which largely reflects middle-class values and norms. In peer-group interactions working-class children were found to be as linguistically agile and skilled as their middle-class peers.

In the USA the deficit hypothesis was framed in terms of ethnicity, and the language of African American children was interpreted as a 'basically non-logical mode of behaviour' (Bereiter and Engelmann, 1966), which was believed to impede educational attainment. This claim was refuted by William LABOV (1972c) in his article the 'Logic of Non-Standard English'. Labov showed that AFRICAN AMERICAN VERNACULAR ENGLISH is a structurally complex and rule-governed linguistic system which, just like standard English, allows the expression of complex abstract reasoning. The position adopted by Labov and other sociolinguists is sometimes referred to as the DIFFERENCE position. The deficit position has been associated with Basil BERNSTEIN's theory of ELABORATED and restricted codes, though Bernstein himself rejected this association.

2. **Deficit** has also been used to characterise an early perspective on female and male language use which saw women's language as deficient in certain respects. This contrasts with DIFFERENCE and DOMINANCE perspectives on female and male language use.

deixis (deictic)   Deixis is often glossed as 'pointing', and encompasses those features of language (**deictics**, or **deictic** expressions) that indicate something relative to the speaker (or writer, narrator etc.), or the situation in which an utterance occurs: for example, *here* and *there* may locate positions spatially relative to a speaker; *now* and *then* may locate points in time relative to a speaker. Pronouns are also commonly considered to be deictic expressions. The term **social deixis** is found for words such as T AND V PRONOUNS or terms of ADDRESS that indicate aspects of the relationship between people.

density
1. As an attribute of SOCIAL NETWORKS, 'density' refers to the number of cross-cutting **ties** (or links) in a network: if the people whom an individual knows, and interacts with, also know and interact with one another, the individual is a member of a **high-density network**; if the people an individual knows and interacts with do not know and interact with one another, the individual is part of a **low-density network**. See also MULTIPLEXITY; STRONG TIES; WEAK TIES.
2. Density (lexical): see LEXICAL DENSITY.

dental   A term used in the description and classification of CONSONANTS, relating to their PLACE OF ARTICULATION. Dental sounds are produced when the tongue comes into contact with the teeth. Examples from English include: [θ] and [ð] (the first sounds in *thin* and *then*, respectively). See also INTERNATIONAL PHONETIC ALPHABET; PHONETICS.

dependent variable   See LINGUISTIC VARIABLE.

depidginisation   Generally used to signify the replacement of features of a PIDGIN by more complex structures like a well-developed tense system, subordinate clauses etc. In one sense the term is almost synonymous with creolisation, if a pidgin expands into a CREOLE, as is happening with Tok Pisin in Papua New Guinea (Jourdan, 1991). In another sense the two terms are not synonymous: if speakers of a pidgin should later gain sufficient access to its LEXIFIER LANGUAGE (the language from which the pidgin derives its vocabulary) so as to elaborate the pidgin into a second-language version of the lexifier rather than into a Creole, then depidginisation would have occurred without creolisation. This appears to be happening as speakers of Fanakalo pidgin acquire Zulu as a second language on some farms in KwaZulu-Natal, South Africa.

descriptive statistics   Statistical methods which help researchers to summarise the QUANTITATIVE aspects of a study. Descriptive statistics are used to uncover patterns or general tendencies in a data set. Methods used include simple frequency counts (e.g. the frequency with which particular linguistic features occur in a text); the transformation of absolute frequencies into percentages; the use of graphs (such as histograms or line plots) to display data; the calculation of data averages (such as the mean) and data distribution (such as the standard deviation). Information on descriptive statistical techniques can be found in many textbooks (e.g. Reid, 1987).

Descriptive statistics contrast with INFERENTIAL STATISTICS. The latter aim to confirm whether interpretations can be extended beyond the immediate data, i.e. whether any patterns observed could also be expected to be valid for the POPULATION from which the SAMPLE was drawn.

descriptivism (descriptive, descriptivist)   An approach within linguistics that aims to describe objectively the rules of a language as they are actually used by its speakers, irrespective of beliefs about what constitutes good or bad usage. For the **descriptive** linguist, the rules of a language reside in the unconscious NORMS embodied in speech, rather than in the prescriptive judgements of teachers, editors and other language professionals. Thus, if a descriptive linguist encounters a form like *I ain't going* in a particular dialect of English, he or she is obliged to analyse it as part of the grammatical system of that dialect, appropriate in informal contexts (see APPROPRIATENESS). Contrast PRESCRIPTIVISM. See also CORRECTNESS; VERBAL HYGIENE.

design
   1. Used descriptively to refer to the fact that individuals construct or 'design' their communication from a wide range of SEMIOTIC

resources, including, for example, the verbal, visual and sound ('sound' here refers to aspects of communication which extend well beyond the sounds of verbal language, such as music). See Kress (1998).

2. Design refers to what is described as the transformation stage ('transformed practice') in the teaching and learning of language and literacy as advocated by the New London Group of academics (see MULTILITERACIES).

3. Design is also used as a theoretical construct to stand in contrast to 'critique' or critical approaches to language and language use, for example work in CRITICAL DISCOURSE ANALYSIS. Kress states 'Design rests on a chain of processes of which critique . . . is one: it [critique] can, however, no longer be the focal one, or be the major goal of textual practices. Critique leaves the initial definition of the domain of analysis to the past, to past production' (Kress, 2000: 160). Kress argues for a need to build on critical approaches but to focus centrally on new ways of designing meaning and communication. See also CRITICAL LANGUAGE AWARENESS; MULTIMODAL.

desire   While desire has long been associated with language in psychoanalysis, this is a fairly recent object of enquiry within sociolinguistics. 'Desire', in this sense, may include any form of desire – for example, the desire for certain types of food, the desire to get someone to do something for you. Much of the research, however, is concerned with the expression of erotic desire. Deborah Cameron and Don Kulick (2003a) argue that research on language and SEXUALITY has much to gain from focusing on desire, including an engagement with psychoanalytic and other theory that can provide insights and challenges for linguistic research. For Cameron and Kulick, however, desire is not simply a psychological process but an interactional accomplishment that may be understood through empirical enquiry. For examples of specific studies, and discussion of 'language and desire' as an area, see Cameron and Kulick (2003a, 2003b), and Harvey and Shalom (1997).

destandardisation   A type of LANGUAGE CHANGE which leads to variability in the NORMS of an existing STANDARD variety, and which supports the development of multiple standard norms. Processes of destandardisation have been described for a number of European standard languages, including Danish, Dutch, German and Swedish

(Deumert and Vandenbussche, 2003). See also PLURICENTRIC
LANGUAGE; STANDARDISATION CYCLE.

deterioration   See PEJORATION; contrast AMELIORATION.

determiner   Determiners are words such as (in English) the articles *the*
and *a(n)*, as well as *this, these, that, those, some, each* and similar
terms that may precede a noun, or an adjective plus noun. Determiners indicate various features of the noun, e.g. number (singular or
plural). The use of determiners differs between languages (e.g. not all
languages have articles) and may also distinguish different DIALECTS
or varieties (see VARIETY), for example different varieties of English.
In varieties of English spoken in West Africa, India and Singapore
utterances such as *she is student* may be heard (i.e. without the article
a), probably influenced by local languages. In Scottish English the
article *the* is used in phrases such as *she's in the hospital,* where no
specific hospital is referred to and *she's in hospital* would be more
usual in standard English in England. See Thomas (1996) for a brief
discussion of variation in the use of determiners in English, and
Miller (1993) on determiners in Scottish English. See also NOUN
PHRASE.

determinism   See LINGUISTIC DETERMINISM.

developmental linguistics
1. An area of linguistics which describes and analyses **language
   development**, in the sense of the acquisition of language by
   children (see CHILD LANGUAGE, LANGUAGE ACQUISITION).
2. A term used by Bailey (1973, 1996) to describe his view of
   language as a system characterised by historically dynamic variation patterns, i.e. the DIACHRONIC dimension is always present in
   language use. This is also referred to as the **dynamic paradigm**.
   In contrast to William LABOV, whose work on CHANGE IN PROGRESS
   is based on the analysis of the linguistic behaviour of social groups,
   Bailey sees the INDIVIDUAL as the central unit of sociolinguistic
   analysis. Speech communities and social groups, according to
   Bailey, can be described as exhibiting POLYLECTAL GRAMMARS
   (understood as series or sets of IDIOLECTS), which cannot always
   be correlated directly and unambiguously with social group
   membership. The polylectal grammar spectrum of a speech
   community can be modelled in IMPLICATIONAL SCALES.

diachronic An approach to the study of language that focuses on its development through time, sometimes termed **diachronic linguistics**. An example would be a study of the changes that separate Old English from Middle English and Modern English. The term was introduced by the Swiss linguist Ferdinand de Saussure (1857–1913), who contrasted diachronic linguistics with SYNCHRONIC linguistics. The latter refers to the study of language at a given point in time, past or present. An example of a synchronic study would be the analysis of the verb system of Old English or the vowel system of Hawai'ian Creole English in the 1990s. Sociolinguistic work on LANGUAGE CHANGE (such as William LABOV's New York Study, 1972a) has shown that it is not always possible to separate **synchrony** from **diachrony**; rather, diachronic CHANGE IN PROGRESS is visible in the synchronic variation spectrum of a speech community. The term PANCHRONIC has been suggested to describe studies which pay attention to both diachronic and synchronic aspects of language variation. See also DEVELOPMENTAL LINGUISTICS (2).

dialect Describes the speech habits (pronunciation, lexicon, grammar, pragmatics) characteristic of a geographical area or region, or of a specific social group. Sociolinguists, therefore, may talk about **social dialects** and **regional dialects**. The term **class dialect** is also found for clearly defined varieties distinguishable along class lines. (Note, however, that in continental European linguistics the term 'dialect' refers primarily to regional varieties and is rarely used to describe the social varieties of a language.) A distinction is sometimes made between **rural dialects**, spoken in rural areas and often showing maintenance of older dialect structures (i.e. they are said to be CONSERVATIVE), and **urban dialects**, spoken in the cities, and often characterised by dialect CONVERGENCE and mixing as speakers of different dialects come into contact with one another (urban dialects are often INNOVATIVE).

In its popular usage the term 'dialect' is commonly contrasted with the supra-regional and prestigious STANDARD 'language'. This evaluative and hierarchical usage has been questioned by sociolinguists, who would see a language as a composite of all its dialects including its standard norm (sometimes also called **standard dialect**), which in many cases emerged historically from one or more regional or social dialects. In this sense, a language may be described as a **diasystem** (e.g. Weinreich, 1954), i.e. an abstract system comprising various regional and social dialects. It is also recognised, however, that a straightforward distinction between 'dialect' and 'language' is problematical (see LANGUAGE). For further discussion, see Chambers and Trudgill (1998). See also ACCENT; DIALECT CONTINUUM; DIALECTALISATION; DIALECTOLOGY.

dialect boundary   See ISOGLOSS.

dialect chain   See DIALECT CONTINUUM.

dialect continuum   Not all regional speech areas have well-defined geographical boundaries (see ISOGLOSS) which can be plotted on dialect maps in a LINGUISTIC ATLAS. In many cases the geographical organisation of language is best described as a finely graded continuum characterised by **chains** of mutually intelligible LECTs. Speakers are typically able to communicate with their neighbours and next-neighbours (i.e. across a number of villages), but communication becomes increasingly difficult the further they move away from their own geographical area. Thus, for instance, speaker A will understand speaker B from the neighbouring area and also speaker C from a little further away. Speaker A will not be able to understand speaker D, who lives even further away, but both speakers B and C will able to communicate with D. Speaker C will also be able to communicate with speaker E and so forth. The term **speech continuum** is also found for this phenomenon.

Examples of dialect continua can be found all over the world, e.g. the Scandinavian language continuum in Northern Europe, the Nguni continuum in South Africa, the Hindi/Urdu continuum in India, the Eskimo-Aleut continuum, which stretches across Alaska, Yukon, Northwest Territories and British Columbia. See also AUTONOMY, HETERONOMY; MUTUAL INTELLIGIBILITY.

dialect convergence   See CONVERGENCE.

dialect divergence   See DIVERGENCE.

dialect levelling   A process whereby dialects that come into regular contact with each other start to lose some of their features that are not widely shared with the others. Such contact may occur because of urbanisation of rural speakers, the formation of new towns, migration and other population movements (see Kerswill and Williams, 2000). In dialect levelling less frequent and less regular grammatical and phonetic forms are generally lost in favour of features that are more widespread in the various dialects. The term overlaps with dialect

CONVERGENCE, but levelling and convergence are not identical: if contact between two or more dialects leads to the addition of features to both/all dialects, rather than the loss or replacement of features, this would involve convergence without levelling. See also KOINÈ.

dialect mixing   See CODE-SWITCHING.

dialect switching   See CODE-SWITCHING.

dialectalisation
1. A historical process by which a relatively homogenous language splits into several dialects (cf. Haugen, 1972: 265ff.): often the result of geographical or political separation.
2. The classification of a MINORITY LANGUAGE as a dialect of a related MAJORITY LANGUAGE. Such sociolinguistic processes of 'covert language endangerment' have been reported, for example, in northern Germany, where North Frisian, a minority language spoken by about 8,000 speakers, is in danger of losing its status as an independent language through its gradual CONVERGENCE with Standard German. See also STANDARDISATION CYCLE; ÜBERDACHUNG.

dialectic (-al)   Used in several ways and often with some slippage between meanings:
1. To refer to the tensions surrounding the interrelationship between different elements. For example, the relationship between individuals and the social world is often described as dialectical because people both reflect the social world, and contribute to its construction, through their interaction with others. This tension is also often emphasised in discussions about the relationship between DISCOURSE and the individual or subject, where the subject is both constituted by discourse and constitutes the discourse (see SUBJECT POSITION).
2. To refer to a process of logical reasoning towards an abstract conclusion, which involves thesis–antithesis–synthesis (i.e. an argument, followed by a counter, argument, and on the basis of both a third argument or position is reached). (See Hegel, 1974.)
3. To refer to Marxist philosophy, in particular to **dialectical materialism**, in which all phenomena are viewed as material (rather than ideal or mental) and emphasis is on the tensions and struggles between different material elements, for example between the working and capitalist classes. The idea of dialectic as in

(2) above, an abstract process of reasoning, within dialectical materialism becomes a focus on material or real world tensions. Here the notions of thesis–antithesis–synthesis are used to refer to social and historical processes which ultimately lead to change or social revolution.

dialectology   The systematic study of DIALECTs, which dates back to the nineteenth century. Traditionally, dialectology has focused on the description and documentation of regional, mostly rural dialects, and the study of REGIONAL VARIATION and LANGUAGE CHANGE. From the 1960s, however, urban dialects have become a focus of interest and attention has been paid to the social dimensions of variation and change, for example in relation to social class, age, gender and ethnicity. A distinction is sometimes drawn between **regional dialectology** and SOCIAL DIALECTOLOGY or **urban dialectology**.

dialogic (dialogism)   A central notion in BAKHTIN's theory of language, used to emphasise that language is a living, social phenomenon which constructs, rather than simply reflects, meaning. A dialogic theory of language (or **dialogism**) stands in contrast to MONOLOGIC theories of language, such as idealist theories where consciousness or thought is often treated as prior to language; it also contrasts with AUTONOMOUS models of language where language is treated as independent of social CONTEXT. In dialogic theory, UTTERANCES are always understood as facing in two directions: they address a particular person and context, yet are also (explicitly or implicitly) a response to a previous word, person, question and context. Thus, for example, a doctor who addresses a patient is not only engaging in a specific communicative act, but is also engaging in a long, standing tradition of a particular type of communication between doctors and patients. The meanings of utterances thus depend on both the more immediate ADDRESSIVITY and more distant addressivity, and the particular senses, or ACCENTS, that wordings develop within specific sociohistorical contexts.

In dialogic theory the struggle to take control over meaning making is often emphasised. The nature of language itself is seen as heteroglossic (see HETEROGLOSSIA) and the pre-existence of language in relation to any individual user means that all language is always already populated 'with the intentions of others' (Bakhtin, [1935] 1981: 294). Hence, individual control over meaning involves engaging with these previous intentions.

diary See LANGUAGE DIARY.

diasystem See DIALECT.

dictionaries Dictionaries list and describe the LEXICON (vocabulary) of a language: the term **lexicography** is used to refer to dictionary making. The compilation and publication of dictionaries is a central aspect of LANGUAGE PLANNING and STANDARDISATION, contributing to the CODIFICATION of word meanings, spelling (orthography) and pronunciation (dictionaries often include a model pronunciation for each word, given in phonetic transcription).

Dictionaries are not neutral compilations of words but tend to reflect certain cultural values in relation to the words and meanings included, the meanings that are prioritised, how words/meanings are described (e.g. whether a usage is identified as 'slang' or 'informal'), and who is cited as an authority (in illustrative quotations). Traditionally, dictionaries have relied on a fairly restricted range of sources (written, usually published, often from more 'respected' authors or publications); contemporary dictionaries tend to draw on large electronic corpora (see CORPUS) including a more diverse range of written and spoken texts, and may therefore appear more democratic, but there is still a need for selectivity in identifying appropriate sources to include in the corpus. Some researchers writing from a critical perspective have discussed the gatekeeping function of dictionaries, and the potential for social/cultural bias in their coverage. For a discussion of feminist concerns about sexism in dictionaries, and feminist interventions in lexicography, see Cameron (1992). See also PRESCRIPTIVISM.

difference (position)
1. A view of language variation that may be contrasted with a DEFICIT position. Whereas US deficit theorists argued (in the 1960s) that many black children had limited verbal abilities that were associated with educational failure, those who took a 'difference' position argued that the children's language could not be considered deficient: instead, there was a clash between the standard language used in education and the non-standard variety spoken by black children. This non-standard variety was, however, as systematic, rule-governed and 'logical' as standard English. William LABOV's paper, first written in 1969, on 'The logic of non-standard English' is a classic statement of the difference position (see Labov, 1972c). The difference position is consistent with the

LINGUISTIC EQUALITY and linguistic DESCRIPTIVISM.
iberal ideas still play an important part in socio-
ing, but they may be critiqued from a more
ctive: e.g. they stop short of examining why the
in people is devalued. For an alternative approach
education, see CRITICAL LANGUAGE AWARENESS.
RICAN AMERICAN VERNACULAR ENGLISH (AAVE);
APPROPRIATENESS; CORRECTNESS; EBONICS; ELABORATED, RESTRICTED
(CODES).

2. Difference has also been used to characterise a perspective on female and male language use which saw this as culturally different (Maltz and Borker (1982) provide a classic statement of this position). This may be contrasted with an (earlier) DEFICIT position, which saw WOMEN'S LANGUAGE as deficient in certain respects; and a DOMINANCE position, which focused on differences in POWER between female and male speakers. The difference, or **cultural difference** position has been influential – for example in explorations of female and male MISCOMMUNICATION and popular books designed to help people communicate more effectively (e.g. Tannen, 1990). It has, however, been critiqued for assuming that women's and men's language is simply different and ignoring the interaction between GENDER and power; and for its assumption that female and male speakers constitute relatively homogeneous social groups (for critiques of Tannen in these respects, see Troemel Ploetz, 1991; and Cameron, 1995). See also LANGUAGE AND GENDER.

diffusion

1. A process by which the linguistic behaviour of speakers becomes more variable (see FOCUSING, DIFFUSION).
2. The spread of new linguistic variants across time, geographical areas, groups of speakers and/or spoken or written language styles. Some sociolinguists distinguish **relocation diffusion** (diffusion of linguistic forms as a result of permanent speaker MIGRATION) and **expansion diffusion** (the spread of innovations across space without permanent geographical relocation of speakers). The unmarked use of the term 'diffusion' in sociolinguistics usually refers to 'expansion diffusion'.

Diffusion across time and groups of speakers is usually gradual and follows the S-CURVE pattern. Geographical (expansion) diffusion, by contrast, has been described as constituting a steady, unidirectional spread from the centre of the innovation to neighbouring areas (see WAVE MODEL). However, diffusion can also be discontinuous as in the case of uvular /r/ which replaced the trilled variant in many French and German dialects (see Trudgill, 1983). In this case, the innovation 'hopped' or 'jumped' from one city (or **focal area**) to another but did not initially affect the areas between urban centres (see GRAVITY MODEL). Discontinuous diffusion across urban centres is typical of contemporary urban societies.

The term **lexical diffusion** is used to refer to the related observation that new pronunciations do not affect all words of a language simultaneously but spread gradually through the lexicon (Chen, 1977).

diglossia   The term was first used by Charles FERGUSON (1959) to denote a situation in which two forms of what are considered the same language co-exist in a complementary relationship in a society (see 'H' VARIETY, 'L' VARIETY). One form (the 'H' or 'high' form) is typically an older or classical form, which is used in functions associated with 'high' culture, like literature, the media, formal speech-making and prayer. The other form (the 'L' or 'low' form) is a VERNACULAR form associated with everyday experiences like casual conversation, shopping and the recital of folk tales, riddles, etc. The H and L forms of the language are grammatically distinct; they do not overlap or shade into each other, nor do the DOMAINS associated with them. Arabic in Egypt was cited as an exemplar of diglossia, with its classical and contemporary, colloquial versions existing side by side.

Several special cases and a generalisation of Ferguson's formulation exist. The generalisation made by Joshua FISHMAN, known as **Fishman's extension**, or **broad diglossia**, refers to situations where two *different* languages (rather than a classical and modern form of the same language) show a complementary relationship found in diglossia (or **narrow diglossia**, as Ferguson's original relationship is sometimes termed). Fishman's examples included the kind of bilingualism found in Paraguay, where Spanish played the role of H language and Guarani the role of L language for all speakers. **Triglossia** exists in a bilingual community in which speakers share two L languages and a common H form or two H varieties with a single L form. An example of the latter is the use of Arabic as L language in Tunisia and both classical Arabic and French as H languages. Similarly, the term **polyglossia** is used for a situation in which several H and L languages co-exist in a complex multilingual society like Singapore, which Platt (1977) describes as having L and H varieties and an intermediate set of M (or mid) varieties. See also Fasold (1984: Chapter 2).

diphthong   See VOWEL.

directive   An utterance designed to get someone to do something (e.g. *Shut the door,* or *Would you mind helping with this?*). Directives have been of interest to sociolinguists because they take different forms, as in the examples above. The use of greater or less MITIGATION may be associated with particular contexts or relations between speakers. Directives may also be analysed in terms of POLITENESS.

discourse (analysis)   Discourse is a difficult term widely used in sociolinguistics with a range of meanings. Whilst there is slippage, and in some instances intentional overlap between usages, it is useful to distinguish three broad meanings:

1. A stretch of language longer than a single sentence or utterance, such as a written paragraph or a spoken dialogue. In this usage discourse is similar to TEXT.
2. A type of language used in a particular context, for example the language used by teachers and students in classrooms (classroom discourse) or the written language of medicine or law (medical or legal discourse).
3. In a more critical and abstract sense a way of representing, understanding and being in the world. Discourse here refers not only to particular uses of language in context, as in (2) above, but also to the world views and ideologies (see IDEOLOGY) which are implicit or explicit in such uses. For example, it is argued that formal schooling involves particular conventionalised language practices, such as those associated with classroom teaching and learning, assembly, playtime, staff meetings. These embody particular ideologies and make available particular kinds of SUBJECT POSITIONS which individuals feel implicitly obliged to take up. Most obviously in the context of schooling, they are those of teacher and the pupil, whose actions, behaviours and identities are regulated by the ORDER OF DISCOURSE of schooling (see Fairclough, 2001). This last definition is closely associated with the work of Michel FOUCAULT and a philosophical approach known as POST-STRUCTURALISM.

Discourse analysis may refer to analytical approaches at any of these levels. In relation to (1) above a well-known example of discourse analysis is John Sinclair and Malcolm Coulthard's (1975) system of analysing classroom talk. Sinclair and Coulthard's analysis is functional, focusing on the ACTS carried out within classroom discourse. An often-cited aspect of the analysis is the identification of the INITIATION–RESPONSE–FEEDBACK (IRF) exchange, used by teachers to elicit information from students. In relation to (2) above, analysis might focus on the use of certain types of language to construct certain relationships between speakers/writers, or certain forms of knowledge – for example, the extensive use of impersonal language in science texts. Discourse analysis in sense (3) above would include the analysis of different ways of constructing and representing social reality by analysing DISCURSIVE PRACTICES and orders of discourse (see CRITICAL DISCOURSE ANALYSIS; DISCURSIVE PSYCHOLOGY; INTERPRETATIVE REPERTOIRES). The first two of the three approaches to discourse outlined above tend to focus on language at the level of CONTEXT OF SITUATION. The third focuses on language at the level of CONTEXT OF CULTURE, drawing on social theory and philosophy in order to theorise the social and cultural meanings that are being constructed in a text. However, several attempts have been made to integrate analyses at different levels. James Gee (1996) uses the terms little 'd' and big 'D' discourse to discuss how specific instances of language use, little 'd' (1 and 2 above) involve particular ways of being and doing in the world, big D (3 above). And Norman Fairclough (1992a) has developed a three-layered framework, a Textually Oriented Discourse Analysis (TODA), which also attempts to integrate analyses on these three levels.

'Discourse analysis' is also found as a cover term for any form of analysis of communication, in which case it would include approaches that are not themselves termed 'discourse analysis' (e.g. CONVERSATION ANALYSIS).

discourse community   Used like SPEECH COMMUNITY to emphasise that individual language use is embedded in social relations and is regulated by conventions specific to particular groups or communities. However, it is often distinguished from 'speech community' on the grounds that speech communities are sociolinguistic groupings with communicative needs such as socialisation and group solidarity, whereas discourse communities are groupings based on common interests. 'Discourse community' is also often used to signal a focus on written rather than spoken texts, such as the writing of the academic discourse community or the reading of magazines by adolescents. An influential model of the defining characteristics of a discourse community was developed by Swales (1990), who lists the following characteristics.

A discourse community:
- has a broadly agreed set of common public goals;
- has mechanisms of intercommunication among its members;
- uses its participatory mechanisms to provide information and feedback;
- utilises and hence possesses one or more GENRES in the communicative furtherance of its aims;
- has acquired some specific LEXIS;
- has a threshold level of members with a suitable degree of relevant content and discoursal expertise (25–7).

A principal criticism of the term discourse community, as of speech community and another related term, COMMUNITY OF PRACTICE, is the implied homogeneous, often idealised, nature of the community and its associated language practices.

discourse practice(s)   Refers to the different types of communicative activities which take place in specific contexts or which are associated with specific domains, for example the discourse practices of schooling, business, or medicine. An example of a discourse practice from schooling in the UK is when pupils take turns to read from a Shakespeare play while sitting at desks in classroom; an example from medicine is the common practice of the patient answering a doctor's questions about her illness. See also CRITICAL DISCOURSE ANALYSIS; DISCOURSE; DISCURSIVE PRACTICE; PRACTICE.

discourse-related, preference-related (code-switching)   A distinction made by Peter Auer (1984, 1998) between different types of CODE-SWITCHING (or 'language/code alternation', to use Auer's alternative terms for the general phenomenon of code-switching). **Discourse-related** switching (or discourse-related alternation) contributes to the organisation of the interaction, for example a switch that marks a shift in topic. To interpret discourse-related switching, participants would search for an account of 'why that language now?'

On the other hand, **preference-related**, or sometimes **participant-related** switching, is connected to attributes of participants, for example a speaker's linguistic preference or ability. Auer acknowledges that discourse-related and preference-related switching are not always strictly separate.

discursive practice   Term drawn from the work of FOUCAULT to emphasise the importance of language in constituting domains of social life. Whilst there is slippage in use between discursive practice and DISCOURSE PRACTICE, the former often signals an explicit interest in power relations within society. Analysis of discursive practice involves a focus on ORDERS OF DISCOURSE including the processes of text production, distribution and consumption (see Fairclough, 1992a). See also CRITICAL DISCOURSE ANALYSIS; DISCOURSE.

discursive psychology   An approach in psychology which emphasises the importance of the study of DISCOURSE. Discursive psychologists do not treat language as a transparent medium which reflects thought or reality but rather as a medium which shapes those phenomena under study (see Harre and Stearns, 1995; and Wetherell et al., 2001). Discursive psychologists have used approaches to DISCOURSE analysis developed in applied linguistics and sociolinguistics, for example CONVERSATION ANALYSIS and CRITICAL DISCOURSE ANALYSIS, as well as developing new approaches, for example, Potter and Wetherell's (1987) conception of INTERPRETATIVE REPERTOIRES.

diverge (-ence)
1. Used in studies of speech ACCOMMODATION to refer to the process whereby speakers increase linguistic differences between themselves and the people they are talking to. Speakers may diverge along a number of dimensions, for example choice of language (in bilingual contexts), ACCENT, DIALECT, speech rate and other vocal characteristics. Traditionally, divergence has been said to be a means of increasing social distance, but more recent studies acknowledge a wider range of potential motivations: for example, a teacher may use a standard variety of language in the classroom because this is expected behaviour, rather than to distance herself from students.
2. A DIACHRONIC process by which the differences between language varieties increase over time. LABOV and Harris (1986), for example, found that in Philadelphia the speech of African Americans and

white Americans is diverging, i.e. African American and white dialects are becoming more dissimilar.

In both cases, contrast CONVERGENCE.

diversity (in language)   See LANGUAGE DIVERSITY.

do (unstressed)   A dialect form of the AUXILIARY verb *do* which retains a function long lost in standard English. *Do* in contemporary standard English is used either in emphatic statements (*I did tell you*) or as a DUMMY verb in questions and negative sentences (*I didn't tell you, Did I tell you?*). However, utterances such as *I did tell you*, in which *did* is unstressed and unemphatic, persist in regional varieties of English in the south-west of England and Wales and – with slight modifications – in Ireland and in English-oriented contact varieties in the Caribbean. In these cases, unstressed *do* signals habitual activity. In Trinidad Creole unstressed *do* can also be used to express completive aspect (*I done know you clever* – 'I have always known that you are clever'). Unstressed *do* has also served other functions in the history of English (and other related languages such as Dutch and German), e.g. as a 'carrier' of tense (*the woman what do own this house*), and even rhythm (as in Wordsworth's poem 'A slumber did my spirit seal').

doctrine of correctness   See CORRECTNESS.

domain   Term introduced by Joshua FISHMAN for a sphere of activity representing a combination of specific times, settings and role relationships, and resulting in a specific choice of language or style. In their study of bilingualism in the New York Puerto Rican community, Fishman et al. (1971) identified five domains which elicited behavioural patterns favouring either Spanish or English: family, friendship, religion, employment and education. These abstract domains may be more concretely realised in physical and institutional settings like the home, street, church, workplace and school respectively. The concept of domain has proved very useful in the study of LANGUAGE CHOICE, DIGLOSSIA (an extreme form of domain specialisation) and LANGUAGE SHIFT.

dominance (interactional)   Refers to the phenomenon whereby one or more participants **dominate** in an interaction, so that their interests are better served than those of other participants. The term has often been used in studies of LANGUAGE AND GENDER, where **male dominance** has been associated with specific interactional features, such as the use of INTERRUPTIONS that prevent another speaker from finishing their speaking turn. In practice, interactional dominance is not as straightforward as this may suggest: participants' interactional strategies are culturally and contextually variable, attempts at dominance may be contested and control may be exercised without the use of linguistic forms associated with dominance. Accounts of language and gender research have sometimes distinguished 'dominance' studies both from those that adopt a DEFICIT perspective (seeing female speech as deficient in certain respects) and those that adopt a DIFFERENCE, or sometimes 'cultural difference' perspective (seeing female and male speakers as culturally different rather than unequal). This distinction applies better to relatively early (e.g. 1970s–80s) work than to more recent work, which is characterised by a wider range of approaches and orientations.

dominant (group, etc.)   Used in many socially oriented studies of language in a number of ways. Whilst there is slippage between uses, the following can be identified.

1. To refer to socially powerful groups, for example, middle and upper social classes as compared with the working class (see SOCIAL CLASS), or professional groups such as doctors or lawyers, who have considerably more POWER in interactions than their patients or clients; such groups may be in a position to dominate within an interaction – see DOMINANCE.
2. To refer to the language(s) which are most powerful within any given context, for example English at global level (see GLOBAL LANGUAGE; LINGUISTIC IMPERIALISM).
3. To refer to the language in which a BILINGUAL is thought to be more competent.
4. To refer to a way of representing, acting or being in the world, for example HEGEMONIC MASCULINITY would be a dominant discourse or practice in relation to gendered behaviour.
5. To refer to ways of understanding which have assumed the status of 'common sense' in any given sociohistorical context, for example the dominant view that a standard language is superior to other language varieties (see STANDARD LANGUAGE IDEOLOGY).

double-languaging   See DOUBLE-VOICING.

double-voice discourse Used by Amy Sheldon to refer to an interactional style that allowed speakers to manage potentially conflictual
talk in a co-operative way. Double-voice discourse involves merging
'the "voice" of MITIGATION and social sensitivity' with 'the "voice"
of self-interest and egocentricity'. This could be contrasted with
single-voice discourse, in which speakers 'have the single orientation of pursuing their own self-interest without orienting to the
perspective of the partner or tempering their self-interest with
mitigation' (Sheldon, 1997: 231). The notion of double-voice discourse is relevant to LANGUAGE AND GENDER research, as this way of
speaking has been associated more with female speakers than with
male in certain contexts.

double-voicing A term used originally by BAKHTIN to refer to instances
when a speaker draws on another speaker's language, 'inserting a new
semantic intention into a discourse which already has, and which
retains, an intention of its own. [...] In one discourse, two semantic
intentions appear, two voices' ([1929] 1984a: 189). An example might
be a narrator telling a story and quoting from another speaker in such
a way that (e.g. by tone of voice) the narrator's viewpoint is evident
behind that of the quoted speaker. Bakhtin distinguished between
'uni-directional double-voicing', in which, although there are two
voices, the semantic intentions are consistent; and 'vari-directional
double-voicing', in which the speaker 'introduces a semantic intention directly opposed to the original one' ([1929] 1984a: 189–93). An
example of the latter is political satire, where the words of the original
speaker are repeated but with a different purpose than those originally intended. The notion of double-voicing has been drawn on in
relation to several sociolinguistic phenomena, including LANGUAGE
CROSSING, where a speaker may use features of a language repertoire
not usually associated with her or his social group in order to enact a
particular kind of identity.

dual standardisation A process whereby two different STANDARD
languages were developed from the same dialectal basis and
now exist side by side as standard varieties in the larger SPEECH
COMMUNITY, for example in south-east Africa the dialects of Gwamba
were codified by different missionaries. As a result two different
(though largely mutually intelligible) standard languages, Tsonga
and Ronga, exist today in South Africa and Mozambique (Harries,
1995). Another often-cited example of dual standardisation is the
CODIFICATION of Norwegian in the nineteenth century (with Bokmål

based on the speech of the urban upper classes and Nynorsk based on the rural dialects).

duetting   Within research on CONVERSATION MANAGEMENT or TURN-TAKING, duetting refers to a co-operative practice whereby two or more speakers jointly construct a SPEAKING TURN, for example:
A: And so he came along quite
B: happily.

dummy   A syntactic element that fills a place in a sentence to render it grammatical; dummy elements are, however, semantically 'empty' – i.e. have no meaning in themselves. In English *it* in sentences like *It's snowing* is a dummy pronoun; in sentences like *It's getting away*, it is not considered a dummy, since it refers to some previously mentioned noun (perhaps a cat) – see ANAPHORIC (REFERENCE). The AUXILIARY verb *do* has a similar function in a sentence like *I don't like cabbage*, where its function is that of a 'dummy' element on to which the negative element *n't* attaches. Compare the positive equivalent *I like cabbage*, where such a dummy is not needed.

E

EAL   Acronym for ENGLISH AS AN ADDITIONAL LANGUAGE.

early adopter   Early adopters are the first speakers to accept and to promote a linguistic change after it has been introduced to the SPEECH COMMUNITY. They show a specific pattern of SOCIAL NETWORK membership: they are closely integrated into their local network but also interact regularly (although not necessarily frequently) with people who are outside of their social group. This network pattern is important for the spread of the innovation: early adopters encounter the innovation in social interactions outside of their local social network; they then carry the innovation back to their local network, where it spreads and develops into a new communicative norm. The term was originally introduced by Rogers (1978) in his monograph *Diffusion of Innovations*. The term was applied to the sociolinguistic study of LANGUAGE CHANGE by James and Lesley Milroy (e.g. J. Milroy, 1992). LABOV (2001) refers to this group as **leaders** (of linguistic change). See also INNOVATOR.

Ebonics   Term combining *ebony* with *phonics*, first introduced by Robert Williams to refer to 'the linguistic and paralinguistic features which on a concentric continuum represent the communicative competence of the West African, Caribbean and United States slave descendants of African origin' (Williams, 1975). Controversy surrounds this term and it became a focus of national US debate after the Oakland California School Board adopted an Ebonics resolution in 1996 declaring Ebonics to be the official language of 28,000 African American schoolchildren (Baugh, 2000). Sociolinguistic debate often centres on the relationship between Ebonics and English, particularly the claim that Ebonics has different origins to English, and the extent to which Ebonics is synonymous or not with the term AFRICAN AMERICAN VERNACULAR ENGLISH (AAVE).

ecology   See LANGUAGE ECOLOGY.

educational linguistics   Used to refer to the application of linguistic theories and research to educational contexts and/or the development of linguistic theory based on research on language and literacy in educational contexts. The broad aim of educational linguistics is to emphasise the relevance of explicit linguistic knowledge to issues of teaching and learning (see e.g. Stubbs, 1986). Interests include the relationship between language and learning, the nature of educational DISCOURSE, the differences between spoken and written language, the importance of implicit and explicit KNOWLEDGE ABOUT LANGUAGE (KAL), the GENRES of education, MULTILINGUALISM and education, the place of VERNACULAR and STANDARD varieties in education. The relevance of SYSTEMIC FUNCTIONAL LINGUISTICS to education has been emphasised notably by M. A. K. HALLIDAY (see e.g. Halliday, 1989, 1993).

EFL   Acronym for ENGLISH AS A FOREIGN LANGUAGE.

elaborated, restricted (codes)   Terms introduced by Basil BERNSTEIN (1977) to describe a particular orientation to language use. **Elaborated code** refers to an orientation to language where shared assumptions and background knowledge are not presupposed by participants. Meanings are therefore made explicit through more complex or 'elaborated' language use, such as substantial use of subordinate clauses, complex sentence structure and a wider range of vocabulary. Bernstein contrasts this with a **restricted code**, which refers to an orientation to language where participants assume a greater shared knowledge, cultural and social history. This leads to a use of language where meanings are left implicit and the language itself is seen as more 'restricted', often focusing on the concrete rather than the theoretical or analytical. Whilst Bernstein states that these codes cannot solely be associated with particular social groups, he argues that the elaborated code is more typically an orientation found in middle-class communication, whereas the restricted code is more typical in working-class communication. These different codes both reflect different socialisation patterns within the family and serve to maintain socially structured relations.

Criticisms of Bernstein's proposed two-code theory have focused on the ways in which they were used to support a DEFICIT hypothesis about working-class children's language (though Bernstein himself rejected this association). The deficit hypothesis has been strongly challenged by sociolinguists.

elaboration   Describes two different but interrelated aspects of language STANDARISATION: (a) the process of extending the social functions in which a language is used (e.g.MEDIUM OF INSTRUCTION, legal language, scientific language); (b) the ongoing terminological, grammatical and stylistic development of a language to meet the demands of modern life and technology. See also CORPUS PLANNING, STATUS PLANNING; MODERNISATION.

electronic communication   See COMPUTER-MEDIATED COMMUNICATION.

elicitation   A method for obtaining linguistic data through carefully designed questioning strategies which allow for the systematic collection of information about words and/or grammatical structures from a native speaker. It is used in linguistics for the description of previously undocumented languages. The researcher first asks for some basic words (e.g. body parts, names of animals, simple verbs etc.) to establish the basic phonological structure of the language. Then simple sentences are elicited to obtain information on verbal paradigms and basic phrase structure. Finally, complex sentences (e.g. relative clauses, embedded clauses, infinitive constructions) as well as whole texts are elicited (the latter are important for the description of discourse phenomena). See also LANGUAGE DOCUMENTATION.

elite   Those members of a society who are most powerful within a specific institutional context, for example religious elites, political elites, economic elites, cultural elites, educational elites. **Counter-elites** are less well-established, newly-emerging elite groups which challenge the power basis of the traditional elite, and establish oppositional (cultural and linguistic) practices and discourses. In sociolinguistics the concepts of 'elite' and 'counter-elite' have been influential in the analysis of LANGUAGE PLANNING (see Cooper, 1989). Elite conflicts have characterised the history of many of the European national standard languages. Latin was supported by members of the religious and educational elite up until the seventeenth century, while a literary counter-elite (e.g. writers, poets, journalists) had begun to develop the European vernaculars (Italian, French, Dutch, German, etc.) as national languages. See also DUAL STANDARDISATION; ELITE CLOSURE.

elite closure   Cultural and linguistic practices of ELITE groups which support the stabilisation of boundaries and the exclusion of the majority of the population from the centres of power (see also GATE-KEEPING). In nineteenth-century Russia, for example, the educated and political elite usually conversed in French, not Russian. Thus, knowledge of French – whose acquisition was time-consuming, costly and out-of-reach for the majority of the population – served as a linguistic and cultural boundary marker.

ELT   An acronym for **English Language Teaching**: see TEACHING ENGLISH TO SPEAKERS OF OTHER LANGUAGES (TESOL).

embedding
1. An aspect of the sociolinguistic study of LANGUAGE CHANGE. 'Embedding' refers to the process by which a variant (e.g. a pronunciation feature) becomes established within a language. Accounts of the embedding of a change would include the identification of the social location of the most INNOVATIVE speakers (that is, their social class membership, their networks, their gender and/or age) as well as the study of the DIFFUSION of new linguistic forms across social groups. William LABOV's study of social differences with regard to the use of POST-VOCALIC /r/ in New York is a classic example of such an approach.
2. 'Embedding' is also found in grammatical description to refer to instances where a clause is included (or **embedded**) within another, as in: 'The place *that I really want to visit* is Kerala.'

emic   See ETIC, EMIC.

empirical linguistics   A methodological approach to the study of
language which argues that linguistic hypotheses and theories should
be based on the empirical data of ordinary language use. William
LABOV (1972a: xvi) also described this perspective as **secular linguistics**, a term which is now rarely used. The empirical principle is
central to the sociolinguistic research paradigm. While structuralists
(such as, for example, Leonard Bloomfield) worked mostly with
formally elicited data (a method still used in research where the aim is
to describe the linguistic structures of a previously undocumented or
minimally documented language – see ELICITATION), and generative
linguists (following Noam Chomsky) with intuitive judgements of
GRAMMATICALITY, sociolinguists tend to rely on naturally occurring
speech recorded in ordinary social settings. See also AUDIO-
RECORDING; INTERVIEW; FIELDWORK; VARIATIONIST (SOCIOLINGUISTICS).

endangered language   A language is classified as endangered if there
is an immediate risk that it will no longer be spoken. Many languages
are endangered because of a generational decline in the percentage of
children who learn to speak them. Languages that have small
numbers of speakers are also considered to be endangered, even if
there is no decline in the proportion of children learning them. While
statistics on all 6,000 or so languages of the world are not equally
reliable, most analysts point to an alarming rate of endangerment at
the turn of the twentieth century. Some researchers (e.g. Krauss,
1992) caution that up to 90 per cent of the world's languages cannot
be considered 'safe'. Accordingly, a number of countries have
instituted **endangered language projects** aimed at revitalising
or even resuscitating languages. See also LANGUAGE DEATH; LANGUAGE
SHIFT.

endearment (terms of)   Terms of ADDRESS such as (in English) *love*,
pet, *dear*, usually used to express intimacy. Such terms have been of
interest in sociolinguistics because there is some cultural variation in
their use. They may also be used asymmetrically and, in certain
contexts, associated with POWER and GENDER (e.g. used more to
women than to men) – see LANGUAGE AND GENDER.

endogenous communication   Communication practices that take
place within a particular ethnic or social group. For example, the
Old Order Amish in North America (groups of German Anabaptists

who arrived in the USA and Canada from the eighteenth century) use a variety of German (called 'Pennsylvania Dutch' or *Deitsch*) for communication within the religious group. English is used primarily for communication with outsiders. The term contrasts with EXOGENOUS COMMUNICATION.

endoglossic language   A language which has developed and is spoken as a native language within a specific geographical area or country, for example English in England, Breton or Basque in France. An endoglossic LANGUAGE POLICY supports the use of the local language in official functions. The term contrasts with EXOGLOSSIC LANGUAGE.

endophoric (reference)   Grammatical term used to describe forms of REFERENCE made within any given TEXT to other elements within the text. For example in the following sentences: 'She gave the book to John. *He* left the room,' *He* is an example of endophoric reference, referring to *John*. Endophoric relations are categorised either as ANAPHORIC (referring to a previous textual element) or CATAPHORIC (referring to an element that comes later in the text). Focusing on endophoric reference within a text is one way of analysing its internal structure or COHESION. Endophoric reference contrasts with EXOPHORIC reference to elements outside the text.

engineering (linguistic)   See LINGUISTIC ENGINEERING.

English as a Foreign Language (EFL), 'X' as a Foreign Language (XFL)   'English as a Foreign Language' (EFL) signifies the status and role of English in countries which were not settled by a body of English speakers. This contrasts with ENGLISH AS A SECOND LANGUAGE (ESL), though the difference between the two is not always clear-cut, especially in deciding how large the settlement of English speakers has to be. In EFL countries such as China, Japan and Columbia, English is used for international communication or for special purposes like tourism rather than internal communication between citizens of the country. Though English might be a subject in school curricula in EFL territories, it is not a medium of instruction nor is it usually used in creative writing. This has implications for teaching techniques, the design of course materials etc. As a general sociolinguistic concept, EFL may well be generalised to XFL for any language X existing under similar circumstances as a foreign language in a particular territory. See also TEACHING

ENGLISH TO SPEAKERS OF OTHER LANGUAGES (TESOL); THREE CIRCLES OF ENGLISH.

English as a Native Language (ENL)   Term used for English spoken as a dominant MOTHER TONGUE in places like the UK, USA, Australia etc. This contrasts with ENGLISH AS A SECOND LANGUAGE, ENGLISH AS A FOREIGN LANGUAGE, ENGLISH AS AN ADDITIONAL LANGUAGE.

English as a Second Language (ESL), 'X' as a Second Language (XSL)   'English as a Second Language' (ESL) is most typically used to refer to the acquisition of English in territories where, although English is not a majority language, its influence is directly felt by the presence of a significant body of English settlers and/or by its use in education, administration and the media. Former British colonies such as Kenya and India are examples of ESL territories. In contrast to ENGLISH AS A FOREIGN LANGUAGE, ESL varieties tend to develop indigenised norms (see INDIGENISATION), which may also be used strategically in creative writing. This has implications for the design of teaching materials and teaching techniques. However, advocates of the notion of ENGLISH AS AN ADDITIONAL LANGUAGE (EAL) or ENGLISH FOR SPEAKERS OF OTHER LANGUAGES (ESOL) tend to blur the ESL/EFL distinction.

In another, more general sense, ESL refers to the INTERLANGUAGES of learners of English either in ESL territories or in countries where English is a dominant, NATIVE language. In this sense ESL contrasts with ENGLISH AS A NATIVE LANGUAGE (ENL). As a general socio-linguistic concept, ESL may well be generalised to **XSL** for any international language X existing under similar conditions. See also TEACHING ENGLISH TO SPEAKERS OF OTHER LANGUAGES (TESOL), THREE CIRCLES OF ENGLISH.

English as an Additional Language (EAL), 'X' as an Additional Language (XAL)   A cover term for ENGLISH AS A SECOND LANGUAGE (ESL) and ENGLISH AS A FOREIGN LANGUAGE (EFL), which also leaves open whether English has been acquired as a second or third or later language for individuals. ENGLISH FOR SPEAKERS OF OTHER LANGUAGES is found with similar meaning. In the educational sphere courses in EAL train teachers for a variety of situations, rather than catering specifically for second- or foreign-language classrooms; see also TEACHING ENGLISH TO SPEAKERS OF OTHER LANGUAGES (TESOL). As a more general concept, EAL may be generalised to **XAL**, where X is any additional language acquired by a speech community. See also THREE CIRCLES OF ENGLISH.

English for Speakers of Other Languages (ESOL) A US term, used as a cover term incorporating ENGLISH AS A SECOND LANGUAGE (ESL) and ENGLISH AS A FOREIGN LANGUAGE (EFL), particularly in relation to English teaching, i.e. includes English teaching for all except those who have English as a MOTHER TONGUE. See TEACHING ENGLISH TO SPEAKERS OF OTHER LANGUAGES (TESOL); and ENGLISH AS AN ADDITIONAL LANGUAGE (EAL).

English Language Teaching (ELT) See TEACHING ENGLISH TO SPEAKERS OF OTHER LANGUAGES (TESOL).

English-only Name given to a LANGUAGE MOVEMENT which emerged in the United States during the 1980s (including groups such as 'English First' and 'US English') to lobby for the introduction of English as a constitutionally recognised OFFICIAL LANGUAGE. An unsuccessful attempt to introduce a constitutional amendment was made in 1981 by Senator S. I. Hayakawa. Over twenty US states have passed active 'Official English' legislation since the 1980s but to date no national policy exists. Sociolinguists are highly critical of the proposed legislation as it would most probably end political and financial support for BILINGUAL EDUCATION, and marginalise the increasingly large numbers of Hispanic speakers and other migrant groups as well as Native Americans. See Crawford (2000) for a critical discussion.

ENL Acronym for ENGLISH AS A NATIVE LANGUAGE.

environment (linguistic) Refers to the linguistic CONTEXT in which a linguistic form (e.g. a specific phoneme, morpheme, syntactic construction) occurs, i.e. the elements (phonemes, words, syntactic constructions) which are near or adjacent to the linguistic form under study. The term CO-TEXT is found with similar meaning. See also VARIABLE RULE.

epistemic (modality) A type of MODALITY that expresses the level of confidence a speaker or writer has in the truth of a proposition. For example, in a study of GENDER and POLITENESS in language, Janet Holmes (1995) identified tag questions such as 'I did my exams in sixty-three, *was it?*' as 'epistemic modal tags' which expressed uncertainty, and suggested that these were used more frequently by male than female speakers.

equilingual   Synonym for BALANCED BILINGUAL.

equivalence constraint   A concept used in CODE-SWITCHING research, introduced by Poplack (1980). Poplack suggested that code-switching between languages could only occur at certain points, when the surface structure of the languages mapped on to one another so that switches did not violate the grammar of either language. (This is disputed; see e.g. the alternative MATRIX LANGUAGE FRAME MODEL of code-switching.)

error
1. In linguistics, a form like a random mistake or 'slip of the tongue', made by a NATIVE speaker (who is, by definition, fluent in at least one variety of the language and has a command of all of its rules). The term thus differs from its everyday sense, which refers to forms that differ from accepted formal standard norms (see PRESCRIPTIVISM; CORRECTNESS).
2. In applied linguistics, forms produced by SECOND LANGUAGE learners that differ from the forms produced by adult FIRST LANGUAGE speakers. Such forms are usually temporary ones produced during the language-learning process and are typically replaced in time by forms from the TARGET language. Sometimes an error shared by groups of speakers may stabilise (see FOSSILISATION) and become a regular 'feature' rather than a random mistake. **Error Analysis** refers to a branch of Applied Linguistics that undertakes a systematic study of the errors made by language learners, with a view to characterising the language-learning process. See also INTERLANGUAGE.

ESL   Acronym for ENGLISH AS A SECOND LANGUAGE.

ESOL   Acronym for ENGLISH FOR SPEAKERS OF OTHER LANGUAGES.

essayist literacy   Sometimes referred to as **essay-text literacy** or **essayist technique**, to indicate a particular kind of LITERACY PRACTICE associated with Western education systems. Key features of essayist literacy have been identified as (a) the linear presentation of ideas, and (b) the explicit marking of relationships between ideas through particular uses of METADISCOURSE. The epistemological assumption underlying essayist literacy, that it is possible, even desirable, for all meaning to reside in a written text, has been strongly criticised (see Gee, 1996). Also, the assumption that essayist literacy is (or should be) a universal practice has been challenged: Scollon and Scollon (1981) argue that the features of essayist literacy embody a particular approach to knowledge making which is premised upon notions of rationality from the Enlightenment tradition. In NEW LITERACY STUDIES essayist literacy is associated with AUTONOMOUS models of literacy.

Estuary English   A term first used by David Rosewarne (in 1984, but see Rosewarne, 1994) for a variety of English seen as becoming widely used in south-east England (initially, along the river Thames and its estuary). Rosewarne identified Estuary English as a variety lying between the prestige accent RECEIVED PRONUNCIATION (RP) and Cockney (popular or working-class London speech). Estuary English would therefore be characterised by intermediate use of features such as t-glottaling (see GLOTTAL), a common feature in London speech, less commonly found in RP. Estuary English has sometimes been termed the new RP (i.e. used by many high-status speakers). Several linguists have discussed related phenomena, such as the spread of features of working-class urban speech into 'mainstream RP' (Wells, 1982a, 1982b).

ethics   Within sociolinguistics and related empirical traditions of research (e.g. anthropology, sociology), **ethical** considerations include the responsibilities of researchers towards their INFORMANTS, and informants' rights in the research process. Ethical considerations have received extensive discussion within the research profession. There is general agreement that researchers must show proper respect to the people they study and should attempt to incorporate their informants' concerns and interests into the research framework; researchers should also minimise potential negative effects on communities under study, and maximise positive effects. This might include, for example, developing, in collaboration with the community, materials describing their cultural and linguistic heritage, or becoming an advocate for the linguistic rights of the community: see Cameron et al. (1992). Although official guidelines (e.g. university policies, professional guidelines) usually require researchers to protect the anonymity of their sources, this can be problematical in some anthropologically-oriented research where the narrators of texts, stories and songs usually have a clear sense of ownership regarding their artistic creations, and are therefore often acknowledged in research publications. See also Ann Arbor Trial; informed consent; surreptitious recording.

ethnic revival A term closely connected with the work of Joshua A. Fishman on language maintenance in immigrant communities (cf. Fishman et al., 1985). 'Ethnic revival' refers to the renewed interest in ethnic identity which was observed in the 1960s and 1970s in North America. Between 1960 and 1970 the number of people in the United States who claimed to speak a language other than English increased by over 70 per cent (during the same period the general population rose only by about 13 per cent). Following Marcus Hansen's (1938) sociopsychological work on ethnicity, Fishman argued that ethnic revival is a third-generation phenomenon typical of many migrant communities. While the second generation of migrants is mainly occupied with finding and establishing its place in the new society, the third generation is confident about its position in society and is eager to rediscover its linguistic and cultural heritage. However, not everyone who claims to speak a language other than English is necessarily a fluent speaker of this language. Richard Alba (1990) has shown that ethnic revival is probably best understood as a symbolic process which supports the overt enactment and maintenance of salient aspects of ethnicity. Ethnic identity is frequently marked by what Alba calls 'ethnic signalling', i.e. the use of individual words (and other cultural markers such as dress, food, etc.) is often sufficient to affirm one's ethnic identity. See also ethnolinguistic vitality.

ethnicity An aspect of an individual's social identity which is closely associated with language. Ethnicity is usually assigned on the basis of descent. In addition, the subjective experience of belonging to a culturally and historically distinct social group is often included in definitions of ethnicity. Thus, Deaf people usually consider themselves to be part of the Deaf community, which is defined by specific cultural and linguistic practices, although they may not have been born into the community (they may have become Deaf only later in life, or they may have grown up among hearing people). Questions of identity and ethnicity are also problematical in the context of migration. Second-generation migrants may not wish to identify with their traditional ethnic group but with the new society (e.g. second-generation German migrants in the USA may see themselves not as German but as American; such shifts in identity are often accompanied by symbolic actions such as name changes – Karl Müller to Chuck Miller). To assign individuals unambiguously to distinct ethnic groups can be difficult in such contexts. Sometimes RELIGION is also considered to form part of ethnicity.

Language forms a central aspect and symbol of ethnic identity (see e.g. Smolicz (1981) on language as a 'core value' of an **ethnic group**). Sociolinguists who study multicultural societies have often included ethnicity as a SOCIAL VARIABLE. Horvath (1985), for example, included speakers from different ethnic groups (Australians of English, Italian and Greek background) in her study of English in Sydney. See also ETHNIC REVIVAL; ETHNOLINGUISTIC VITALITY; RACE.

ethnography   Ethnography is an attempt to study systematically the beliefs and practices – or more generally the CULTURE – of a community or social group. It is associated with a particular methodological approach: groups are studied in their natural settings; categories used to interpret activities tend to emerge during the study rather than being fixed at the outset; researchers try to obtain an 'insider' perspective so that activities are understood from the standpoint of group members; data may come from a range of sources, but generally involve close observation of activities, including PARTICIPANT OBSERVATION; the approach is broadly QUALITATIVE. The term **ethnography of speaking** (subsequently and often interchangeably **ethnography of communication**) was coined by Dell HYMES in 1962 to refer to the ethnographic study of the WAYS OF SPEAKING evident in a speech community. Language is viewed here as a cultural activity that needs to be studied in CONTEXT rather than as a more abstract decontextualised system. A concern is with speakers' COMMUNICATIVE COMPETENCE: what they need to know to interact appropriately within a particular community. Hymes' ideas have influenced a large number of studies carried out from the early 1970s to the present day: for early examples see for instance Baumann and Sherzer ([1974] 1989), and Gumperz and Hymes ([1972] 1986); for a recent overview of methods and approaches see Saville-Troike (2003). **Linguistic ethnography** is also found for approaches to the study of language use that draw on ethnographic methods and procedures. **Ethnographically-oriented sociolinguistics** may be used to distinguish sociolinguistic approaches that take an ethnographic perspective. See also INTERACTIONAL SOCIOLINGUISTICS; LINGUISTIC ANTHROPOLOGY.

ethnolect   See LECT.

ethnolinguistic vitality   Describes the attitudinal and sociohistorical conditions which support the maintenance of an ethnic language in an intergroup setting. Ethnolinguistic vitality was said by Giles et al. (1977) to be affected by (a) an ethnic group's attitudes (i.e. whether or not language is seen as a symbolic marker of ethnic identity; this can be measured, for example, by the **Subjective Vitality Questionnaire**, see Bourhis et al., 1981); and (b) the presence or absence of a number of extra-linguistic factors including the group's economic, political and social status, its demographic strength (i.e. speaker numbers and concentrations, birth rates, migration patterns) and the institutional support given to the ethnic language (e.g. in education, the church, government and media). See also ETHNIC REVIVAL; ETHNICITY; LANGUAGE MAINTENANCE.

ethnolinguistics   Sometimes used for the study of the interrelationship between language and other aspects of CULTURE, drawing on insights from **ethnology** (defined as the science of culture) and linguistics. Ethnolinguistic interests include the linguistic features of particular language varieties; the lexicon of a language as a reflection of culture (e.g. terminology for physical, social and cultural concepts in a particular language); the relationship between language use and social groups (e.g. social STATUS, GENDER); language ATTITUDES; language practices in specific communities (e.g. greetings, BABY TALK). Ethnolinguistics therefore overlaps with LINGUISTIC ANTHROPOLOGY, and with SOCIOLINGUISTICS, including the ETHNOGRAPHY of communication.

Ethnologue   A publication of the SUMMER INSTITUTE OF LINGUISTICS (SIL). The *Ethnologue*, a comprehensive SURVEY of the world's languages, is currently in its fourteenth edition and is available on-line (www.ethnologue.com), in print and on CD-Rom. Language entries represent languages or 'probable' languages (i.e. highly divergent DIALECTS). The information provided by the *Ethnologue* includes number of speakers, location, alternate language names, dialects, linguistic affiliation according to LANGUAGE FAMILY, multilingualism of speakers, availability of Bible, grammars and dictionaries as well as bibliographical information and language maps.

ethnomethodology   A tradition associated with the sociologist Harold Garfinkel and developed during the 1960s and 1970s, of interest within sociolinguistics because it gave rise to CONVERSATION ANALYSIS.

Ethnomethodology contrasts with other sociological approaches in focusing on how human social activities are orderly, in the sense of being intelligible to participants. It argues that this order is locally produced, through use of shared methods by which people make sense of others' actions and construct their own. Ethnomethodologists study these methods as they are used in practice within different settings. Garfinkel's own work covered such diverse activities as how jury members deliberated to reach a decision, how researchers made coding decisions, and the work of staff in a suicide prevention centre. Ethnomethodological analysis focuses on participants' own understandings, insofar as these are demonstrated in everyday activity, rather than trying to impose analysts' preconceptions on the interpretation of an event. For an example of Garfinkel's work, see Garfinkel ([1967] 1984) (but note that Garfinkel's writing is notoriously difficult). See also Button (1991), Heritage (1984) and Lynch (1993).

ethnopoetics   The study of POETIC texts in specific cultural contexts, and particularly non-Western contexts. Ethnopoetics attempts to understand such texts from the perspective of the cultures in which they occur. For instance, Dell HYMES (1981, 2003), in his study of Native American narratives, sets these out in lines and stanzas, rather than paragraphs, to illustrate their poetic quality.

ethnosemantics   The study of linguistic classifications made by particular cultural and linguistic groups: this might include the terminology for local flora and fauna, KINSHIP relations etc.

etic, emic   The etic/emic distinction derives from the linguist Kenneth Pike's 'tagmemic' analysis of language, extended to provide an integrated approach to the analysis of language and culture. Based on the distinction between the linguistic terms PHONETIC and PHONEMIC, an **etic** approach describes observable behaviour from a standpoint outside a particular linguistic/cultural system. By contrast, an **emic** account relates to the internal characteristics of the system: how behaviour functions within the system, and how it relates to and contrasts with other linguistically and culturally significant behaviour. An emic account would reflect what is seen as relevant by members of the linguistic/cultural group. In a church service, for instance, it might identify segments such as a hymn, a sermon, a series of announcements (further subdivided into segments at different levels – e.g. the stanzas of a hymn). An etic account would include a wider range of behaviour that is not culturally significant: in the case of the church service, behaviour not seen as relevant to the conduct of a service – e.g. people chatting as they take their seats or wetting their finger to turn the pages of the hymn book. For Pike (e.g. 1967), etic data provide initial access to the system – they are the starting point for analysis. But the final analysis would be in emic units.

evaluation

1. Used by sociolinguists and social psychologists to refer to people's propensity to make judgements about different language forms; these judgements reflect certain ATTITUDES towards languages and language varieties (and, by implication, their speakers). Language evaluation plays an important role in LANGUAGE CHANGE: positive evaluations of a variety, or specific variants, may support the DIFFUSION of a change; conversely, a change may be 'arrested' because of negative evaluations.

   A range of methods has been used to study listeners' evaluation of specific languages or language varieties, as well as vocal characteristics such as speaking rate. One of the best-known methods is the MATCHED GUISE test, in which listeners rate voices in terms of their speakers' competence, social attractiveness etc. (e.g. Giles and Powesland, 1975). Other research has focused on speakers' 'self reports', or on listeners' identification of speakers' ethnic, social or regional background (see Labov, 2001). Early studies in particular have operated with a notion of listeners' attitudes as relatively fixed and enduring, a belief that has since been questioned within social psychology (e.g. Potter and Wetherell, 1987). In practice, it is likely that meanings attributed to language varieties will be relatively ambiguous and dependent on a range of contextual factors.

2. Also used to refer to a speaker or writer's attitudes towards objects, people and events which may be inferred from the way they speak/write about these (e.g. their choice of vocabulary or the use of modal verbs such as *may* or *should*: compare *She is the winner* with *She may be the winner*). Evaluation has been studied as an aspect of NARRATIVE. In this sense it conveys the point of the story: why the narrator has chosen to tell it (see Labov, 1972c).

3. In LANGUAGE PLANNING, evaluation refers to the critical assessment of the success of a LANGUAGE POLICY or of specific language-planning activities, i.e. the comparison of predicted and actual outcomes.

exchange   An element in an interaction between two or more people. In the system of DISCOURSE analysis devised by John Sinclair and Malcolm Coulthard (1975) to analyse classroom interaction, 'exchange' refers more specifically to a sequence of turns or part-turns that perform a particular function and may be considered a minimal interactional unit. For an example, see INITIATION–RESPONSE–FEEDBACK (IRF).

exogenous communication   Communication and interaction with people who are located outside of a particular ethnic or social reference group, i.e. linguistic interactions with the wider community. Contrasts with ENDOGENEOUS COMMUNICATION.

exoglossic language   A language which has been TRANSPLANTED to another area where it is now used as an official or co-official language: for example, English in Tanzania or Malaysia. Contrasts with ENDO-GLOSSIC LANGUAGE.

exophoric (reference)   Grammatical term used to describe a linguistic feature in a TEXT which refers to something outside of that text. Examples are words such as *there*, *that*, or *here*, when these are not further elucidated in the text: e.g. 'The book is over *there*.' This stands in contrast to ENDOPHORIC REFERENCE, which describes forms of REFERENCE made within texts to other elements of the text.

expanded pidgin   See PIDGIN.

expansion diffusion   See DIFFUSION (2.)

experiential   See METAFUNCTIONS.

experiment   The study of any phenomenon under controlled conditions designed to assess the effect of one variable on another, generally using one or more **experimental** and **control groups**. For example, an experimental study of whether teacher response (feedback) plays a role in improving students' writing in a foreign language might include two groups of learners, one who received extensive feedback on their writing (the experimental group) and the other who received no or minimal feedback (the control group). All other factors (class size, age of learners, social background of learners, etc.) would be kept constant. At the end of the instruction period the writing skills of both groups would be tested and compared (see Robb et al., 1986).

Linguistic investigations which are carried out in a controlled environment but which only involve one group of SUBJECTS (i.e. there is no control group) are called **weak experiments**. Weak experiments have been used in research on second language acquisition where rudimentary language input was given to participants who were then asked to construct more complex sentences and engage in spoken and written communications about a range of topics (e.g. Master et al., 1989).

extended pidgin   See PIDGIN.

external history (of language)   See HISTORICAL LINGUISTICS.

extra-territorial dialect   See TRANSPLANTED (DIALECT, LANGUAGE).

eye-dialect   The use of non-standard spelling conventions to represent pronunciation, for example *We wuz jus goin*. Sometimes eye-dialect is used in the TRANSCRIPTION of conversations, in preference to phonetic symbols which may make transcripts harder to read. The danger of this, however, is that the speech may appear inaccurate or inarticulate. This is a particular problem when eye-dialect is used to represent NON-STANDARD (but not STANDARD) dialect forms, thus making the former appear deviant.

F

face   A concept associated with the work of Erving GOFFMAN (1955). Goffman defined face as 'the positive social value a person effectively claims for himself by the line others assume he has taken during a particular contact' (1972: 319). Face, therefore, refers to a person's public self-image, which needs to be managed during an interaction. If someone's face is not confirmed they are said to lose face, or in Goffman's terms to be 'in wrong face' or 'out of face'. During an interaction participants need to have regard both to their own face and that of others. The work required to maintain face is referred to as **facework**. This might involve, for instance, avoidance strategies such as pretending not to have noticed a social gaffe. Face is a fundamental concept in POLITENESS theory. Penelope Brown and

Stephen Levinson (1987) distinguished **positive face** and **negative face** (respectively, the desire for approval by others and the desire not to be imposed on by others), and argued that participants in an interaction need to employ a range of politeness strategies to maintain the face of other participants.

Fairclough, Norman (1941–)   One of the founders of CRITICAL DISCOURSE ANALYSIS (CDA) which brings together the tools of linguistic theory, discourse theory and social theory to establish connections between LANGUAGE, IDEOLOGY and POWER. Fairclough sees language as a means of domination, a carrier of ideology; at the same time, the analysis of language via CDA is a means of unveiling and contesting relations of domination. A related area in which Fairclough has played a key role, CRITICAL LANGUAGE AWARE-NESS (CLA), involves more practical, educational application of CDA. In his edited collection *Critical Language Awareness* Fair-clough demonstrates how the conservative force of APPROPRIATENESS favours the language of socially powerful groups in the 'sociolinguistic order'. Fairclough is Professor of Language and Social Life at Lancaster University.

false consciousness   A Marxist concept (see MARXISM) which refers to what are assumed to be the mistaken or false set of understandings held by some members of socially oppressed groups, such as members of the WORKING CLASS, which prevents them from recognising their exploitation by the ruling or capitalist class. A key interest in CRITICAL DISCOURSE ANALYSIS (CDA) is to uncover ways in which language serves to maintain false or mistaken understandings through MANIPULATION.

fast speech   See CONNECTED SPEECH.

fatherese   See CHILD–DIRECTED SPEECH.

feature   While 'feature' has a technical meaning in some linguistic theories it may also be used as a general term for an aspect of language at any linguistic level (e.g. a grammatical feature, pronunciation feature, conversational feature).

felicity conditions   A term from SPEECH ACT theory. Speech act theory is concerned with the acts that are carried out by utterances (e.g. an utterance may promise, warn or threaten someone). It is argued that, in order for such speech acts to be satisfactorily performed, they need to satisfy certain conditions, and these are often termed felicity conditions. In the case of promising, felicity conditions would include:

- the utterance predicates a future act (i.e. you promise to do something in the future: you cannot promise to have done something). An utterance such as *I promise, I've cleaned my room* does not constitute a promise in speech act terms: it functions as an assurance that the speaker has done something;
- the speaker believes the hearer wishes the promised action to be carried out, and the hearer does in fact wish this;
- the speaker would not be expected to carry out the promised action in the normal course of events;
- the speaker intends to carry out the action;
- the speaker intends that the utterance commits her or him to carry out the action.

For a full and more formal specification of the conditions for a successful promise, see Searle (1969).

femininity (-ies)   Within early (1970s and 1980s) research on LANGUAGE AND GENDER, **femininity**, like MASCULINITY, was seen as an attribute of speakers that could be reflected in language and perceived by listeners. Social psychological research on language EVALUATION, for instance, suggested that different accents, or other aspects of speech, could be perceived as feminine or masculine (or in some studies as feminine, masculine, undifferentiated or androgynous – see Smith, 1985). More recent models of GENDER as a social phenomenon would see femininity as relatively heterogeneous (i.e. emphasising the existence of different types of femininity – the plural **femininities** is often used for this purpose). There is also a focus on femininity/ femininities as a contextualised PRACTICE rather than a fixed attribute (so that speakers could be seen as 'doing femininity', or a certain type of femininity, by speaking in a certain way).

feminism (and sociolinguistics)   Feminism may be broadly defined as a movement concerned with identifying and seeking to combat the social, cultural, political and economic oppression of women and girls. The aim is not simply to produce gender equality: Deborah Cameron argues that feminism is a movement for the 'full humanity of women' (1992: 4), on the grounds that it has also challenged the (male-oriented) standards against which 'equality' might be judged. Within this broad definition, feminism is characterised by diversity:

the focus of feminist enquiry has changed over time and, at any one time, has been informed by different beliefs, values, approaches and theoretical understandings, so that the plural term **feminisms** is sometimes preferred. Feminism has had diverse and changing relationships to (socio)linguistic research and theory. The terms **feminist linguistics** or **feminist sociolinguistics** may be used for research that takes an explicitly feminist approach; feminism also underpins research on LANGUAGE AND GENDER.

Feminist researchers have been interested in the relationship between GENDER (as a social phenomenon) and language, and in how this relationship is studied. Feminists have critiqued traditional (socio)linguistic theories and research practices, for example the selection and classification of female and male informants in early VARIATIONIST studies, and stereotyped interpretations of gendered language use. Several aspects of language have been studied from a more overtly feminist perspective, for example the linguistic representation of women and men, and sexist imbalances in the structure of a range of languages (see SEXISM); perceptions of, and prescriptions about, female and male language use; and differences/ inequalities in female and male speakers' actual linguistic behaviour. Since the late 1980s/1990s, feminist linguistic research, influenced broadly by intellectual developments such as POSTSTRUCTURALISM and POSTMODERNISM, has focused on the language practices of particular groups of women and men and on the contextualised performance of gender and other aspects of identity, rather than seeing gender as a fixed social category related to language use. Feminism has also engendered a number of linguistic reforms, or LANGUAGE PLANNING initiatives, for example the production of guide-lines to avoid 'sexist language', or to challenge traditional speaking practices in public discussion or debate. These themselves have become an object of study (see Pauwels, 1998). For a discussion of feminism and linguistic theory, see Cameron (1992). See also WOMEN'S LANGUAGE.

Ferguson, Charles A. (1921–98)   As first director of the centre for Applied Linguistics, at Washington D.C. in 1959, and as chairperson of the Social Science Research Council's Committee on SOCIO-LINGUISTICS between 1964 and 1970, Ferguson is acknowledged as one of the founding figures of sociolinguistics. He was the first chairperson of the linguistics programme at Stanford University in 1967. His own contribution to sociolinguistics included seminal studies of DIGLOSSIA, FOREIGNER TALK and language in RELIGION.

Within APPLIED LINGUISTICS he has made significant contributions in the area of LANGUAGE PLANNING.

field

1. In SEMANTICS, refers to the way in which particular words form conceptual groups or fields (see SEMANTIC FIELD).
2. In SYSTEMIC FUNCTIONAL LINGUISTICS, refers to one of the three aspects of REGISTER, the other two being MODE and TENOR. Field, or **field of discourse**, here refers to the subject matter, activity or topic of any particular text. For example, in the following inter-action: *Good morning, Dr Wang's surgery, can I help you?/ Yes, I'd like to make an appointment for my daughter* the field is medical appointment making.

fieldwork   A research activity which involves the systematic collection of linguistic material directly from individual speakers, for example, through PARTICIPANT OBSERVATION, QUESTIONNAIRES, ELICITATION or the recording of INTERVIEWS. Fieldwork can be carried out in distant places as well as in one's own city or country. See also EMPIRICAL LINGUISTICS.

fingerspelling   An important part of SIGN LANGUAGE. Each letter of the alphabet is represented by a specific hand shape. Fingerspelling is mostly used when referring to, for example, people, places, films or book titles. Different manual alphabets exist in different countries, e.g. Auslan (Australian Sign Language) uses a two-handed alphabet, American Sign Language or South African Sign Language both use one-handed alphabets. The term **manual alphabet** is also found.

first language   Used generally to refer to the first language that an individual learns. The shortened formulation L1 (in contrast to L2, L3 etc.) is also used. However, 'first language', or 'L1', may also refer to the language in which an individual is most competent at any one point in her life, and this may be different from first language in a chronological sense. For example, the first language of a young child growing up in the USA in terms of chronology of exposure and learning may be Spanish. However, by the time she becomes an adult, her first language in the sense of competence, the extent to which she uses the language and even her identification with the language, may become English because of the DOMINANT status of English in the USA. The term 'primary language' is also found for the language which a speaker uses most commonly. 'First language' is also found with reference to the language of a community rather than an individual. See also MOTHER TONGUE; SECOND LANGUAGE.

Firth, J. R. (1890–1960)   Firth was Britain's first and – until 1960 – only Chair of Linguistics (at the University of London's School of Oriental and African Studies). His early work was mainly in the area of PHONOLOGY. He is best known for his sociolinguistic work on CONTEXT OF SITUATION, partly based on the ideas of the anthropologist Bronislaw MALINOWSKI. Firth viewed context in a more general and abstract way and was concerned to analyse how a particular 'type' of situation accounts for the specific features of language used. In this he influenced a later generation of scholars including M. A. K. HALLIDAY and Braj KACHRU.

Fishman, Joshua (1926–)   The founder of the SOCIOLOGY OF LANGUAGE, a spirited advocate of BILINGUAL EDUCATION in the USA and a leader in applied linguistic issues pertaining to ENDANGERED LANGUAGES. He has shaped and defined the modern scholarly study of BILINGUALISM and MULTILINGUALISM: standard terms like DOMAIN, LANGUAGE LOYALTY, and LANGUAGE MAINTENANCE and LANGUAGE SHIFT stem from his writings. He also played a central role in the fields of LANGUAGE PLANNING, ETHNICITY and language, and the relation between language, culture, and thought (see SAPIR-WHORF HYPOTHESIS). More recently, he has proposed an incisive analysis leading to a programme to 'reverse language shift' in beleaguered communities. From his first-hand and scholarly experience with Hebrew and Yiddish, Fishman has insisted that 'there is no language for which nothing can be done'. Fishman was born in Philadelphia, and has taught at the University of Pennsylvania, Yeshiva University, Ferkauf Graduate School, and most recently at Stanford University. He is the founding editor of the *International Journal of the Sociology of Language*.

Fishman's extension   See DIGLOSSIA.

flap   A term used in the description and classification of CONSONANTS, relating to their MANNER OF ARTICULATION. Flaps are produced when one articulator touches another briefly. An example is the sound [ɾ], produced by brief contact between the tongue and ALVEOLAR ridge, which may occasionally be heard as a realisation of /r/ in English. The term **tap** may be used interchangeably with flap, though a distinction between these terms is found in the description of some languages. See also INTERNATIONAL PHONETIC ALPHABET; PHONETICS.

floor Often used loosely in the sense of the interactional 'space' occupied by speakers. In a classic account of floor in interactions, Carole Edelsky (1981) defined this more precisely as 'the acknowledged what's-going-on within a psychological time-space'. This definition recognises that not all SPEAKING TURNS constitute part of the floor (a brief question seeking clarification would be an example of a non-floor-holding turn). It also allows researchers to identify different kinds of floor. Edelsky distinguished between two types of floor, related to different patterns of TURN-TAKING: 'singly developed floors', where one speaker holds the floor at a time, and 'collaboratively developed floors', where several speakers hold the floor together. See also CONVERSATION MANAGEMENT.

focusing, diffusion The concepts of 'focusing' and 'diffusion' were introduced by Robert Le Page and Andrée Tabouret-Keller (Le Page and Tabouret-Keller, 1985) in the context of their sociopsychological ACTS OF IDENTITY model of language variation and use. **Focusing** describes a process in which the individual varieties of speakers become more and more similar to one another as individuals gradually adjust their own speech patterns so that they resemble the speech of the larger group. Such linguistic adjustments are motivated by the speakers' desire to be identified with the larger group (a process of identity formation which is called PROJECTION). To describe a language variety as **focused** implies that it is relatively homogeneous, that is, speakers are similar to one another in their linguistic behaviour. A **diffuse** variety, on the other hand, shows much internal variation and processes of diffusion are the outcome of diverging speaker behaviour. STANDARDISATION, i.e. the deliberate development of relatively uniform varieties for supra-regional communication, often interacts with gradual processes of interpersonal ACCOMMODATION and focusing. See also CONVERGENCE; LANGUAGE STANDARD.

folk linguistics Used by some linguists to refer to popular beliefs about language, many of which differ from (professional) linguistic understandings. These might include judgements about the aesthetic qualities of a language or dialect; stereotypes about languages/

dialects; judgements about the borders of a dialect; and **folk etymology**, or beliefs about the origins of certain words. Folk-linguistic perceptions have themselves been the object of sociolinguistic study – for an example see Niedzielski and Preston (2000). See also LANGUAGE IDEOLOGY; STANDARD LANGUAGE IDEOLOGY.

footing   A term derived from the work of Erving GOFFMAN. Footing relates to a person's alignment or stance in relation to others, or to a situation. A change in footing suggests a change in relations with others, or a change in the way events are framed. For Goffman, changes in footing are a routine characteristic of interaction between people, and may be occasioned by or reflected in language use: for instance, a change to 'small talk' after a meeting indicating a more informal relationship. Style shifting (see STYLISTIC VARIATION) or CODE-SWITCHING may be interpreted in terms of a change in footing between participants. See also FRAME.

foreign language   A language that is not generally spoken in a particular territory. As there is no opportunity to learn it by 'natural' interactive means in this case, it has to be learnt consciously via schooling or special classes. Contrasts with SECOND LANGUAGE, which is an additional language available to learners in a particular territory. Hence French is a foreign language in South Africa, where there is no French-speaking community. It would, however, be learnt as a second language by immigrants in France. In a country formerly ruled by France, and still under French cultural influence, like the Ivory Coast, French is also considered a second language. See also ENGLISH AS A FOREIGN LANGUAGE (X AS A FOREIGN LANGUAGE).

foreigner talk   A term coined by Charles FERGUSON (1971) for the special way in which NATIVE speakers of a language speak to those who lack a command of the language. Foreigner talk is thus a special REGISTER, typically involving grammatically simplified forms, including COPULA absence and a lack of suffixes, and a slower tempo of speech with greater use of stress and loudness. Sociolinguists have been interested in the possible influence of such a simplified register and modified INPUT upon the processes of SECOND LANGUAGE acquisition and PIDGINISATION.

forensic linguistics   A branch of APPLIED LINGUISTICS, concerned with the analysis of language to assist in legal processes. Many sociolinguists have had some involvement in forensic linguistics: for instance, variationist sociolinguists may draw on their expertise in the study of particular dialects to establish the geographical area a particular speaker comes from; or discourse analysts may analyse interview data or other forms of evidence to help evaluate the validity of motives attributed to a speaker. Sociolinguists have also contributed to the development of policy and practice in legal contexts (e.g. on the conduct of interviews or cross-examinations with speakers from different linguistic or cultural backgrounds – for an example, see Eades, 1992).

form (vs function)   Many sociolinguistic studies have taken linguistic forms as their starting point, for example looking at speakers' variable use of pronunciation or grammatical features. In order to interpret patterns in the incidence of linguistic forms, however, analysts need to make inferences about their meanings or functions. It is generally recognised that this is not straightforward – i.e. that functions cannot simply be read off from forms – and there is sometimes disagreement between analysts in their interpretations. For instance, many researchers interested in LANGUAGE AND GENDER have disputed a claim, made in some early studies of language variation, that women's greater use of standard or prestige linguistic features is an indication of their linguistic insecurity. Alternative interpretations have also been given of gendered patterns in the use of discourse features such as TAG QUESTIONS or apparent INTERRUPTIONS. Studies in INTER-ACTIONAL SOCIOLINGUISTICS have tended to focus more directly on functions or meanings, for example on speakers' communicative strategies rather than the distribution of specific forms between groups of speakers. Recent studies in particular acknowledge the potential for ambiguity and multiple meanings in such strategies.

form word   See GRAMMATICAL WORD.

formal (-ity)   An important dimension related to variation in both speech and writing. Generally, speakers and writers will adopt different styles depending on the degree of formality associated with a task or situation. Within sociolinguistics, formality is usually thought of as a continuum running from more to less formal. The concept may be applied, rather confusingly, both to the CON-TEXT in which communication takes place and the different styles that result from this. In his now classic study of variation in the speech of New York City, William LABOV (1966) conceptualised STYLISTIC VARIATION in terms of a series of speaking styles that differed in formality. Formal styles were said to involve speakers paying more ATTENTION to their speech and were associated with greater use of PRESTIGE pronunciations (see STYLISTIC CONTINUUM for more detail and critique). Other VARIATIONIST studies have produced similar findings.

formalism   Formalism is an approach to the study of texts which focuses on their FORM and structure and is often contrasted with a FUNCTIONAL approach. The term is also used to refer to a particular linguistic and literary movement, including Russian Formalism, the proponents of which were interested in identifying the formal distinguishing features of different literary genres. **Formalist** scholars included Viktor Shklovsky, Vladimir Propp and Roman Jakobson (for an account of this tradition, see Bennett, 1979). The formalist tradition stands in contrast to other contemporaneous traditions of language and literary study, such as that advocated by the Bakhtin circle (see BAKHTIN; DIALOGIC).

formant   A term used in the acoustic measurement of speech, particularly in relation to the analysis of VOWEL quality. During the articulation of vowels, the vocal cords vibrate allowing pulses of air to pass through. The frequency of vocal cord vibration is termed the 'fundamental frequency' and corresponds roughly to our perception of pitch of voice. In addition, certain overtones or 'harmonics' are produced, which have higher frequencies. These frequencies are modified as the air passes through the vocal tract: certain frequency bands are amplified, depending on the shape of the vocal tract. These amplified frequency bands are known as **formants,** and it is **formant frequencies** that give each vowel its characteristic quality. Typically, vowels are analysed in terms of the first and second formants (sometimes termed F1 and F2) which correspond, respectively, to vowel height and the 'frontness' or 'backness' of a vowel (see Ladefoged, 2001). Sociolinguistic studies of LANGUAGE VARIATION or LANGUAGE CHANGE which draw on acoustic techniques may use formant frequencies to provide an objective measurement of vowel quality (see e.g. Labov, 1994). See also SOCIOPHONETICS.

formulaic language   Refers to set phrases or expressions: for example, idioms, fixed metaphors, or other frequent or conventionalised COLLOCATIONS. Examples in English would include *(letting) the cat out of the bag, to all intents and purposes*, greetings formulae such as *pleased to meet you.* Language may be more or less formulaic – i.e. there isn't a strict cut-off point between 'formulaic' and 'free' expression. Formulaic language is said to facilitate language use (by providing 'ready-made' expressions). Certain formulae may also characterise particular GENRES or CONTEXTS – for example, *once upon a time* to begin a story; or establish a relationship between speakers – for example, the relationship between storyteller and audience. Formulaic language is often associated with RITUAL; see also REPETITION.

fort Creole, plantation Creole   Derek BICKERTON drew a distinction between **fort** and **plantation** CREOLES. The former typically developed in the coastal areas of north-west Africa when slaves were held in forts prior to being shipped overseas, and where there was interethnic communication between Europeans and Africans in mixed households where European men lived with African women. **Plantation Creoles** typically developed out of the experiences of slaves and their children in the New World plantations, away from the predominant influence of the languages of the coastal forts and trading posts of Africa. Bickerton argued that a fort Creole like Guinea Coast Creole English was different from a plantation Creole like Jamaican Creole English – the latter showing more clearly the effects of the BIOPROGRAMME in creolisation.

fossilisation (fossilised)
1. Refers to fixed expressions (i.e. whose form does not change) such as *the more the merrier* – such expressions are said to be **fossilised**. See also FORMULAIC LANGUAGE.
2. In SECOND LANGUAGE ACQUISITION, fossilisation refers to the stabilisation of some features of an INTERLANGUAGE (in terms of pronunciation, grammar and semantics): i.e. when an individual or group retains such interlanguage features rather than equivalent features of the TARGET language.

Foucault, Michel (1926–84)   Michel Foucault is a French philosopher whose writings on DISCOURSE have been highly influential in all areas of the social sciences including sociolinguistics. A fundamental claim by Foucault is that individuals do not exist outside of language or discourse but rather are constituted by it. His work is most obviously used in CRITICAL DISCOURSE ANALYSIS and feminist theories of language – see FEMINISM. See also POSTSTRUCTURALISM; SUBJECTIVITY.

founder (principle, population)   A term from human biology and evolutionary theory (coined by Harrison et al., 1988) and popularised by the creolist Salikoko Mufwene (1996) in connection with the influence of specific TRANSPLANTED dialects or languages on the formation of a new language or language variety. Mufwene was interested in how structural features of CREOLES have been predetermined to a large extent by characteristics of the speech of the populations that founded the colonies in which they developed (the **founder principle**). The influence of this **founder population** is held to outlast the influence of later incoming groups, who accommodate to the founder population, irrespective of the size of the respective populations. This principle has not proved infallible: it is likely that in some cases the dialects or speech characteristics of founder populations will be 'swamped' by incoming groups.

frame (framing)

1. A concept generally attributed to Gregory Bateson (see Bateson's collected essays, 1972) and used within several academic disciplines, including artificial intelligence, linguistics and sociology. It is Erving GOFFMAN's sociological study of frames and **framing** (Goffman, 1974) that is principally drawn on in INTERACTIONAL SOCIOLINGUISTICS. 'Frame' refers to our knowledge, based on previous experience, about the typical organisation of an event or activity. The way a particular activity is framed is said to affect participants' interpretation of that activity, as well as the forms of behaviour, including language behaviour, they might be expected to engage in. For instance, an activity might be framed as making a purchase in a shop, an academic seminar, a conversation with friends or a child's birthday party, with an associated set of expectations about the structure of that activity, types of participant involved, appropriate forms of language use etc. Goffman argues that frames may have successive **laminations**, or layers: for example, an activity may be framed as a joke within a conversation with friends. As a means of establishing expectations about an activity, frame is related to the notions of SCHEMA and SCRIPT, and these terms are sometimes used in a similar way. They may also, however, be distinguished. For instance, Deborah Tannen distinguishes *interactive frames* ('what is going on') from *knowledge schemas* ('expectations about people, objects, events and settings') (see Tannen and Wallat, 1993). See also FOOTING; KEY.

2. In John Sinclair and Malcolm Coulthard's (1975) system of DISCOURSE ANALYSIS, frame is used rather differently to refer to boundary markers such as *right, now, OK* that, in an interaction, indicate the end of one stage and the beginning of the next.

free variation   LANGUAGE VARIATION which is not constrained by linguistic or social factors.

Freire, Paulo (1922–97)   A Brazilian educator and academic whose published works focus on literacy, education, power and poverty. He is particularly well known for his work on CRITICAL LITERACY and CRITICAL PEDAGOGY, which has influenced the development of adult literacy campaigns around the world as well as debates about teaching and learning at school level.

fricative   A term used in the description and classification of CONSONANTS, relating to their MANNER OF ARTICULATION. Fricatives are produced when the air stream is constricted causing friction. Examples include [f], [v], [θ], [ð] (the initial sounds in English *thin* and *then* respectively), [s] and [z]. See also PHONETICS; INTERNATIONAL PHONETIC ALPHABET.

friend of a friend   An approach to FIELDWORK and sampling (see SAMPLE) used by Lesley Milroy (1987a) in her study of Belfast working-class speech. Lesley Milroy entered the community as a friend-of-a-friend; her first contact was a member of the community who knew about the purpose of the research and who provided her with lists of friends and acquaintances. She then contacted these people introducing herself as a 'friend of X'. This helped her quickly to establish relationships of trust within the community. The 'friend of a friend' approach is closely linked to the anthropological fieldwork tradition of PARTICIPANT OBSERVATION and draws on insights from SOCIAL NETWORK analysis.

front (-ed, -ing)
1. Of speech sounds, refers to sounds produced with the front of the tongue and/or at the front of the mouth. In the description and analysis of VOWELS, this is part of a three-way distinction, contrasted with BACK and CENTRAL vowels. Examples of front vowels from English include [i] (the vowel sound in *beat*) and [ɛ] (the vowel sound in *bet*). The terms **fronting** and **fronted** are used when sounds are produced further forward in the mouth

relative to a point of reference such as an earlier pronunciation. In their study of DIALECT LEVELLING in south-eastern British English, Paul Kerswill and Ann Williams found that some of their LINGUISTIC VARIABLES showed evidence of fronting: for example, the back vowel /uː/ (the vowel sound in *shoe*) was fronted to give a pronunciation closer to the vowel in French *tu* (Kerswill and Williams, 2000). See also PHONETICS; INTERNATIONAL PHONETIC ALPHABET.

2. Fronting is also a general term in syntax for a process that places certain elements of a sentence in initial position to give them greater prominence. For example, the following response to the question *Do you like cats?* involves fronting of the object (and special intonation): *Cats, I love.* IT-CLEFTING (*It's cats that I love*) also involves fronting (see Harris (1993) for a discussion of this feature in Irish English).

fudged lect, dialect   See BORDER DIALECT.

function word   See GRAMMATICAL WORD.

functional   An approach to the analysis of language that takes account of the meanings or **functions** of utterances rather than (simply) their formal characteristics. See FORM (VS FUNCTION). On **functional grammar,** see SYSTEMIC FUNCTIONAL LINGUISTICS.

functional literacy   A term that has been in widespread use particularly in the contexts of adult literacy and of national and international educational programmes (for example under the auspices of UNESCO, United Nations Educational, Scientific and Cultural Organisation). It is used to refer to, and often measure, individuals' capacity to carry out what are thought to be basic or everyday reading and writing activities. Tests have been devised to measure functional literacy levels which are seen as an indicator of a nation's level of development. However there is considerable debate about what constitutes basic or functional literacy (see the examples in Street, 2001). See LITERACY.

functionalism   A major approach in sociology, associated with the American scholar Talcott Parsons, that studies society as a system of interlocking parts, which contribute to the maintenance of the overall whole. Taking a society as an abstract aggregate, joined by consensus among its members over certain values, functionalism studies the composition and function of subsystems like the family, law, education, etc. It is also concerned with how such units are maintained or modified over time and how individuals are socialised within their society. Early sociolinguistic research of LABOV, FISHMAN and others largely followed the premises of functionalism, but just as sociology became influenced by views stressing conflict of interests rather than consensus among societal groups, the influence of functionalism in current sociolinguistics has dissipated. See also MARXISM.

G

Gastarbeiterdeutsch ('guest workers' German') A variety of German spoken by first-generation migrants from Turkey, Italy, Greece and Yugoslavia. Some have described *Gastarbeiterdeutsch* as a PIDGIN variety (e.g. Clyne, 1968), while others (e.g. Klein and Dittmar, 1979) have argued that it should be seen as an unstable INTERLANGUAGE since learners' proficiency has been found to be dependent on factors such as length of stay and degree of interaction with the German community.

gate-keeping The practice of restricting access to powerful social and cultural resources. A range of language practices (e.g. interviews by which people gain access to education, training etc.; the compilation of DICTIONARIES and other reference works based on prestige norms; the use of high-status languages or language varieties in contexts such as education and professional employment) have been said to have a gate-keeping function. See also ELITE CLOSURE in this respect.

gay language See LESBIAN AND GAY LANGUAGE.

gender
1. Gender as a linguistic category: 'gender' refers to a means of classifying nouns into certain groups, or classes. This occurs in several languages, including many Indo-European languages, the Dravidian languages of south India, the Bantu languages spoken in southern Africa, many Australian languages. Gender in this grammatical sense may affect the form of words and indicates relationships between words. For example, in German, nouns may be feminine, masculine or neuter. *Sun* is a feminine noun,

and in the phrases *die helle Sonne . . . sie scheint* ('the bright sun
. . . it shines') the article *die*, the adjective *helle* and the pronoun
sie take a feminine form to agree with the noun. Masculine/
feminine, or masculine/feminine/neuter classifications are common across languages, but gender classifications also include
animate/inanimate or human/non-human. Bantu languages have
between ten and twenty classes. In some languages, nouns are
assigned to genders on semantic criteria (e.g. a male human being
would be masculine, a female feminine, an inanimate object
neuter). Many languages are like German, however, and assign
words to a gender largely on the basis of their formal characteristics. These languages may still have a semantic 'core'. For
example in German when nouns refer to people there is a high
level of correspondence between grammatical gender and the sex
of the person referred to: *der Mann*, 'man', is masculine and
die Frau, 'woman', is feminine (there are also exceptions: *das
Mädchen*, 'girl', is neuter).

Languages that make distinctions based on gender are sometimes termed **gender languages**. The term **grammatical
gender** may be used with reference to any gender system, but
is sometimes restricted to languages like German where nouns
are assigned to gender primarily on formal criteria. In this case, a
contrast may be made with **natural gender** – i.e. a semantically
based system, or one where classifications such as 'feminine',
'masculine' and 'neuter' correspond to real-world distinctions.
Modern English is often referred to as a language that has natural
gender: for instance, *sun*, as a word referring to an inanimate
object, would be thought of as neuter and replaced by the pronoun
it. With rare exceptions (such as *ship*), the categories feminine and
masculine are restricted to words referring to female and male
people or animals.

In the case of words for people, gender categorisation is rarely a
neutral process, and this has been of interest within LANGUAGE AND
GENDER research. For instance, masculine words may be used as
GENERIC MASCULINE forms, referring to people in general; and
feminine words often acquire negative connotations. Grammatical
gender is also one way in which languages may reflect, and,
arguably, facilitate the construction of social differences and
inequalities. For a general account of gender as a linguistic
category, see Corbett (1991); for a discussion in terms of 'language
and gender' research, see Hellinger and Bussman (2001, 2002,
2003). See also SEXISM.

2. Gender as a social phenomenon: 'gender' as a social grouping, or an aspect of social IDENTITY, has been of considerable interest in sociolinguistics and related areas (e.g. linguistic anthropology, social psychology). The term SEX is found in earlier (1960s, 1970s) studies, but gender has been preferred since around the 1980s, reflecting a common distinction made in the social sciences between 'sex' as a biological attribute and 'gender' as social attribute. Sex/gender has been a SOCIAL VARIABLE in several VARIATIONIST studies of LANGUAGE VARIATION and LANGUAGE CHANGE; it has also been of interest in studies in INTERACTIONAL SOCIOLINGUISTICS, which have identified 'feminine' and 'masculine' conversational styles: LANGUAGE AND GENDER is now a substantial interdisciplinary research area. A focus of earlier sociolinguistic research was on the establishment of gender differences in language use: for instance, variationist studies found that women used more prestige and men more vernacular linguistic features. Many studies also focused on gender and POWER – for example, male DOMINANCE of mixed-gender interactions. Such approaches take gender as a pre-existing social category and examine how it relates to language use. More recent approaches (since the late 1980s and 1990s) have seen identity (including gender) as more differentiated, context dependent and ambiguous (i.e. different aspects of identity may be foregrounded in different contexts and there may be a certain ambiguity in the representation of identities); such approaches have also seen gender as something that is performed in interactions – i.e. as an interactional outcome rather than a pre-existing social category that affects interactions (see FEMININITY; MASCULINITY; PERFORMATIVITY). For overviews of the relationship between language and gender, see Eckert and McConnell-Ginet (2003); Talbot (1998); Romaine (1998). On contemporary approaches to identity, see POSTMODERNISM; POST-STRUCTURALISM; SOCIAL CONSTRUCTIONISM; SUBJECTIVITY; see also WOMEN'S LANGUAGE.

genderlect   A constellation of linguistic features associated either with female or male speakers. See LANGUAGE AND GENDER; LECT.

General American   Term used by some linguists for US speech that is not perceived as having strong localised features, especially not having features associated with the southern states and the northeast. In the older dialect models of the 1940s, the three dialects of US

English were held to be 'Eastern' (i.e. the Northeastern sea-board), 'Southern' and 'General American'. Subsequent work casts this model into doubt, with General American being divided into 'Inland Northern' and 'Midland' dialects. However, the notion of 'General American' persists, especially for the UNMARKED variety used by broadcasters who drop the more local features of their own speech. General American is therefore a descriptive term for a set of regional dialects, the more prestigious forms of which tend to be accepted as a 'network' or 'broadcasting' standard. See also RECEIVED PRONUNCIATION.

generic masculine A masculine form used to refer to people in general (i.e. including both females and males). Hellinger and Bussmann (2001) cite the use of grammatically masculine forms such as *ministre* (French, 'minister'), *vrač* (Russian, 'physician') and *muḥami* (Arabic, 'lawyer') to refer to males, people whose gender is unknown or not considered relevant, or even females. Examples from English would include the generic use of *man*, or of the pronouns *he*, *his* etc. (as in *Everyone should tidy his own room*). Some analysts restrict the use of 'generic masculine' to languages such as French, Russian or Arabic, which have grammatical GENDER, preferring the term **male generic** in the case of languages without grammatical gender, such as English. Generic masculine/male generic forms have been the subject of feminist intervention. In many languages alternative forms are found in contemporary usage, for example in the case of English pronouns *he or she*, *s/he*, generic *she*, or singular *they* may be used. New 'gender-neutral' pronoun forms (such as *e*, *tey*) have been suggested, but these have not been successful. See also LANGUAGE AND GENDER; SEXISM (IN LANGUAGE).

genre (analysis) Genre is a term in widespread use to indicate an approach to communication which emphasises social function and purpose. Significant debate surrounds the definition of genre, particularly the extent to which it refers to TEXTS or the activities in which texts are embedded. It is often vaguely defined but several uses of the term can be identified which are illustrated in different types of **genre analysis**. It may refer to:
1. Different types of literary texts, such as poetry, novels, plays. Genre analysis here often involves a focus on the stylistic features of different 'subgenres', for example the subgenres of poetry include lyric, epic, ballad, sonnet (see STYLISTICS).

2. Clusters of different types of spoken and written TEXTS grouped according to their function, formal characteristics and/or rhetorical purposes such as jokes, greetings, school essays, advertisements (see discussion in Swales 1990, see also SPEAKING). Genre here is often used in the sense of TEXT TYPE and the term **text genre** is occasionally found. Genres or text types can be analysed in a number of ways. These include analyses which focus on rhetorical purposes alongside a formal or schematic approach. In the field of English for Specific Purposes (ESP), for example, the rhetorical purposes of different parts of a text have been analysed in terms of stages or moves (Swales, 1990; see also, CARS).

3. Language and communication seen as a social activity or PRACTICE. Genre analysis in this sense involves focusing on language as one of many activities or practices which take place in a particular CONTEXT (see Miller, 1984; see also ACTIVITY THEORY; COMMUNITY OF PRACTICE).

4. In SYSTEMIC FUNCTIONAL LINGUISTICS the notion of genre is similar to that outlined in (3). It is one of the three levels of analysis of communication (the other two being REGISTER and language or clause level; see LEXICOGRAMMAR). An example of a genre is the activity of a group of school pupils writing an account of a visit to a museum; this in turn can be analysed in terms of three typical functions: an 'orientation' (stating where they went); a 'record of events' (listing what they did and saw); and a 'personal evaluation' (statement of enjoyment). (For this sense, see Martin, 2001.)

5. Genre is also a key notion in the work of BAKHTIN, who distinguishes between **primary** and **secondary genres**. The former are everyday communication activities, such as greetings, buying bread or writing short notes; the latter are more explicitly contrived, such as literary works, political speeches. These categories have been used in NEW LITERACY STUDIES.

6. In recent work on MULTIMODALITY, genre is used as a way of exploring the nature of multimodal texts where the term **mixed genres** seems to more accurately indicate the functions of the different modes in any text (see Kress, 2003). Genre analysis here involves developing tools which can deal with the range of modes in a text (see e.g. VECTORS).

geographical linguistics   See LINGUISTIC GEOGRAPHY.

geographical variation   Variation in language across geographical areas; see REGIONAL VARIATION.

geolinguistics   See LINGUISTIC GEOGRAPHY.

given, new   Contrasting terms used in some linguistic approaches to distinguish between the types of information in texts, usually at CLAUSE level and often on the basis of intonation patterns (as identified in speech, or as inferred from written texts). They are key terms in SYSTEMIC FUNCTIONAL LINGUISTICS. **Given** refers to information which a speaker/listener or reader/writer are presumed to share; **new** refers to information which the speaker or writer is introducing to the listener/reader in the message. For example, if a mechanic says to a customer: *The car is ready*, then *the car* is given, as they both know what car they are talking about, and *is ready* is new because this is new information the mechanic is providing. In English, given information is usually at the beginning of a clause, and new information at the end.

global language   Refers to languages of the world which are spoken by large numbers of people and/or across a number of national contexts. Sometimes used synonymously with INTERNATIONAL LANGUAGE. For example, Spanish is sometimes referred to as a global language because it is spoken by some 400 million people and is the official language of twenty-one countries. Increasingly, however, 'global language' is used in the context of English to refer to its widespread use. English has official status in some 45 countries as well as being widely used in many other contexts. There are now more speakers using ENGLISH AS A SECOND LANGUAGE or ENGLISH AS A FOREIGN LANGUAGE in the world than there are speakers using ENGLISH AS A NATIVE LANGUAGE (see Crystal, 1997; Graddol, 1997). See also GLOBALISATION; WORLD ENGLISH(ES).

globalisation   Refers to a phenomenon which emphasises inter-connectedness across the globe and which encompasses a number of significant economic, technological and cultural aspects. Whilst the term is often used in vague or ambiguous ways, there are several key dimensions to globalisation which have been explored within sociolinguistics. (a) *Economic* – this refers to the way in which processes of production and consumption, and the consequent flows of capital, operate increasingly on a global, rather than 'local' or national levels: large corporations may employ labour in a number of national contexts and target consumers around the world. An example of a sociolinguistic study focusing on these practices is Deborah Cameron's (2000) study of 'call centres'. (b) *Technological* – rapid changes in information technology have profoundly affected the ways in which people communicate across the globe, not least in terms of speed. Rapid communication is possible via the internet, fax, mobile phones and this in turn influences how people experience space within the world: notably, the world feels smaller. (c) *Cultural* – cultural practices no longer remain tied to one particular location but are rather dispersed across the world, predominantly through the possibilities afforded by information technology (for discussions, see Giddens, 1990; Castells, 2000). One obvious area in sociolinguistics which has focused on local/global relations is that of NEW ENGLISHES or WORLD ENGLISHES.

A key concern about different aspects of globalisation is homogenisation resulting from the HEGEMONY of the Western world. Cultural and economic models are imported from the more powerful countries, notably the USA, to the rest of the world, and these disrupt local practices and values. However, whilst much emphasis is placed on the negative consequences of globalisation, positive outcomes are also noted: for example, the opportunities provided by information technology for collaborative and collective communication across geographical locations centring on mutual support or political campaigning. It is also argued that globalisation is contributing to **localisation** – the maintenance and development of local cultural practices and identity – as a reaction against powerful centralising and homogenising forces.

glottal   A term used in the description and classification of sounds, indicating their PLACE OF ARTICULATION (the glottis is the opening between the vocal cords in the larynx). A much commented-on feature of British English is the increasing use of the **glottal stop** [ʔ] as a realisation of /t/ between vowels (e.g. *butter*); before /l/ (e.g. *little*) and at the end of words (e.g. *but*). This is sometimes termed **t-glottalling**. Other consonants may also be realised as glottal stops: in London speech this may occur for the PLOSIVES /p/, /k/, /d/ at the end of words, and also sometimes for FRICATIVES /f/, /v/, /θ/ and /ð/ (e.g. Wells, 1982a, 1982b). The glottal stop is a highly salient, and stigmatised pronunciation feature in British English. While associated particularly with the speech of London and south-east England it is now widespread and is increasingly found in high-status speakers and in the prestige accent RECEIVED PRONUNCIATION (RP).

Other forms of **glottalisation** include 'preglottalisation' or 'glottal reinforcement', when certain sounds are preceded by a glottal stop. This may occur in different linguistic environments in different varieties of English. Milroy, et al. (1994) discuss aspects of glottalisation in British English, relating their use to gender and social class.

Goffman, Erving (1922–82) A pioneer in the study of face-to-face interaction through naturalistic observation. Whereas other scholars stressed the self as a 'being' constantly interpreting events, Goffman characterised the self as constantly being made/remade by an audience. Goffman's 'dramaturgical' model includes concepts such as 'backstage', 'frontstage' and 'role'. Associated concepts in the field that are synonymous with Goffman are FACE, 'impression management', 'encounter', 'remedial work', etc. In later work Goffman concentrated on FRAMES, speakers' knowledge and expectations about the typical organisation of an activity or event based on previous experience. A related term coined by him, FOOTING, denotes the speaker's stance in relation to what he or she says. Goffman has exerted a profound influence on the related fields of ETHNOMETHO-DOLOGY, CONVERSATION ANALYSIS and INTERACTIONAL SOCIOLINGUISTICS. His insistence on the study of speech in natural encounters has also influenced variationist sociolinguists like William LABOV.

gradual shift See LANGUAGE SHIFT.

gradualism A theory of creolisation that holds that CREOLES evolve gradually over time from simple to more complex forms of communication as circumstances require. **Gradualists** like Ellen Woolford, Philip Baker, Jacques Arends and John Singler also hold that some Creoles may have evolved without a preceding PIDGIN phase. With their careful attention to sociohistorical details gradualists have offered the greatest challenge to the BIOPROGRAMME theory of Derek BICKERTON, which once dominated the field of Creole linguistics. See also CREOLE CONTINUUM.

grammar Grammar refers both to the structure of language, and to attempts to describe that structure. It is also found with more specific meanings in different areas of linguistics. Grammar may refer to the structural properties of human language in general (sometimes termed **theoretical grammar**); or attempt to describe the structure of a specific language (termed **descriptive grammar**); it may refer broadly to several aspects of language structure, including

PHONOLOGY, SEMANTICS, SYNTAX and MORPHOLOGY; or, more narrowly, to syntax and morphology. Within these different categories, there are several different approaches to grammatical description and analysis. Sociolinguistic studies of **grammatical variation** tend to focus on syntax and morphology and to draw on categories from descriptive grammars of particular languages. For instance, studies may investigate the variable use of certain verb forms or sentence structures. Critical studies (e.g. in CRITICAL DISCOURSE ANALYSIS) are often informed by insights from HALLIDAY's SYSTEMIC FUNCTIONAL LINGUISTICS.

Contemporary published grammars of particular languages have an overtly descriptive function but they are also likely to become PRESCRIPTIVE (i.e. prescribing norms of acceptability). Grammars are a form of CODIFICATION and thus play an important part in language STANDARDISATION.

grammatical (-ity) 'Grammatical' is the adjective from GRAMMAR in phrases such as 'grammatical variation'. It is also used to refer to structures that are regarded as possible within the grammar of a particular language. In this sense one may speak about the **grammaticality** of a structure: whether it is possible within a language. Sentences that are not regarded as possible are termed **ungrammatical** and are conventionally indicated by an asterisk. It is the task of a grammar (as constructed by linguists) to account for all grammatical structures. In this sense, 'grammatical' and 'un-grammatical' are not evaluative terms – i.e. they are not intended to refer respectively to 'good' and 'bad' uses of language; contrast CORRECTNESS.

grammatical gender　See GENDER (1).

grammatical intricacy　See LEXICAL DENSITY.

grammatical word　Sometimes applied to words such as articles (*a*, *the* in English), conjunctions (*and*, *but*), some prepositions (*in*, *on*) and adverbs (*often*) that have a primarily grammatical function, linking other words together. Such word may also be said to carry **grammatical meaning**. The term **grammatical items** may be used to include words and grammatical MORPHEMES such as inflections (eg. the plural -*s* on nouns in English). Grammatical words may be contrasted with LEXICAL WORDS (e.g. nouns, adjectives). Other terms (e.g. **form word** or **function word** vs content word) are also found for this distinction.

grammaticalisation
1. Introduced by the French linguist Antoine Meillet (1912) to describe a type of LANGUAGE CHANGE by which a full LEXICAL WORD gradually acquires grammatical functions. Such a word typically loses its phonetic substance and semantic complexity. An often-cited example from the history of English is the use of purposive 'be going to' as an independent future marker (*I am going to go to Hawai'i next week/ I will go to Hawai'i next week*), and its phonologically reduced form *gonna* (Hopper and Traugott, 1993).
2. Also refers to the process whereby certain concepts are encoded in the GRAMMAR of a language. In many languages relations between speakers are **grammaticalised** (reflected, for instance, in T AND V PRONOUNS or different language LEVELS).

gravity model   A model of LANGUAGE CHANGE and DIFFUSION proposed by Peter Trudgill (1974a; following the geographer Torsten Hager-strand) to describe the likelihood that patterns of language use which emerged in one urban centre will influence the speech of another urban centre. According to Trudgill, linguistic influence across geographical regions is a function of the distance between places as well as their relative population size. The model is based on the idea that places with larger populations show more interaction with each other than with smaller places, but this interaction decreases with distance. A change will spread from the largest to the next largest city with influence diminishing the greater the distance between them. Unlike the WAVE MODEL, which focuses on the spread of a change across a geographical area, the gravity model describes the pattern or direction in which changes move from one city to another city.

Great Vowel Shift (GVS)   A series of SOUND CHANGES, termed a CHAIN SHIFT, that took place in the English VOWEL system between around 1400 and 1600, during which LONG, HIGH vowels became diphthongs, and other long vowels moved one step upwards. Thus in the FRONT vowels, schematically we may say that [aː] took the place of [ɛː], which took the place of [eː], which took the place of [iː], which became the diphthong [aɪ]. A similar shift applied to the BACK vowels [ɔː], [ʊː] and [uː]. Many spellings give an indication of the 'pre-shift' pronunciations of words. Thus the [iː] in *geese* is spelt with 'ee', which reflects the earlier pronunciation [eː]. A reflection of the GVS can also be seen in pairs of words like *crime* – *criminal*; *please* – *pleasant*. The underlined vowel in the first word of each pair has undergone shift, while the equivalent vowel in the second word of each pair retains a pre-shift pronunciation except that they are shortened (and therefore escaped the effects of the shift). The GVS began in the south of England and spread northwards; hence it did not affect the north-ernmost dialects of English as much, and residual forms like [hu:s] for *house* (often spelt *hoose*) occur in Scots whereas southern dialects show the diphthong [au]. See also NORTHERN CITIES SHIFT; SOUTHERN SHIFT; SOUTHERN HEMISPHERE SHIFT.

Grice's maxims   See CONVERSATIONAL MAXIMS.

group
1. Social: see SOCIAL GROUP.
2. As a grammatical term: used in some grammatical approaches, such as SYSTEMIC FUNCTIONAL LINGUISTICS, to refer to a unit of language which is bigger than a word and smaller than a CLAUSE. In the clause: *The girl was playing the piano in the kitchen*, *The girl* is a **nominal group**, *was playing* a **verbal group** and *in the kitchen* an **adverbial group**. Groups are generally equivalent to **phrases** in other grammatical approaches.

Gumperz, John J. (1922–)   Considered one of the central figures in the birth and growth of sociolinguistics, Gumperz has contributed seminal papers and texts in the fields of ethnography of commu-nication (see ETHNOGRAPHY), INTERETHNIC COMMUNICATION, CODE-SWITCHING and, above all, the subfield he founded, INTERACTIONAL SO-CIOLINGUISTICS. His early fieldwork, based in India and Norway, drew him to studying how social groups retain their identities in complex societies. His subsequent interactional work in institutional settings drew on a wide variety of analytic tools from PRAGMATICS and CONVERSATION ANALYSIS, and ETHNICITY and network studies (see SO-CIAL NETWORK), enabling him to link the macro-sociological to the micro-conversational. An important concept here is CONTEXTUALISA-TION, as set out in his book *Discourse Stategies* (Gumperz, 1982).

Gumperz grew up in Germany and emigrated as a teenager with his family to the USA. He gained his Ph.D. at the University of Michigan (Ann Arbor) and was professor at Berkeley, where he is now Professor Emeritus.

Guttman scalogram analysis   See IMPLICATIONAL SCALE.

H

h-dropping Popularly conceived of as the lack ('dropping') of the phonetic realisation of word-initial /h/ where it is pronounced in standard English (often represented as an apostrophe as in *'appy, 'opeful*). Phoneticians also point to a concomitant change in the initial vowel (which is produced with a discernible rise in pitch). H-dropping is widespread in urban non-standard varieties of English in England and Wales. It is typically evaluated as 'un-educated' and 'vulgar'. Upwardly-mobile speakers tend to avoid it but also show HYPERCORRECTION (i.e. overapplication of /h/ to words where it is not present in standard English). H-dropping is not generally found in the north of England, the USA, Canada, Australia, New Zealand and South Africa (see Milroy, 1992: 137–45).

'H' variety, 'L' variety The terms 'H' and 'L' were used by Charles FERGUSON (1959) for two forms of the same language used in non-overlapping contexts. His example was of Arabic in Cairo, which had two forms: a classical (or **H**) variety reserved for DOMAINS associated with public and prestigious functions (like the law, education, government, the media) and a colloquial (or **L**) variety used in informal domains, like the home, street and shopping centre. While 'H' and 'L' stand for 'high' and 'low' respectively, sociolinguists prefer the abbreviated forms so as to avoid the everyday connotations of 'high' and 'low'. The distinction between H and L forms of the same language has been generalised to describe a similar relationship shared by two languages that are not necessarily related. Thus in Paraguay Spanish plays the role of H language, while Guarani fulfils L functions (see Fishman, 1967). See also DIGLOSSIA; LANGUAGE CHOICE.

habitus Term used by the sociologist Pierre BOURDIEU to refer to the way in which CULTURE is enacted at the level of the individual (1977). Habitus is the embodied culture, that is the set of dispositions or habits that are learned throughout childhood and beyond and lead people to act and react in certain ways. These dispositions are socially structured, with different dispositions being acquired by different social groups. Language and communication are viewed as key aspects of these dispositions. See also CULTURAL CAPITAL; SYMBOLIC POWER.

Halliday, M. A. K. (1925–)   Michael Halliday is an English linguist who is most famous for his foundational contribution to the theory of SYSTEMIC FUNCTIONAL LINGUISTICS. A basic premise of this theory is that language is *functional*, that is, it is a resource for meaning-making that has evolved, and continues to evolve, to meet human needs. A key aim has been to develop ways of describing language as a system from this functional perspective. Halliday has applied this approach primarily to the field of education but his work has been used by researchers with many different interests who study language in CONTEXT. See also COHESION; CRITICAL DISCOURSE ANALYSIS; CRITICAL LINGUISTICS; GENRE; REGISTER; TRANSITIVITY.

Heath, Shirley Brice   An educational linguist who has worked in the interdisciplinary areas of educational anthropology, ethnography of speaking (see ETHNOGRAPHY) and SOCIOLINGUISTICS. She is best known for her classic work *Ways with Words* (Heath, 1983), which is probably the most widely-cited work dealing with children's language use in and out of school. The work details the home and school language practices of three communities in a south-eastern area of the USA – poor white, poor black, and middle-class white and black – as they sent their children to the then newly-integrated public schools. Literacy and literacy development, language planning, multilingualism, multidialectism and multiculturalism feature in Heath's other work. Heath has taught at Winthrop College, South Carolina, University of Pennsylviania Graduate School of Education and Stanford University, where she is currently Professor of English and Linguistics and has links with Anthropology and Education.

hedge   A hedge, or **hedging**, involves the use of words or phrases that express some degree of qualification or uncertainty, for example *some degree of* (!), *sort of*, *kind of*, *perhaps*. Hedges may be analysed in terms of MODALITY (they have to do with EPISTEMIC MODALITY – the extent to which a speaker expresses confidence in the truth of what they are saying). Hedges have been associated with certain groups of speakers (e.g. women, relatively powerless speakers) but, like many similar conversational features, their use and their specific meanings are likely to be highly context-dependent.

hegemonic masculinity   A culturally-dominant form of MASCULINITY that ensures the subordination of women but also of certain groups of men (e.g. gay men in contemporary Western contexts). The notion of hegemonic masculinity emphasises the interplay between different masculinities as well as between masculinities and FEMININITIES. It is consistent with a model of masculinity as a set of contextualised PRACTICES, rather than a fixed attribute: a hegemonic masculinity occupies the dominant position in a given set of gender relations, but this position may be contested. Hegemonic masculinity may be supported or contested linguistically as well as by other means, and the concept has therefore been drawn on in studies of LANGUAGE AND GENDER (see e.g. Johnson and Meinhof (1997) on language and masculinity; on hegemonic masculinity more generally see Connell (1995)). See also HEGEMONY.

hegemony (hegemonic)   Concept developed by Antonio Gramsci (1971) to describe and account for the way in which power relations are enacted in society, in particular how one social class dominates another. Such domination can be maintained through coercion, such as physical force through the use of armies. However, Gramsci argues that in capitalist societies domination is achieved through hegemonic power, that is alliances between social institutions such as the church and the family, who secure consent through ideological means (see IDEOLOGY). Hegemonic power is dynamic, involving alliances between different social groups, including both the more and the less powerful. It is because of this dynamic set of relations that hegemony is never complete: alliances shift between and across social groups thus allowing for the possibility of challenge and change.

   Hegemony is a key concept in studies focusing on language and power such as CRITICAL DISCOURSE ANALYSIS. See also the notion of HEGEMONIC MASCULINITY.

heritage language   The ancestral or background language(s) of groups whose members have shifted or are in the process of shifting to the MAJORITY LANGUAGE. The term 'heritage language' thus includes indigenous languages (e.g. Australian Aboriginal languages), colonial languages (German in Namibia) and migrant languages (Russian or Polish in the USA). Some heritage languages are no longer spoken within the speech community while others are still spoken, but no longer (or only partially) acquired by the younger generation (e.g. Italian in Australia or the USA). **Heritage language education** is a rapidly developing area. It focuses on the development of appropriate language teaching materials for especially younger speakers of heritage languages who typically have at least passive knowledge of the language (and culture) they are studying.

heterogeneity of production   A defining aspect of the SPEECH COMMUNITY in LABOVian sociolinguistics. A speech community is homogeneous in terms of speakers' EVALUATION of and ATTITUDES to linguistic variants (**homogeneity of interpretation**): i.e. irrespective of their social background, speakers agree which linguistic forms or varieties are most prestigious and should thus be used in formal, high-status domains. However, speech community members are differentiated socially by their use of linguistic forms (**heterogeneity of production**). Thus in the case of POST-VOCALIC /r/ in New York (the pronunciation of /r/ in words like *car*), all speakers evaluated this feature as prestigious but only the highest social groups made frequent use of post-vocalic /r/ in their speech.

heteroglossia   Term used by BAKHTIN ([1935] 1981) to refer to the fact that language is not one unified thing but is rather constituted by many social languages, for example the language used by professionals, younger people, older people, and the language used in different historical epochs and contexts. Heteroglossia is also used to signal the struggles between different social languages or GENRES, VOICES, worldviews or DISCOURSES in any instance of language use. This struggle between worldviews is described by Bakhtin in terms of a relationship between **centripetal** (centralising or unifying) forces and **centrifugal** (diversifying) forces. The former can be exemplified as official languages, discourses or socially powerful genres and the latter as unofficial languages, discourses or genres with lower social status. Some sociolinguists use heteroglossia to emphasise the fact of the co-existence of diverse social languages; others use the term to emphasise the tensions and struggles between such languages. See also POLYPHONY.

heteronormativity   The process by which HETEROSEXUALITY is established as an unquestioned norm, with other sexualities regarded as deviant, or at least a departure from the norm. Heteronormativity is associated with GENDER as well as SEXUALITY, in that heterosexuality is seen as a feature of 'appropriate' forms of MASCULINITY and FEMININITY. Heteronormativity may act as a constraint on language use but may also be reproduced and subverted through language and discourse: see discussion of language, heterosexuality and hetero-normativity in Cameron and Kulick (2003b).

heteronym(y)
1. In SEMANTICS, **heteronyms** are words that have the same form in either speech or writing but different forms in the other mode, and different meanings. Examples are *tear* (verb) and *tear* (noun) (same spelling, different sound and meaning); and *bough* and *bow* (verb) (same sound, different spelling and meaning). The relationship between such words is termed **heteronymy**.
2. Manfred Görlach uses the term for different names for identical referents as used in different dialects. Heteronymy in this sense has been studied particularly in relation to the spread of international languages like English to colonies that did not have a great deal of contact with each other. Well-known international English heteronyms are US *gas* versus UK *petrol*. In some instances the more recent prestige of US English has resulted in the replacement of British-English forms in some territories. Thus *motorway* (the British term) has been replaced by *freeway* or *expressway* in Australia, and *freeway* in South Africa. New Zealand retains the British form *motorway*. Sometimes heteronyms co-occur in the same dialect because of competing British and US norms: thus South Africa has both *truck* (originally US) and *lorry* (originally UK) and likewise both *trunk* and *boot* (of a car).

heterosexuality   Studies of SEXUALITY and language have often focused on marginalised sexualities (e.g. LESBIAN, GAY, BISEXUAL, TRANSGEN-DERED AND QUEER (LGBTQ) sexualities) with more limited scrutiny given to heterosexuality. Heterosexuality has also been taken as an unacknowledged norm, a position critiqued within, for instance, lesbian feminism. Some studies have, however, begun to focus explicitly on heterosexuality or, more accurately, particular hetero-sexualities and how these are constructed; see e.g. studies by Cameron (1997), Kiesling (2002) and discussion/examples in Cameron and Kulick (2003b).

high (variety)   See 'H' VARIETY, 'L' VARIETY.

high (vowel)   Part of a three-way classification of VOWELs depending on the height of the tongue during their articulation. High vowels contrast with MID and LOW vowels. See CLOSE.

high involvement (conversational style)   See INVOLVEMENT.

high modality   See MODALITY.

high rising tone (HRT)   A feature that has been observed in some dialects of English: the use of a rising INTONATION in declarative statements, which in most dialects would show a falling intonation; also called **Australian Questioning Intonation (AQI)**, or 'uptalk'. HRT is of interest to the study of language change because of its increasing use: it is particularly common among adolescents. The phenomenon was first described for Australia by Mitchell and Delbridge (1965). It has also been reported for the USA, Canada, New Zealand and more recently Britain. It has been suggested that HRT has an interactive function, i.e. the speaker is checking on his or her interlocutor's understanding (see Guy et al. 1986). See also PROSODY.

historic present   The use of the present TENSE to recount a past event. This often occurs in conversational narratives to dramatise an event. Wolfson (1982: 73) provides an example of an excerpt from a narrative about a break-in, told by a member of a community action group on crime. The narrator begins in the past tense: 'A woman came to us and aah—after I gave her this scare tactic, you know she went out and had a lock put on her door. She lived in an apartment.' He then switches to the present for stylistic effect: 'And when she came home that night, she goes to insert the key and the door goes open. Well, she's petrified now because she knows that this particular lock requires a key to open the door. So she calls the police . . .' This conversational use of the historic present is sometimes termed **conversational historic present (CHP)**. CHP provides an example of **narrative tense**, the use of tense for narration, rather than time sequencing. The historic present is also found in other contexts (e.g. news reporting).

historical linguistics   The study of the history of language and languages, and how languages have changed over time. The term DIACHRONIC linguistics is also found. A central part of the discipline involves the comparison of languages with a view to ascertaining which ones are related, and to reconstructing earlier stages of related languages, for example Indo-European as the common ancestor of languages such as Latin, Greek, Sanskrit, Anglo-Saxon etc. Historical linguistics has also been interested in the development of individual languages (e.g. the development of English from Old English to contemporary varieties) and in identifying general principles of LANGUAGE CHANGE. Research has focused both on the **internal history** of languages (e.g. changes to pronunciation, grammar and vocabulary) and the **external history** (e.g. the changing status of a language, where and by whom it was spoken at different points in time). Accounts of language change may also draw on internal and external evidence, or suggest internal or external factors that may bring about change. For instance, the loss of Old English inflections has been attributed to changing stress patterns so that the inflections became more weakly stressed and, eventually, less distinctive (an internal factor); and to contact with Scandinavian languages, spoken by the Vikings who settled in northern areas, where inflectional loss began (an explanation that includes external factors). A **social history of language** would take into account social and contextual factors that were bound up with language change (e.g. Burke and Porter, 1995; Leith, 1997). Historical linguistics has been influenced by the contemporary sociolinguistic study of language change, most notably the work of William LABOV; see also SOCIO-HISTORICAL LINGUISTICS.

history (of language)   See HISTORICAL LINGUISTICS.

holophrasis (holophrastic)   A sentence or utterance comprising a single word. Typical of children in the early stages of language acquisition, for example an utterance like *kitty* might stand for *The cat is approaching*; or *allgone* for *The food is all eaten up*. This phase of language production is called the **holophrastic stage**, and the term **holophrastic language** may also be found.

home language   See MOTHER TONGUE.

homogeneity of interpretation   See HETEROGENEITY OF PRODUCTION.

honorific   Honorifics are linguistic forms that express POLITENESS or respect, i.e. where politeness/respect are encoded in the language, or grammaticalised (see GRAMMATICALISATION). One example of this would be the T AND V PRONOUNS found in many languages. Honorifics may be used as terms of ADDRESS (as in the case of T and V pronouns), but some languages have elaborate honorific systems where any utterance may be modified to indicate respect for the person

addressed or referred to. Examples would include the language
LEVELS found in certain Asian languages such as Japanese, Javanese,
Korean, where higher or more 'refined' styles may be used to convey
respect.

host language   A language that 'borrows' a word from another language – see BORROWING, contrast SOURCE LANGUAGE.

hybrid (-ity, -isation)
1. **Hybridisation** is a concept from biology sometimes drawn on to
   distinguish PIDGINISATION from other forms of language development. Keith Whinnom (1971) described pidginisation as a process
   of **tertiary hybridisation,** in contrast with other analogues from
   biology – **primary hybridisation** and **secondary hybridisation.** Primary hybridisation denotes the 'smooth' development of
   several different species from one ancestral species, as with a
   LANGUAGE gradually splitting up into DIALECTS which become
   languages themselves. Secondary hybridisation denotes the inter-
   breeding of distinct species to form a new one. A linguistic
   analogue given by Whinnom was when speakers of language A
   and language B use a simplified form of A for communication with
   each other (see INTERLANGUAGE). Whinnom argued that tertiary
   hybridisation, resulting in the development of a PIDGIN, occurs
   when a third group, speaking neither language A nor B, begins to
   use the simplified form of A not just with speakers of A but with
   speakers of B as well. Whereas this principle seems to apply in a
   number of pidgins, there are one or two counter-examples of
   pidgins based on two languages (e.g. Russenorsk, a pidgin based
   on Russian and Norwegian used by fishermen in the nineteenth
   century). See also WHINNOM FORMULA.
2. In discourse and genre analysis, **hybrid** and **hybridisation** are
   increasingly used to signal the mixing or bringing together of what
   might often be thought of as distinct GENRES, VOICES or DISCOURSES
   (the concept derives from the work of BAKHTIN). Hybridisation has
   become a prominent focus in some areas of sociolinguistics and is
   discussed in terms of BORDER CROSSING, LANGUAGE CROSSING and
   INTERTEXTUALITY. The term **hybridity** is also found, for example
   to refer to the hybrid nature of texts that draw on different
   discourses.
3. In LANGUAGE CONTACT situations a **hybrid** is a synonym for a MIXED
   CODE, for example MacArthur (1998) describes 'Hybrid Englishes'
   arising in modern urban settings. One such variety is Tex-Mex, a

variety that involves extensive code-mixing, spoken in the border areas of Texas and Mexico.

Hymes, Dell H. (1927–) One of the founders of contemporary sociolinguistics: Hymes' work has had a huge influence on the development of the discipline, as well as in related areas such as anthropology, folklore and the study of language in education. He was a founding editor of the journal *Language in Society*. Hymes' view of language as fundamentally social led him to argue that the concern of sociolinguistics was not simply to bring together linguistic and social data and analyses, but to 'rethink received categories and assumptions as to the bases of linguistic work, and as to the place of language in social life' (1974: vii). His development of the concept of COMMUNICATIVE COMPETENCE, for instance, stood as a challenge to Chomsky's narrower conception of linguistic competence. Much of Hymes' work has been concerned to map out a properly social linguistics based on ethnographic principles and procedures. He has done much to develop an area of sociolinguistics, sometimes termed the ETHNOGRAPHY of speaking/ communication (see e.g. the studies in Gumperz and Hymes, [1972] 1986); and the field of ETHNOPOETICS, based on his study of Native-American narratives (see Hymes, 1981, 2003). Hymes is Commonwealth Professor of Anthropology, Emeritus, at the University of Virginia. See also Hymes' concepts of SPEAKING; SPEECH EVENT; WAYS OF SPEAKING.

hypercorrection The overgeneralisation of linguistic forms which carry social prestige. Traditionally 'hypercorrection' describes cases where speakers (or writers) misapply linguistic rules which are considered prestigious (e.g. the pronunciation *heggs* instead of *eggs*, see H-DROPPING). In sociolinguistics the term was extended by William LABOV to describe a situation in which members of a lower-status group show a greater frequency of prestige/standard variants in formal situations than members of higher-status groups (see CROSS-OVER PATTERN). Janda and Auger (1992) refer to the former as 'qualitative hypercorrection' and to the latter as 'quantitative hypercorrection'. See also SCHIZOGLOSSIA.

I

icon (-ic)   In semiotics as developed by Charles Peirce, an icon is a kind of SIGN which, rather than having an arbitrary or conventional relation with the object it denotes, represents some aspect of the object itself (contrast INDEX; SYMBOL). Thus drawings are **iconic**, as are the images or figures used in religious worship. The signs of language (words) are not usually iconic, apart from instances of onomatopoeia, for example a word like *buzz* simulates the sound of the bee. A particular kind of emphasis in which one may draw out the vowels in *huge* or *big* to denote size is also an iconic use of language.

ideational   Term used in SYSTEMIC FUNCTIONAL LINGUISTICS to refer to one of three communicative functions, or METAFUNCTIONS of language. The ideational (or sometimes **experiential**) metafunction refers to the means by which language represents the world (i.e. the communication of what is happening, or what is being discussed). See also INTERPERSONAL and TEXTUAL metafunctions.

identity   A term used to refer to an individual's or group's sense of who they are, as defined by them and/or others. Identity can be expressed in a number of ways, for example in terms of nationality, geographical location, ETHNICITY, GENDER, SOCIAL CLASS, occupation etc. The relationship between language and identity has been studied in numerous ways in different sociolinguistic traditions. In QUANTITATIVE approaches to the study of LANGUAGE VARIATION, aspects of identity have been treated as SOCIAL VARIABLES to be mapped against LINGUISTIC VARIABLES: for example studies have identified relationships between age, gender, and social class and the frequency of use of certain linguistic features. Studies of code-switching have often seen this as indexing different aspects of bilingual speakers' identities. In NEW LITERACY STUDIES the identity of communities has sometimes been categorised in terms of social class and ethnicity and these communities have been associated with particular kinds of LITERACY PRACTICES (see e.g. Heath, 1983).

Early studies on the relationship between language and identity tended to treat identity as a fixed set of attributes, often as something external to language and pre-existing language. More recent approaches, drawing on POSTSTRUCTURALISM, conceptualise identity as something that is in constant process and argue that language, or more accurately DISCOURSE, is the principal means through which identity is forged (see PERFORMATIVITY). In order to signal identity as a process rather than something fixed, the term SUBJECTIVITY is often used in preference to identity, although identity is now often used with this more processual meaning in mind. See also AGENCY.

ideological model (of literacy)   See NEW LITERACY STUDIES.

ideology
1. A particular set of beliefs that individuals or groups of individuals have about the way society works, similar to the notion of **worldview**.
2. In a Marxist or neo-Marxist sense, ideology refers to a system of ideas and practices that disguise and distort the social, economic and political relations between dominant and dominated classes (see MARXISM). In classical Marxist writings, ideology is seen as distinct from material social conditions. In neo-Marxist approaches, the relationship between ideology and material social conditions is seen as more dynamic, each serving to support each other in the service of maintaining unequal power relations between groups in society. Language is seen as central to this process as it is through language – verbal and non-verbal – that ideology is expressed. Ideology in this Neo-Marxist sense is a key concept in CRITICAL DISCOURSE ANALYSIS. See also LANGUAGE IDEOLOGY; STANDARD LANGUAGE IDEOLOGY.

idiolect   The linguistic system (pronunciation, lexicon, grammar, pragmatics) used by an individual speaker. Social and regional dialects can be understood as clusters of similar (but not identical) idiolects, and their linguistic description is an abstraction from the variable speech habits of individuals.

illiteracy   See LITERACY.

illocutionary (act, force)   See SPEECH ACT.

immersion (education)   Refers to programmes of education where students are taught a foreign or second language by being immersed in this language through constant use. For example, in Canadian immersion education programmes students whose first language is English are immersed in the target language of French, by being taught most of their subjects in French. The outcomes of such programmes have generally proved to be positive, with strong indications that they lead to ADDITIVE BILINGUALISM. See also BILINGUAL EDUCATION.

implementation   An aspect of language STANDARDISATION and LANGUAGE PLANNING: the practical realisation of decisions taken by language planners. Implementation includes a range of steps taken to ensure that a policy is put into practice, e.g. the popularisation of a chosen linguistic NORM by publishing GRAMMARS and DICTIONARIES, by propagating newly coined words through word lists or administrative guidelines, or by encouraging people to learn an official language (e.g. by providing affordable languages courses). Implementation of a language policy can also include legislation, as in the case of the French Language Charter (Bill 101) in Quebec, which regulates the use of French in the public domain. See also ACCEPTANCE.

implicational scale (- scaling)   A method for data representation. Also called **Guttman scalogram analysis** (Guttman, 1944). **Implicational scaling** was first used in linguistics by David DeCamp (1971) in his analysis of the Jamaican CREOLE CONTINUUM to show the ordered transitions from basilect to acrolect (see BASILECT, MESOLECT, ACROLECT). Among other forms DeCamp looked at lexical co-occurrence rules. In the Jamaican acrolect, for example, speakers use the English words *eat*, *granny*, *child* and the verb form *didn't*; in the basilect these would be *nyam*, *nana*, *pikni* and *na bin*. DeCamp noticed that use of these words by individual speakers was not random but followed a well-structured pattern. Figure 4 represents this pattern as an implicational scale (also termed **panlectal grid**). It demonstrates that, if a speaker used a basilectal form to the left of the implicational scale, he or she would also use all the basilectal forms to right of that form: use of form B (*nana*) implies use of C and D but not A; use of form C (*na bin*) implies use of D but not A and B, and so on.

	A	**B**	**C**	**D**
speaker 1	eat	granny	didn't	child
speaker 2	eat	granny	didn't	pikni
speaker 3	eat	granny	na bin	pikni
speaker 4	eat	nana	na bin	pikni
speaker 5	nyam	nana	na bin	pikni

Figure 4   Implicational scale showing lexical co-occurrence rules in Jamaican Creole (based on the more complex scale given in DeCamp, 1971: 355)

Implicational scales have also been used to describe the process of LANGUAGE SHIFT according to interlocutor. In her study of the bilingual Austrian town of Oberwart, in which both German and Hungarian were spoken, Susan Gal (1979) found there was a general shift towards the use of German. German was also used more to younger people and Hungarian more to older people. She was able to plot individual speakers' use of German or Hungarian towards older and younger family members on an implicational scale. Implicational scales may therefore reflect a CHANGE IN PROGRESS (Rickford, 1987; Bailey, 1973), illustrating the path by which the change moves across the language system and/or the social contexts in which language is used.

implicature   See CONVERSATIONAL IMPLICATURE.

independence (in conversation)   See INVOLVEMENT.

independent variable   See LINGUISTIC VARIABLE.

index (-ical, -icality)   In the SEMIOTICS developed by Charles Peirce, an index is a particular kind of SIGN, which has some kind of logical relation to the object it stands for, rather than having an arbitrary relationship with it (contrast SYMBOL and ICON). Thus smoke 'signals' a fire, but is also a result of a fire being kindled and is therefore an index of it. In sociolinguistics and related areas (e.g. LINGUISTIC ANTHROPOLOGY) the term is extended to refer to the way in which aspects of language are connected to a sociocultural context as when words or phrases 'index' a past or present experience. This property of language may be referred to as **indexicality**. An example is CODE-SWITCHING: by uttering a word from another language a speaker might evoke another place, time or experience. Similarly, use of a particular speaking style might index ethnicity, gender, membership of an urban teenage group, a particular attitude, etc. (see Duranti, 1997: 17–19).

The phenomenon of DEIXIS is often seen as an aspect of indexicality, in the sense that deictic terms such as *I, you, now, here, tomorrow* etc. index people or events in relation to the context of speaking and, more broadly, may index relations between speakers and particular cultural contexts.

indicator   Indicators are LINGUISTIC VARIABLES of which speakers are not consciously aware. They contrast with MARKERS (variables of which speakers are aware); and STEREOTYPES (associated with stereotyped perceptions of varieties). Indicators show SOCIAL VAR- IATION but no STYLISTIC VARIATION between formal and informal speech styles. For example, Trudgill (1974b) found that in Nor- wich, England, the degree of FRONTING of (ɑː) in the LEXICAL SET *part, path, half, banana*, etc., did not show variation according to speaking style. There was, however, social variation: fronted vowels were associated with working-class speakers and centralised vowels with middle-class speakers. It has been suggested that indicators often reflect linguistic changes which are still at an early stage; alternatively they might be indicative of STABLE VARIATION (Labov, 1965; Trudgill, 1986).

indigenisation   A term coined by Braj KACHRU to describe the pro- cesses by which a language changes in response to a new environ- ment to which it is transported; it includes the adoption of alternative forms of language and the development of local indi- genised NORMS of language use. Indigenisation may include the incorporation of local terms for flora, fauna, customs, topographical features, etc. It also includes the influence of the phonetic and grammatical patterns of indigenous languages as local people adopt the new language as a second language. This process of cultural transformation has been studied most extensively in relation to the spread of English (see LANGUAGE SPREAD). See also NATIVISATION; NEW ENGLISH(ES); WORLD ENGLISH(ES).

individual   There has been considerable debate in linguistics and sociolinguistics about whether language should be seen as being located in the individual or in the community. The debate goes back to the late nineteenth/early twentieth centuries (e.g. Hermann Paul, *Principien der Sprachgeschichte*, 1880 vs W. D. Whitney, *Language and the Study of Language*, 1867), and constitutes a basic and unresolved issue in sociolinguistic theory. Sociolinguists who have advocated a strongly 'individualist view' of language include C.-J. N. Bailey (1973), R. A. Hudson (1996) and Robert Le Page (Le Page and Tabouret-Keller, 1985). LABOVian approaches to the study of lan- guage, on the other hand, define the speech community or social group as the unit of analysis and describe 'social' (rather than a series of 'idiolectal') grammars. See also DEVELOPMENTAL LINGUISTICS; SAUSSUREAN PARADOX.

inductive, deductive (methods)   Two different modes of reasoning. **Induction** means that one moves from specific observations to broader generalisations and theories. Sociolinguistics, with its strong empirical orientation is usually described as based on the inductive method: sociolinguists would typically engage in some kind of FIELD-WORK and systematic data collection, then formulate theories on the basis of their observations of patterns in the data. **Deduction**, on the other hand, moves from general principles and theories to the confirmation of these theories by specific observations. Deductive reasoning, in which individual structures are deduced from general theories about the nature of language, is common in generative linguistics (see LINGUISTICS).

inferential statistics   Statistical methods which enable researchers to test whether the patterns observed in a data set are likely to exist in the POPULATION from which the sample was drawn. Contrasts with DESCRIPTIVE STATISTICS. See also SIGNIFICANCE TESTING; P-LEVEL.

informalisation   See CONVERSATIONALISATION.

informant   Linguists have used different terms to refer to those who provide data on language use, attitudes and beliefs etc. The traditional term in linguistics and anthropology is **informant**. However, this term has come under critique as it does not reflect the complex, collaborative relationships that often exist between researchers and language users. Other designations include: (native speaker) **consultant, interviewee, source, subject, assistant** and **co-researcher**. These terms indicate that participants can play quite different roles in the research and data-gathering process, and that there are different potential relationships between researchers and those on, with, or for whom they carry out research. 'Subject', for instance, is most common in experimental contexts where research is usually more directly under the control of the researcher; 'co-researcher' suggests a more collaborative relationship where the co-researcher may have some input into the research process. For further discussion, see Newman and Ratliff (2001). See also ETHICS; FIELDWORK; PARTICIPANT.

informed consent   Refers to the practice whereby participants in a research study give their consent to take part and confirm that they understand the aims and research format etc. of the study. Participants usually give consent in writing, but in contexts where writing is not widespread or integrated into community structures, consent may be given orally (sometimes audio- or video-taped by the researcher). See also ETHICS.

-ing   The unstressed *-ing* ending in words such as *running* or *jumping* in English, where the final consonant may be pronounced as [n] or [ŋ]. *-ing* is a common LINGUISTIC VARIABLE in studies of SOCIAL VARIATION and STYLISTIC VARIATION: as a variable, it is commonly represented as **(ng)**. For an example, see Peter Trudgill's study of variation in the English of Norwich (Trudgill, 1974b), which found that the final [n] pronunciation occurred more frequently in informal speaking styles, among WORKING CLASS (rather than MIDDLE CLASS) speakers and among male (rather than female) speakers.

Initiation–Response–Feedback   (IRF)   Initiation–Response–Feedback (or sometimes 'Follow-up') is a pattern of interaction which has been identified as common in classroom talk. An example of IRF is as follows:

Teacher:	What is the capital of England?	**I** (Initiation)
Student:	London.	**R** (Response)
Teacher:	Well done.	**F** (Feedback)

The term comes from the system of DISCOURSE analysis devised by John Sinclair and Malcolm Coulthard (see e.g. Sinclair and Coulthard, 1975). Mehan (1979) uses the expression IRE (Initiation–Response–Evaluation) to refer to a similar classroom interaction pattern. The extent to which such patterning is common across distinct cultural contexts has been explored by Alexander (2000).

innovator (innovative)   Innovators are speakers who introduce new linguistic forms into the REPERTOIRE of the SPEECH COMMUNITY. Their behaviour may therefore be said to be **innovative**. Research has found that innovators are typically located outside of close-knit SOCIAL NETWORKS; they are marginal members of the speech community and only interact infrequently with other speakers. Because of their social position, innovators are not constrained by community norms and are thus believed to be more experimental in their social and linguistic behaviour. Contrast CONSERVATIVE. See also ACTUATION; EARLY ADOPTER.

input   A term in LANGUAGE ACQUISITION studies that refers to the sum total of forms and varieties of a language that a learner is exposed to. In first-language acquisition the input to the child-learner may comprise not just adult forms of the local DIALECT, but special varieties like the BABY TALK of caregivers, the speech of other young children, etc. In the acquisition of a foreign language the input may be limited to classroom language. In PIDGIN and CREOLE formation, it is believed that the input in any pre-existing language is inadequate for the learning of those languages, hence resulting in a pidgin/ Creole. See also CHILD-DIRECTED SPEECH; FOREIGNER TALK.

insiders   See INTERLOPERS, INSIDERS, OUTSIDERS, ASPIRERS.

institutional (discourse)   The DISCOURSE and DISCOURSE PRACTICES of institutions. Substantial work has been carried out with three principal emphases: (a) the language used in institutional texts (spoken and written); for example legal documents, academic publications, medical reports, political speeches using forms of GENRE analysis (see e.g. Bhatia, 1993) and CRITICAL DISCOURSE ANALYSIS (see Fairclough, 2000; Reisgl and Wodak, 2000); (b) the kinds of encounters that take place within institutions, often emphasising the asymmetrical power relations between institutional representatives and clients. Here the tools of CONVERSATION ANALYSIS and INTERACTIONAL SOCIOLINGUISTICS are key methods (see Drew and Heritage, 1992; Boden, 1994; Sarangi and Roberts, 1999); (c) the institutional activities or practices in which communication is embedded, using a range of ethnographic methods (see Mumby and Clair, 1997; Cameron, 2000; Swales, 1998).

institutionalised variety, performance variety   Braj Kachru (1992) drew a distinction between two types of ENGLISH AS AN ADDITIONAL LANGUAGE (EAL). **Institutionalised varieties** of English are common in ENGLISH AS A SECOND LANGUAGE (ESL) contexts: they are introduced via the education system and used to some extent in administrative spheres and in the media; they are also used as a medium of education and in creative writing. **Performance varieties**, by contrast, are used in a relatively restricted functional range within certain countries, in contexts of international trade, tourism and study as a foreign language. Performance varieties may arise solely out of education in ENGLISH AS A FOREIGN LANGUAGE (EFL) or out of the ad hoc skills of communication that individuals pick up via brief contacts with tourists, traders, etc. Although the difference between institutional and performance varieties to a large extent replicates the ESL–EFL distinction, there are differences. One difference is that performance varieties include English-based PIDGINS. Thus a country which might be broadly defined as an ESL territory could have both institutional (ESL) English as well as performance varieties (like a pidgin or simplified English used by some tour guides). See also DOMAIN; THREE CIRCLES OF ENGLISH.

integrational linguistics Proposed initially by Roy Harris, integrational linguistics involves the study of language in context, alongside other forms of behaviour, rather than as an independent linguistic system: it is 'a linguistics which takes as its point of departure the individual linguistic act in its communicational setting' (Harris, 1981: 166). Harris was concerned with the reconceptualisation of formal linguistics. While integrational linguistics seems to share many of the concerns of sociolinguistics, it has been developed, initially at least, as a separate project.

interactional sociolinguistics A major branch of sociolinguistics associated particularly with the work of John GUMPERZ and his associates (e.g. Gumperz, 1982), but also referring more broadly to the sociolinguistic study of language and interaction. Interactional sociolinguistics involves the study of contextualised language use: traditionally face-to-face spoken interactions, but similar methods and principles may also be used in the study of other forms of communication, including written communication (e.g. letter writing) and electronic communication. Studies may focus on a range of interactional features (e.g. CODE-SWITCHING or 'style shifting' between language varieties, TURN-TAKING and other aspects of CONVERSATION MANAGEMENT, patterns of speaking and SILENCE). They tend to investigate patterns of language use in specific social/cultural contexts, with interests in issues such as the construction of relationships between speakers/writers, language and IDENTITY, INTERCULTURAL COMMUNICATION, language and POWER, LANGUAGE AND GENDER. Methodological approaches tend to be broadly QUALITATIVE, often drawing on insights from ETHNOGRAPHY or anthropology. For a brief overview, see Mesthrie et al. (2000). See also INTERPRETIVE (APPROACH); LINGUISTIC ANTHROPOLOGY.

interactionism See SYMBOLIC INTERACTIONISM.

interactive sociolinguistics See INTERACTIONAL SOCIOLINGUISTICS.

intercultural communication   Communication between members of different cultural groups, who may bring different language PRAC-TICES or WAYS OF SPEAKING, and different expectations and cultural understandings to an interaction (see e.g. Scollon and Scollon, 1995). The term **cross-cultural communication** is also found. Studies focus on the characteristics of different communication styles and often on communication difficulties such as misinterpretations and MISCOMMUNICATION. A key area of interest is communication between people from different ethnic or language backgrounds, for example an interaction in English between NATIVE and non-native speakers (see also INTERETHNIC COMMUNICATION); but there is also interest in the language of other social/cultural groupings, for example interactions between women and men. Studies taking an intercultural approach to LANGUAGE AND GENDER have been criticised for focusing simply on cultural difference and not taking sufficient account of differences in POWER between women and men.

interdialect   A term coined by Peter Trudgill for a new DIALECT that emerges from contact between speakers of different dialects of a language. Such a dialect typically arises during migration. The term 'interdialect' – like INTERLANGUAGE, on which it is based – stresses the processes of ACCOMMODATION between speakers as well as the unstable nature of the new dialect in its formative stages. If an interdialect stabilises as the first language of a speech community it is termed a KOINÈ.

interdiscursivity   Used in a general way to refer to the relations and interconnections between distinct DISCOURSES (senses (2) and (3)). It is used in a more specific way by Norman Fairclough to distinguish between different kinds of relations, particularly between what he refers to as **manifest intertextuality** and interdiscursivity. Fair-clough uses 'manifest intertextuality' (see INTERTEXTUALITY) for rela-tions between TEXTS, and 'interdiscursivity' for relations between discourses (Fairclough, 1992a). The former refers to explicit refer-ence, in a text, to other texts or inclusion of items from other texts: for example a magazine article quoting what a celebrity has said in an interview. Interdiscursivity refers to a more abstract set of relations: for example the embedding of a particular discourse on MASCULINITY in the discourse of science. **Constitutive intertextuality** is often used synonymously with interdiscursivity.

interethnic communication   Communication between members of different ethnic groups. Researchers have been interested in how this may be characterised by differences in linguistic and cultural knowledge and assumptions, leading to MISCOMMUNICATION and sometimes to discrimination against relatively powerless groups (see e.g. Gumperz, 1982). See also INTERCULTURAL COMMUNICATION.

interference   See TRANSFER.

interlanguage   The term 'interlanguage' was coined by Larry Selinker (1972) for the version of a language produced by a second- or foreign-language learner. The term drew attention to learners' unstable but continually developing system, which displays properties that derive neither wholly from their first language nor wholly from the language they are acquiring (the TARGET language). Although an interlanguage does contain errors based on TRANSFER from a speaker's first language, analysts have shown that many of these are similar to the forms produced by children learning their first language. However, an interlanguage differs from first-language development in that it may 'fossilise' when an individual shows no further development in the second language. FOSSILISATION involves the stabilisation of some features of an interlanguage by an individual or group, instead of an equivalent feature of the target language.

interlocutor   The person with whom one is engaged in conversation. The term implies a degree of interaction and reciprocity not implied in related terms like ADDRESSEE and AUDIENCE (in its conventional sense).

interlopers, insiders, outsiders, aspirers   A set of terms introduced by J. K. Chambers (2003) to describe types of speakers who show anomalous language behaviour in an otherwise homogeneous SAMPLE. **Interlopers** are individuals who have not fully mastered the dialect features of a region (or social group) because they arrived in the area (or joined the social group) as adolescents or adults (see CRITICAL AGE). Their language use thus differs from that of the larger group. **Insiders** are those at the centre of a social group and are closely involved with its activities. They show patterns of language use which are somewhat different from those of the rank-and-file. With regard to language change, they often seem to be racing ahead of the rest of the group. **Outsiders** (see also LAMES) are isolated individuals at the fringes of a social group: they do not participate fully in the patterns of language use and change that are characteristic of the group. **Aspirers** are those 'with social ambitions that stretch beyond their immediate social domain' (Chambers, 1995: 95). This includes not only upwardly-mobile speakers, but anyone who wants to achieve membership in a different social group (e.g. migrants who want to became part of the new society, middle-class adolescents who want to participate in African American Hip-hop culture, etc.).

internal history (of language)   See HISTORICAL LINGUISTICS.

international language   A language that is in widespread use across national boundaries as a LINGUA FRANCA. Among these are English, French, German, Russian, Mandarin Chinese and Swahili. The current spread of English makes it a language reaching global proportions and therefore of especial sociolinguistic interest; see GLOBAL LANGUAGE; WORLD ENGLISH(ES); THREE CIRCLES OF ENGLISH.

International Phonetic Alphabet (IPA)   A system frequently used for the phonetic TRANSCRIPTION of speech sounds. For the full set of IPA symbols see the International Phonetic Association consonant and vowel charts, available on the association's web site: http:// www.arts.gla.ac.uk/IPA/ipachart.html (accessed October 2003). See also PHONETICS.

interpellation   Term associated with the philosopher Louis Althusser, who emphasised the centrality of IDEOLOGY in reproducing economic and political relations, and in particular the role of institutions in ideological processes. Althusser refers to those institutions which are most closely aligned with the power, culture and values of the state (such as organised religion, the legal system, the family and the education system) as 'Institutional State Apparatuses' (or ISAs). Althusser explores the process by which individuals become influenced by such institutions and consequently become 'subjects' of them. Any one institution represents a coherent set of beliefs, which 'hail' or 'interpellate' the individual, that is implicitly directs her into a particular way of being and acting, referred to as a SUBJECT POSITION (see Althusser, 1971). See also SUBJECTIVITY.

interpersonal   Refers to relations between people, for example in phrases such as 'interpersonal communication'. In SYSTEMIC FUNCTIONAL LINGUISTICS, the interpersonal is one of three META-FUNCTIONS of language, referring to the way language is used to construct relationships between speakers/listeners and writers/readers (e.g. a formal or informal relationship); and between language users and what they are talking/writing about (e.g. a speaker's attitude to something she is describing). See also IDEATIONAL and TEXTUAL metafunctions.

interpretative repertoires   A concept derived from work on scientific discourse by Gilbert and Mulkay (1984) and introduced into SOCIAL PSYCHOLOGY by Jonathon Potter and Margaret Wetherell (e.g. Potter and Wetherell, 1987). Interpretative repertoires are internally coherent ways of speaking about objects, actions or events. The concept is defined more specifically as: 'basically a lexicon or register of terms and metaphors drawn upon to characterise and evaluate actions and events' (Potter and Wetherell, 1987: 138). As an example, Wetherell (1998) refers to different interpretative repertoires of sexuality drawn on by a group of young men in providing an account of one young man's sexual exploits. Interpretative repertoires are similar in some respects to DISCOURSES (senses (2) and (3)), although they are seen as less abstract, and there is a focus on their use as contextualised practices. See also DISCURSIVE PSYCHOLOGY.

interpretive (approach)   Within INTERACTIONAL SOCIOLINGUISTICS, the term refers to the attempt to take participants' perspectives into account in analysing an interaction. This derives particularly from the work of John GUMPERZ (e.g. Gumperz, 1982). Gumperz was concerned with the discourse strategies employed by participants in an interaction, and particularly with how participants drew on linguistic and social/cultural knowledge in order to produce and interpret utterances in context. This involved consultation with participants to discover their understandings of utterances. Gumperz suggested that the analyst should: 'make an in-depth study of selected instances of verbal interaction, observe whether or not actors understand each other, elicit participants' interpretations of what goes on, and then (a) deduce the social assumptions that speakers must have made in order to act as they do, and (b) determine empirically how linguistic signs communicate in the interpretation process' (1982: 35–6). This may help illuminate several aspects of interaction, including MISCOMMUNICATION, when participants do not share relevant linguistic or cultural knowledge.

interpretive frame   See FRAME.

interruption   'Interruption' tends to be used in its everyday sense of a hostile or at least unwelcome incursion by a speaker into another's

SPEAKING TURN. Interruptions have been of interest within socio-linguistics because they have been found to be differentially distributed among groups of speakers (one of the most notable findings has been that men interrupt women more than vice versa). However, there have been problems in reliably identifying interruptions. Different formal definitions have been adopted, which makes it difficult to compare evidence from different studies. More importantly, simple formal definitions are often inadequate. For example, an interruption may be defined as an instance where someone begins speaking at some point before the current speaker has reached a TRANSITION RELEVANCE PLACE, but this kind of definition is unsuitable for multi-party talk with significant amounts of overlapping speech. Furthermore, such formal definitions tell us nothing about the interactional function, or the interactional effect of the (apparent) interruption (see FORM (VS FUNCTION); on problems in the interpretation of interruptions, see e.g. Graddol et al., 1994). Some studies (e.g. Coates, 1996) have found examples of overlapping speech that match earlier formal definitions of interruptions but that in fact have a highly co-operative function. There are also cultural differences in the extent to which speakers will tolerate overlapping speech (e.g. Tannen, 1984). See also CONVERSATION MANAGEMENT; LANGUAGE AND GENDER; OVERLAP; TURN-TAKING.

intersentential code-switching   See CODE-SWITCHING.

interspeaker variation   Refers to variation in the language used by different speakers, or groups of speakers: for example, differences between female and male speakers (see GENDER); members of different SOCIAL CLASSes; AGE groups; ethnic groups (see ETHNICITY). Much recent research has given more weight to the complexity of social groupings and to differences within social groups. See also SOCIAL VARIATION; contrast INTRA-SPEAKER VARIATION.

intersubjectivity   See SUBJECTIVITY.

intertextuality   Term coined by Julia Kristeva drawing on work of BAKHTIN to refer to the ways in which all UTTERANCES form part of a 'chain of speech communication' (Kristeva, 1986). All utterances or TEXTS are inherently intertextual, made up of wordings and meanings from other texts. An obvious example is the insertion of other people's comments into newspaper articles. A distinction is sometimes made between **manifest** intertextuality and **constitutive intertextuality** (the latter is also termed INTERDISCURSIVITY; see Fairclough, 1992a). 'Manifest intertextuality' refers to texts which are explicitly present or marked in other texts, for example direct speech from one text quoted in another. 'Constitutive intertextuality' refers to more abstract relations at the level of DISCOURSE, for example incorporating everyday or 'commonsense' discourse about language into academic/linguistic discourse. Fairclough identifies three principal types of intertextual (or interdiscursive) relations: **sequential**, where different texts or discourses alternate within a text; **embedded**, where one text or discourse is clearly embedded within another; and **mixed**, where texts or discourses are merged in a less obviously distinct way (Fairclough, 1992a: 118).

intertwined language   A term coined by Peter Bakker and Peter Muysken (1995) for a special type of bilingual MIXED CODE which draws on one language for its lexical morphemes and another for its grammatical morphemes. Bakker and Muysken provided the example of Media Lengua, a language of Ecuador, which has lexical elements almost entirely from Spanish and grammatical elements almost entirely from Quecha. In an intertwined language the mixing is permanent.

interview   A method of data collection in which a researcher asks questions of an informant to obtain data for analysis. Interviews are used in sociolinguistics to gather information on language use (e.g. self-reports, linguistic biographies) as well as on language ATTITUDES. Sociolinguists also use interviews as a means of obtaining large quantities of naturalistic language data. To capture the individual's full linguistic repertoire, William LABOV developed the so-called **sociolinguistic interview**. The Labovian interview is divided into five speech styles which are distinguished on the basis of relative formality (see STYLISTIC CONTINUUM). This allows researchers to document linguistic differences between speech styles. The greatest challenge for interviewers is to gain access to the VERNACULAR, i.e. speakers' most informal variety which they use in relaxed settings. Labov encouraged people to talk about topics of everyday interest which would divert their attention from the artificial and formal setting of the interview (see the DANGER OF DEATH interview question). Some examples of the interviews conducted by Labov between 1963 and 1973 can be found under http://ldc.upenn.edu/Projects/DASL/SLX_corpus.html (last accessed October 2003).

An important advantage of the Labovian sociolinguistic interview is that it allows researchers to collect large quantities of easily comparable linguistic data as all speech samples are structured according to the same interview schedule. However, the Labovian interview has been criticised as an artificial and non-natural speech event (e.g. Wolfson, 1976). Research has also included different interview formats to take account of the influence of different types of interviewer, different settings etc. (e.g. Edwards, 1986). Instead of relying on interview data, some sociolinguists prefer to record naturally occurring conversations, often taped by the participants themselves without the presence of the researcher (e.g. Sebba, 1993).

interviewee   See INFORMANT.

intonation   Systematic variation in PITCH in an utterance: what is important, in intonation, is not absolute pitch but changes in pitch, as when an utterance is pronounced with a rising intonation to indicate a question. Utterances are often divided into intonational groups, which may then be analysed in various ways. Most relevant to sociolinguistic studies is the identification of a nuclear tone – the last stressed syllable of an intonational group which carries the main pitch movement. There are different types of pitch movement, including a 'fall', 'fall-rise', 'high rise', 'low rise' (for a brief discussion, see Graddol et al., 1994). Intonation has an important grammatical function – for instance, it may mark clause boundaries, and distinguish statements from questions. It may play a part in TURN-TAKING by signalling the approach of a TRANSITION RELEVANCE PLACE. Accents may be characterised by distinctive intonation patterns: for instance, there has been considerable interest in the HIGH RISING TONE that is increasingly heard among speakers of English in Australia and several other countries. Intonation also conveys information about speakers' emotions and attitudes – in the expression of surprise, dismay etc. See also PROSODY.

intra-sentential code-switching   See CODE-SWITCHING.

intra-speaker variation   Refers to variation in the language use of an individual speaker – i.e. how individuals vary the way they speak in different contexts (depending on such factors as the SETTING or physical context, who they are talking to, what they are talking about, their interactional goals etc.). See also CODE-SWITCHING; CONTEXTUAL VARIATION; STYLISTIC VARIATION; contrast INTERSPEAKER VARIATION.

intrusive *r*   See LINKING *r*.

involvement (in conversation)   Refers to participants' active participation in an interaction. The sociolinguist John GUMPERZ (1982) argued that involvement is fundamental to participants' understanding or interpretation of the interaction, and that it needs to be signalled verbally or non-verbally (e.g. by gesture or eye-contact). Gumperz and other sociolinguists have been interested in the strategies employed to create and sustain involvement, how these may differ between different cultural groups and the potential for misunderstandings or MISCOMMUNICATION when they are not shared (e.g. in INTERCULTURAL COMMUNICATION). It is also argued that participants need to balance involvement and 'independence', i.e. participants' need to maintain their own independence and respect that of others (see e.g. Ron Scollon and Suzanne Wong Scollon, 1995). Speaking styles may be characterised by different levels of involvement: Deborah Tannen (1984) discusses the characteristics of a **high involvement** style, which 'put[s] the signalling load' on interpersonal involvement – e.g. faster rate of speech and turn-taking, cooperative OVERLAPs, telling stories in rounds, marked shifts in PITCH. This is contrasted with a style that expresses 'considerateness' – the need to avoid imposing on others. Although the connection is not always made, involvement may be related to the concepts of FACE and POLITENESS (e.g. (high) involvement may be compared to positive politeness and independence or considerateness to negative politeness). For discussion, see Scollon and Scollon (1995).

IRF   See INITIATION – RESPONSE – FEEDBACK.

irrealis   A grammatical term for a verb form referring to something that has not been realised or is not likely to happen. It is a cover term for categories like hypotheticals, conditionals and counter-factuals. In English the hypothetical (or subjunctive) *were* in *If I were to come over* . . . counts as irrealis. Derek BICKERTON has argued that the irrealis category is an important one in CREOLE languages, in the verb system as well as in subsystems like verb complements. An example from Guyanese Creole English is *Awi bin go kom out seef* meaning

'We would have come out safe/all right', where the AUXILIARY verb *go* marks irrealis. See also TENSE–MODALITY–ASPECT.

isogloss   In DIALECTOLOGY, a dividing line or boundary, plotted on a map, showing where one linguistic form (e.g. a particular REALISA-TION of a PHONEME) gives way to another. Sometimes, isoglosses 'bundle', that is, isoglosses for several different linguistic features are found close to one another, and this can be interpreted as representing a **dialect boundary**. In the United Kingdom, for example, 'bundled' or intersecting isoglosses constitute a well-defined line which distinguishes northern from southern dialects. However, boundaries between DIALECTS are not always clear-cut, and frequently isoglosses form complex criss-cross patterns in a geographical area. See also LINGUISTIC ATLAS; SURVEY OF ENGLISH DIALECTS (SED).

it-clefting   A syntactic construction used to make part of a sentence more prominent: for instance, in the sentence: 'It's stars that Helen can see', *stars* occurs in an initial CLAUSE preceded by *it's*, giving it prominence or greater emphasis; compare 'Helen can see stars.' 'It-clefting' is interesting as a dialect feature: for instance it is found more frequently, and with a wider range of functions, in Irish English than in standard English English (see Harris, 1993).

jargon
1. A rudimentary PIDGIN, also known as a **pre-pidgin**, which has an unstable structure and limited vocabulary on account of sporadic use and restriction to a few DOMAINS like trade or labour. Jargons contrast with **stable pidgins**, which they may evolve into if the circumstances of contact change.
2. Technical or other specialist vocabulary used within a certain social group – most frequently a professional or special interest group – and that may not be understood by outsiders. Jargon may be used to facilitate professional communication but it also has social functions, for example marking group membership and excluding non-members (see also SLANG).

3. The popular sense of jargon for unnecessary use of technical terms in colloquial speech is rare in sociolinguistics. Jargon in this sense refers to the inappropriate use of a technical REGISTER in informal speech.

Jocks and Burnouts   Two ADOLESCENT groups who were distinguished by participants in Penelope Eckert's study of young people's language use in a Detroit high-school (see e.g. Eckert, 1989, 2000). 'Jocks' and 'Burnouts' differed with regard to their integration into the norms of high school culture and their attitudes towards further education: 'Jocks' participated actively in school activities and were planning to continue with their education after school; 'Burnouts', on the other hand, positioned themselves in opposition to the school environment, did not participate in extra-curricular activities and intended to leave school as soon as possible to join the local (blue-collar) workforce. The two groups mirrored the SOCIAL CLASS division of society: 'Jocks' could be seen as adolescent representatives of the American middle class, 'Burnouts' as representatives of the American working class. The linguistic differences between the two groups also reflected their social position: 'Burnouts' used more low-prestige vernacular variants, while 'Jocks' reproduced socially prestigious middle-class variants. Eckert also found that gender interacted with these patterns of language use: girls asserted their social identities more clearly through symbolic systems such as language (and also clothing) than boys. The 'Jocks' and 'Burnouts' distinction is common in US high schools, although many people in Eckert's study referred to themselves as 'In-betweens', with some allegiance to either the 'Jocks' or the 'Burnouts'.

judgement sample   A SAMPLE which is systematically constructed to include certain pre-determined social groups. For example, in order to study dialect attitudes researchers might wish to include representatives of different age groups – ADOLESCENTS, adults and older people – as well as people from different dialect regions and social classes. The sample would be constructed in such a way as to include equal numbers of individuals in each specified category (sometimes called **cells**), i.e. young, middle class, southern; adult, working class, northern, etc. Most quantitative sociolinguistic studies are based on judgement samples. Contrast RANDOM SAMPLE.

K

Kachru, Braj B. (1932–)   A leading scholar in the field of WORLD
ENGLISHES. Kachru has insisted that varieties of English that arose
and developed as second languages in the era of British colonialism
are not makeshift INTERLANGUAGES. Rather, they are stable varieties
which have developed their own norms according to the local CON-
TEXT OF SITUATION. Kachru's pioneering papers on Indian English,
reproduced in book form as *The Indianisation of English* (1983),
provided the model and inspiration for scholars attempting to
characterise English in diverse parts of the world, using key concepts
like INDIGENISATION, and acknowledging the creativity of bilinguals.
Kachru's general model of the THREE CIRCLES OF ENGLISH is widely
used in characterising relations between the CENTRE and periphery
in World English studies. He has been a spirited advocate of the
recognition of World Englishes in the classroom, and of the acceptance of multiple norms in English around the world. The adjective
Kachruvian is sometimes used to refer to Kachru's ideas, especially
in relation to the 'Three Circles of English'.

key (-ing)

1. One of the terms used by Dell HYMES to characterise a SPEECH
   EVENT, key refers to the tone, manner or spirit of a particular
   SPEECH ACT, for example whether this is mock or serious. See
   Hymes' mnemonic SPEAKING.
2. In the analysis of FRAMES, key refers to the set of conventions that
   transforms an activity already meaningful within a primary interpretive frame so that it is understood as a different type of activity
   (the process is referred to as **keying**: Goffman, 1974: 43–5). For
   instance, an activity such as a family conversation may be **keyed** as
   make-believe (in pretend play between children), or as a dramatic
   performance of a conversation, etc. Activities may be successively
   rekeyed, as when a dramatic performance of a conversation is sent
   up, or satirised.

kinship (terms)   Kinship terminology has a long history of study in
linguistics and anthropology. Researchers have identified similarities
and differences between the sets of kinship terms used in different
linguistic and cultural groups. For instance, most CULTURES distin-

guish between generations and between genders; some also mark age differences within a generation; some distinguish cousins from brothers and sisters, others have the same term for sisters/female cousins and brothers/male cousins. Kinship terms have been of interest partly because of the insights they are said to provide into cultural beliefs and practices.

Knowledge About Language (KAL)   Term used particularly in the UK educational context to refer to the importance of developing teachers' and students' knowledge about language in the context of school education. It is strongly associated with the LINC (Language In the National Curriculum) project and with materials developed in the late 1980s aimed at improving teachers' and students' understanding of language, for example how language works as a system, the social contexts and uses of different kinds of language, the relationship between language and learning. A key focus of debate within LINC was the relative importance of teachers' and students' explicit knowledge about language (including knowledge about GRAMMAR) as compared with the implicit knowledge about language that all users possess (see Carter, 1990). See also LANGUAGE AWARENESS; METALINGUISTIC.

koinè (-isation)   A new variety which develops when population movements bring mutually intelligible dialects of the same language into contact with each other. The original Koinè was the variety of Greek that developed between 450–200 BC at Piraeus, the seaport of Athens, where there was contact between people from all parts of the Mediterranean speaking several Greek dialects, especially Attic. Koinès are frequently characterised by DIALECT LEVELLING as less frequent and less regular grammatical and phonetic forms are lost in favour of features that are more widespread in the various dialects. Though frequently held in low esteem in their early stages, koinès may stabilise to become bearers of a new social and regional identity. Australian English fits this mould – see Trudgill (1986). **Koinèisation** refers to the process of koinè formation. See also INTERDIALECT.

Kultursprache   'Cultured' or 'culture-bearing language'. Used to describe standardised literary varieties which function as the dominant language in a society and which are employed in a wide-range of functions. The term is rarely used in sociolinguistics because of the connotation that non-standard varieties would thus be 'un-cultured'.

'L' variety   See 'H' VARIETY, 'L' VARIETY.

L1, L2 etc.   In studies of BILINGUALISM, SECOND LANGUAGE ACQUISITION and other areas relating to the use of more than one language, L1 refers to a speaker's first language, L2 to his or her second language, and so on. See also FIRST LANGUAGE; MOTHER TONGUE.

labio-dental   A term used in the description and classification of CONSONANTS, relating to their PLACE OF ARTICULATION. Labio-dental sounds are produced when the lower lip comes into contact with the teeth. Examples from English include: [f] and [v]. See also PHONETICS; INTERNATIONAL PHONETIC ALPHABET.

labio-velar   A term used in the description and classification of CONSONANTS, relating to their PLACE OF ARTICULATION. Labio-velar sounds are produced by the lips while the back of the tongue is raised towards or touches the velum, at the back of the mouth. In English, [w] is a labio-velar sound. See also INTERNATIONAL PHONETIC ALPHABET; PHONETICS.

Labov, William (1927–)   Labov has been the dominant figure in sociolinguistics since the early 1960s, when the results of his M.A. thesis on the social motivation for sound change in Martha's Vineyard and of his Ph.D. thesis on the sociolinguistic stratification of New York City were published. His work was notable not only for uncovering the finely grained variation and stratification in a complex urban setting, but also for his field methods and sampling techniques. Labov is generally credited with developing an empirical, rigorous and reproducible approach to the study of language as it is actually used. At the same time he revitalised the fields of HISTORICAL LINGUISTICS and DIALECTOLOGY by showing the connections between LANGUAGE VARIATION and social group membership. More recently, his interest in CHAIN SHIFTs that are current in urban English dialects world-wide has continued to unite and influence these two fields profoundly (see e.g. NORTHERN CITIES SHIFT). **Labovian linguistics** thus refers to an approach to language that highlights variation and change within a linguistic and social context. Labov is also known for his work on NARRATIVE and for descriptive work on AFRICAN AMERICAN VERNACULAR ENGLISH. His commitment to making the results of his research available to serve the community is well documented, notably in his expert testimony in courtrooms and his ongoing research on reading difficulties among dialect speakers.

Labov studied and taught at Columbia University before moving to the University of Pennsylvania to found the sociolinguistics programme. See also QUANTITATIVE; VARIATIONIST.

Lakoff, Robin   Widely recognised as one of the first linguists to analyse GENDER as a powerful, complex and nuanced influence on linguistic form and language as a social practice. Her position as a feminist-sociolinguist pioneer rests against a broader concern with power, discourse and linguistics. Her best-known work is *Language and Woman's Place* (1975), written against the background of the feminist movement of the 1970s in the USA, as an initial exploration of the thesis that gender had a significant impact upon language structure and use. Some of the phenomena analysed in this context have stimulated continuing debate in subsequent work in the field: the use of HEDGES, TAG QUESTIONS, POLITENESS phenomena. Her more recent work has focused on related sites of inequality and power: the courtroom, psychotherapy, race, the media and so forth. Robin Lakoff graduated with a Ph.D. from Harvard in 1967. She was an Assistant Professor of Linguistics at the University of Michigan before moving to Berkeley, where she has been Professor since 1972. See also LANGUAGE AND GENDER; WOMEN'S LANGUAGE.

lames   A term used by African American PEER GROUPS to refer to peripheral group members (reported by Labov, 1972c). It is now used as a general term in the sociolinguistics literature to refer to marginal members of a social group. Chambers (1995) refers to this group as 'outsiders' (see INTERLOPERS, INSIDERS, OUTSIDERS, ASPIRERS).

language
1. Edward Sapir (1921) defined language as 'a purely human and noninstinctive method of communicating ideas, emotions, and desires by means of a system of voluntarily produced symbols. These symbols are, in the first instance, auditory and they are produced by the so-called "organs of speech."' Today we would add signs, not just vocal symbols, to this characterisation on the basis of SIGN LANGUAGES, in which the symbols are visual rather

than auditory. This technical definition of language avoids mention of writing, since it is not a defining criterion: languages can exist without being written down at all. Sociolinguists are most interested in the 'human communication' aspect of the definition, with a stress on COMMUNICATIVE COMPETENCE. Aspects of language use that are frequently idealised or ignored in other branches of LINGUISTICS, like the context, the background of speakers, the interactive nature of language, the purpose of the communication, the variability of speech and the availability of choices are foregrounded in SOCIOLINGUISTICS.

2. Sapir's definition focused on 'language' rather than 'a language'. The latter turns out to be difficult to define objectively, with the popular opposition between 'a language' and 'a DIALECT' particularly misleading. Such an opposition frequently associates 'a language' with a written STANDARD variety or the prestigious spoken form on which such a standard is based. Linguists, on the other hand, consider all dialects of a language to be 'linguistically' equal, and hence conceive of a language as the sum total of its dialects. VARIETY is often used as a neutral term to avoid the lay associations of 'language' and 'dialect'. Where necessary, a distinction is then made between standard and NON-STANDARD varieties. The standard/non-standard distinction is a sociohistorial one, since political and social factors are responsible for the choice of one variety over others as a possible standard form. Even the idea of a language as a sum total of its dialects is not without problems. Whereas 'common sense' dictates that there are clear-cut languages like 'Dutch' and 'English', this applies to their standard spoken and written manifestations. On the ground, at the level of speech, the distinction is less clear-cut, since there is frequently a DIALECT CONTINUUM over a geographical area, rather than clear-cut language boundaries. MUTUAL INTELLIGIBILITY has sometimes been suggested as a way of deciding whether two varieties belong to 'the same language'. Such tests are difficult to put into practice, since mutual intelligibility may depend on speakers' experience, cultural assumptions and willingness to understand. The criterion of mutual intelligibility does not accord with the 'real world' status of languages: Norwegian and Danish have separate statuses as languages but are more or less mutually intelligible. But for political factors relating to nationhood, they could have been considered part of 'the same language'. Frequently, calls for political separation are accompanied by upgrading what may have been considered 'a dialect' into 'a language'.

Hence many sociolinguists critique the notion of 'a language' as a 'given' entity, stressing that languages are partly inherited and partly made and remade by speakers (see Mühlhäusler, 1996).

language academies   Public institutions which are set up to monitor the development of a language and which publish dictionaries, grammars and orthographies as well as guidelines on, for example, educational or institutional language use. The Italian *Academia della Crusca* (founded in 1512) and the French *Académie Française* (founded in 1635) have served as models for later academies. Language academies exist in many countries: for example, in Bangladesh, Spain, Frisia, Sweden, Hungary, Iceland, Israel, Korea and South Africa (where there are two academies, one for Afrikaans and one for English, as well as a Pan South African Language Board). In many cases language academies have followed highly purist language policies and have actively contributed to the 'purification' of the national language from foreign influences. The terms **language council** and **language board** are also found. See PRESCRIPTIVISM; STANDARDISATION; LANGUAGE PLANNING; PURISM.

language acquisition   In studies of language learning, in monolingual, bilingual and multilingual contexts, a distinction is often made between the 'acquisition' and the 'learning' of language. Acquisition emphasises that language is acquired, often unconsciously, through engagement in everyday activity, whereas learning emphasises that language is explicitly, or formally, taught and learned.

Language acquisition is sometimes used to refer to the early acquisition of one language (also referred to as **child language acquisition**) and considerable research has been carried out into the stages in which different lexical and grammatical items are acquired by children. SECOND LANGUAGE ACQUISITION is used to refer to studies which focus on the ways in which people acquire a second (and sometimes also third etc.) language, with significant emphasis on issues of direct interest to pedagogy, such as individual learner behaviours and error analysis.

Much work focusing on the acquisition of language(s) is drawn from within the fields of linguistics and psychology, often referred to as psycholinguistics, and focusing principally on the ways in which children acquire vocabulary and grammar. More socially oriented studies of language acquisition and learning focus on how individuals acquire language through interaction with others, using such concepts as DISCOURSE PRACTICE and COMMUNITY OF PRACTICE (see e.g. work by Eckert, 2000; Maybin, 2003). See also CHILD LANGUAGE.

language alternation   See CODE-SWITCHING.

language amalgamation   The blending together of two language varieties in a language or dialect contact situation. Language amalgamation can be unplanned (see MIXED CODE), however, the term is usually used to refer to the planned or deliberate merging of language varieties (see LANGUAGE PLANNING; STANDARDISATION). For example, standard Shona, which is today one of Zimbabwe's two national languages (the other is Ndebele), was created by the South African linguist Clement Doke in the 1930s on the basis of a comparative analysis and amalgamation of five different Shona dialects.

language and desire   See DESIRE.

language and gender   The relationship between language and gender has long been of interest within SOCIOLINGUISTICS and related disciplines. Early twentieth-century studies in LINGUISTIC ANTHROPOLOGY looked at differences between women's and men's speech across a range of languages, in many cases identifying distinct female and male language forms (although at this point language and gender did not exist as a distinct research area). GENDER has also been a SOCIAL VARIABLE in studies of LANGUAGE VARIATION carried out since the 1960s, a frequent finding in this case being that, among speakers from similar social class backgrounds, women tend to use more standard or prestige language features and men more vernacular language features. There has been an interest, within INTERACTIONAL SOCIOLINGUISTICS, in female and male interactional styles. Some studies have suggested that women tend to use more supportive or co-operative styles and men more competitive styles, leading to male DOMINANCE of mixed-gender talk. Feminist researchers, in particular, have also been interested in SEXISM, or sexist bias, in language.

Studies that focus simply on gender differences have been criticised by feminist researchers for emphasising difference (rather than similarity); seeing male speech as the norm and female speech as deviant; providing inadequate and often stereotypical interpretations of WOMEN'S LANGUAGE; and ignoring differences in POWER between female and male speakers.

More recently (and particularly in studies carried out since the late

1980s and 1990s) gender has been reconceptualised to a significant extent. It is seen as a less 'fixed' and unitary phenomenon than hitherto, with studies emphasising, or at least acknowledging, considerable diversity among female and male speakers, as well as the importance of CONTEXT in determining how people use language. Within this approach, gender is also seen less as an attribute that affects language use and more as something that is performed (or negotiated and perhaps contested) in interactions – see FEMININITY, MASCULINITY, PERFORMATIVITY. For a sense of the field of language and gender, see the studies in Coates (1998); and Holmes and Meyerhoff (2003); for overviews, see Eckert and McConnell-Ginet (2003); Talbot (1998); Romaine (1998). See also SEX; SEXUALITY; on contemporary approaches to IDENTITY, see POSTMODERNISM; POST-STRUCTURALISM; SOCIAL CONSTRUCTIONISM; SUBJECTIVITY.

language and sex   See LANGUAGE AND GENDER; SEX (VS GENDER).

language attitudes   See ATTITUDES; EVALUATION.

language awareness   Refers to educational initiatives which seek to raise students' explicit METALINGUISTIC awareness, or their knowledge of language (see also KNOWLEDGE ABOUT LANGUAGE (KAL)). Programmes are varied, ranging from a focus on the linguistic features of texts, to discussing the POLITICS OF LANGUAGE. Across this range of interests, there is considerable debate about what kind of METALANGUAGE, that is language to talk about language, is most useful to teachers and students. Different claims are made for the value of language awareness: it may be said to (a) improve students' use of language(s); (b) develop understanding about language as a system; (c) challenge stereotypes about language and language users; (d) promote tolerance, equality of opportunity and pluralism (see Hawkins, 1984; James and Garrett, 1991). By and large, these claims are not easy to assess. Language-awareness programmes or teaching activities which seek explicitly to focus on the relationship between language, power and ideology are often referred to as CRITICAL LANGUAGE AWARENESS.

language change   All natural languages are continuously changing on all linguistic levels (pronunciation, grammar, lexis) and patterns of usage in a speech community are constantly in flux. Language change is normally slow and gradual; sometimes, however, it can be relatively sudden and abrupt (mostly in LANGUAGE CONTACT situations: see CREOLE; PIDGINISATION).

William LABOV has shown that it is not only possible to study completed changes, but that attention to variation and social context allows us to describe CHANGE IN PROGRESS. A comprehensive sociolinguistic research programme for the study of language change was formulated by Weinreich et al. (1968), who argued that an adequate explanation of language change should focus on five central aspects of the process (they referred to these aspects as 'problems' which need to be solved or addressed by historical linguists): the origin/beginning of a change (the ACTUATION problem), the specification of possible and impossible changes (the CONSTRAINTS problem), the role played by the social context (the EMBEDDING problem), the attitudes which accompany the change (the EVALUATION problem) and the stages in the transition from language X to language Y (the TRANSITION problem). While much early sociolinguistic work has focused on language change, later studies have also paid attention to the detailed investigation of processes of LANGUAGE MAINTENANCE (e.g. Milroy, 1987a; see also SOCIAL NETWORK). See also CONVERGENCE; DIACHRONIC; DIVERGENCE; SOCIOHISTORICAL LINGUISTICS.

language choice   Refers to speakers' selection between languages, or language varieties in particular CONTEXTS or DOMAINS of use. Much research on language choice has been carried out in bi- or multilingual communities, where languages are associated with different activities. For instance, an INTERNATIONAL LANGUAGE such as English may be used in formal or public interactions in settings such as educational institutions and professional workplaces, and a local language used in less formal interactions or in settings such as the home. Languages are therefore associated with particular settings, activities etc.: the term 'choice' does not imply that speakers have a completely free choice over which language to adopt. See also CODE-SWITCHING; DIGLOSSIA.

language contact   The co-existence of languages in a geographical area or in a speech community. A degree of BILINGUALISM is usually involved, either throughout the speech community or on the part of some individuals. The field of language contact is concerned with macrosociolinguistic issues like LANGUAGE MAINTENANCE and LANGUAGE SHIFT, as well as microsociolinguistic issues like the effects of BORROWING, CODE-SWITCHING, etc. 'Internal change' and 'contact-induced change' are the two ways in which languages develop over time – see also LANGUAGE CHANGE. The linguistic study of language contact is sometimes termed **contact linguistics**.

language correction   Introduced by Neustupny (1983) as a broad cover term to refer to language modification in general. Language correction includes deliberate and conscious government intervention (LANGUAGE PLANNING) as well as a speaker's ordinary clarifications or rephrasing of statements in conversations. In both cases language correction is used to remedy what is perceived as a communication problem.

language crossing   Used by Ben Rampton to refer to a speaker's use of a variety of language associated with a social or language group that the speaker does not normally belong to. In Rampton's research among young people in a British multi-ethnic urban community, 'crossing' would include Panjabi or Creole spoken by a white monolingual speaker (see Rampton, 1995). Rampton relates such forms of language behaviour to BAKHTIN's concept of DOUBLE-VOICING. Crossing may be seen as a particular form of CODE-SWITCHING: one which involves a disjunction between speaker and expected code (see SITUATIONAL, METAPHORICAL (CODE-SWITCHING)). However, Rampton also sees crossing as both shaped by and potentially able to contest broader patterns of race division and hierarchy.

language cultivation   See CULTIVATION.

language death   The process by which a language ceases to be spoken either because its former speakers die out with no surviving offspring or because its former speakers gradually shift to another distinct language, leaving no speakers of the original language. The former is an instance of language death without LANGUAGE SHIFT; the latter involves both death and shift. There are also cases of language shift without death when a community shifts to a new language, but the 'older' language survives in some other territory. In the technical sense ancient languages like Sanskrit and Latin did not undergo language death, even though they are popularly referred to as 'dead languages'. They gradually evolved by continuous transmission from one generation to another and split into regional varieties that were later recognised as independent languages like Hindi, Gujarati,

Bengali, etc (in the case of Sanskrit) and French, Italian, Spanish, etc. (in the case of Latin). Certain languages like Pictish and Etruscan, on the other hand, have undergone language death, with no modern offshoots. There is currently great concern over the ongoing demise of numerous languages like the Native American languages Luseño and Cupeño. See also ENDANGERED LANGUAGES.

language determination   Introduced by Jernudd (1973) to describe that aspect of LANGUAGE PLANNING which is concerned with the allocation of languages or language varieties to specific functions in a given society. Language determination is concerned with matters such as choice of an OFFICIAL LANGUAGE, MEDIUM OF INSTRUCTION, the regulation of language use in courts and administration, the workplace, religious institutions and the media (newspapers, broadcasting and television). Heinz Kloss (1969) referred to this aspect of language planning as status planning (see CORPUS PLANNING, STATUS PLANNING).

language development   May be found with three meanings:
1. to refer to processes of LANGUAGE ACQUISITION;
2. within the field of LANGUAGE PLANNING, as an alternative term for 'corpus planning' (see CORPUS PLANNING, STATUS PLANNING);
3. to describe DIACHRONIC processes of LANGUAGE CHANGE (see DEVELOPMENTAL LINGUISTICS (2)).

language diary   A method for data collection frequently used in research on BILINGUALISM and LANGUAGE CHOICE. Language diaries include self-reports on a speaker's language use. Speakers not only indicate the languages they have used over a given period but also their interlocutors, topics spoken about and the settings in which the languages are used (e.g. Gibbons, 1983). Language diaries are also used in LANGUAGE ACQUISITION studies, where they include regular notes made by parents on children's language development.

language diversity   The co-existence of structurally and sociolinguistically varied linguistic codes (DIALECTS and LANGUAGES) within a SPEECH COMMUNITY, a country or countries or across the world as a whole. Language diversity has often been identified as a problem for national and international communication, and many LANGUAGE PLANNING activities have been directed at combatting this, following an ideology of **linguistic assimilation** (see Cobarrubias, 1983). Linguistic assimilation policies are based on the political principle of 'one nation, one language' and assert the importance of a single language for national as well as international communication and administration. Policies of **linguistic pluralism**, on the other hand, acknowledge language diversity and support the co-existence of different language groups. In some cases assimilatory and pluralist policies have been combined. India, for example, recognises language diversity on the regional level but promotes Hindi and English as official languages for national communication.

Worldwide language diversity is currently under threat, with most smaller languages considered to be ENDANGERED LANGUAGES, used by only a few (mostly older) speakers and no longer transmitted intergenerationally. See also LANGUAGE DEATH; LANGUAGE POLICY; LINGUISTIC RIGHTS.

language documentation   The systematic recording, transcription and translation of spoken (and written) language samples. Comprehensive language documentation is important in the current situation of ENDANGERED LANGUAGES and accelerated LANGUAGE DEATH. Such documentation includes an outline of the sociolinguistic context in which a given language is used as well as audio (and, if possible, video) recordings of a wide range of different language GENRES and DOMAINS of usage. Language documentation differs from traditional linguistic descriptions which have focused almost exclusively on the grammatical and lexical aspects of a language, and paid little attention to patterns of sociolinguistic variation. See also SURVEY.

language ecology   Ecology, in the sense of the sets of relationships surrounding an organism and its environment, has been extended to the study of the interaction between languages and their broader social, linguistic, historical and political environment. (The term **linguistic ecology** is also found.) The metaphor of 'language ecology' was introduced to sociolinguistics by Einar Haugen (1972). According to Haugen, the 'ecological questions' a linguist tries to answer include questions such as: what is the linguistic relationship of a given language to other languages (e.g. in South Africa both Zulu and Xhosa are closely related members of the Nguni LANGUAGE FAMILY and thus show MUTUAL INTELLIGIBILITY)? Who and where are its users? What are its domains of usage? Are its users monolingual or bilingual? Are there language-internal varieties or dialects? Does the language have a written tradition and is it standardised? Is there political and institutional support? What are the attitudes of the speakers towards the varieties of the language? Is the language a symbol of group or national identity? The metaphor of 'language ecology' has also been used by Peter Mühlhäusler (1996), who has, however, criticised Haugen's list for its underlying assumption that there is such as thing as 'a given language' (and that languages can be enumerated). Mühlhäusler emphasises that ecological approaches to language should not be formulated as a list of separate questions but as a holistic enterprise.

language entrepreneurs   See LANGUAGE STRATEGISTS.

language evaluation   See EVALUATION.

language family   A group of languages which emerged through processes of linguistic DIVERGENCE from a single ancestor. English, German, Dutch, Yiddish, Frisian, Afrikaans, etc. are all so-called **daughter languages** of West-Germanic, which in turn is one of the daughter languages of Germanic ('North-Germanic' or 'Scandinavian' is another daughter language of Germanic). Languages which belong to a language family are said to be **related**.

language ideology   In its broadest sense, the term refers to a set of shared ATTITUDES and beliefs about language, underpinned by certain social or cultural values (for examples and discussion see e.g. Blommaert, 1999; Schieffelin et al., 1998). Language ideologies often serve to rationalise existing social structures, relationships and dominant linguistic habits. For example, standard language varieties spoken by higher-status groups may be seen as markers of 'educatedness' and 'refinement', whereas speakers of non-standard varieties are considered 'vulgar' or 'inarticulate'. Language ideologies play a significant role in processes of language STANDARDISATION (see also STANDARD LANGUAGE IDEOLOGY) and also in the formulation of LANGUAGE POLICY. Linguistics itself has been shaped by various ideologies. An example is the set of beliefs about language and identity which has been referred to as 'MOTHER TONGUE fascism' in the context of the historiography of German linguistics (Hutton, 1998). It is argued that activities directed at 'saving' the national language from foreign intrusions and at 'helping' those outside of the country (e.g. Germans in the United States) to maintain their linguistic and cultural identity are based on a mother-tongue ideology, resting on a simplistic idea of cultural identity and ignoring the fact that people often have several 'mother tongues' and linguistic identities. See also FOLK LINGUISTICS; VERBAL HYGIENE.

language-in-education planning   LANGUAGE PLANNING activities which are directed at the formal educational sector (Kaplan and Baldauf, 1997). Overlaps with Robert Cooper's (1989) concept of ACQUISITION PLANNING.

language legislation   Legal provisions which regulate the use of language within a political system (state or province): see LANGUAGE PLANNING.

language levels   See LEVEL (2).

language loyalty   A term coined by Joshua FISHMAN (1966) for the attachment to their home or religious language that causes a minority group to maintain or try to maintain this in the face of competition from other dominant languages. Language loyalty thus denotes the impulse behind LANGUAGE MAINTENANCE efforts. See also ATTITUDES.

language maintenance   Term coined by Joshua FISHMAN (1964) for the preservation of a language or language variety in a context where there is considerable pressure for speakers to shift towards the more prestigious or politically dominant language. Studies of language maintenance often draw on SOCIAL NETWORK analysis to explain patterns of language retention: for instance, Lesley Milroy's work in Belfast (1987a) showed that speakers who were closely integrated into local community networks maintained linguistic forms characteristic of the local dialect more frequently than other speakers. Contrast LANGUAGE SHIFT.

language mixing   See CODE-SWITCHING.

language movement   A single-issue social movement which focuses on questions of language status and use in a society. Frequently language movements concentrate on advocacy for a national language or minority LINGUISTIC RIGHTS (e.g. medium of instruction, access to government services and the media, etc.). Examples of language movements include the ENGLISH ONLY movement in the USA and the PLAIN LANGUAGE MOVEMENT, which is active across the English-speaking world. See also LANGUAGE PLANNING; LANGUAGE SOCIETIES.

language of wider communication   See LINGUA FRANCA.

language planning   An area of APPLIED LINGUISTICS. Language planning refers to deliberate and future-oriented activities aimed at influencing or modifying the language behaviour of a speech community or society. Language-planning activities include the creation of a STANDARD variety, the selection of OFFICIAL LANGUAGES, NATIONAL LANGUAGES or educational languages (see MEDIUM OF INSTRUCTION), the support of MINORITY LANGUAGES; as well as changes to the structure of a given variety (e.g. the promotion of gender-neutral variants such as *chair/chairperson* instead of *chairman*, or the systematic formation of new scientific or technological terms such as German *Rechner* (lit. 'calculator') for English *computer*). A distinction is sometimes made between 'corpus planning' (focusing on language structure) and 'status planning' (concerned with the social position, or status of a language) – see CORPUS PLANNING, STATUS PLANNING.

Language planning can be undertaken by governments and governmental agencies (e.g. ministries of education, a LANGUAGE ACADEMIES), non-governmental interest groups (e.g. LANGUAGE SOCIETIES, the feminist movement – see LANGUAGE MOVEMENT) as well as individuals (e.g. the linguist Ivar Aasen, who wrote the first grammar of Nynorsk, one of Norway's two standard languages). Other terms which occur in the literature and which overlap with language planning are: CULTIVATION; **language management**; **language reform**; LANGUAGE TREATMENT; LINGUISTIC ENGINEERING; STANDARDISATION; VERBAL HYGIENE.

language-planning agencies   Governmental and non-governmental institutions which participate in LANGUAGE PLANNING. These include, for example, government departments of education at national and regional level; language institutes (e.g. the *British Council*, the *Goethe Institut*, the *Alliance Française*) and language academies (see LANGUAGE ACADEMIES); non-governmental organisations (including professional bodies, e.g. the Australian Federation of Modern Language Teachers); broadcasting organisations (sometimes governmental); as well as informally constituted language societies (see LANGUAGE SOCIETY).

language play   Refers to instances when language is manipulated to playful effect: puns, riddles, BACK SLANG and VERBAL DUELLING are all examples of language play. Sociolinguists have been interested not just in the forms language play may take but also in its functions (e.g. how play may be used, in certain contexts to maintain solidarity between participants). It is also argued more broadly that play is pervasive in everyday language, and that it has an important role in human development and human cognition (e.g. Carter, 2004; Cook, 2000; Crystal, 1998).

language policy Sometimes used as a synonym for LANGUAGE PLANNING. However, more often used to refer to the more general linguistic, political and social (implicit and explicit) goals underlying the actual activities of language planners (e.g. Cooper, 1989). Language policies typically reflect general beliefs about and attitudes towards language which exist within a given society (see LANGUAGE IDEOLOGY). A pluralist language policy, for example, is based on the belief that it is worthwhile to support the co-existence of different language groups within a state or society. Its supporters may decide on language-planning measures such as the publication of school books in all the languages spoken in the community, the training of teachers, the provision of translation services, radio and TV programmes in different languages, etc. South Africa, which acknowledges eleven official languages in its constitution, is an example of a country with a pluralist policy. Other countries support policies of assimilation which are based on the belief that a state or society should only have one language and that speakers of other languages should assimilate to the majority language. Policies are formulated not only at national level but also by LANGUAGE MOVEMENTS, pressure groups, institutions such as the church, businesses etc. For instance, the ENGLISH ONLY movement in the USA has an assimilationist policy with respect to minority languages. Not all countries or institutions have explicit language policies; in many cases language policies are implicit, a question of tradition and habit rather than overt and explicit decision making.

language reform See LANGUAGE PLANNING; RENOVATION.

language re-genesis See RE-NATIVISATION.

language revitalisation See RE-NATIVISATION.

language revival See RE-NATIVISATION.

language shift Term coined by Joshua FISHMAN (1964) for the inability of a SPEECH COMMUNITY to maintain its language in the face of competition from a regionally and socially more powerful or numerically stronger language. Sociolinguists have studied the causes of shift (noting the impact of political domination and economic change) and the course of shift (frequently via DOMAINS of use), noting that the home and religion are often the last bastions of survival for beleaguered languages. Gender relations may also play a role (see Gal, 1978). Linguists have also been interested in changes to the structures of languages undergoing shift. Fishman (1991) has outlined a programme of 'reversing language shift' by pinpointing the possible stages of shift and suggesting policies and activities appropriate to counter shift at each stage. See also ENDANGERED LANGUAGE; LANGUAGE DEATH. Contrast LANGUAGE MAINTENANCE.

language societies   Informal groups set up for the promotion of languages and language varieties. Language societies are a familiar aspect of many language histories, in particular in the context of language STANDARDISATION. They not only function as single-issue pressure groups (see LANGUAGE MOVEMENTS) but also often contribute to language CODIFICATION by publishing dictionaries and grammars, by devising orthographies and by promoting the production of literary and popular scientific texts. Examples of language societies include the German *Fruchtbringende Gesellschaft* ('Fruitbearing Society'), which initiated the publication of early German grammars and promoted the use of German as a literary language in the seventeenth century; the *Genootskap van Regte Afrikaners* ('Society of True Afrikaners', founded 1875, dissolved around 1900), which promoted Afrikaans against Dutch and English in South Africa, and which followed a strongly nationalist agenda; the *Cymdeithas yr laith Gymraeg* ('Welsh Language Society', founded in 1962; www.cymdeithas.com), which launches campaigns supporting the use of Welsh.

language spread   A term coined by Robert Cooper (1982) to denote the processes via which the uses or the users of a language increase. Language spread usually occurs under processes of political expansion as a dominant group imposes its language directly or indirectly via the prestige of its speakers, culture and technology on other speech communities. It may also be the outcome of ACQUISITION PLANNING (e.g. the teaching of English as a second language by the British Council across the world), and language promotion (such as the 'Speak Hebrew' campaign in Israel). The field tends to be studied under more specific subfields. See also LANGUAGE DEATH; LANGUAGE SHIFT; LINGUISTIC IMPERIALISM; NEW ENGLISH(ES).

language standard   A term introduced by Joseph (1987) to describe a linguistic variety which (a) is relatively uniform, and (b) functions as a measure (or standard) against which the quality of an individual's speech is evaluated. However, language standards lack the overtly prescriptive norms and codification characteristic of STANDARD varieties. An example of language standards are the so-called **chancery languages** of the Middle Ages, which have been described by language historians for several European countries (including Germany, England, Frisia and Sweden). These were relatively focused written varieties which were used in the government document offices and which were understood across the different regions of the country. However, chancery languages were not codified in grammars or dictionaries. The norms of these varieties were acquired by scribes primarily through exposure to and imitation of model texts rather than the explicit teaching of rules and norms. Language standards exist in most speech communities and are similar to what Le Page and Tabouret-Keller (1985) have described as 'focused' systems (see FOCUSING, DIFFUSION).

language strategists   Individuals who consciously try to influence the patterns of language use in a society by encouraging or discouraging the use of certain linguistic forms, languages or language varieties. The term was introduced by Weinstein (1979). Rubin (1977) uses the term **language entrepreneurs**. See also LANGUAGE PLANNING.

language switching   See CODE-SWITCHING.

language treatment   Sometimes used as a synonym for LANGUAGE PLANNING, i.e. organised and co-ordinated activities of a social group which are directed at solving communication problems (Neustupny, 1983).

language variation   A fundamental characteristic of language. Language variation most often refers to the variable use of forms from a single language but is also found for the use of more than one language in bilingual communities; the latter is also referred to as LANGUAGE DIVERSITY. Sociolinguistic research has shown that variation is not random but structured along linguistic, stylistic and social dimensions. For example, the pronunciation *-in* instead of *-ing* is more common in PROGRESSIVE constructions (such as *she is singing*) than in nouns (such as *morning* or *ceiling*). In an early study of children's language, John Fischer (1958) also found that the *-ing* pronunciation was used more by girls than by boys, more by children from middle-class backgrounds than those from working-class backgrounds, and more in 'formal' than 'informal' contexts. Evidence from more recent sociolinguistic studies supports Fischer's findings, documenting systematic patterns in SOCIAL VARIATION (relationships between language use and factors such as speakers' SOCIAL CLASS, GENDER, AGE, ETHNICITY; aspects of their lifestyles such as the SOCIAL NETWORKS they form part of and their degree of integration within such networks); and STYLISTIC VARIATION (variation across different speaking styles). Research has also documented how LANGUAGE CHANGE spreads within a speech community. The term **sociolinguistic variation** is sometimes used for such patterns of variation. William LABOV's (1966, 1972a) study of the variable use of certain pronunciation features in New York City is a foundational study of sociolinguistic variation. See also Lesley Milroy's (1987a) study of language and SOCIAL NETWORKS; and Penelope Eckert's (2000) more recent ethnographic study of language variation as social practice. See also QUANTITATIVE; VARIATIONIST.

language variety   See VARIETY.

langue, parole   Langue is a term introduced by Ferdinand de Saussure ([1916] 1959) for the language system or CODE, in contrast to **parole**, the act of using the system by an individual. Saussure conceived of 'langue' as an abstract system which speakers deduce on the basis of social interaction. In separating 'langue' from 'parole', Saussure argued that he was separating what is social from what is individual and what is essential from what is ancillary or accidental. If the word *I* referred to *John*, *Mary* or *Jack* in different circumstances (depending on who was uttering the word), this would be a fact of parole. In terms of the abstract system (langue) the 'value' of *I* is that of 'first-person pronoun', contrasting with other pronouns in the language. The langue/parole distinction overlaps with Chomsky's later distinction between 'competence' and PERFORMANCE. However, while langue is characterised as a system and as a social entity, competence is a system that is conceived of as individual, rather than social. See also DIACHRONIC; SAUSSUREAN PARADOX; SYNCHRONIC.

latching   Within conversational TURN-TAKING, an instance where one speaker's turn follows on from a previous speaker's turn with no perceptible gap. This is often represented in TRANSCRIPTION by an ' = ' sign, for example:

A: and so the dog is running like crazy =

B: = yeah you should see him

lateral   A term used in the description and classification of CONSONANTS, relating to their MANNER OF ARTICULATION. Lateral sounds are produced when the airflow is blocked or restricted by the tongue at a particular point in the mouth, but escapes around the sides of the tongue. For instance, in the articulation of /l/ in English, the front of the tongue touches the alveolar ridge, but air escapes at the sides. See also INTERNATIONAL PHONETIC ALPHABET; PHONETICS.

lavender linguistics, language(s)   **Lavender linguistics** is used by William Leap and some other researchers to refer to the study of the language used by lesbian, gay, bisexual, transgendered and queer (LGBTQ) speakers, usually from an insider (i.e. engaged rather than detached) perspective – see e.g. studies in Leap (1995). The term derives from the association of lavender as a colour with lesbian and gay experience (the origins of this use are not known). **Lavender language(s)** is found for language used by LGBTQ speakers/ writers, and which represents LGBTQ lives (the plural emphasises diversity). Leap argues that, as an object of study, this should not be restricted to erotic language but should encompass a wide range of everyday language practices (including conversation, written language, media and literary language). See also LESBIAN AND GAY LANGUAGE; LESBIAN, GAY, BISEXUAL, TRANSGENDERED AND QUEER (LGBTQ) LANGUAGE; QUEER LINGUISTICS; SEXUALITY.

leader (of linguistic change)   See EARLY ADOPTER.

lect   From Greek *lego* 'to speak'. The term is used by linguists (cf. Bailey, 1973) to distinguish and label linguistic varieties, e.g. DIALECT (a regionally or socially distinct variety), **ethnolect** (an ethnically or culturally distinct variety), GENDERLECT (a variety associated with female or male speakers), **sociolect** (a socially distinct variety) or IDIOLECT (the language variety used by an individual speaker).

Furthermore, it underlies the terms BASILECT, mesolect and acrolect, which are used in PIDGIN and CREOLE studies. 'Lect' can also be used as a separate term to refer to a linguistic CODE in general. See also LECTAL SHIFTING; PANLECTAL.

lectal shifting A particular type of style shifting (see STYLISTIC VARIATION), common to the CREOLE CONTINUUM (BASILECT, MESOLECT, ACROLECT) and to analogous varieties in NEW ENGLISH settings like Singapore. Some speakers shift 'up' and 'down' this continuum in response to the formality of the context and the status of their interlocutor. Since basilectal speakers are by definition those who only command the basilect, most speakers accommodate 'downwards' in speaking to them. Thus **lectal shifting** typically occurs between acrolect and mesolect or mesolect and basilect. It differs from other types of style shifting in the greater degree of grammatical adjustments made. See also BACKSLIDING; LECT.

lesbian and gay language Forms of language and language practices associated with lesbian and/or gay speakers and writers. **Gay language** may also be found as a general term (i.e. including language use among both lesbian women and gay men). In practice, however, there are more studies of the language of gay men than lesbian women. While earlier studies exist (e.g. a collection on **Gayspeak** – Chesebro, 1981), interest in this area within sociolinguistics has increased dramatically since the late 1980s and 1990s. This is consistent with broader developments in LANGUAGE AND GENDER research: for example, the acknowledgement of a diverse range of MASCULINITIES and FEMININITIES; and with developing interest in lesbian and gay studies and Queer studies across the social sciences.

Studies of lesbian and gay language have investigated certain language forms, for example the idea of a 'gay voice' – distinctive pronunciations and intonation patterns; and gay ARGOTS or SECRET LANGUAGES (see Paul Baker's (2002) study of the British gay language Polari as an example of the latter). They have also been interested in subtle practices of, for example, identity negotiation that are harder to tie to specific linguistic features (see William Leap's (1996) account of US gay men's English). Studies may focus on specifically (and stereotypically) lesbian/gay language, including overtly erotic language, or include a wider range of language practices (again, see Leap, 1996). There has been debate over the validity of the idea of a distinct lesbian and/or gay language: Don Kulick (2000) points to the danger of circularity if, for instance, whatever gay men do with language is termed 'gay language' (for discussion and counter-argument, see Liz Morrish and William Leap, 2003).

In line with recent preoccupations in language and gender research, lesbian and gay identity is generally seen as something that is performed (emphasised, played down, subverted etc.) through language use in specific contexts, rather than an attribute that affects language use (see PERFORMATIVITY). There is also increasing recognition of and interest in a wider range of sexualities (the term LESBIAN, GAY, BISEXUAL, TRANSGENDERED, QUEER (LGBTQ) language is sometimes preferred as an acknowledgement of this diversity). And there is an acknowledgement of cultural and geographical difference in the identification of lesbian/gay identities and language practices. For examples of studies see Leap (1995); and Livia and Hall (1997). See also discussion in Cameron and Kulick (2003b). See also DESIRE; LAVENDER LINGUISTICS, LANGUAGE(S); QUEER LINGUISTICS; SEXUALITY.

lesbian, gay, bisexual, transgendered, queer (LGBTQ) language
This phrase (usually found in its abbreviated form) is used as a catch-all term for language use associated with a range of non-mainstream or marginalised sexualities. LESBIAN AND GAY LANGUAGE is also commonly found, but LGBTQ is sometimes preferred to emphasise greater diversity in sexual identities. See also LAVENDER LINGUISTICS, LANGUAGE(S); QUEER LINGUISTICS; SEXUALITY.

level
1. Of linguistic description/analysis: in describing and analysing language, linguists conventionally distinguish between different linguistic levels. Precise levels differ in different analytical frameworks, but a common distinction is drawn between the levels of sound (PHONETICS and PHONOLOGY), grammar (SYNTAX and MORPHOLOGY) and meaning (LEXIS and SEMANTICS). Within sociolinguistics this is reflected in research on LANGUAGE VARIATION, where studies tend to focus on one linguistic level, or to distinguish between levels in their analysis.
2. As an aspect of style: 'level' may also refer to different speaking styles, for example in the sense of level of FORMALITY. Certain languages have an elaborate system of **language levels** (the terms **speech levels** and **speech styles** are also found) that allow a range of social and contextual distinctions to be made. Javanese, for instance, has a series of styles running from high or 'refined' to

low or 'coarse'. The higher styles may be used to convey respect – for example, to a high-ranking addressee; but they are also affected by topic (e.g. they are perceived as more impersonal, and not to be used for the expression of strong emotion). High-status speakers are said to have command of a wider range of styles, including more refined levels. The use of language levels is, however, changing in line with broader social and cultural changes and contact with other languages: see Errington (1988). Language levels may be analysed in terms of POLITENESS (see also HONORIFIC).

levelling   See DIALECT LEVELLING.

lexeme   Used by some linguists as an alternative to 'word', in recognition of the fact that there are different word forms that may be seen as part of the same linguistic unit. For instance, the lexeme *play* would include the forms *play, plays, played, playing*. A lexeme may also include more than one word, for example *break down*.

lexical density   Used to refer to the proportion of LEXICAL WORDS (i.e. 'content' words) in any given text. Thus in the clause *The president travelled to Australia* there are three lexical items, *president, travelled, Australia*. *The* and *to* are GRAMMATICAL WORDS. The lexical density of a text is calculated in a number of ways, for example on the basis of the percentage of lexical words per text, or the average number of lexical words per clause. Higher lexical density is associated with written texts, particularly formal or academic texts. M. A. K. HALLIDAY contrasts the lexical density evident in formal written texts, with the **grammatical intricacy** of spoken texts, where there is usually a greater number of clauses (see Halliday, 1989). Lexical density is sometimes used to indicate the level of difficulty of a text: the more lexical items there are in a text, the more difficult a text is presumed to be for the reader to follow.

lexical diffusion   See DIFFUSION.

lexical gap   A perceived gap in the lexicon or vocabulary of a language, usually identified by comparison with other languages or with the representation of related concepts in the same language. For instance, different sets of KINSHIP terms are available in different languages: relationships that are 'lexicalised' or represented in the vocabulary of one language may not be in another. In the English language, feminist researchers in the 1970s noted that there were fewer words to represent women's sexual experience than to represent men's; by contrast there were fewer words for a promiscuous man than for a promiscuous woman. See also LEXICALISATION; SEXISM.

lexical set   A means of enabling comparisons of the VOWELS of different DIALECTs without having to use any particular dialect as a norm. A lexical set is a group of words whose vowels are uniformly pronounced within a given dialect. Thus *bath, brass, ask, dance, sample, calf* form a lexical set whose vowel is uniformly [ɑː] in the south of England and uniformly [æː] in most US dialects of English. The phonetician J. C. Wells specified **standard lexical sets,** each having a keyword intended to be unmistakable, irrespective of the dialect in which it occurs (see Wells, 1982). The above set is thus referred to as 'the BATH vowel'. Wells specified twenty-four such keywords, since modified slightly by Foulkes and Docherty (1999) on the basis of their study of urban British dialects.

lexical word   A word that carries content, for example nouns, adjectives, most adverbs. Such words may also be said to carry **lexical meaning**. Lexical words may be contrasted with GRAMMATICAL WORDs, which have a primarily grammatical function. A similar distinction is sometimes made in terms of **lexical items** vs grammatical items. Other terms (e.g. **content word** vs function word) are found for this distinction.

lexicalisation   The representation of concepts in the LEXICON, or vocabulary, of a language. This is of interest within sociolinguistics because the range of concepts that are **lexicalised** differs between languages and language varieties, and lexicalisation is said to be an indicator of cultural preoccupations and values within a speech community. In his discussion of ANTI-LANGUAGES, M. A. K. HALLIDAY (1978) refers to several aspects of lexicalisation that characterise these varieties. **Relexicalisation** refers to the introduction of new or alternative words, not found in the mainstream language, particularly relating to areas of interest that are central to the users of the anti-language. Such central areas of interest are also prone to **overlexicalisation** – when several words are available to refer to the same or similar concepts. By analogy, **underlexicalisation** refers to a lack of words for certain concepts (in this respect see also LEXICAL GAP). These ideas may be applied to the study of any language or language variety: for example, in English the existence of several pejorative terms for a gay man is an instance of overlexicalisation, and the existence of relatively few terms for women's sexual experiences (but rather more for men's) is an example of underlexicalisation. They may also be applied to the analysis of texts, or to make comparisons between texts in terms of their vocabulary. They have been drawn on particularly in CRITICAL approaches to language study, e.g. CRITICAL LINGUISTICS and CRITICAL DISCOURSE ANALYSIS.

lexicogrammar   Used in SYSTEMIC FUNCTIONAL LINGUISTICS to refer to the micro elements or features of TEXTS such as MORPHEMES, words, phrases (or GROUPS) and CLAUSES. Using one term to refer to all these features contrasts with a distinction commonly made in other systems or models of language, between GRAMMAR (as syntax and morphology) and LEXIS (vocabulary). Halliday argues that lexicogrammar or **wording** is preferable because 'grammar and vocabulary are merely different ends of the same continuum – they are the same phenomenon as seen from opposite perspectives' (Halliday, 1994b: 15).

lexicography   See DICTIONARIES.

lexicon   Used more or less as the equivalent of 'vocabulary': the lexicon of a language contains all the words or LEXEMES in the language. It is possible to talk of the lexicon of a subvariety – for example, ARGOTS are frequently characterised as a particular set of terms, or a lexicon; it is also possible to refer to the lexicon of an individual speaker.

lexifier language   If a new MIXED CODE arises in situations of LANGUAGE CONTACT showing vocabulary from one language and grammar from another, the language supplying the vocabulary is called the 'lexifier language'. PIDGINS and CREOLES are usually classified as varieties of their **lexifiers**, for example Jamaican Creole English or West African Pidgin English, though this classification is called into doubt by studies of their grammar. See also INTERTWINED LANGUAGE.

lexis (lexical)   General term referring to the vocabulary system of a language. Lexis may be seen as a linguistic level of description and analysis. Sociolinguistic research has investigated several phenomena at the **lexical** level. **Lexical variation** refers to variation in language use (social, regional, contextual etc.) at the level of lexis, for example *burn*, *beck* and *brook* or *stream* as alternatives for 'stream' in dialects of British English. See also DIFFUSION; LEXICAL DENSITY; LEXICAL GAP; LEXICALISATION.

184   **liminal (-ity)**

liminal (-ity)   Liminality refers to 'in-betweenness' – to the ambiguous status occupied by speakers/writers, texts or practices which do not fit into obvious categories. The concept was developed by the anthropologist Victor Turner (1969) in relation to the study of RITUAL. For Turner, liminality describes transitional, indeterminate and ambiguous phases which are a characteristic feature of, for example, initiation rituals. For example, before a boy becomes a man he usually goes through an in-between stage, in which he is perceived as being neither boy nor man: 'Liminal entities are neither here nor there, they are betwixt and between the positions assigned and arrayed by law, custom, convention and ceremonial' (Turner, 1969: 95). These ideas have been drawn on by Ben Rampton in his account of LANGUAGE CROSSING. Rampton (1995) argues that crossing is a linguistic practice employed strategically and often playfully by speakers to create moments of symbolic in-betweenness and ambiguity.

lingua franca   Refers to any form of language serving as a means of communication between speakers of different languages. Lingua francas (or **lingue franche**) may be 'natural' languages (e.g. French used between a speaker of Lingala and one of Bambara in Africa), PIDGINS (e.g. Tok Pisin used between speakers of Bolo and Tolai in Papua New Guinea) or an ARTIFICIAL LANGUAGE like Esperanto (at some international academic conferences). The term 'lingua franca', literally 'Frankish language' or 'French', referred originally to a vernacular Romance variety related to Italian and Provençal, spoken along the Mediterranean coast. It became mixed with Arabic, Greek, Spanish and other elements as it was adopted as an AUXILIARY language of the Crusades.

linguicism   Introduced by Tove Skutnabb-Kangas (1986) to describe processes and policies of **linguistic discrimination**. The term was coined in analogy with racism and sexism, and refers to the stigmatisation and (social, economic and political) marginalisation of speakers of NON-STANDARD varieties and MINORITY LANGUAGES. Linguistic discrimination can be open and deliberate (e.g. the former Turkish language policy towards Kurdish, which banned the speaking of Kurdish in public places, government offices and schools), or hidden and implicit (e.g. lack of political and financial support for minority language groups). See also LINGUISTIC RIGHTS.

linguistic anthropology   The study of language and language use from an anthropological perspective, drawing on anthropological methods and procedures. Linguistic anthropology is defined by Alessandro Duranti as 'The study of language as a cultural resource and speaking as a cultural practice' (1997: 2). It concerns itself with the different WAYS OF SPEAKING (or writing) evident in a community and how language, or specific languages, contributes to a range of social and cultural activities (including everyday activities such as greetings, asking for a drink, children's pretend play and more formal activities such as religious ceremonies). The emphasis, then, is on contextualised language PRACTICES rather than (for instance) the social distribution of linguistic features within a community. The term **anthropological linguistics** is also found, and while this may be seen as a branch of linguistics (rather than anthropology) and may orient more towards linguistic concerns (e.g. the documentation of previously undescribed languages) the two terms also overlap and are used to refer to the same traditions and bodies of work. There is also a significant overlap with the interests and approaches of INTERACTIONAL SOCIOLINGUISTICS, ethnographically-oriented sociolinguistics and linguistic ethnography (see ETHNOGRAPHY). See also CULTURE; ETHNOLINGUISTICS; ETHNOPOETICS; ETHNOSEMANTICS.

linguistic area   A geographical area where a number of unrelated or distantly related languages are spoken. As a result of intensive language contact and CONVERGENCE, these languages share a large number of structural properties, and are more similar to one another than to other languages of their LANGUAGE FAMILY. Examples of linguistic areas include: the Balkans (Romance, Slavic, Albanian and Greek languages), the Ethiopian highlands (Cushitic, Omotic and Ethiopic Semitic languages), South Asia (Dravidian, Indo-European and Austro-Asiatic languages) and the Pacific Northwest (Salishan, Wakashan and Chimakuan languages). **Areal linguistics** is concerned with the description and analysis of such linguistic areas. The term *Sprachbund* is also found. See Thomason, 2001 (chapter 5), for further details. See also SOCIOLINGUISTIC AREA.

linguistic assimilation   See LANGUAGE DIVERSITY.

linguistic atlas   Collections of maps which plot the geographical distribution of (a) individual linguistic items (e.g. pronunciation features, grammatical inflections, words), and the location of ISOGLOSSes, or (b) languages in multilingual societies. An example of the former is the atlas produced by the SURVEY OF ENGLISH DIALECTS (Orton et al, 1978) showing the distribution of linguistic features across dialect areas in England. An example of the latter is the *Language Atlas of South Africa*, showing the geographical distribution of the South African languages: i.e. KwaZulu/Natal is mostly Zulu-speaking, the Orange Free State mostly Sotho-speaking and Xhosa is spoken primarily in the Western and Eastern Cape; in the Western Cape and the Orange Free State there are also many speakers of Afrikaans (Grobler et al., 1990). Linguistic atlases have been produced since the late nineteenth century for many countries, areas and also cities (see Baker and Eversley (2000) for maps illustrating the distribution of migrant languages in London). Maps on the global distribution of languages are also provided by the ETHNOLOGUE. See also DIALECTOLOGY.

linguistic culture   Introduced by Harold Schiffman (1996) to refer to the beliefs and values, ATTITUDES, historical experiences, religious or mythological traditions (including myths about the origin of languages), taboos, SHIBBOLETHS, etc. that are associated with a particular language or SPEECH COMMUNITY. Schiffman has argued that a community's linguistic culture functions as an interpretative filter and implicitly influences the formulation of any LANGUAGE POLICY, the specification of LANGUAGE PLANNING measures and the responses of the community to policies and language-planning activities (i.e. the ACCEPTANCE or otherwise of a language policy as well as the maintenance and transmission of language in general). For example, DIGLOSSIA is maintained by a specific set of linguistic beliefs about the antiquity and purity of the 'H' VARIETY. Efforts to change the linguistic form of this variety to make it more similar to the 'L' VARIETY may therefore be resisted by the speech community. However, linguistic cultures are not stable, unchanging entities and a speech community's beliefs and ideas about language can change gradually or rapidly across time. See also CULTURE; FOLK LINGUISTICS; LANGUAGE IDEOLOGY.

linguistic determinism, linguistic relativity   Linguistic determinism is the thesis that the structure of a language determines or limits the world view of its speakers. An early proponent of this thesis was Alexander van Humboldt in the eighteenth century. These ideas were developed independently in the twentieth century by Edward Sapir and Benjamin Lee Whorf, who were struck by the radically different ways in which American Indian languages structured natural phenomena compared to most European languages. This is also known as a theory of **linguistic relativity**, since the phenomena of nature can only be conceptualised relative to one's language, rather than on absolute 'natural' grounds. This is captured in Wittgenstein's dictum 'The limits of my language are the limits of my world.' These ideas have few adherents today, since detailed investigation of languages shows that there are limits to the ways in which languages vary. Hence close translation between structurally very different languages is not impossible. See also SAPIR-WHORF HYPOTHESIS; WHORFIAN.

linguistic discrimination   See LINGUICISM.

linguistic ecology   See LANGUAGE ECOLOGY.

linguistic engineering   Although it sometimes occurs as a synonym for LANGUAGE PLANNING, the term 'linguistic engineering' is used mainly to emphasise the technical aspects of this process, focusing in particular on corpus-planning activities (see CORPUS PLANNING, STATUS PLANNING). From the perspective of linguistic engineering, language is seen as a tool or instrument for communication which can be systematically improved so that it is easier to learn and use, maximally unambiguous and grammatically regular and uniform (see e.g. Ray, 1963; Tauli, 1968). Language attitudes which are unfavourable to such proposed changes are believed to be changeable by promotion and political power. Such technocratic approaches to language planning are no longer current and have been replaced by more sociolinguistically oriented approaches which pay attention to, for example, LANGUAGE IDEOLOGY/ies and LINGUISTIC CULTURES as complex social constructs based on a large number of (sometimes conflicting) beliefs, ATTITUDES, values etc.

linguistic equality   The idea prevalent within linguistics that there are no linguistic grounds for regarding any language VARIETY as inferior to another: all language varieties are regarded as valid systems with their own linguistic conventions, and beliefs in the superiority of one variety over another are based on social rather than linguistic considerations (e.g. preferred varieties tend to be spoken by social elites). This idea has been questioned to some extent within linguistics (e.g. learner varieties and some contact varieties are problematical in this respect) but remains broadly accepted across the discipline. It is consistent with a set of related ideas: an adherence to DESCRIPTIVISM rather than PRESCRIPTIVISM and a belief that the use of NON-STANDARD linguistic features is better dealt with in terms of APPROPRIATENESS than in terms of CORRECTNESS. These ideas frequently underpin linguists' engagement in public debate about language and their participation in the development of policy and practice in areas such as education. In this respect they have faced challenges from a CRITICAL perspective. For instance, it is argued that in educational debates about the teaching and learning of standard English in England, some linguists have focused on a small range of linguistic features said to distinguish 'standard' from 'non–standard' English, rather than considering the more complex range of language practices children need to learn; that in engaging in policy-making (in any context) linguists necessarily have to make evaluative judgements about language; and, more generally, that both linguistic and popular conceptions of language need to be understood and theorised, rather than simply dismissing popular conceptions as 'wrong' (for discussion of these and related issues, see e.g. Cameron, 1995; Swann, 1998; see also LANGUAGE IDEOLOGY; VERBAL HYGIENE).

linguistic geography   A field of linguistics which studies the geographical (or **areal**) distribution of dialects and languages, and creates language and dialect maps (see LINGUISTIC ATLAS). The terms **geolinguistics** and **geographical linguistics** are also used. See also DIALECTOLOGY.

linguistic habitus   Based on the concept of HABITUS developed by Pierre BOURDIEU: 'habitus' refers to a set of dispositions or habits learned during childhood that lead people to act in certain ways. 'Linguistic habitus' refers to dispositions acquired in relation to language: an individual's or a community's conception of a language VARIETY, linguistic NORMS, 'good' and 'bad' language, etc.

linguistic ideology   See LANGUAGE IDEOLOGY.

linguistic imperialism   Refers principally to the dominance of English as an INTERNATIONAL LANGUAGE or GLOBAL LANGUAGE, but may also be applied to other internationally powerful languages. In his account of English linguistic imperialism, Robert Phillipson claimed: 'the [international] dominance of English is asserted and maintained by the establishment and continuous reconstruction of structural and cultural inequalities between English and other languages' (1992: 47).

The argument here is that English linguistic imperialism is associated with other forms of imperialism (e.g. cultural, economic) that systematically assert the dominance of Western 'Europeanised' countries and their cultures.

linguistic insecurity   A result of speakers' negative ATTITUDES to their own speech and their inability to emulate the prestige norms of society. This would include instances when speakers who belong to socially subordinate groups perceive their speech styles as inappropriate for use in formal contexts or for communication with members of high-status social groups. In these situations the PRESTIGE norms of the wider society are usually expected. Speakers who do not have access to the prestige variety may experience 'linguistic insecurity' in such situations and show a tendency towards HYPERCORRECTION. Similarly speakers of highly divergent regional DIALECTs and also CREOLE languages may feel insecure in situations which are dominated by the STANDARD variety (e.g. the education system, political administration, etc.). The term SCHIZOGLOSSIA is also found. The notion of 'linguistic insecurity' implies a negative characterisation of many speakers' attitudes towards their language, but clearly speakers may also value non-standard or local language varieties or have more critical perceptions of socially powerful varieties.

linguistic marketplace   The metaphor of a **linguistic market** is used in sociolinguistics to describe differences in the evaluation and usage of linguistic varieties. The market metaphor links sociolinguistic practices to aspects of social and political power and authority. That is, not all forms of language have the same 'value' in the market since their EVALUATION depends on the power and authority of the groups which use them (see BOURDIEU, 1991). The unification of the market is, however, never complete and in alternative markets different hierarchies and value systems exist. Linguistic variants or varieties which are usually described as commanding covert PRESTIGE can be conceptualised as being exchanged on alternative markets, that is markets in which the law of 'price formation' reflects group solidarity rather than status difference. See also SYMBOLIC POWER.

linguistic minority   See MINORITY LANGUAGE.

linguistic phonetics   See PHONETICS.

linguistic pluralism   See LANGUAGE DIVERSITY.

linguistic relativity　See LINGUISTIC DETERMINISM.

linguistic rights　The idea that people have certain rights in relation to their use of language. Such rights may be the subject of legal provisions which aim to create a standard for the protection of linguistic groups (especially minority groups). Central aspects of linguistic rights include non-discrimination, use of the MOTHER TONGUE in the public domain, and education in and about the mother tongue.

　　Early provisions for linguistic protection can be found in some nineteenth-century trans-national legal documents. Since the end of the Second World War linguistic rights have explicitly been understood as forming part of universal human rights. The United Nations Declaration of Human Rights (1948) guarantees that no one should be discriminated against on the basis of language (article 2.1), and that people have a right to maintain their cultural identity (article 27). This was most recently reaffirmed in the United Nations Declaration of Cultural Diversity (2001), which also emphasises (in the current context of LANGUAGE DEATH) the need to safeguard 'the linguistic heritage of humanity' and to encourage the maintenance of LANGUAGE DIVERSITY (further information can be found on www.unesco.org/most/ – last accessed October 2003).

　　Since the early 1990s, language planners have increasingly focused their attention on the promotion and realisation of linguistic rights (see Varennes, 1996; Skutnabb-Kangas, 2000). However, the concepts of language and cultural identity which seem to underlie these policies and LANGUAGE PLANNING activities have been criticised by some linguists. Blommaert (2001) and Pennycook (2002) have argued that debate about linguistic rights often assumes a 'fixity' of people, languages and places, which is at odds with what we know about language contact, mixed and indigenous varieties and complex multilingual speech communities, where the concept of the mother tongue (which still forms the basis of many of these declarations) is inherently problematical.

linguistic sexism　See SEXISM (IN LANGUAGE).

linguistic variable　A theoretical construct introduced by William LABOV (1966) to describe patterns of LANGUAGE VARIATION. The term **sociolinguistic variable** is also found. A linguistic or sociolinguistic variable is a feature that has two or more identifiable linguistic forms, or realisations (termed VARIANTS). For instance, in some parts of Britain alternative forms are found for the third-person singular (with and without an inflectional marker: *he reads* and *he read*). These function as two variants (*-s* and 'zero') of a linguistic variable (third-person singular verbal inflection). In this case, the variable is grammatical, but variables occur on different linguistic levels: many studies have used phonological variables because of the prevalence of pronunciation features (i.e. the ease with which these may be collected).

While variants differ in form, such differences do not affect their linguistic meaning. However, they differ in their distribution across speaking styles and across social groups (forms like *he reads* would be more common in formal styles, and among middle-class speakers). The analysis of their distribution has provided evidence of systematic SOCIAL VARIATION and STYLISTIC VARIATION within speech communities. The concept of the linguistic variable is also used in DIALECTOLOGY, where alternating forms help to determine dialect boundaries (see ISOGLOSS). For example, in the northern part of Germany dialect speakers say *Appel* ('apple') and in the south *Apfel* – the variable has thus two variants [p] and [pf]. While early dialectological work focused on determining patterns of categorical variation between dialects, Labov argued that variation is rarely categorical but must be described in terms of relative frequencies, i.e. linguistic variation reflects relations of 'more or less'.

In sociolinguistic research linguistic variables constitute what statisticians call **dependent variables**, i.e. the variable about which one wants to find out more and which is influenced by the presence or absence of other factors. These factors (the social attributes of the speakers such as age, gender or social class, contextual or stylistic factors etc.) are termed **independent variables**.

linguistics The study of LANGUAGE, with attention to its structure, acquisition, use and history. Linguists study language as a general phenomenon, a specific endowment of the human species. Noam Chomsky (1957, 1965) set the goals of linguistics as accounting for the child's capacity to acquire the language or languages in common use in the environment. Since, in theory, a child can pick up any language he or she is adequately exposed to (see INPUT), Chomsky argues that languages share a common ('universal') base. Chomsky's research paradigm is dominant in linguistics, and seeks to ascertain what general properties of language exist and what aspects are specific to individual languages. Chomsky's approach is characterised as **generative**, since he aims to formulate a small core of rules or principles that underlie (or 'generate') the sentences possible in a language. It is also 'modular', since it analyses language as composed of distinct but interlocking components: SYNTAX, SEMANTICS, PHONOLOGY and the LEXICON (or vocabulary component). Chomsky's goals involve a necessarily abstract view of language. Other branches of linguistics are less concerned with abstract 'universals'. HISTORICAL LINGUISTICS is generally concerned with the histories of individual languages and language families (see LANGUAGE FAMILY) and with LANGUAGE CHANGE at a less abstract level. Descriptive linguistics remains interested in the structure of individual languages, again at a less abstract level. Language use is stressed in areas such as PRAGMATICS. Whereas Chomsky's research goals require the simplifying assumption of a uniform society where everyone uses language in the same way, SOCIOLINGUISTICS emphasises the shortfalls in this approach (see COMMUNICATIVE COMPETENCE). William LABOV takes the view that there can be no linguistics that is asocial. Generally, sociolinguists have been less concerned with 'essentialising' language and focus on the interrelation between language and social life, rather than focusing narrowly on linguistic structure. See also PERFORMANCE.

linking *r*   'Linking' is a term in PHONOLOGY for the introduction of a sound between other sounds for ease of pronunciation. 'Linking *r*' refers to the use of [r] as such an element. In many dialects of English the *r* in words like *far* is not pronounced; but if the following word begins with a vowel (e.g. *far out*) then *r* appears as a linking element. When *r* occurs in this role with words that have no *r* in the spelling, it is known as **intrusive** *r* – for example, some speakers pronounce *law and order* with an *r* between the first two words, especially in CONNECTED SPEECH. See also POSTVOCALIC /r/; RHOTIC.

linking verb   See COPULA.

literacy (-ies)   Literacy refers to communication which involves the use of written language. However, the meaning of the term literacy, and thus 'illiteracy', is hotly contested, with debates centring on a number of key questions. (a) What does it mean to be literate – does it, for example, mean the ability to read street signs, newspapers, scientific writings? (b) What are people doing as they read and write: are they simply decoding and encoding symbols from/to a page or also learning particular social and cultural PRACTICES? (c) How should literacy be measured? In many international indices the emphasis is on measuring 'basic' or FUNCTIONAL LITERACY levels in order to distinguish between 'literacy' and 'illiteracy' in the population, but controversy surrounds the ways in which different countries do this, making international comparisons problematical. (d) What are the social benefits of literacy? For example, literacy is used as an indicator of economic development and considered a cause of development, but the causal relationship between literacy and economic development is strongly contested. (e) What is the relationship between literacy and cognitive development or ways of reasoning? Claims are variously made that literacy has a particular and universal impact on cognition or reasoning, that different kinds of literacies have different cognitive effects, or that literacy has no significant impact on reasoning – for discussion, see Graff (1987); papers in Street (2001).

Understandings about literacy are shaped by the particular ideological and disciplinary traditions researchers work within: for example, psychologists have tended to focus on individuals' perceptive and cognitive capacities, whereas anthropologists and sociolinguists focus on the social contexts and purposes of literacy.

The plural form **literacies** is in widespread use in NEW LITERACY STUDIES. At one level it is used descriptively to distinguish different types of reading and writing activities in different social DOMAINS, for example academic literacy, everyday literacies, workplace literacy, local literacy, e-literacy. At another level, it indicates a particular theoretical perspective on literacy, sometimes referred to as **ideological** (see NEW LITERACY STUDIES): namely, that literacy is not one universal phenomenon which leads to one unified set of outcomes – cognitive, economic or otherwise – but rather is multiple (hence 'literacies'), and thus varies in nature and consequences.

literacy event   Used to describe an event in which written texts play an important part, for example, reading a letter at the breakfast table, reading a story to a child at bedtime, writing a letter (see Heath, 1983). A focus on literacy events emphasises the importance of CONTEXT in understanding the nature of literacy; compare SPEECH EVENT.

literacy planning   A type of LANGUAGE-IN-EDUCATION PLANNING or ACQUISITION PLANNING which is directed at increasing the number of literate people in a society. See also LANGUAGE PLANNING.

literacy practice(s)   'Literacy practice' or 'literacy as social practice' are phrases widely used by those working within NEW LITERACY STUDIES to emphasise that reading and writing are activities which always take place in specific social and cultural contexts (see also PRACTICE). Whilst there is slippage between meanings, three distinct uses of the term can be identified:

1. To describe the range of observable communication activities in which people engage. Scribner and Cole (1981) were among the first to talk of literacy as social practice in their research on literacy use among the Vai people of North Africa. They identified three literacy practices specific to particular languages and social contexts: literacy in English was associated with school functions; literacy in Arabic with religious practices; literacy in Vai with personal communication.

2. In addition to (1), to describe language and literacy from the perspectives of participants in order to explore the meanings and values they attribute to different communicative activities (see Street, 1993).

3. To refer to socially patterned ways of using language and literacy, for example the analysis of different kinds of literacy activities in which people engage on the basis of social class or gender (see discussions in Barton and Hamilton, 1998).

literacy studies   Used to refer to the wide range of research and theory focusing on LITERACY. A distinction is sometimes made between literacy studies and NEW LITERACY STUDIES, with the former drawing on, broadly speaking, psychological theories and the latter drawing on anthropology and sociolinguistics.

literary language
1. A language which is primarily used for literary purposes. In the history of German, for example, the medieval poets' language (*mittelhochdeutsche Dichtersprache*) was used only for court poetry and knightly epics. In the context of LANGUAGE PLANNING literary development is generally seen as important: it shows that the VERNACULAR language is suitable for the domains of high culture (see KULTURSPRACHE). For example, in the case of Bengali, the national language of Bangladesh and the major language of the Indian state of West Bengal, the writings of the 1913 Nobel prize-winner Rabindranath Tagore contributed much to the general acceptance and prestige of the 'L' language 'Colit Bhasa' (the 'current language', i.e. the general colloquial), which differed

from the traditional, heavily Sanskritised written 'H' language ('Sadhu Bhasa', the 'pedantic language'). See 'H' VARIETY, 'L' VARIETY.

2. Used also in the sense of the style of language used in literature, in which case it is sometimes contrasted with more 'everyday' language. STYLISTICS has often focused on the analysis of literary language. Recently, however, there has been considerable interest in the everyday uses of 'literary' forms and a tendency to question the distinctiveness of 'literature' on formal grounds. See CREATIVITY; LANGUAGE PLAY; POETIC.

loan translation See CALQUE.

loanblend A new vocabulary item in a language made up of a borrowed MORPHEME combined with a native one. For example, the compound noun *muti-man* in South African English is a loanblend meaning 'traditional healer', formed from the borrowed Zulu word *umuthi* 'tree, shrub, herb, traditional medicine' and English *man*. See also BORROWING.

loanword A word that has been introduced into one language from another: see BORROWING.

localisation See GLOBALISATION.

locutionary (act, force) See SPEECH ACT.

long, short (speech sounds) **Long** and **short** refer to the duration of a sound. Many languages distinguish speech sounds in terms of their length. In English certain VOWELS may be termed long or short, for example /iː/ (the vowel in *seat*) is long and /ɪ/ (the vowel in *sit*) is short. In this case, the vowels also differ in quality. In phonetic TRANSCRIPTION the symbol [ː] indicates vowel length.

longitudinal study A study that collects information about an individual or a group of individuals over a period of time. The aim of longitudinal studies is the description of developmental processes or LANGUAGE CHANGE. Contrast CROSS-SECTIONAL STUDY. See also REAL TIME.

low (variety) See 'H' VARIETY, 'L' VARIETY.

low (vowel)   Part of a three-way classification of VOWELS, relating to the height of the tongue during their articulation. Low vowels contrast with HIGH and MID vowels. Vowels are said to be **lowered** when they become articulated in a lower position, for example in one dialect compared to other dialects, a later pronunciation compared to an earlier one, or in one linguistic environment compared to another. For instance, the vowel spelt 'e' in Xhosa is lowered to [ɛ] whenever it occurs before a NASAL sound like [m] or [n]. See also OPEN.

low modality   See MODALITY.

ludic   Refers to the playful use of language: see LANGUAGE PLAY.

macrosociolinguistics   SOCIOLINGUISTICS that studies language in society with a relatively large-scale perspective, concerned with the distribution of languages and their broader functions, rather than a close examination of the details of internal language structure and variation. Macrosociolinguistics covers topics such as LANGUAGE CHOICE, DOMAINS, LANGUAGE PLANNING, educational policy, etc. The term is broadly synonymous with the SOCIOLOGY OF LANGUAGE; contrast MICROSOCIOLINGUISTICS.

maintenance   See LANGUAGE MAINTENANCE.

majority language   In sociolinguistics the language spoken by the majority of the population in a country or geographical area. In sociology a distinction is sometimes made between **numerical majority** and **political majority**. The latter term refers to the most powerful group in society which, however, need not be the numerical majority. Issues of power, authority and dominance can thus interact with the identification of a language as a majority language (Coulmas, 1985). For example, English and Afrikaans were political majority languages in South Africa during the time of apartheid, although they were spoken by a numerical minority of the population. Xhosa, Sotho and Zulu, on the other hand, were numerical majority languages. Contrast MINORITY LANGUAGE.

male generic   See GENERIC MASCULINE.

male-as-norm   A practice highlighted by feminist researchers (see FEMINISM), in which men's behaviour, including language behaviour, represents an unacknowledged norm against which women's behaviour is judged. In sociolinguistic research, this would occur when the results of research on male informants were generalised to a community as a whole; or when WOMEN'S LANGUAGE was seen as deviant (differing from the norm) and therefore in need of specific explanation.

Malinowski, Bronislaw (1884–1942)   An anthropologist who exerted a profound influence on British linguists with his concept of the CONTEXT OF SITUATION, based on his fieldwork in the Trobriand Islands. His three great ethnographies of the islands, *Argonauts*, *Sexual Life* and *Coral Gardens*, established the tradition of intensive fieldwork in anthropology and later in sociolinguistics. He insisted on understanding matters 'from the natives' point of view', particularly emphasising the value of learning and using indigenous languages. 'Context of situation' emphasised that the meaning of words lay in their use. In this regard another term of Malinowski's that has been adopted in linguistics, PHATIC COMMUNION, is significant. This type of language, which includes gossip and pleasantries, makes it clear that language not only communicates ideas, but is a mode of action used to establish personal bonds between people. Malinowski's conception of CONTEXT OF CULTURE emphasised, further, that some meanings can only be understood within a particular cultural framework. Malinowski influenced subsequent generations of linguists via his impact on J. R. FIRTH, the first British Chair of Linguistics. Malinowski was born in Cracow, Poland, gained a Ph.D. in Physics and Mathematics, and held appointments at the Universities of London and, later, Yale.

manipulation   Linguistic manipulation refers to the ways in which people can be manipulated through specific uses of language or DISCOURSES. Fairclough defines linguistic manipulation as an activity which consciously involves hiding one's objectives (see Fairclough, 2001). The ways in which texts, for example newspaper articles, are constructed explicitly and implicitly POSITION readers in particular ways in order to impose or encourage a particular reading (or interpretation) of an event (see SUBJECT POSITION). CRITICAL DISCOURSE ANALYSIS aims to make such constructions

visible. See also CRITICAL LANGUAGE AWARENESS; FALSE CONSCIOUS-
NESS; POINT OF VIEW.

manner of articulation   One of the dimensions commonly used in
the description and classification of speech sounds. 'Manner of
articulation' refers to the way in which a sound is produced. For
instance, the sound [t] in English *tip* is a PLOSIVE, produced when
the air stream is blocked and then released. On the other hand, [s]
in English *sip* is a FRICATIVE, produced when the air stream is
constricted, causing friction. CONSONANT sounds are commonly
classified according to their PLACE OF ARTICULATION, manner of
articulation, and whether or not they are VOICED. See also INTER-
NATIONAL PHONETIC ALPHABET; PHONETICS.

manual alphabet   See FINGERSPELLING.

markedness   In language description a distinction is often made
between **marked** and UNMARKED forms. Unmarked forms constitute the base form and are generally seen as more 'neutral' in
meaning; marked forms typically show the presence of additional
characteristics. For example, *actor* (unmarked), *actress* (marked,
for GENDER).
   With regard to grammar the marked/unmarked distinction is
applied to regular/irregular verbal and nominal forms: regular
forms (e.g. past tense forms such as *talked* and *looked*) are
considered unmarked, whereas irregular forms (*spoke*, *brought*)
are marked. Markedness is a productive heuristic in linguistic
research as it allows for the formulation of clearly defined
hypotheses about e.g. LANGUAGE ACQUISITION and LANGUAGE CHANGE.
In language acquisition the marked member of an opposition is
believed to be acquired later and with more difficulty than the
unmarked member (e.g. language learners first acquire regular
verbs, later they acquire irregular forms). In language change,
marked forms are usually lost earlier and would typically join the
unmarked class (e.g. formerly irregular verbs may be inflected
according to the paradigm of regular verbs – see ANALOGY). The
idea of markedness has also been applied to CODE-SWITCHING in
Carol Myers-Scotton's MARKEDNESS MODEL.

markedness model   A concept introduced by Carol Myers-Scotton
(see e.g. Myers-Scotton, 1993b) to explain speakers' motivations
for CODE-SWITCHING. The model distinguishes code-switching as an

UNMARKED choice – i.e. the selection of a LANGUAGE VARIETY or CODE that would be expected within a certain context; from code-switching as a **marked** choice, often an attempt to signal a shift in relations between participants. A further concept is code-switching as an **exploratory** choice, made when speakers are uncertain about aspects of the social context or other participants and need to negotiate a mutually acceptable code. The model is premised on the belief that language varieties are indexical of social relationships and of the particular rights and obligations that will obtain between participants in an interaction.

marker   A LINGUISTIC VARIABLE that shows variation according to speaking style (STYLISTIC VARIATION) as well as SOCIAL VARIATION. People are generally aware of linguistic markers and respond to them in MATCHED-GUISE tests. Markers are thus consciously perceived carriers of social information, i.e. they 'mark' the social identity of speakers. Markers contrast with INDICATORS (variables of which speakers are unaware) and STEREOTYPES (variables associated with stereotyped perceptions of varieties).

Peter Trudgill (1986) found that markers are subject to ACCOMMODATION, whereas indicators remain stable. Thus, in his interviews in Norwich, England, Trudgill found that he (as interviewer) approximated the speech of his informants with regard to linguistic markers. With regard to his pronunciation of indicators, on the other hand, he maintained his middle-class norm irrespective of the class position of his informants. Trudgill explains this as a result of the greater awareness attached to markers.

marketisation   Term used to refer to the extension of market models and terminology to other spheres of life (Fairclough, 1992a: 6). Examples in English are found in the DISCOURSE of education, where teaching and learning are often reworded as 'delivery', learners as 'clients', courses as 'packages'. See also BORDER CROSSING; CRITICAL DISCOURSE ANALYSIS.

Marxism   A theory founded by Karl Marx that posits conflict as a common and persistent feature of society. The theory stresses the inherent contradiction in human economic systems in which power and wealth are not distributed equally. CRITICAL DISCOURSE ANALYSIS draws extensively on Marxist assumptions about power, in studying the relation between language and IDEOLOGY and the ways in which social differentiation and inequality are 'naturalised'. Some analysts advocate a **Marxist** rather than the widespread functionalist approach (see FUNCTIONALISM) to the study of SOCIAL CLASS and other differences in language (see Rickford, 1986; Bourdieu, 1991).

masculinity (-ies)　Masculinity has been seen, like FEMININITY, as an attribute of speakers that could be reflected in language and perceived by listeners. Both sociolinguistic and social psychological studies, for instance, have identified an association between WORKING CLASS or VERNACULAR speech and masculinity. Other research in LANGUAGE AND GENDER studied differences between female and male speech but in this case, masculinity, as a construct, was rarely examined. Recently there has been an upsurge of interest in language and masculinity (see e.g. studies in Johnson and Meinhof (1997), and Coates' (2003) book-length treatment). Contemporary studies, however, would reject the notion of masculinity as a relatively fixed and undifferentiated social attribute. In line with current models of language and gender, studies are often concerned to problematise masculinity, focusing on the differing forms this may take, and on relations between different **masculinities** (the plural form emphasises diversity). In this connection, see the notion of HEGEMONIC MASCULINITY. Masculinity is seen here as a contextualised PRACTICE rather than a fixed attribute, and speakers are seen to use language as a resource to 'do' or 'perform' certain types of masculinity. See also PERFORMATIVITY.

matched guise　A technique designed to investigate listeners' responses to different languages or language varieties, developed in the late 1950s (e.g. Lambert et al., 1960) and widely used by social psychologists through the 1970s and 1980s (e.g. Giles and Powesland, 1975). The same speaker is recorded reading a passage in different language varieties, or 'guises'. This is presented to listeners as coming from different speakers, and listeners are asked to rate these speakers according to certain dimensions (e.g. how competent, intelligent or friendly they are). The technique provided evidence of the social meanings attributed to language varieties. It has, however, been criticised because of its artificiality. See also EVALUATION.

Matrix Language Frame model　A model proposed by Carol Myers-Scotton (e.g. 1993a) to explain grammatical constraints on CODE-SWITCHING. Myers-Scotton proposed that, within any stretch of intra-sentential code-switching, one language can be seen as the main or **matrix language** into which items from other language varieties are embedded. It is the matrix language that then supplies the grammar for the utterance; the matrix language word order applies, and the matrix language supplies what Myers-Scotton terms 'syntactically relevant morphemes'. These are MORPHEMES that function as **grammatical items** (see GRAMMATI-CAL WORD), and that signal relations between items in a sentence.

maxims of conversation   See CONVERSATIONAL MAXIMS.

Mean Length of Utterance (MLU)   The average number of gram-matical elements (MORPHEMES) per utterance produced by an individual at a particular moment of time. The measure was introduced by Roger Brown in studies of CHILD LANGUAGE, where it is used to chart the increasing length of a child's utterances over time, as an indication of the increasing complexity of sentence structure. It is believed that comparing the linguistic behaviour of children with the same MLU is more accurate than grouping children on the basis of age. Similarly, the MLU is useful in bypassing age and establishing a means of grouping SECOND-LANGUAGE learners. The features used by second-language learners who are at the same level in terms of MLU may then be fruitfully compared.

meaning   The study of meaning is a fundamental concern within linguistics, although it is approached differently within different areas of the discipline. For instance, SEMANTICS is concerned with **linguistic meaning** in a relatively abstract sense – the 'diction-ary' meanings of words; the meaning of sentences; and relations between words (e.g. the relation of 'opposition' that exists between words such as *good* and *bad*). PRAGMATICS, on the other hand, is concerned with the meaning of UTTERANCES: how words are used, and what speakers mean by them in specific contexts. Pragmatics needs to take account of speakers' world knowledge, or 'general reasoning', in addition to their linguistic knowledge to study such aspects of meaning. Many areas of sociolinguistics (e.g. INTER-ACTIONAL SOCIOLINGUISTICS, ETHNOGRAPHY of communication, var-ious forms of DISCOURSE analysis) are also concerned with meaning in this latter contextualised sense. Sociolinguists have also studied the social meanings attributed to different languages and language varieties, accents etc. (see EVALUATION). Meaning is sometimes used, like function, in contrast to 'form', for example when studies are said to focus on the meanings of utterances rather than just their linguistic form (see FORM (VS FUNCTION)).

medium

1. A language used for communication in particular contexts: for example, 'English-medium education', meaning education through the language of English. In this sense see MEDIUM OF INSTRUCTION; MEDIUM FOR INTERETHNIC COMMUNICATION.
2. A means for communicating via language: media in this sense would include speech, signing and writing. Medium in this sense is similar to the term MODE.
3. More generally (and loosely) a means of communication that would include verbal language but also NON-VERBAL COMMUNICATION, pictures and other visual signs, etc.

medium for interethnic communication (MIC)

Term used by Philip Baker (1994) to characterise the manner in which PIDGINS and CREOLES are formed. Most theories assume that during the formation of pidgins and Creoles the linguistic outcome was not what the participants wanted – that these languages reflect a failure to acquire a TARGET language (usually the dominant European language in slave-holding, or other forced-migration, situations). Baker, however, argued that participants in such contact situations were motivated by the desire to solve the problem of interethnic communication, since slaves frequently were drawn from different areas and lacked a common language. They set about creating a means of communication (i.e. a new language that was not 'targeted' at the dominant European language) and succeeded in that endeavour. The new medium could be subsequently altered by changing circumstances – for example access to the dominant European language and motivation to acquire it. Baker's account, which does not draw a sharp distinction between 'pidgin' and 'Creole', is a major influence on current research (see GRADUALISM). See also BIOPROGRAMME; CREATIONISM.

medium of instruction (MoI)

A language variety which is used in educational settings for purposes of teaching and learning. In some MULTILINGUAL countries several languages are used in the school system. In Luxemburg, for example, Luxemburgish is used at kindergarten, German is the MoI at primary schools while French (which is taught as a second language at primary school level) is the MoI in secondary schools. In Bangladesh, the national language Bengali was used in the 1960s up to university level in the humanities but only up to higher secondary-school level in the natural sciences. Today English is increasingly used as the MoI in Bangladesh's higher education system. See also LANGUAGE PLANNING; THREE-LANGUAGE FORMULA.

membership categorisation (device, analysis) Drawn on by some analysts to explore how inferences may be made about social categories represented in conversation. The notion of membership categorisation (or sometimes just **categorisation**) derives from early work carried out by the sociologist Harvey Sacks. Sacks used the following example of a story told by a young child to illustrate membership categorisation:

The baby cried. The mommy picked it up.

Most people would interpret *the mommy* as the mother of the baby who was crying. To explain this, Sacks suggested that *baby* and *mommy* were **categories** that formed part of the same **membership categorisation device** (a collection of categories that go together – in this case, the family). This device allows hearers to relate the baby to the mommy. Categories are also linked to certain activities which affect hearers' interpretations, for example in this case we would expect a mother to soothe her crying baby. (For the full discussion and analysis, see Sacks, 1972.) **Membership categorisation analysis** involves an appeal to analysts' cultural knowledge. It was not pursued in Sacks' later work and is not widely accepted within CONVERSATION ANALYSIS. For an introduction to this form of analysis, see Lepper (2000). For examples of studies in conversational analysis that take a range of approaches to identity categories in talk, see Antaki and Widdicombe (1998).

merger The loss of a previous linguistic contrast. An example of a phonological merger would be the vowel sounds in words such as *meat* and *meet* in English (pronounced respectively [ɛː] and [eː] in Middle English, both now pronounced [iː]). These changes result from the GREAT VOWEL SHIFT. In the context of morphology the loss of a previous grammatical contrast is often termed **syncretism**. An example of this is the loss of the accusative/dative distinction in the Modern English pronoun system, where there now exists only one object case, e.g. English *him* (accusative and dative) vs German *ihn* (accusative) and *ihm* (dative). See NEAR-MERGER.

mesolang   See BASILANG, MESOLANG, ACROLANG.

mesolect   See BASILECT, MESOLECT, ACROLECT.

metadiscourse   Refers to those features of a TEXT which help the listener or reader follow or make sense of it. For this reason metadiscourse is sometimes referred to as 'signposting' in teaching contexts. Examples include connectives or link words such as *first*, *second*, and conjunctions such as *however*, *nevertheless*.

metafunctions   In SYSTEMIC FUNCTIONAL LINGUISTICS language is understood as being organised along three fundamental dimensions or metafunctions, referred to as the IDEATIONAL (what is happening, what is being discussed); the INTERPERSONAL (the relationship between participants); and the TEXTUAL (the organisation of language into meaningful texts). All uses of language involve these three metafunctions. These metafunctions of language as a system correspond to three contextual aspects of language and communication, respectively FIELD, TENOR and MODE (see also REGISTER).
   The three metafunctions are sometimes referred to by different sets of terms. For example, Iedema in analysing film language refers to **representation, orientation** and **organisation** (Iedema, 2001, after Lemke, 1989).

metalanguage   Refers to language about language, that is language used to describe aspects of language itself. Metalanguage can be of various types. One example of a fully developed metalanguage from within linguistics is SYSTEMIC FUNCTIONAL LINGUISTICS. Most of the entries in this dictionary are examples of different kinds of metalanguage. See also KNOWLEDGE ABOUT LANGUAGE; LANGUAGE AWARENESS.

metalinguistic   Found in phrases such as **metalinguistic awareness, metalinguistic knowledge, metalinguistic skills** etc. to refer to speakers'/writers' ability to think about language. It is thus similar to LANGUAGE AWARENESS or KNOWLEDGE ABOUT LANGUAGE, except that the latter tend to refer to knowledge that is taught (i.e. made explicit) in schools; this is not necessarily implied in expressions such as metalinguistic awareness.

metaphorical (code-switching) See SITUATIONAL, METAPHORICAL (CODE-SWITCHING).

microsociolinguistics SOCIOLINGUISTICS that studies language in society with attention to details of the internal structure of language, variation within a language and how language is used strategically in interaction and negotiations between individuals; contrast MACROSOCIOLINGUISTICS. Many sociolinguists consider the study of LANGUAGE VARIATION to be the central part of micro-sociolinguistics. However, fine-grained studies of topics such as CONVERSATION ANALYSIS, CODE-SWITCHING, LANGUAGE CONTACT, etc., also have a 'micro' focus, though this label is seldom applied to them. There are many instances in which both micro- and macrosociolinguistics seem to be two sides of the same coin, and several topics like LANGUAGE SHIFT, BILINGUALISM, ACTS OF IDENTITY, and code-switching have been informed by both approaches.

mid (vowel) Part of a three-way classification of VOWELS, relating to the height of the tongue during their articulation. Mid vowels contrast with HIGH and LOW vowels. See also OPEN and CLOSE.

middle class The SOCIAL CLASS in the middle of the social hierarchy. Members of the middles class typically work in 'white-collar' professions, i.e. they work in banks, insurance companies, universities, schools, government offices, etc. They are distinguished from the WORKING CLASS (whose members work in 'blue-collar' professions) and the **upper class**. Many sociolinguistic studies have discussed differences between middle-class and working-class speakers. Studies of the language use of the upper class are rare (see Kroch (1996) for an example of such a study). Some sociolinguistic studies further distinguish between **upper middle class** and **lower middle class**.

migration The movement of individuals or groups of people from one area to another. Migration can occur trans-nationally (i.e. across national borders) as well as nationally (within a national border, e.g. urbanisation). Migration affects the distribution of languages and the history of linguistic groups. It can interact with political expansion and can support LANGUAGE SPREAD (e.g. the settlement of Celtic-speaking areas of the British Isles by speakers of English in the Middle Ages). Migration can also lead to the development of discontinuous speech communities and the formation of SPEECH ISLANDS (e.g. German settlements in Russia and the Americas, or the Indian community in South Africa). Horvath (1985) has shown for Sydney how non-English-speaking migrant communities (Italians, Greeks) are gradually incorporated into the host speech community. See LANGUAGE MAINTENANCE; LANGUAGE SHIFT; NEW DIALECT; NEW ENGLISH(ES).

minimal pair   A pair of words which have different meanings but which are distinguished only by one sound, for example *cat – mat*. Minimal pairs are used to establish the PHONEME inventory of a language.

minimal response   Minimal responses are expressions such as *mmh* or *yeah* which are used by listeners in conversation. While usually associated with coversational support, they have a variety of functions: for example, to signal attention, agreement or sometimes an upcoming bid for the next speaking turn. They are of interest as an aspect of CONVERSATION MANAGEMENT, and also because some studies have found they are used differently, or to different effect, by different speakers (e.g. by female and male speakers). See also BACK CHANNEL.

minority language   A language which is spoken by a numerical minority (or by a politically subordinate group): the language group is referred to as a **linguistic minority**. A minority language is sometimes also referred to as a **community language**, **ethnic language** or HERITAGE LANGUAGE. Linguistic minorities are found in most countries. Sometimes a distinction is made between **native minorities** or **indigenous minorities** (e.g. the Aboriginal communities in Australia), and **immigrant minorities** (the Greek, Italian, Ukranian, Vietnamese, Chinese minorities in Australian cities and towns). Contrast MAJORITY LANGUAGE.

miscommunication   Used particularly within studies of INTERCULTURAL COMMUNICATION and INTERETHNIC COMMUNICATION to refer to misunderstandings between speakers resulting from differences in language background or communication styles.

missionaries Missionaries of all regions have inevitably had to confront linguistic barriers and have sought ways to deal with them. In the era of European colonisation of Asia, Africa, Australia and the Americas, missionaries were often the first outsiders to make prolonged contact with indigenous groups of people. Missionaries have therefore been closely associated with linguistic description and applied linguistic activities like compiling word lists, making dictionaries, translation, developing orthographies and developing teaching methods. In some instances (as in Southern Africa), they were involved consciously or unwittingly in the process of standardising languages (see STANDARDISATION), where previously a DIALECT CONTINUUM was in existence. Today, missionaries have kept up with and contributed to sociolinguistic approaches to language description, including perspectives from the SOCIOLOGY OF LANGUAGE, LINGUISTIC ANTHROPOLOGY and MICRO-SOCIOLINGUISTICS. Their position in relation to ENDANGERED LANGUAGES is, however, an ambiguous one. Critics charge missionaries with being agents of language and cultural change that leads to language loss (see Headland, 1996). Missionaries see the encroachment of ideas from the Western world as inevitable and see themselves as supporters of VERNACULAR languages, helping them to face competition from DOMINANT languages with tools like literacy. See also SUMMER INSTITUTE OF LINGUISTICS.

mitigation (mitigate(d)) Mitigation involves reducing the force of an utterance as an expression of courtesy or deference, or so as not to give offence. For instance, a DIRECTIVE may be more, or less **mitigated**: 'I wonder if you'd mind closing the door,' vs 'Close the door.' The latter example may also be referred to as **unmitigated**. Mitigation may involve a range of linguistic and other strategies, for example the use of certain syntactic structures, intonation, voice quality. Mitigation is a component of POLITENESS – it demonstrates a concern with the listener's FACE. Contrast AGGRAVATION.

mixed code A new language variety arising out of intimate BILINGUALISM, in which frequent CODE-SWITCHING and mixing have become the norm, rather than optional strategies dependent upon style, intention and interlocutor. The terms **(bilingual) mixed language** or sometimes **syncretic language** may also be found for this phenomenon. The new variety is an amalgam that often draws upon each pre-existing language for different spheres of vocabulary and different facets of grammar. A subset of such mixed codes draws upon one language for vocabulary and another for grammar: these are sometimes called INTERTWINED LANGUAGES. There is not a hard and fast line between CODE-SWITCHING and the development of a mixed code: Peter Auer (1998: 16ff.) charts a possible continuum between the two.

mixed lect, dialect   See BORDER DIALECT.

mixing   See CODE-SWITCHING.

mock language   Use of another language or dialect in an exaggerated or distorted way by speakers of a DOMINANT variety with the intent of stereotyping and parodying speakers of the dominated variety. Jane Hill (1993) used the term 'mock Spanish' for the APPROPRIATION of presumed linguistic features of Spanish by English speakers in the south-west USA in casual speech. Hill provides the example *Hasta la vista, baby*, which parodies and devalues the Spanish formal phrase *hasta la vista*, which signals a sincere hope for the pleasure of a future meeting. The juxtaposition with the slang term *baby* renders the original colloquial and vulgar, as does the exaggerated intonation in which the phrase would be rendered. Another example is 'mock Ebonics', used by Ronkin and Karn (1999) to describe the vast number of materials on the internet that parody EBONICS, or AFRICAN AMERICAN VERNACULAR ENGLISH. The authors suggest that the parody is used to articulate an anti-Ebonics LANGUAGE IDEOLOGY and to stereotype its speakers. See also STEREOTYPE; VARIETY IMITATION.

modal (-ity)   **Modality** refers to the ways in which speakers and writers express attitudes to, beliefs about and degress of certainty about what they are saying or writing. In its broadest interpretation, modality encompasses many if not all aspects of a TEXT. In English, it is most frequently identified in relation to a subclass of auxiliary verbs, termed **modal verbs,** or **modal auxiliaries,** as in 'she *will/may/can/ought to/should* come'. Modal verbs have special properties, for example the absence of inflections such as *-s* or *-ing*. Other modal elements in English include 'modal adverbs', as in 'she will *certainly/probably/definitely* come'.

Modality is also sometimes described as high or low. A statement claiming certainty is said to have **high modality**, such as 'I got the job', as compared with 'I may have got the job', where there is **low modality**. High modality is a common feature in particular kinds of texts, such as newspapers, where truth is presented as clear and categorical as in for example, 'Maggie plans the invasion' (Fairclough, 2001; see also discussions in Fowler, 1991). See also MOOD; TENSE–MODALITY–ASPECT.

mode Term used in SYSTEMIC FUNCTIONAL LINGUISTICS to refer to what may be more generally known as the MEDIUM (2) or CHANNEL of communication, such as the spoken or written mode. Mode is one of the three aspects of REGISTER, the others being FIELD and TENOR.

More recently emphasis has also been placed on non-verbal modes of communication, such as visual images and sound (e.g. music) in addition to written or spoken language, and the ways in which different modes combine to represent meaning in particular texts (see MULTIMODALITY).

modernisation Used as a synonym for language ELABORATION. Ferguson (1968) defined modernisation as the development of **inter-translatability** with internationally established, mature STANDARD languages in everyday, political, cultural, educational as well as, in particular, technical/scientific domains.

modernism Refers to a broad artistic and literary movement in Europe and the USA at the end of the nineteenth century. A key dimension to the movement was to self-consciously focus on the SEMIOTIC modes used in different contexts, such as language, art, dress, architecture. Modernism involved a shift away from treating such modes as transparent, that is as representing reality or reflecting real life, towards focusing on them as representations in their own right (see discussions in Smith, 1998; Childs, 2000). POSTMODERNISM is seen as a continuation of these ideas.

modernity Term used by social scientists to refer to a period in history characterised by industrialisation and the rise in importance of the nation state. There are debates around the actual historic period which constitutes modernity, with some sociologists characterising the fourteenth to eighteenth centuries as the modern period, and others pointing to the late eighteenth and nineteenth centuries. Modernity is often contrasted in a number of ways with the subsequent historic period, referred to variously as **late, post** or **high modernity**. The contrasts include a shift from stable to more fluid social structures; changes in the means of production from large-scale industrial production to increasing numbers of small specialist companies; a shift from highly centralised governments providing all key services to independent, often privately run organisations. A key characteristic of late modernity is GLOBALISATION (see Giddens, 1990, 1991).

The importance of DISCOURSE in the period of late modernity and the ways in which discourse shapes the individual, her identity and social relations at this historical moment is a focus in some areas of language study, in particular CRITICAL DISCOURSE ANALYSIS (see Chouliaraki and Fairclough, 1999).

monitored speech
1. Speech during which an individual pays ATTENTION to the act of speaking. Also known as FORMAL or CAREFUL style. Contrasts with VERNACULAR speech in which the individual speaks freely, without attention to PRESCRIPTIVE or other norms.
2. In SECOND LANGUAGE acquisition studies, careful speech during which a language learner consciously tries to apply rules of the TARGET language that he or she has been taught or has learnt. Stephen Krashen (1987) hypothesised that LANGUAGE ACQUISITION (as opposed to 'language learning') takes place in the absence of such monitoring. Acquisition occurs when rules are processed and internalised unconsciously.

monogenesis   A theory in PIDGIN and CREOLE studies that attributes all European-based pidgins (and, ultimately, Creoles) to the same source – a pidgin form of Portuguese that developed out of Sabir, a Portuguese form of the LINGUA FRANCA of the medieval Crusades. The theory holds that, as the Portuguese were often the first Europeans to set up trade in various parts of the world, a Portuguese-based pidgin developed in those coastal areas, which was modified by subsequent European traders and colonists. The structure of the original pidgin was not radically changed, but its vocabulary was replaced by items from subsequent languages like Spanish, Dutch, French or English (see RELEXIFICATION). This theory is no longer widely supported; its opponents believe that PIDGINISATION could well have occurred independently in different times and places.

monolingual (-ism) The fact of speaking only one language: the term **monolinguality** may also be found. Individuals, communities or entire states may be characterised as monolingual (contrast BILINGUAL; MULTILINGUAL). This may suggest a degree of homogeneity that does not exist in practice. Even in communities where only one language is available, speakers need to understand and make choices between different varieties of language, WAYS OF SPEAKING etc. Monolingualism at both individual and state level is sometimes taken as a norm (e.g. in LANGUAGE POLICY and LANGUAGE PLANNING). This has been referred to as a **monolingual habitus** (an example of LINGUISTIC HABITUS). It has been discussed in relation to the development of nation states in Europe, where states were associated with a particular NATIONAL LANGUAGE. The monolingual habitus leads to a failure to take account of language diversity in education and other institutional contexts; see discussion and further sources in Gogolin (2001). See also HABITUS.

monologic (monologism) Used by BAKHTIN to refer to approaches to language which stand in stark contrast with his DIALOGIC approach. Monologic approaches (or **monologism**) emphasise unity and authority in actual and ideal language use and focus on language as a discrete system, often in an idealised way. Dialogism, in contrast, emphasises diversity and POLYPHONY, which Bakhtin sees as both a description of actual language use and an ideal to be struggled for. See also HETEROGLOSSIA.

monophthong See VOWEL.

mood A category used to classify the form of a verb and consequently the sentence that contains it in terms of the speaker's attitude to, or beliefs about, the action expressed. These attitudes involve 'certainty', 'wish' (or 'desire for the action'), 'possibility', etc. Mood may be expressed in various ways: by an inflection in languages like Latin, by an auxiliary verb in English, by a prefix in Zulu. **Subjunctive mood** usually denotes a hypothetical state of affairs; **optative mood** a desire ('will' or 'wish'); **imperative mood** designates a command; **indicative mood** is the UNMARKED or neutral form, typically denoting a statement or DECLARATIVE sentence. MODALITY is a general and abstract term more or less synonymous with 'mood' – see also TENSE–MODALITY–ASPECT.

moral panic   Term used by the cultural historian S. Cohen (1987) for the manner in which a social phenomenon or problem is suddenly foregrounded and exaggerated in public discussion. This is frequently done in an alarmist and moralistic manner disproportionate to the problem, with warnings of impending catastrophe over issues like immigration, rock music, pornography, prostitution etc. Deborah Cameron (1995) applies the concept to the way language is treated in some societies. For example, in Britain in the 1980s and early 1990s there was considerable debate about the state of grammar teaching in schools, with allegations that the neglect (or perceived neglect) of formal grammar teaching was leading to illiteracy, indiscipline and even moral decay. Liberal educational policies, drawing in part upon linguistic and sociolinguistic research, were held to blame. Cameron argues that this controversy fulfilled the criteria for 'moral panic' in that (a) there was the initial 'discovery' of a problem; (b) there was a prompt identification of scapegoats; (c) uncovering and reporting more instances of the problem fostered a sense of crisis; and (d) there was a shift towards more and more authoritarian attempts at solutions. Cameron holds that the controversy did not have a single cause and was certainly not about grammar alone. Rather, grammar was used as a symbol of SOCIAL CLASS and the debates were ultimately political in nature, with language being used to uphold conservative rather than liberal or progressive values and policies, not just in education but in the society at large. See also PRESCRIPTIVISM; PURISM; VERBAL HYGIENE.

morpheme   Considered to be the minimal unit of grammatical analysis. 'Morpheme' is a concept drawn on in the study of word structure, or MORPHOLOGY. The word *dogs* consists of two morphemes, *dog* + *-s*. The morpheme *-s* is an inflection, denoting plurality. It is possible to break up other words in a similar way: for example, *played* also consists of two morphemes, *play* + *-ed*, a past tense marker. These morphemes are of different types: forms such as *dog* and *play*, which can occur on their own, are termed 'free morphemes'. Forms such as *-s*, and *-ed*, which cannot occur on their own, are termed 'bound morphemes'. Morpheme is an abstract category, and morphemes may be realised differently. The plural morpheme in English may be realised as *-s* (as in *dogs*) but other forms are possible: for example, [əz] (phonetically) in *houses*; zero in *sheep*. The realisation of morphemes may differ in different language varieties and this may be studied as an aspect of morphological variation (see MORPHOLOGY).

morphology Refers to word structure and its study. Morphology is an aspect of GRAMMAR, along with SYNTAX, or sentence structure. The main unit of analysis in morphology is the MORPHEME. Sociolinguists have studied several aspects of **morphological variation**, including verb inflections in different varieties of English (e.g. the incidence of forms such as *she love* as opposed to standard English *she loves*); and COPULA contraction and deletion in varieties such as AFRICAN AMERICAN VERNACULAR ENGLISH.

mother tongue Together with NATIVE language, **home language, primary language** and FIRST LANGUAGE or L1, a set of overlapping terms for the language used by an individual from birth, the usual language of the home and community. In the simplest case, of an individual who is part of a family and community with stable MONOLINGUAL norms, the terms designate the same entity: the individual's native language ('language spoken from birth') is the mother tongue ('native language usually transmitted by parents') and home language ('language of the home'), which is spoken as a first language and is the **primary language** ('the most commonly-used language').

However, according to circumstances, especially in a BILINGUAL or MULTILINGUAL community or a community undergoing LANGUAGE SHIFT to a new language, the terms may signal important differences and be somewhat ambiguous, and used differently by different writers. Thus, in certain communities, the 'mother tongue' of a child might not be the same as that of parents. In the same situation the notion of 'home language' would also be ambiguous: is it the traditional language used by elders or the new native language of the children, or both? One of those home languages might not be a native language for some family members. Whereas 'first language' or 'L1' usually denotes a language acquired first, or a native language, there are situations in which a child might have shifted from language A to language B at an early age and stopped speaking A altogether, i.e. its L1 would have changed. Some applied linguists therefore prefer to reserve 'L1' (L2, L3, etc.) for a chronological sense, with 'primary language' reserved for the extent to which a language is used. In the example above, language A would be the (chronological) L1 for the child, but language B would be its primary language from a certain age.

motherese   See CHILD-DIRECTED SPEECH.

mother-in-law vocabulary, style   See AVOIDANCE.

move   A functional unit of analysis in some forms of DISCOURSE ANA-
LYSIS; the specific meaning varies within different analytical frameworks. For instance:
1. Within the system of discourse analysis devised by John Sinclair
   and Malcolm Coulthard (e.g. 1975), moves are constituents in an
   EXCHANGE between speakers. In classroom interaction, an exchange
   designed to elicit information from pupils typically consists of
   three moves, an initiation from the teacher, a response from one or
   more pupils and feedback from the teacher (see INITIATION–
   RESPONSE–FEEDBACK). A move may perform one or more ACTS:
   for instance an initiating move such as 'Can you tell us a bit more
   about that, Anna?' both elicits information and nominates a
   particular pupil to provide this.
2. Move analysis has also been carried out on written texts, notably
   introductions to academic research articles, where the different
   moves writers make in constructing an argument in relation to
   their specific field of enquiry have been identified (see Swales
   1981, 1990). Each move can be broken down into **steps**. For
   example move 1 in introductions to research articles may be to
   'establish a territory'. This can be broken down into several
   optional steps, such as 'claim centrality' and/or 'make topic
   generalisation' and/or 'review items of previous research' (Swales,
   1990).

multidimensional scaling   A statistical technique which allows
researchers to represent similarities and dissimilarities between,
for example, speakers or languages in a two- or three-dimensional
space. The closer speakers or languages are located to each other in
the diagram, the more similar they are to each other. See also
CLUSTER ANALYSIS.

multilingual (-ism)
1. In much linguistic writing, multilingualism is a synonym for
   BILINGUALISM, the use of two or more languages by an individual
   or by a SPEECH COMMUNITY.
2. More recently, sociolinguists believe that it is important to keep
   the two terms apart, reserving 'bilingualism' for the use of two
   languages and 'multilingualism' for the use of more than two

languages. The *Journal of Multilingualism*, for example, solicits research papers from 'multilingual', not 'bilingual', contexts. Likewise, in South Africa it seems significant to differentiate the policy of the previous constitution, which promulgated two official languages, from the new constitution's multilingual policy, recognising eleven official languages.

multiliteracies   Term associated with a group of academics known as the New London Group (2000) and used in three ways. (a) To refer to the diverse contexts in which people live and the existence of correspondingly multiple language and literacy practices. (b) To refer to the increasing range of what are known as semiotic or RE-PRESENTATIONAL RESOURCES being used other than just the verbal, particularly in new technologies such as e-mails, web pages, computer games. (c) To raise questions about the kinds of languages and literacies that should be taught in schools. Four elements are considered essential for a meaningful educational literacy programme: **situated practice** – that is, students being immersed in a range of literacy practices; **overt instruction** – that is, students being taught explicit and systematic ways of analysing texts; **critical framing** – that is, students critically examining the texts they are reading/writing/designing; **transformed practice** – that is, students developing new ways of designing or constructing meaning. The critical framing stage closely parallels approaches advocated in CRITICAL LANGUAGE AWARENESS. See also DESIGN.

multimodal (-ity)   Term particularly associated with the work of Gunther Kress and Theo Van Leeuwen (2001) and their emphasis on the multimodal nature of all communication. In contrast to much work in Western applied linguistics and sociolinguistics where the emphasis has been on the verbal mode of communication (spoken and written), Kress and van Leeuwen argue that all communication is multimodal and that there is a need to analyse all modes – sound (e.g. music), visual images, smell – systematically. In developing a systematic approach to the analysis of modes they draw on SYSTEMIC FUNCTIONAL LINGUISTICS.

A key reason they advance for focusing on **multimodality**, and in particular on the visual mode, is the profound change taking place in communication practices, primarily the shift towards greater use of visual images due to the increased availability of information technology. However, it is acknowledged that multimodality has a much longer history (e.g. medieval manuscripts were highly visual) and considerable cultural diversity (for an example of Brazilian multimodal practices, see Menezes de Souza, 2003). Other frameworks have been used in the analysis of multi-modality: see for instance the anthropologically-influenced approach adopted by Ruth Finnegan (2002). See also DESIGN; NON-VERBAL COMMUNICATION.

multiple negation   Negation refers to a syntactic construction which negates or contradicts the meaning of an utterance. Negative particles are commonly used (e.g. English *not*). In many non-standard varieties of English multiple, emphatic negations are common, e.g. *Nobody didn't do nothing*, corresponding to standard English *Nobody did anything*. Such constructions are also known as **negative spread** or **negative concord** (see CONCORD). However, not all multiple negations are emphatic (e.g. the grammaticalised multiple negation in French and Afrikaans).

multiplex (-ity)   **Multiplexity** is an attribute of close-knit social networks (see SOCIAL NETWORK). In a **multiplex** network people are linked by multiple ties, e.g. two network members might be linked to one another in several different ways: as workmates, kin, friends, members of the same political party, etc. A network in which members are linked to each other only in one capacity (e.g. members of the same political party) is called a **uniplex** network. See also STRONG TIES; WEAK TIES.

muted group   Term derived from the work of the anthropologists Shirley Ardener and Edwin Ardener. Muted groups are less powerful social groups whose sense of reality is not adequately represented through a society's DOMINANT 'modes of expression'. These are controlled by dominant social groups and better re-present the sense of reality of these groups. Muted groups are 'muted' in that they need to express themselves through the relevant dominant mode in any situation in order to be heard, but cannot properly articulate any alternative model of the world through this mode. The existence of dominant modes of expression may even inhibit muted groups from generating such alternative models (e.g. Ardener, 1978). This latter argument would be consistent with a determinist conception of language (see LINGUISTIC DETERMINISM). The Ardeners focused on women as a muted group, and their ideas have been taken up by feminists concerned about women's linguistic oppression: for discussion and critique see Cameron (1992). See also FEMINISM; LANGUAGE AND GENDER; WO-MEN'S LANGUAGE.

mutual intelligibility Two language varieties are said to be mutually intelligible if their speakers can understand each other. The criterion of mutual intelligibility is sometimes invoked to distinguish DIALECTs (mutually intelligible) from LANGUAGES (mutually unintelligible). However, there are serious problems with such an approach. Sociocultural factors may lead to speakers claiming unintelligibility for closely related language varieties. For example, Zulu and Xhosa, two Bantu languages spoken in South Africa, are very similar to one another and form part of a DIALECT CONTINUUM. However, speakers frequently claim that it is difficult for them to understand one another. The fact that Zulu and Xhosa speakers have distinct cultural identities and traditionally support different political parties may influence their intelligibility assessments. Similarly, Dutch and German, which are considered to be different languages by their speakers (and which, like Zulu and Xhosa, have different STANDARD forms), are very closely related and to some extent mutually intelligible (especially along the German–Dutch border). Their identification as separate languages is a result of the separate political and cultural histories of the territories in which they are spoken. In Scandinavia, on the other hand, speakers of different national languages (Danish, Swedish, Norwegian) see themselves as belonging to a more general Scandinavian culture. Communication across national language boundaries, although not perfect, is common. Intelligibility is thus not a yes–no phenomenon but a matter of degree. It is strongly affected by motivation and experience as well as interpersonal factors. See also ABSTAND, AUSBAU; SEMI-COMMUNICATION.

$$\boxed{\text{N}}$$

narrative At its simplest, narrative is a term used to refer to a story which has a sequence of events, with one or more key characters. Different kinds of analysis have been carried out on different types of narratives. Analysis of fairy tale narratives was famously carried out by Vladimir Propp (1968), who identified a basic set of structures common across this GENRE. Narratives can be in any MODE – spoken, written, visual, sound (e.g. music).

Sociolinguistic studies of everyday narratives were pioneered by Labov (1972c), who identified the following six-part structure of oral narratives:

- Orientation; sets the scene – who? what? where? when?
- Complicating action; central part of the story – and then what happened?
- Evaluation; narrator's point in telling the story – so what?
- Abstract; summary of the story – what is the story about?
- Resolution; conclusion – what finally happened, what was the outcome?
- Coda; the end of the narrative – narrator returns from the events of the narrative to the current conversation.

This structure has been used and adapted to analyse a range of narratives including older people's life experiences (Hill, 1995); children's interests and family experiences (Maybin, 1997); women's sex encounters (Caldas-Coulthard, 1996); men's life stories (Freccero, 1986); and newspaper articles (Bell, 1991). In many studies emphasis has been on the ways in which narratives are co-authored, particularly in spoken interaction (see e.g. Ochs, 1997).

Narratives are often viewed as more than simply stories about events or other people. Rather they are seen as an important way of making sense of both individual and collective experience. Simply put, it is said that in telling particular stories about others and ourselves we are actively constructing a sense of who we are as individuals, and as cultural collectives (see e.g. Bruner, 1990; Schiffrin, 2001; Gee, 1999).

narrow (transcription) See TRANSCRIPTION.

nasal A term used in the description and classification of speech sounds, relating to their MANNER OF ARTICULATION. Nasal sounds are produced when the velum (or soft palate) is lowered, allowing air to escape through the nose. Nasal CONSONANTS in English include: [m], [n] and [ŋ] (the final consonant in *ring*). Nasal VOWELS occur in languages such as French, and vowels in English may also be **nasalised** in certain environments (e.g. the [i] sound in *mean*). See also INTERNATIONAL PHONETIC ALPHABET; PHONETICS.

national language A language associated with a particular country where it is recognised as a symbol of national identity. In many postcolonial states the language of the former colonial power was retained after independence as an OFFICIAL LANGUAGE, while indigenous languages of wider communication were chosen as national languages. In Kenya, English is the main official language and medium of instruction; Kiswahili, the East African lingua franca, is promoted as the national language. It is used in parliamentary debates and is taught as a school subject. In some countries more than one national language exists. Switzerland, for example, has four national languages: German, French, Italian and Romansh. See also CORPUS PLANNING, STATUS PLANNING.

nationalism, nationism A distinction introduced by Joshua A. FISHMAN (1972). **Nationalism** refers to the attitudes and sentiments that support the collective identity of national communities as culturally distinct and linguistically homogenous political units. Language is commonly identified as a central marker of the national community (i.e. Italians speak Italian, Greeks speak Greek and Icelanders speak Icelandic). **Nationism**, on the other hand, refers to behaviours and beliefs pertaining to the development and maintenance of political-territorial autonomy (e.g. the postcolonial, multi-ethnic nations of Africa and Asia). In nationism there is no (real or believed) isomorphy between citizenship and language use (i.e. South Africans speak Zulu, Xhosa, Sotho, Afrikaans, English, Hindi, Telugu, Portuguese and so forth; Malaysians speak Malay, Mandarin, English, Tamil, Iban, and so forth; Swiss speak German, Swiss German, Italian, Romansh and French).

native (speaker, language)   A **native speaker** is as someone who acquires a particular LANGUAGE from birth to early childhood naturally, via interaction with family and community members, rather than by formal instruction. As such, everyone is a native speaker of at least one language. Such a language is termed the **native language**. Thus it is assumed, broadly speaking, that most people in the UK are native speakers of English, whereas most people in Spain are native speakers of Spanish. In establishing the rules of a language linguists often prefer to study the NORMS and intuitions of native speakers.

The term is, however, highly controversial for a number of related reasons. (a) It idealises both speakers and actual language usage, rather than acknowledging the wide variety of 'native speakers' and 'native language' varieties. (b) It often presupposes MONOLINGUALISM rather than BILINGUALISM or MULTILINGUALISM as the norm. In many multilingual societies, people may be native speakers of more than one language, whose rules of grammar and pronunciation influence each other. (c) The distinction between 'native' and 'non-native' speakers is not clear cut: a language introduced via the educational system (e.g., English in India) can produce speakers who have native (or native-like) proficiency and whose intuitions are no less reliable than their counterparts in monolingual societies. (d) More critically, in the context of the global spread of English the 'native speaker' of English possesses considerably more symbolic capital (see SYMBOLIC POWER) than the 'non-native' speaker. The monolingual bias of the notion of native speaker has been critiqued by scholars such as Singh (1998). See also FIRST LANGUAGE; MOTHER TONGUE; NATIVISATION.

nativisation
1. In CREOLE studies the process by which a PIDGIN is made into a FIRST LANGUAGE (or NATIVE language) by expansion of its vocabulary, and grammatical and phonological structures. In this process the expanded variety 'acquires' native speakers.
2. More generally, the process by which a former second language is adopted as a first language (or native language) by a community undergoing LANGUAGE SHIFT.
3. In the study of WORLD ENGLISHES or NEW ENGLISHES the term is used synonymously with INDIGENISATION, to denote the adaptation of English by second-language speakers outside 'inner circle' contexts such as the United Kingdom and United States to fit into the sociocultural and linguistic milieu of its new environment,

without implying that it is in the process of becoming a first language. See also THREE CIRCLES OF ENGLISH.

natural gender   See GENDER (1).

near-merger   The close approximation of two sounds (generally vowels). The sounds, however, remain phonetically distinct and do not actually merge. It has been shown in empirical studies that speakers perceive near-mergers as phonetically identical (Labov, 1975, 1994). One such near-merger which has attracted socio-linguistic attention is the relation between the vowels of *meet* and *mate* which constituted a 'near-merger' in the early Modern English period. Today the vowels are distinct in most varieties of English (see Milroy, 1992: 155–8). In Belfast the two vowels still show all the signs of a near-merger: they are phonetically very close for older speakers and are usually considered to be 'the same'. See also MERGER.

negative concord   See CONCORD.

negative face   See FACE.

negative politeness   See POLITENESS.

negative spread   See MULTIPLE NEGATION.

neighbourhood   A socially relatively homogenous section of a city. Urban dialectologists have frequently avoided the collection of large RANDOM SAMPLES and have instead conducted ethnographi-cally-inspired 'neighbourhood' studies (often adopting the FRIEND OF A FRIEND approach). An early example of a neighbourhood study is LABOV's (1972c) *Language in the Inner City*, a study of the linguistic practices of African American male peer groups in South Harlem. Neighbourhood studies (such as e.g. Lesley Milroy's work in three Belfast neighbourhoods – Milroy, 1987a) have also made use of SOCIAL NETWORK analysis.

network   See SOCIAL NETWORK.

new   See GIVEN, NEW.

new dialect   If dialect speakers move to new areas where they come into contact with speakers of different dialects, new dialects may emerge via processes of DIALECT LEVELLING and CONVERGENCE. Paul Kerswill (1996) studied the emergence of such a 'new dialect' in Milton Keynes, UK. See also TRANSPLANTED (DIALECT, LANGUAGE).

New English (-es)

1. A cover term for the varieties of English that developed outside the UK, irrespective of whether they are first or second languages.
2. More specifically, a cover term for English that developed initially as a SECOND LANGUAGE outside England, typically in territories colonised by the UK and USA. In this sense, many North American and Australasian varieties of English do not count as 'New Englishes'.
3. A further refinement occurs in Platt et al.'s (1984) work, which used the term for certain second-language varieties that developed under British colonialism. They limited their characterisation of 'New English' to territories where English was (mainly) introduced via the classroom rather than by a large body of settlers, but soon became adopted as a LINGUA FRANCA among speakers of different languages, stabilising indigenous words and other facets of language (e.g. accent, grammar) in the process. Excluded from their characterisation were second-language English varieties in places like Australia or Canada, on the grounds that a considerable body of NATIVE speakers of English exerted a counter-influence.

   Most definitions exclude PIDGIN and CREOLE Englishes and ENGLISH AS A FOREIGN LANGUAGE (EFL) from their jurisdiction. Study of the features of different varieties of English are of considerable interest and have included PHONOLOGY, GRAMMAR, LEXIS and DISCOURSE (see e.g. Kachru, 1992). See also WORLD ENGLISH(ES); THREE CIRCLES OF ENGLISH.

New Literacy Studies   Refers to a body of work on literacy which views literacy as a social phenomenon implicated in relations of power and identity. The 'new' is used to contrast this approach with a more widespread focus on literacy as an individual or cognitive phenomenon. Work in New Literacy Studies emphasises the importance of CONTEXT for researching literacy and involves the use of notions such as LITERACY EVENT and LITERACY PRACTICE.

Brian Street (1984) argues that debates around literacy can be conceptualised in terms of two models of literacy, AUTONOMOUS and **ideological**. The autonomous model treats literacy as independent of social context, and as a phenomenon which of itself has an impact on social and cognitive practices. In contrast, an ideological model sees literacy as a socially and culturally situated phenomenon, the nature and impact of which varies according to the context in which it is used.

nominalisation   Grammatical term used to refer to the process of forming a noun or noun phrase from another linguistic item such as a verb or adjective. For example, 'The *building* of the school took place in 1987' rather than 'They *built* the school in 1987.' Considerable attention has been paid in SYSTEMIC FUNCTIONAL LINGUISTICS and CRITICAL LINGUISTICS to the relationship between nominalisation and meaning. It is argued that nominalisation tends to obscure human action and agency. For example, a key difference between the two clauses, *the strikers picket a factory* and *picketing curtailed coal deliveries* is that in the first the actors are visible and in the second they are not. Linguistic features such as nominalisations are thus viewed not as formal linguistic items but as FUNCTIONAL items, contributing to particular ways of meaning and offering particular representations of events (Hodge and Kress, 1993).

nonce (borrowing)   See BORROWING.

non-prevocalic /r/   See POST-VOCALIC /r/.

non-rhotic   See RHOTIC.

non-sexist (language)   See SEXISM.

non-standard (language, variety)   **Non-standard language** refers to elements of a language that are not considered STANDARD (i.e. appropriate in formal speech and writing), like localised vocabulary, items of grammar and pronunciations of individual words that are not sanctioned by teachers, editors and other norm-setters. A **non-standard variety** is one whose norms are not accepted in formal speech and writing. The term is intended to avoid the pejorative overtones of **substandard**, a term previously used in educational circles, since sociolinguists have demonstrated the regular and rule-governed nature of many non-standard constructions like COPULA DELETION. Since most sociolinguists consider the standard form of a language to be a dialect (or at least to have developed from one or more dialects) a distinction between **standard dialect** and **non-standard dialect** is sometimes made. Matters of pronunciation are less clear. Some linguists suggest that it is possible to speak the standard variety of a language in any ACCENT, with 'standardness' referring instead to degrees of prestige. Others argue that since broad localised accents are seldom paired with the standard variety, accent is part of 'standardness' and one may therefore refer to non-standard accents.

non-stative   See STATIVE.

non-verbal communication (NVC)   'Non-verbal communication', or sometimes **non-verbal behaviour**, refers to features used by people to communicate but that are not part of VERBAL language. Many non-verbal systems are associated with speech, including gesture, proxemics (degree of physical distance between speakers), body contact or haptics, posture and body orientation, facial expression and gaze or eye contact. Such aspects of NVC have different communicative functions: they may convey specific conventionalised meanings (as in a nod for 'yes'); they may convey certain attributes of a person such as their emotional state, or their relative status; or they may be more closely integrated with speech (for instance the use of gesture or eye-contact may contribute to the management of TURN-TAKING). NVC may be extended to other SEMIOTIC systems such as clothing, and in this broader sense it is not clear where the concept should stop. Semiotic systems that are more distant from the person (such as room layout) are usually considered as part of the CONTEXT of an interaction rather than as NVC.

NORM   An ironic acronym introduced by Chambers and Trudgill (1998) to describe the typical informant of traditional dialect research: 'non-mobile, older rural males' (NORMs). It was believed that these older male speakers who had never left their area of residence spoke 'pure' dialect, i.e. dialect which was un-contaminated by other dialects or by the standard variety.

norm (linguistic) Linguistic practices which are typical or representative of a group. Two types of social norms are commonly distinguished in sociolinguistics and sociology (e.g. Hechter and Opp, 2001): (a) **regularity norms**, i.e. linguistic practices or customs as well as behaviour patterns which occur repeatedly and habitually within a speech community (sometimes also called **subsistent norms**; Gloy, 1975); and (b) **oughtness norms**, i.e. behaviours which are expected within a community: individuals who do not conform to these norms will be ridiculed, excluded or even punished. Thus, in the German-speaking part of Switzerland private conversations take place in Swiss German (a regional variety) and not in standard German. This is a regularity norm (reflecting a custom, a regular type of behaviour) as well as an oughtness norm (use of standard German in private conversations will lead to ridicule and possibly even exclusion from the conversation). The overtly prescriptive norms of STANDARD languages (see PRESCRIPTIVISM) are a special type of oughtness norms.

normal transmission, abnormal transmission Terms coined by Sarah Grey Thomason and Thomas Kaufman (1988) to characterise different ways in which a community acquires a first language. **Normal transmission** usually denotes a situation in which a community acquires its first language from the previous generation, with all components of the language (phonology, grammar, vocabulary) 'intact'. Normal transmission would also include those cases of LANGUAGE SHIFT in which children learn a first language from a new reference group with which they are in regular contact, with all components coming from this language. **Abnormal transmission** denotes a situation where, through force of circumstances, a group of speakers is unable to maintain its former languages and aims at a TARGET language associated with a dominant reference group, but lacks sufficient access to this language to acquire all its components. Typically, speakers acquire the vocabulary of the target language but retain the grammatical structures of the 'ancestral' languages spoken by their parents' generation. In so doing they come up with a new language, a CREOLE. Abnormal transmission thus implies that different sub-components of a new language derive historically from different languages. Whilst the negative tones of 'abnormal transmission' have not been critiqued, linguists would insist that Creole languages are not 'abnormal' in any sense – they are fully-fledged systems. See also ABRUPT CREOLISATION.

Northern Cities Shift   A series of related vowel changes that are taking place in the northern parts of the United States, especially in the cities. The shift involves six vowels (PHONEMES) which may be heard as instances of another phoneme by listeners from another dialect area, with some resultant confusion of meanings: *Ann* may be heard as *Ian*, *bit* as *bet*, *bet* as *bat* or *but*, *lunch* as *launch*, *talk* as *tock* and *locks* as *lax*. Phonetically, this involves a 'clockwise' rotation or CHAIN SHIFT of a whole set of vowels, initially 'triggered' by the raising of /æ/ (the vowel in *Ann*) to the position occupied by /ɪə/ (in *Ian*). These changes are being studied as part of a major research project headed by William LABOV, *The Atlas of North American English*. The shift is most advanced in the Inland North – the industrial region stretching along the Great Lakes from Western New York State to Southern Wisconsin, including major cities like Syracuse, Rochester, Buffalo, Cleveland, Toledo, Detroit and Chicago. See also GREAT VOWEL SHIFT; SOUTHERN HEMISPHERE SHIFT; SOUTHERN SHIFT.

notation   See TRANSCRIPTION.

noun phrase   A phrase that has a noun (or PRONOUN) as its head: a noun phrase may consist of a single noun or pronoun, or a noun/pronoun with any features that modify it. So, *Toby*, *he*, *the big cat* or *the big cat with bright orange fur* are all noun phrases. In some grammatical frameworks, e.g. SYSTEMIC FUNCTIONAL LINGUISTICS, the term **nominal group** is used (see GROUP). Several sociolinguists have looked at variation at the level of the noun phrase: for example, differences in pronoun forms in different language varieties; differences in the use of determiners such as the articles *a* and *the* (see DETERMINER).

observer's paradox   Used by William LABOV to refer to the fact that speakers' language behaviour is affected by the presence of linguists who wish to observe that behaviour. Linguists who wish to capture VERNACULAR speech may, by their presence, cause speakers to adopt a more formal speaking STYLE. This is similar to the notion of 'experimenter effect' in other disciplines. The term **observer effect** is also sometimes found. A number of strategies have been devised to minimise the effects of observation. In sociolinguistic INTERVIEWS this could involve playing down the interviewer's status and introducing topics that would involve the speaker and elicit an informal speaking style (see DANGER OF DEATH). In other studies, researchers have talked informally to speakers in friendship pairs or groups, carried out PARTICIPANT OBSERVATION, asked speakers to record themselves at home or with friends, or sometimes recorded speakers surreptitiously. This last method would now, however, generally be regarded as unethical (see ETHICS).

official language   A language which is used for political, legal and administrative communications within a given political territory. The legal status of official languages is usually constitutionally guaranteed and official languages are also taught in the education system. Some countries have more than one official language (South Africa, for example, has eleven; Luxembourg has three). In such cases there is often a 'division of labour' and not all official languages are used in all functions (e.g. certain documents may not be available in all languages). To grant official status to a language is a symbolic and political act. IMPLEMENTATION of such decisions, however, is often slow or only partial. See also NATIONAL LANGUAGE.

ontogeny   A biological term for the origin and development of an individual organism. In linguistics, the development of language in the individual, especially at the stage that it is acquired in childhood. Contrasts with PHYLOGENY, the development of language in the human species. See also CHILD LANGUAGE; LANGUAGE ACQUISITION.

open

1. A term used in the description and classification of VOWELS: open vowels are produced when the the tongue is relatively low in the mouth (the term LOW vowel is also found). This is part of a four-way classification of vowels depending on tongue height: CLOSE – half close – **half open** – open. Open vowels would include [a] (similar to the vowel in *pat* in varieties of English found in northern England) and [ɑ] (the vowel in English *part*). A half-open vowel would be [ɛ], as in English *pet*. See also INTERNATIONAL PHONETIC ALPHABET; PHONETICS.

2. A distinction is sometimes made between **open** and **closed** word classes. Open classes include nouns, verbs, adjectives and adverbs: in principle these classes may be expanded infinitely as new terms are added to the language. Closed classes include conjunctions, prepositions, DETERMINERS, PRONOUNS etc. These are seen as a 'closed' system, to which new items are not commonly added. The lack of success experienced by attempts to add a gender-neutral third-person pronoun to the English language (i.e. as an alternative to *she* and *he*) has sometimes been attributed to the fact that pronouns are a closed system.

oracy (-ies)   The term 'oracy' was introduced in educational contexts to refer to skills and competence in spoken language – speaking and listening – and to argue that these should be considered as important in the school curriculum as the development of LITERACY (see Wilkinson et al., 1965; Wilkinson et al., 1974). In the UK a National Oracy Project was carried out and has influenced national policies and curricular programmes (see Maclure et al, 1988; Department of Education and Science, 1989). The plural form **oracies** is sometimes used, in a similar way to 'literacies', to indicate that there are different types of oracy and different rationales underlying these. Maggie Maclure, for example, has pointed to four oracies: for personal growth, cultural transformation, the improvement of learning, and functional competence (Maclure, 1993).

oral

1. Term used in general sense to refer to spoken as compared with written forms of communication.

2. In the description of speech sounds, oral is found in opposition to NASAL, to refer to sounds which are made with air being

passed through the mouth rather than through the nose. For instance, [b] is an oral consonant whereas [m] is nasal (see also PHONETICS).

orality   Used to refer to cultural traditions which use mainly or solely spoken communication. Orality is often juxtaposed with LITERACY to refer not only to different modes of communication but to different outcomes in culture, cognition and economic development. Most famously Walter Ong argues that literacy has a profound effect on both individual and collective cognitive capacities, being seen as a necessary prerequisite for the development of science, technology and philosophy (Ong, 1982). **Residual orality** is a term sometimes used to refer to cultures where oral traditions remain strong.

The dichotomy between orality and literacy, and their presumed differential outcomes for the individual mind and society more generally have been strongly criticised, particularly by researchers within NEW LITERACY STUDIES. Criticism is made of the simple dichotomy used to describe whole societies and cultures, when, it is argued, a wide range of literate and oral practices take place within any one cultural or geographical context.

order of discourse   Term from the work of FOUCAULT used to account for the relationship between language and POWER. It refers to the sets of conventions and norms which govern the ways in which language can be used, by whom, in what contexts and under what conditions. For example, the order of discourse of higher education involves particular ways of constructing knowledge and relationships around knowledge making which are enacted in specific DISCURSIVE PRACTICES, such as seminars, lectures, ESSAYIST LITERACY. Orders of discourse also account for the power and prestige attached to different varieties of language use and different types of language user. Control over the orders of discourse is an aspect of HEGEMONY, and is sometimes referred to as the 'power behind discourse'. See also DISCOURSE (3); SYMBOLIC POWER.

orthography   See WRITING SYSTEM.

outsiders   See INTERLOPERS, INSIDERS, OUTSIDERS, ASPIRERS.

overgeneralisation   See ANALOGY.

overlap (in conversation)   In studies of conversation, an overlap refers to overlapping speech – i.e. when a speaker begins to talk before the current speaker has finished his or her SPEAKING TURN. In models of conversation that assume one person talks at a time, anything other than a brief overlap may be treated as an example of disfluency that needs to be explained. Overlapping speech is, however, common among certain groups of speakers and in certain contexts: for example, Coates (1996) found frequent overlaps in informal interaction among women friends in Britain. Such forms of overlapping speech are seen as indicators of highly co-operative talk and may be contrasted with INTERRUPTIONS, or more competitive or hostile incursions into another speaker's turn. See also CONVERSATION MANAGEMENT; TURN–TAKING.

overlexicalisation   See LEXICALISATION.

overt prestige   See PRESTIGE.

p-level   A statistical measure. The p-level estimates the likelihood that the patterns observed in a SAMPLE would also be present in the POPULATION from which the sample was drawn. Results that yield $p < 0.05$ are generally considered statistically significant, i.e. in this case the patterns observed in the sample can be generalised to the population with a specifiable degree of confidence (the figure means that the probability of error is less than 5 per cent). See also SIGNIFICANCE TESTING.

palatal   A descriptive term for CONSONANTs relating to their PLACE OF ARTICULATION: palatal sounds are produced when the tongue touches or comes close to the hard palate. An example from English is [j], the initial sound in *yeast*.

Palato-alveolar refers to sounds produced when the tongue touches or comes close to the alveolar ridge and the front of the hard palate. Examples from English are [ʃ], the initial consonant in *she*; and [ʒ], the consonant in the middle of *pleasure*. See also INTERNATIONAL PHONETIC ALPHABET; PHONETICS.

panchronic   Originally used by Ferdinand de Saussure as a term that embraced both SYNCHRONIC and DIACHRONIC approaches to language study. Saussure raised the question whether there could be laws of LANGUAGE CHANGE which existed panchronically – i.e. which hold in all cases (synchronically) and forever (diachronically). He dismissed this possibility, arguing that linguistic rules and changes to them were unlike laws in the natural and physical sciences. In a weaker sense, however, some phonologists such as Kuryłowicz have attempted to characterise SOUND CHANGE panchronically – i.e. by paying attention to how an earlier phonological system of a language evolved into a later one. Within sociolinguistics, something nearing a panchronic approach has been adopted in DIALECTOLOGY, when dialectologists attempt to describe the rules of a language by paying attention to variation in space (REGIONAL VARIATION) and in time (LANGUAGE CHANGE). In LANGUAGE CONTACT studies a panchronic approach has proved fruitful in characterising how a rudimentary INTERLANGUAGE or PIDGIN develops over time into a fuller system (stable SECOND LANGUAGE or CREOLE) while also characterising subsystems associated with different speakers (see CREOLE CONTINUUM).

pandialectal   Sometimes used in DIALECTOLOGY to refer to linguistic phenomena (e.g. particular linguistic features, an aspect of language change) that are found across all the DIALECTs of a language.

panlectal   Describes an approach to grammar which sees a LANGUAGE as a union of subsystems (varieties or LECTs) which can be ordered implicationally on a **panlectal grid** (see IMPLICATIONAL SCALE).

paradigmatic   A relation between linguistic elements that can be substituted for each other in a given sequence. In the sentence *The cow walked over the bridge*, the word *cow* may be substituted by *dog*, *cat*, *girl*, etc., and is said to have a paradigmatic relation to each of these elements. Similarly, in English the sounds [p] and [t] have a paradigmatic relation, since they can be substituted in sequences like *p-i-n and t-i-n*. Contrast SYNTAGMATIC.

paralinguistic   Paralinguistic phenomena include features of VOICE QUALITY and other vocal features that accompany language (e.g. giggling, laughing or moaning while speaking). Such features are not generally regarded as part of verbal language, although they contribute to the meaning of an utterance. Sometimes the term is used more broadly to include gesture, facial expression etc and in this case it becomes similar in meaning to NON-VERBAL COMMUNICATION.

parole   See LANGUE, PAROLE.

participant
1. Normally used in the analysis of spoken language as a general term to refer to all those who participate in an interaction. Studies sometimes identify different types of participant: for example, speaker and listener, ADDRESSEE (these may also be referred to as **participant roles**). See also INFORMANT; PARTICIPANT OBSERVATION.
2. **Participant** and **participant role** are also categories in SYSTEMIC FUNCTIONAL LINGUISTICS (see TRANSITIVITY).

participant observation   A technique used in ethnographic research, when a researcher becomes part of the group he or she wishes to study, often for an extended period. Researchers are able to collect a range of language data in naturally-occurring settings, and gain an insight into community practices and values. Problematical issues (both practical and ethical) include the potential effects of the research, and the researcher's presence, on the community; how the researcher relates to other community members; how the researcher eventually 'disengages' from the community. See also ETHNOGRAPHY.

passive bilingual   A term for an individual who has a full understanding of a language, but is unable to speak it with any fluency. This typically occurs in a situation of LANGUAGE SHIFT when younger speakers retain a 'receptive competence' of the traditional language of their elders, but use the new language being shifted to by the community when speaking among themselves or responding to older speakers. Such receptive competence extends not just to following conversations in the traditional language of the community but to appreciating jokes and word-play, deciphering whispers and even translating from the traditional language into the new one (but not vice versa). See also SEMI-SPEAKER.

passivisation Grammatical term used to refer to the transformation of a clause from an **active** to a **passive** form, for example, changing the clause *the girl kicked the ball* to *the ball was kicked by the girl*. See also VOICE (2).

patois The French expression *patois* refers to non-standard, colloquial varieties of the spoken language and traditionally carries negative associations of 'uneducatedness' and 'coarseness'. It is therefore rarely used by linguists. However, in some speech communities the term is found without negative meaning as a proper name for a variety, for example speakers of Jamaican Creole refer to their language as *Patwa*.

peer group While the family environment provides the first speech models for children, the peer group (or circle of friends) has been shown to be linguistically more influential from about the age of five. As a result, children usually speak more like their peers, and not like their parents, teachers or other adult models. This is clearly visible in migrant speech communities: LANGUAGE SHIFT typically starts in the youngest age group, who encounter the new language in peer-group interaction in the playground and at school. A general pattern of speaking the HERITAGE LANGUAGE to parents and the new majority language to age mates (siblings and peers) is typical of migrant families undergoing language shift (see Chambers, 1995). The process is similar in monolingual speech communities, where sociolinguists have often observed a **generation gap** with regard to, for example, participation in linguistic changes in progress (Labov, 1994). In addition, sociolinguists also study language use in peer groups in its own right (see YOUTH LANGUAGE), and have, for example, linked patterns of language usage to the internal structure of the group (e.g. Cheshire, 1982). See also ADOLESCENCE

pejoration Refers to an aspect of semantic change in language, in which a word develops negative meanings. Linguists interested in the CRITICAL study of language have documented pejoration in words referring to relatively powerless social groups: Dick Leith (1997) cites examples such as *churl*, which was originally a term of rank, referring to the lowest rank of freemen, but became used as a general term of disparagement. Leith argues that, in such cases, connotations that derive from socially powerful groups have become criterial in word meaning. By similar processes, words for women have also systematically acquired negative, and frequently sexual meanings: for example, *hussy* once referred to the mistress of a household, or a thrifty woman. See LANGUAGE AND GENDER; SEXISM.

The terms **deterioration** and **semantic derogation** are also found; contrast AMELIORATION, when words lose negative meanings.

perceptual dialectology   An area of SOCIOLINGUISTICS and DIALECTOLOGY which studies metalinguistic speaker ATTITUDES and FOLK LINGUISTICS. Perceptual dialectologists identify dialect regions and dialect boundaries not on the basis of objective differences in language use, but on the basis of speakers' subjective perceptions (Preston, 1989). Respondents are asked, for example, to evaluate the degree of similarity (or difference) of the speech of surrounding localities, or to draw **mental maps** of where the 'nicest' or most 'standard-like' variety of their language is spoken, where the most 'polite' or 'friendly' variety is spoken, etc. Perceptual dialectology also includes studies of the discoursal and conversational strategies speakers use when talking about their linguistic perceptions (including the labels they use when describing different varieties e.g. Hillbillies, southern drawl, etc.), as well as studies which try to determine which linguistic elements (e.g. lexicon, grammar, pronunciation) influence the speakers' perception of variation and difference most strongly.

perfect (-ive)   A feature of verb forms used to denote a contrast of a temporal or durational nature. It is better described as a feature of ASPECT than TENSE, since it focuses on an event or action as completed, rather than on the time of the action *per se*. Thus while *I saw* is in the (simple) past, *I have seen* is both present and perfective. Here 'perfective' denotes a past situation that is relevant to the present (e.g. *I have seen the movie; now I can read the book*). Similarly, *I had seen* is both past and perfective. **Imperfect(ive)** denotes an action not conceived of as perfective (e.g. *I am watching a movie/I was watching a movie*). These grammatical categories are of interest to sociolinguists since they may be treated differently in different dialects. For example, Indian English allows the perfective in sentences like *I have read this book last month*. Irish English has a 'hot news' perfective involving *after*, as in *She's after winning the lottery*, meaning 'She's just won the lottery.' See also PROGRESSIVE; TENSE–MODALITY–ASPECT.

performance
1. Chomsky's theory of language rests on a crucial distinction between **competence** and **performance**. The former denotes the specific capacity for language characteristic of human beings, which enables one to acquire one's first language (and in theory any language one is adequately exposed to in early childhood). For Chomsky the task of the linguist is to describe the general and rather abstract linguistic principles that make this possible. **Performance** denotes a speaker's actual use of language, i.e. the concrete utterances emanating from his or her competence. Performance sometimes reflects human errors (like slips of the tongue) and contextual limitations like interruptions, incomplete utterances and so forth. The distinction between competence and performance is accepted by few sociolinguists, most of whom find Chomsky's focus on competence to be too narrow, and prefer to work with a wider notion of COMMUNICATIVE COMPETENCE.
2. 'Performance' is also found in a more overtly theatrical sense to suggest that everyday behaviour, including language behaviour, constitutes a performance in which speakers, by their behaviour, represent and bring into being a particular social situation and also a particular version of themselves (a 'performed character') – see GOFFMAN's influential attempt to map out a 'dramaturgical' model of human interaction (Goffman, 1959).
See also PERFORMATIVITY.

performance variety   See INSTITUTIONALISED VARIETY, PERFORMANCE VARIETY.

performative (performativity)
1. In SPEECH ACT theory, as formulated by the philosopher J. L. Austin, **performative utterances** are those that perform an action by virtue of being uttered: for example, *I warn you to keep away from there* constitutes the act of warning. Austin initially contrasted these with CONSTATIVE utterances – statements of fact, such as *I went shopping yesterday*. Although performatives are in statement form, such utterances are not statements of fact, and cannot be considered as true or false. Performative utterances may include **performative verbs**, which make the speech act performed explicit (e.g. *warn, promise, threaten*) but they need not do so (*Don't go over there* may constitute a warning). In developing speech act theory, Austin did not maintain his original distinction between performative and constative

utterances, recognising that all utterances perform some sort of act (including the act of stating). In this sense, all language use may be seen as performative.

2. The idea of **performativity** in language has also informed studies of IDENTITY, which see this as being continually performed or enacted, linguistically and by other means, rather than as an essential attribute of a person. For instance the philosopher Judith Butler ([1990] 1999) has argued that GENDER is achieved by the 'stylisation of the body' – repeated gestures, movements etc. that conform to cultural norms of behaviour. The performative model also allows gender to be transformed (e.g. performed differently, challenged or subverted). These ideas have been drawn on in recent research on LANGUAGE AND GENDER. Echoing Butler, Deborah Cameron argues that speech may be seen as a repeated stylisation of the body: 'the "masculine" or "feminine" styles of talking identified by researchers might be thought of as the "congealed" results of repeated acts of social actors who are striving to constitute themselves as "proper" men and women' (1997: 49). See also FEMININITY; MASCULINITY.

periphery   See CENTRE, PERIPHERY.

perlocutionary (act, force)   See SPEECH ACT.

personality principle   A principle of LANGUAGE LEGISLATION and LANGUAGE POLICY which implies that all citizens have access to government services in their own language, irrespective of the area where they reside. The personality principle underlies the educational language political framework in Sweden: every citizen has (in principle) the right to learn his or her mother tongue at school. If there are a sufficient number of interested students, courses in languages other than Swedish will be established. Contrast TERRITORIAL PRINCIPLE.

phatic (communion)   Introduced by the anthropologist Bronislaw MALINOWSKI (see Malinowski, 1923) to refer to language use designed primarily to foster or maintain social relationships rather than exchange information or ideas, for example in English, comments about the weather.

phoneme (phonemic)   Phonemes are the distinctive units that make up a language's sound system. For instance, the word *cot* in

English is made up of three distinctive sounds or phonemes, represented as /kɒt/ (phonemic transcription is conventionally set between slashes). The word *got* is regarded as a different word, beginning with a different sound: /gɒt/. Words such as *cot* and *got*, differing in terms of just one phoneme, are termed MINI-MAL PAIRS.

As part of the linguistic system, phonemes can be distinguished from the actual sounds produced by speakers. The phonemes /k/ and /g/ differ from one another in terms of just one feature (the presence or absence of VOICE), but this contrast is significant. The contrast between [k] and [kʰ], however, also differing in terms of one feature (ASPIRATION), is not significant in phonemic terms in English. The sounds [k] and [kʰ] would be regarded as different REALISATIONS, or **allophones**, of the same phoneme, and [kɒt] and [kʰɒt], although pronounced differently, would be regarded as the same word. What counts as distinctive varies between languages. In Hindi aspiration is a distinctive feature and [k] and [kʰ] are two separate phonemes. The words *kana* and *khana* have different meanings in Hindi (respectively 'one-eyed' and 'to eat'). The complete set of phonemes in any one language is termed its **phoneme inventory**.

Phonemes are an important category in the analysis of language variation. Varieties may differ in terms of their phoneme inventories, for instance: Scottish English has a phoneme /x/ (the final sound in *loch*) not found in other varieties of English. Varieties may also differ in the distribution of phonemes: /r/ is pronounced in words like *car* and *cart* in some, but not all varieties of English (see POST-VOCALIC /r/ and RHOTIC). And varieties may differ in terms of the phonetic realisation of phonemes: /r/ is pronounced differently in different varieties of English. See also PHONOLOGY.

phonetics (phonetic)   Often described as the scientific study of speech. Phonetics may be distinguished from PHONOLOGY: whereas phonology is concerned with the sound system of a language, phonetics is concerned with the description and analysis of speech, or speech sounds as they are produced. The INTERNATIONAL PHONETIC ALPHABET is frequently used to represent speech sounds, and phonetic TRANSCRIPTIONS are conventionally enclosed within square brackets (as in [pɪn] to represent the word *pin* in English). Phoneticians may focus on the acoustic properties of speech, on how speech is articulated and on speech perception (how speech is perceived by listeners). Of particular relevance in sociolinguistics is the intersection of phonetics and phonology, sometimes termed **linguistic phonetics**. For instance, sociolinguists may draw on phonetic description to identify the **phonetic realisation** of a particular PHONEME, or how this is actually pronounced by speakers: this may differ between different varieties of a language, between individual speakers, between social groups, etc. See also SOCIOPHONETICS.

phonology (phonological)   The study of the sound system of a language. A distinction is often made between **segmental phonology**, concerned with discrete sounds or PHONEMES (e.g. the sounds /p/, /a/ and /t/ in the word *pat*); and **supra-segmental phonology**, concerned with features such as INTONATION that run across individual phonemes. Many VARIATIONIST sociolinguistic studies have focused on **phonological variation**, or how the pronunciation of certain phonological features varies between speakers and contexts. Typically this would involve identifying a set of **phonological variables** (e.g. phonemes whose pronunciation varies – see LINGUISTIC VARIABLE), and charting the distribution of different variants across different social groups or contexts. Milroy and Gordon (2003) discuss relevant aspects of sociolinguistic methodology.

phylogeny   A biological term for the evolution of a species or other subgroup like a phylum. In linguistics, the study of the origins and development of language in general, or of specific languages in speech communities (see SPEECH COMMUNITY). Contrasts with ONTOGENY, the study of how an individual develops into a proficient user of language.

pidgin   A new and initially simple form of language that arises out of LANGUAGE CONTACT between two or more groups of people who do not share a common language. In its early stages the pidgin is frequently makeshift and reduced in structure, referred to in linguistics as a JARGON or **pre-pidgin**. Furthermore, it is not spoken as a NATIVE language by anyone. As social solutions to the problem of communication, especially in trade- and labour-related contexts, pidgins have norms of their own, frequently making maximum use of minimal grammatical resources. Pidgins may develop into more stable and complex varieties (termed **stable** or **crystallised pidgins**) if contact between groups is sustained or if the pidgin is adopted as a LINGUA FRANCA beyond the initial situation of contact. An **expanded pidgin** (sometimes also termed **extended pidgin**) is a further development of a stable pidgin, in terms of increased grammatical and lexical complexity to meet the needs of speakers who use it in informal interactive contexts and not just in labour situations (e.g. Tok Pisin in Papua New Guinea). Pidgins frequently draw on the socially or demographically dominant language (see SUPERSTRATE) for much of their vocabulary, but are more diffuse in their grammar. They are generally classified in terms of the language that provides the bulk of their vocabulary: hence West African Pidgin English, Chinese Pidgin English, etc. Although pidgins based on a 'two-language' contact situation do exist (e.g. Russenorsk, a nineteenth-century pidgin based on contact between Russian and Norwegian fisherman), prototypically they involve contact between speakers of three or more languages (see WHINNOM FORMULA).

Traditionally, pidgins were contrasted with CREOLES – fully developed first languages of a community that were believed to arise from a prior pidgin phase. This 'life-cycle' theory is associated with Robert A. Hall (Jnr) (1966), and pidgins and Creoles are frequently studied as one subject labelled **Pidgin and Creole Linguistics**, or **Creolistics** for short. Increasingly, however, researchers are exploring alternative models which stress (a) that some Creoles, especially those of the Caribbean, may have evolved 'abruptly', without a prior pidgin phase (see ABRUPT CREOLISATION) and (b) that the distinction between a pidgin and a Creole may not be as clear-cut as once believed, if one examines expanded pidgins like West African Pidgin English, which is becoming a first language (e.g. Faraclas, 1996). The label **pidgin/Creole language** is often preferred when the status of the language (between pidgin and Creole) is unclear. See also DEPIDGINISATION; PIDGINISATION.

pidginisation The process of forming a PIDGIN, involving the development of a simple and useful variety when no other means of communication is available to speakers of different languages. Also used, somewhat ambiguously, for certain simplification processes occurring in LANGUAGE CONTACT which are reminiscent of pidgin characteristics (e.g. COPULA absence), without leading to the formation of a pidgin. See also FOREIGNER TALK.

pilot study A preliminary investigation carried out on a small scale to explore whether a planned research project is viable. For example, instead of immediately interviewing a large number of people of different social groups, one might select a few individuals and decide on the basis of the preliminary interview data which characteristics of their speech would be most interesting for a more extensive study.

pitch (of voice)   A perceptual quality, corresponding to whether a voice sounds 'high' or 'low'. In acoustic terms, pitch of voice or **speaking pitch** is related to the fundamental frequency of a sound wave, determined by the frequency at which the vocal cords vibrate. However, other factors also contribute to perceived pitch. Although strictly a perceptual quality, 'pitch' is sometimes also used to refer to measurable attributes of a speaker's voice. Variation in pitch is studied in terms of INTONATION and TONE. Some studies have also looked at the average speaking pitch of different groups of speakers or different language varieties. For instance, differences in the speaking pitch of women and men have been found to vary in different cultures/language groups – for a discussion see Graddol and Swann (1989).

place of articulation   One of the dimensions commonly used in the description and classification of speech sounds. 'Place of articulation' refers to the point in the vocal tract where a sound is produced. For instance, the sound [d] (in English *dot*) is an ALVEOLAR consonant, produced at the alveolar ridge behind the teeth; whereas [g] (in English *got*) is a VELAR consonant, produced at the velum or soft palate. CONSONANT sounds are commonly classified according to their place of articulation, MANNER OF ARTICULATION, and whether or not they are VOICED. See also INTERNATIONAL PHONETIC ALPHABET; PHONETICS.

plain language movement   A broad social movement which campaigns for the use of 'plain' (i.e. easily understandable) language, especially in the legal sector and government publications. The plain language movement has also been concerned with written information accompanying everyday consumer products, including insurance policies, guarantees, medical labels and technical instructions. See also LANGUAGE MOVEMENT; VERBAL HYGIENE.

plantation Creole   See FORT CREOLE, PLANTATION CREOLE.

play (in language)   See LANGUAGE PLAY.

plosive   A descriptive term for CONSONANTS relating to their MANNER OF ARTICULATION; examples from English include: [p], [b]; [t], [d]; [k], [g]. Plosives are produced when the air stream is blocked and then released. The term **stop** is also found. See also INTERNATIONAL PHONETIC ALPHABET; PHONETICS.

pluricentric language   A language which has several centres of STANDARDISATION, i.e. countries where it is used as an official language and where some language CODIFICATION takes place (most commonly dictionary work). Examples of pluricentric languages include: English (UK, USA, Australia, South Africa, Jamaica, etc.); German (Germany, Austria, Switzerland); Portuguese (Portugal and Brazil, but also as a second language in Mozambique, Cape Verde, Angola, etc.); Spanish (Spain, South America); and Kiswahili (Kenya, Tanzania). The different national varieties of pluricentric languages rarely enjoy equal status and their relationship is generally asymmetrical. Thus, British English (and RECEIVED PRONUNCIATION) still function as an overt PRESTIGE norm in countries such as Jamaica, South Africa and Australia, although all three countries also show codification of their local standard norm.

poetic (poetics)   Poetic language, or poetic uses of language, has often been distinguished from more 'everyday' uses, most frequently on formal grounds: for example, poetic language may use features such as rhythm, rhyme, various forms of repetition (e.g. of words, sounds), figures of speech such as metaphor. The **poetic function** of language is said to be one of 'foregrounding', in which such forms of language draw attention to themselves. Poetic language is therefore sometimes said to be 'self-referential' – i.e. in a poetic text, attention is focused on language itself. Such ideas derive from the ideas of FORMALIST scholars (see e.g. Roman Jakobson, 1960). Sociolinguists such as Dell HYMES have been interested in the forms **poetry** may take in different cultural/linguistic contexts (e.g. Hymes, 1981, 2003) – see also ETHNOPOETICS. However, poetic language is not restricted to poetry and other forms of literature, and there is increasing contemporary interest in the use of poetic forms in more everyday discourse (see CREATIVITY; LANGUAGE PLAY; LITERARY LANGUAGE).

point of view Term used to refer to the perspective or, more literally, the view from which something is produced or interpreted. It is used in various, sometimes overlapping ways.

1. In studies of literature, particularly the novel, to refer to the way in which the narrator approaches the material of his/her text – such as the events and characters – and also the reader. For example, an **omnisicient narrator** provides the overarching and authoritative perspective from which a story is intended to be read. A **first-person** narrative, in contrast, explicitly sets out to provide one perspective, often that of the main character, on a series of events. POLYPHONY is the term used by BAKHTIN to refer to the range of voices, thus points of view, represented in the novel, particularly in the works of Dostoevsky (see Bakhtin, [1929] 1984a; for an overview of point of view in fiction, see Fludernik, 1993).
2. To refer to the perspectives evident in the production of a whole range of texts (written and spoken) and in a range of media, such as books, television, film.
3. In CRITICAL approaches, term often synonymous with IDEOLOGY, for example an analysis of a particular ideology represented in a text.
4. Also in critical approaches, to refer to the relationship between producers, texts and their readers/audiences. Texts can be said to be constructed in terms of **preferred readings** around an **ideal reader** or to position readers in particular ways which readers can take up or resist. For example, a teenage magazine may be said to POSITION young women in a particular way: as interested mainly in sex and fashion. Readers can either accept or take up this positioning, or point of view.

(For discussions relating to 2, 3 and 4, see e.g. Fowler, 1977, 1986, 1991; Simpson, 1993; Clark and Ivanic, 1997.)

politeness Politeness relates to the linguistic expression of concern for others (e.g. courtesy, deference). There are different models of politeness, including Leech's **politeness principle**, developed as a refinement to Grice's CO-OPERATIVE PRINCIPLE. The politeness principle states that people need to 'minimise (other things being equal) the expression of impolite beliefs' or, in its positive form, 'maximise (other things being equal) the expression of polite beliefs' (Leech, 1983: 81). This is designed to explain phenomena such as the use of indirect forms in making accusations. **Politeness**

Theory, developed by Penelope Brown and Stephen Levinson (1987) has been drawn on in several areas of sociolinguistics. Politeness Theory is based on the notion of FACE. 'Face' refers to a person's public self-image: it is related to the everyday use of the term in expressions such as 'losing face'. Brown and Levinson distinguish two aspects of face: 'positive face', the desire for appreciation and approval by others; and 'negative face', the desire not to be imposed on by others. In interacting, speakers need to balance a concern for other people's face with a desire to protect their own. Participants in an interaction draw on politeness strategies as a means of paying attention to another person's face and avoiding 'face-threatening acts': **positive politeness** strategies involve the expression of friendliness or approval (an example might be explicitly including someone in a conversation); **negative politeness** strategies involve not imposing on others or threatening their face (an example might be phrasing a request indirectly: 'Could you possibly close the door?'). Forms of ADDRESS (e.g. PRO-NOUN CHOICE) may also be related to politeness. The actual expression of politeness depends upon several factors: e.g. concerns about face may be over-ridden in cases of danger or urgency; the relative status of participants may affect the politeness strategies that are adopted; there will also be cultural differences in the expression of politeness.

Some aspects of Politeness Theory have been questioned: for example, Alessandro Duranti (1992) argues that respectful terms (which would be seen as an expression of negative politeness) may well constitute an imposition, by reminding a listener of the obligations of his or her position. However, the model has been highly influential within sociolinguistics – for instance, in LAN-GUAGE AND GENDER, where it is argued that women and men may make different use of politeness strategies (e.g. Brown, 1980, 1990; Holmes, 1995).

political correctness Term of debated origins which is used with two meanings (see discussions in Cameron, 1995; Lakoff, 2000).
1. It refers to attempts to provide alternative forms of expression for those that serve to exclude, insult or marginalise less powerful groups within society; examples in English include using *men and women* in preference to the generic *man*; *chairperson* in preference to *chairman* (see GENERIC MASCULINE); using *disabled* in preference to *crippled*.

2. It is used pejoratively by those who are critical of attempts to change language usage (exemplified in 1), and who often ridicule such attempts.
See also VERBAL HYGIENE.

politics of language　Refers to debates and decisions surrounding all aspects of policies on language at national, local and international levels. Key areas of focus are policies on OFFICIAL LANGUAGES or STANDARD languages, and ENDANGERED LANGUAGES; LANGUAGE PLANNING; LANGUAGE ACADEMIES and educational curriculum initiatives. Given the complex relationship between language and POWER, and language and IDENTITY, considerable debate usually surrounds the establishment and implementation of any policy on language.

The **language of politics** is sometimes found referring to the language and discourses used by all those involved in public political life, most notably that of politicians. Considerable work has been carried out in this area, from classical rhetorical theory to current studies in CRITICAL DISCOURSE ANALYSIS (see e.g. Wodak, 1989; Reisgl and Wodak, 2000; Fairclough, 2000)

polyglossia　See DIGLOSSIA.

polylectal grammar　A model of language proposed by sociolinguists to account for the varieties (LECTS) of a language that are used by individuals within a SPEECH COMMUNITY. Such a model attempts to factor in REGIONAL VARIATION and SOCIAL VARIATION (as in studies of DIALECT) or command of multiple lects within a CREOLE CONTINUUM. This is in contrast to the idealised, 'monolectal' grammars of other branches of linguistics, which avoid dealing systematically with variation and multiple competences. Critics of the model express doubt about the amount of knowledge that individuals have about other lects that they encounter but do not habitually use. See also DEVELOPMENTAL LINGUISTICS (2); PANLECTAL.

polyphony　A term used by BAKHTIN in his discussions of Dostoevsky's work to refer to the plurality of VOICES or characters evident in his novels (Bakhtin [1929] 1984a). Rather than the author's voice dominating, the different characters or voices are said to exist as if in their own right. This co-existence of many voices within one textual space stands in contrast to texts where only one voice, usually the author's, dominates. The relevance of the notion of polyphony as applied in literature to Bakhtin's DIALOGIC theory of language more generally lies in its emphasis on multivoicedness in any instance of language use.

Whilst there is some slippage between the uses of the terms polyphony and HETEROGLOSSIA, the former is distinguished from the latter in three ways: (a) polyphony is often used to emphasise distinct individual voices (characters, individuals), whereas the latter is used to emphasise social languages; (b) polyphony simply points to the fact of plurality or multivoicedness, whereas heteroglossia often emphasises the tensions and struggles between voices; (c) it is sometimes argued that polyphony is an earlier conceptual version of heteroglossia in Bakhtin's work.

polysemy   Term in semantics for the use of a word in several senses, for example the different (but related in terms of their origins) meanings of 'round' in a *round ball, a round of golf, round the house, to round a bend*.

popular culture   Expressive forms (songs, dances, films, texts, discourses) which are widely disseminated through society, often (but not exclusively) through the mass media (print, radio, TV and computer networks). Examples of popular culture include soap-operas such as *Neighbours* or music styles such as Hip Hop. As a result of GLOBALISATION American popular culture is now accessible in many countries and has begun to influence local cultural and linguistic STYLES (e.g. the adoption of American pronunciations by British pop/rock stars in the late 1970s; see Trudgill, 1983). Contrasts with **high culture**, i.e. classical literature, drama and music.

population   Used in statistics to refer to a group of cases or items (e.g. all members of a speech community or all texts belonging to a particular GENRE) that are the object of interest. For example, one might decide to study the language use of rural primary school children in Kenya. In this case, all children in all primary schools in Kenya would constitute the population and the researcher would need to decide on an appropriate SAMPLE size and design to investigate the children's language. Alternatively, one could decide to study TV adverts in Spain in the 1990s. In this case, all adverts shown on Spanish TV between 1990 and 1999 would constitute the population from which the research sample would be drawn.

position (-ing)   Used in critical approaches to the study of language to suggest that texts or discourses 'position' people in certain ways in order to encourage a particular point of view, or interpretation of an event. For instance a newspaper may position its readers as certain types of people, with particular interests etc. Readers may either take up or resist such **positioning** (see MANIPULATION; POINT OF VIEW (4); SUBJECT POSITION).

positive face   See FACE.

positive politeness   See POLITENESS.

post-Creole continuum   Same as CREOLE CONTINUUM.

postmodernism
1. Refers to a literary and artistic movement which built on MODERNISM. Postmodern literature and art often challenge conventions of representation, particularly any straightforward notions of unity of meaning, emphasising instead the possibility of consciously playing with meaning in any text or art form. In this way postmodernism is often used synonymously with POST-STRUCTURALISM.
2. The term also refers to a broad intellectual movement that problematises the idea that there is an objective truth about the world, which we can come to know or understand (see Lyotard, 1984). Postmodernism has been influential in studies of language, as in the social sciences generally, in raising questions about the nature of the object of study – language and communication – and the processes by which we perceive this object. For example, the object 'language' is assumed to be far more precarious than often assumed, all uses of language having a range of possible meanings. Likewise, the 'objective' role of the researcher in observing language has been problematised, with greater emphasis being placed on making visible and exploring the impact of the researcher's position or 'stance' on the kind of observations and interpretations made.

poststructuralism   Term used to indicate an approach which differs from STRUCTURALISM in fundamental ways. In contrast to the emphasis (explicit and implicit) in structuralism on identifiable and stable structures, poststructuralist approaches emphasise the following: (a) change and fluidity rather than stability as a general principle; (b) the indeterminacy of meaning in language, that is the impossibility of fixing meanings in any straightforward way as these will vary not least according to context and participants; (c) the individual as constantly in process, rather than a stable or fixed entity, which is captured in the term SUBJECTIVITY (see also IDENTITY).

post-vocalic /r/   A feature of some varieties of English, in which the /r/ sound is pronounced in words such as *car* or *garden*. Despite the term 'post-vocalic' (after a vowel), the relevant feature of the linguistic environment is the absence of a succeeding vowel: /r/ is habitually pronounced after a vowel in words such as *carry*, but post-vocalic /r/ is pronounced where there is no following vowel. For this reason the term **non-prevocalic /r/** has sometimes been preferred. Varieties in which /r/ is pronounced in this position are sometimes termed RHOTIC. Post-vocalic /r/ has been used as a LINGUISTIC VARIABLE in several VARIATIONIST studies, most notably William LABOV's study of sociolinguistic patterns in New York City, where the extent to which post-vocalic /r/ is pronounced varies between different social groups and different speaking styles.

power   Significant debate surrounds definitions of power, what it is and where it resides, and its relationship to language. Power is a key focus in CRITICAL LINGUISTICS and CRITICAL DISCOURSE ANALYSIS and in areas of sociolinguistic study such as LANGUAGE AND GENDER. Power is theorised and analysed in different ways. (a) It is analysed at a micro text level – such as who dominates in conversations. Here power is viewed as either residing with the individual or as produced interactionally (see INTERACTIONAL SOCIOLINGUISTICS). (b) Power is also analysed at an institutional level, in relation to INSTITUTIONAL discourse. (c) Power is analysed at a more macro level, drawing on social theories to explore the ways in which relations between different social groups influence language use. Here power is an effect of social structure (see IDEOLOGY; MARXISM; PRACTICE). (d) Drawing on the work of FOUCAULT, the power of language itself is emphasised through the use of the term DISCOURSE, and related terms, such as ORDERS OF DISCOURSE. See also CULTURAL CAPITAL; SYMBOLIC POWER.

practice (social)   Language is referred to as a social practice to indicate that language and communication are embedded in society and not separate from it, or AUTONOMOUS.

In addition, critical approaches such as CRITICAL DISCOURSE ANALYSIS use 'practice' in a more abstract way. Practice is a critical term from neo-Marxist theory which means an intervention in the social and economic order (see Kress and Hodge, 1979). Language is determined by social structures and works towards reproducing those structures (Fairclough, 2001): repeated ways of using language contribute to the maintenance of socially structured relationships in complex ways. For example, in education the routine language practices of children from middle-class backgrounds usually have higher social status than those of children from working-class backgrounds, and are consequently more highly valued in the classroom. This contributes to the differential educational success of children from different social groups, which in turn contributes to the reproduction or maintenance of those very same social groups. See also HABITUS.

pragmatics   Pragmatics is the study of language in use: how language is produced and interpreted in context. Pragmatics shares with SEMANTICS a concern with MEANING, but whereas semantics is concerned with linguistic meaning, pragmatics also takes into account commonsense (non-linguistic) understandings that may be brought to bear on the interpretation of an utterance. For instance, in order to interpret the following extract:

A: There's a great film on this evening.
B: I've got loads of work to finish.

one might infer that A is issuing an invitation to the cinema and B understands this but has too much work and so cannot go, but this cannot be derived simply from an understanding of linguistic meaning. (See CONVERSATIONAL IMPLICATURE in this respect.) See Kempson (2001) for a brief overview of pragmatics.

The interests of pragmatics overlap to some extent with those of sociolinguistics, particularly INTERACTIONAL SOCIOLINGUISTICS. The term **sociopragmatics** (Leech, 1983) is sometimes used to refer to pragmatics research that places an emphasis on social or cultural factors that influence language use. See also WORLD KNOWLEDGE.

preference (in conversation)   See SEQUENTIAL ORGANISATION.

pre-pidgin   Same as JARGON.

prescriptivism (prescriptive, prescriptivist)   A doctrine that holds certain features of a language to be incorrect and in need of replacement by other forms deemed correct on the grounds of logic, existence in classical or older forms of a language or use by 'good' writers. On such grounds split infinitives (*to boldly go*) and double negatives (*I don't see no horses*) are prescribed to be wrong and to be replaced by forms like *to go boldly* and *I don't see any horses* respectively. Most linguists argue that while a degree of **prescription** might be necessary to acquaint schoolchildren with the STANDARD form of their language, it is the task of the linguist to record and describe utterances made by NATIVE speakers rather than to suppress them. This approach within linguistics which aims to describe objectively the rules of a language as they are actually used by its speakers, irrespective of beliefs about good or bad usage is termed DESCRIPTIVISM. Prescriptivism overlaps with PURISM, though the latter is used more frequently in connection with negative attitudes to foreign words in a language. See also CORRECTNESS; APPROPRIATENESS; VERBAL HYGIENE.

prestige   Refers to the positive EVALUATION of linguistic forms. **Prestige pronunciations**, for example, are pronunciations that are evaluated positively in society and are typically associated with the dominant social classes.

   In the study of LANGUAGE CHANGE the notion of prestige is frequently used to explain the adoption and spread of an innovation. Prestige explanations are, however, problematical as different groups within a speech community have different ideas of what counts as prestigious. William LABOV (1972a) therefore introduced a distinction between 'overt' and 'covert' prestige. **Overt prestige** is typically attached to the speech forms of the socio-economically dominant classes. The linguistic norms which command overt prestige are heard for example, in educational contexts (schools, universities) as well as in the media (newspapers, broadcasting). **Covert prestige**, on the other hand, has more 'local' connotations and refers to ways of speaking which are highly valued within smaller groups and communities (see NEIGHBOURHOOD). Overt-prestige variants are thus markers of status, while covert-prestige variants are markers of within-group solidarity. The covert prestige of non-standard varieties has also been linked to perceptions of MASCULINITY. Trudgill (1974b) found in his interviews in

Norwich, England, that men over-reported their use of non-standard forms while women under-reported their use of non-standard forms. Based on his results, Trudgill suggested that in Norwich non-standard forms have associations of 'roughness' and 'toughness', and are used as markers of masculine social identities.

prestige planning   Introduced by Harald Haarmann (1990). PRESTIGE planning describes those aspects of LANGUAGE PLANNING that are directed at creating a favourable attitudinal background for corpus and status planning (see CORPUS PLANNING, STATUS PLANNING) as well as ACQUISITION PLANNING. The aim of prestige planning is to improve the speech community's ATTITUDES towards low-prestige varieties so that speakers are willing to use them in, for example, 'high-culture' domains (such as literature or religious ritual) or the educational system. Often, prestige planning involves the creation of a nationalist language discourse which identifies the VERNACULAR language as a core value of the SPEECH COMMUNITY. Prestige planning is a type of 'language promotion' and has sometimes been approached from an 'advertising' or 'language marketing' perspective (see Cooper, 1989).

primary language   See MOTHER TONGUE.

principal components analysis (PCA)   A statistical method which allows researchers to reduce the complexity of data sets consisting of a large number of interrelated or correlated variables to a smaller number of underlying variables. Principal components analysis allows the investigation of many LINGUISTIC VARIABLES simultaneously and helps to discover the structure of the relationships between variables. PCA was used by Barbara Horvath (1985) in her study of language use in Sydney, where she included over twenty different linguistic variables in her analysis.

progressive   Feature of verb forms used to denote ongoing/continuous/progressive activity. This is better described as a feature of ASPECT rather than TENSE, since it denotes duration rather than the time of the action *per se*. Thus, while *I go* is in the present tense but 'non-progressive', *I am going* is both present and progressive. Similarly, *I went* is in the past tense and non-progressive, whereas *I was going* is past progressive. Progressive forms, and the use of the progressive, are subject to variation. For instance forms such as *I was sat* are found in some northern varieties of English in England, whereas standard English would have *sitting*. STATIVE verbs (such as *know*, *like*) do not normally use progressive aspect in standard (British) English, but forms such as *I am knowing that* . . . are found in other varieties, for example in India and Singapore. See also PERFECT(-IVE); TENSE–MODALITY–ASPECT.

projection   Introduced by Robert Le Page and Andrée Tabouret-Keller (see Le Page and Tabouret-Keller, 1985) to describe the interpretative activities of speakers which underlie the selection of linguistic forms in general, and processes of linguistic FOCUSING in particular. Speakers develop models of the social world as a result of their regular, interpersonal interactions. Le Page and Tabouret-Keller call these models **projections**. The speakers' projections reflect ATTITUDES to group boundaries and group identities, and shape the speakers' linguistic and social behaviour. Ultimately these interpretations of the social world and definitions of group boundaries also contribute to the creation of specific patterns of linguistic variation at the level of the social group. See also ACTS OF IDENTITY.

pronoun, pronoun choice   Pronouns are words such as (in standard English) *I*, *you*, *she*, *he*, *it*, *we*, *they* that can replace a noun phrase or sometimes other sentence constituents. For instance, *she* can replace 'that girl I met at the shops yesterday'. Pronouns have been of interest as an aspect of language variation: different language varieties may be characterised by different pronoun systems (see for instance Joan Beal (1993) for a discussion of the pronoun system in Tyneside English and how this differs from the standard English system). Pronouns are also of interest because they may express certain relationships between speakers. In many languages, such as Japanese, the choice between different pronoun forms expresses varying degrees of familiarity, POLITENESS, FORM-ALITY, etc. – see Mühlhäusler and Harré (1990). See also T AND V PRONOUNS.

prosody   Speech rate, pause structure, variation in loudness and pitch range are aspects of prosody or intonation. Also called **non-segmental** or **supra-segmental phonology**. See also PARA-LINGUISTIC.

purism   A LANGUAGE IDEOLOGY which emphasises the desirability of linguistic 'purity', and which negatively evaluates the presence of foreign lexical or grammatical material in a language. Purist ideologies are frequently motivated by a desire to inhibit LANGUAGE CHANGE and promote the belief that languages should be 'cleansed' from foreign-language influences as well as from the influence of NON-STANDARD varieties (e.g. regional dialects, sociolects). The term is often used pejoratively. See also BORROWING; PRESCRIPTIVISM; VERBAL HYGIENE.

qualitative   Qualitative approaches to research may be contrasted with QUANTITATIVE approaches. Whereas quantitative research in sociolinguistics tends to look for general patterns in the distribution of linguistic features across different groups of speakers or different contexts, qualitative research is more concerned with the close examination of specific instances of speakers' language use. The term **qualitative paradigm** is sometimes found for this approach, in contrast to 'quantitative paradigm'. In the study of language variation, a qualitative approach might analyse the meanings, in specific contexts, of speakers' variable use of certain pronunciation features (for an example, see Coupland, 1985; contrast traditional VARIATIONIST approaches to STYLISTIC VARIATION). Qualitative approaches are usually associated with INTERACTIONAL SOCIOLINGUISTICS; see also ETHNOGRAPHY. Whereas quantitative and qualitative approaches are sometimes regarded as discrete paradigms, it is also possible to use them in combination, for example to use the general distribution of linguistic features in a community to help explain specific instances of language use; for an example, see Holmes (1996).

quantitative   Quantitative approaches to the study of language draw numerically-based comparisons between different types of language use: for instance, they may look at the frequency with which certain linguistic forms are used across speakers, groups of speakers, texts or text types. Quantitative approaches use DESCRIPTIVE STATISTICS and INFERENTIAL STATISTICS for data analysis.

The term **correlational linguistics** is also found for studies that have as their goal the identification of systematic CORRELATIONS, or interrelationships, between LINGUISTIC VARIABLES and SOCIAL VARIABLES.

Quantitative approaches are associated particularly with VARIATIONIST sociolinguistics in the tradition inspired by William LABOV – so much so that the terms **quantitative sociolinguistics** or the **quantitative paradigm** are found for this tradition. For instance, in his study of the language of New York City (e.g. Labov, 1966, 1972a) Labov was able to identify systematic patterns in the frequency distribution of certain pronunciation features across different social groups and speaking styles. Labov's work and other studies in this tradition have made a major contribution to our understanding of LANGUAGE VARIATION and LANGUAGE CHANGE.

A quantitative approach informs other sociolinguistic traditions, for example quantitative patterns have been identified in the use of interactional features such as INTERRUPTIONS. It is also typical for much work in CORPUS linguistics (researchers have analysed corpora of several million words to identify systematic patterns of usage across a range of text types; see e.g. Biber et al., 1998); as well as for work on LANGUAGE SHIFT (e.g. Clyne, 1991, described frequency patterns for the maintenance of HERITAGE LANGUAGES among Australian migrants).

Quantitative approaches are commonly distinguished from QUALITATIVE approaches, which focus more closely on the meaning of language use in specific contexts, but it is also possible to draw on a combination of quantitative and qualitative methods – for an example, see Holmes (1996).

queer linguistics A set of approaches to the study of language and discourse that are broadly poststructuralist (see POSTSTRUCTURALISM), informed by queer theory and aspects of feminist theory. Queer linguistics foregrounds language practices associated with marginalised, 'non-mainstream' sexualities; these would normally incorporate lesbian, gay, bisexual, transgendered and queer (often termed LGBTQ) sexualities, but could also include some marginalised heterosexualities and exclude gay sexualities thought to have been assimilated into the mainstream. In principle, 'queer' may incorporate other marginalised identities – for example, black and disabled identities may be examined from a queer perspective – but these rarely feature in queer linguistic studies.

Queer linguistics is not a single, unified approach, but studies undertaken from this perspective would tend to emphasise some or all of the following: a rejection of the idea of pre-defined stable sexual identities, and a focus on the construction of identities in discourse (see PERFORMATIVITY); a rejection of, and an attempt to deconstruct, binary oppositions such as 'hetero-' and 'homosexuality'; an interrogation and critique of HETEROSEXUALITY and HETERONORMATIVITY; a recognition of diversity and ambiguity (in relation to sexualities and associated language practices); historical and cultural specificity (in the identification of and meanings attributed to different sexualities); a focus on the study of localised practices (see discussion in Anna Livia and Kira Hall, 1997). Sometimes queer linguistics is framed as a linguistics of contact: for example, Rusty Barrett (1997) draws on concepts from CODESWITCHING to consider how African American drag queens use language styles to negotiate their overlapping identities as gay men, African Americans and as drag queens.

Queer, in these senses, has been reclaimed from its earlier meanings as a term of abuse. It is rejected by some researchers on the grounds that it still carries these earlier meanings, and would not be accepted by their research participants. It is also felt by some to be over-elitist and 'Western', and not conducive to political action.

See also DESIRE; LAVENDER LINGUISTICS, LANGUAGE(S); LESBIAN AND GAY LANGUAGE; LESBIAN, GAY, BISEXUAL, TRANSGENDERED, QUEER (LGBTQ) LANGUAGE; SEXUALITY.

question(s)   Questions have been of interest in sociolinguistics because their form may differ in different language varieties. Varieties of English make differential use of subject-verb inversion: for example, in Indian English, *What you would like to do?* is found, whereas *What would you like to do?* would be usual in standard British English. The form of TAG QUESTIONS (as in 'You'd like to go, *wouldn't you?*') is also highly variable across varieties of English.

Questions have also been investigated as an aspect of conversation: for example, some studies of LANGUAGE AND GENDER have suggested that women make more frequent use than men of questions that draw out other participants in conversation. However, question forms have a range of other functions: in classrooms, for instance, they may allow a teacher to control the direction of the interaction.

On **question intonation,** see HIGH RISING TONE.

questionnaire   A tool for data ELICITATION using pre-formulated, written questions. Questionnaire studies are relatively inexpensive and allow researchers to gather data from a large number of respondents in a relatively short time. Contrast INTERVIEW.

$$R$$

r-full, r-less   See RHOTIC.

race   Highly contested term. Whilst it has no basis in biological or scientific fact, 'race' is in widespread everyday usage to refer to particular groups or 'races' of people, usually on the basis of physical appearance or geographical location, who are presumed to share a set of definable characteristics. The term ETHNICITY is sometimes used to refer to the identity of different groups on the basis of their assumed or presumed genealogical descent. 'Race' in social studies of language is viewed as a social construct rather than a fact (hence the use of inverted commas around 'race'): that is, 'race' or 'racial groups' only exist because particular physical characteristics (such as skin colour, facial features) are attributed a special kind of significance in society. This attribution usually involves differentiation between 'races' in terms of status and power, resulting from a particular IDEOLOGY. It is acknowledged that 'race' has considerable force in continuing to inform policies, behaviour and attitudes, including those relating to language and behaviour (see discussions in Omi and Winant, 1994). For this reason, 'race', usually within the context of RACISM, has been a focus of study in sociolinguistic research (e.g. Reisgl and Wodak, 2000).

racism   Racism in language refers to discriminatory language and DISCOURSE practices concerning particular groups of people who are presumed to share a set of definable characteristics, usually on the basis of physical appearance or geographical location. Racism has been studied in sociolinguistic research in a number of ways, including studies which focus directly on racism in language use and studies which focus on the racist assumptions underlying language policy and practice.

Studies focusing directly on racism and language include research on discrimination in interaction in the workplace (e.g. Roberts et al., 1992); discrimination in encounters in legal contexts, such as interviews with the police and in court (e.g. Eades, 1995); the analysis of racist discourse in newspaper articles and political speeches (e.g. Krishnamurthy, 1996; Reisgl and Wodak, 2000).

Studies focusing on the racist assumptions underlying policies and practice include: challenges to DEFICIT approaches to language varieties associated with particular 'racial' or ethnic groups, for example the stigmatisation of AFRICAN AMERICAN VERNACULAR ENGLISH (see Labov, 1972c); the questioning of the prestige attached to standard languages (see STANDARD LANGUAGE IDEOLOGY): this effectively discriminates against all other varieties, including language varieties used by less socially powerful 'racial' or ethnic groups; challenges to the 'imperialist' role of English as a global language (see LINGUISTIC IMPERIALISM).

radical Creole   Term coined by Derek BICKERTON for a CREOLE that formed relatively rapidly from an unstable JARGON (or pre-pidgin) rather than gradually from a stable PIDGIN. Bickerton argued that such early-creolised varieties were 'true' Creoles, which differed most drastically from their SUPERSTRATES (the dominant colonial language on the plantations where many pidgins and Creoles were formed). Saramaccan, a language of Suriname, is thought to be a radical Creole. See Byrne (1987). See also ABRUPT CREOLISATION.

raise (-ed, -ing)   In the description of speech sounds, a process whereby a sound becomes articulated at a higher point in the mouth. During the sound change known as the GREAT VOWEL SHIFT, English LONG vowels were raised so that (for instance) the vowel sound in *meat*, pronounced [eː] in Middle English (similar to north of England *mate*), became raised to give its present pronunciation [iː].

random sample   A SAMPLE which is drawn in such a way that every member (or item) of a POPULATION has an equal chance of being selected. For example, researchers who wish to study language use in cities such as London or Johannesburg could simply select every nth person from the local electoral register or the telephone book. Alternatively (i.e. if they didn't want to restrict their sample to those who are entitled to vote or own a telephone), they could select every nth house in every nth street in each suburb or metropolitan area. Random samples are rare in sociolinguistics, where JUDGEMENT SAMPLES are more common.

rapport (talk)   'Rapport' refers to an emphasis on interconnectedness or mutuality in conversation – a meaning similar to that of conversational INVOLVEMENT. A distinction has also been made between **rapport talk** and **report talk** – see Deborah Tannen (1990). Tannen suggested that, in rapport talk, there would be a focus on relationships and participants would be concerned to emphasise similarity. Report talk, on the other hand, would emphasise independence; it would be characterised by, for instance, individual speakers holding the floor. Report talk would also be associated with a more hierarchical social order. Tannen suggested that women felt more comfortable with rapport talk and men with report talk, and that this could be a source of mutual misunderstanding. Claims about this sort of distinction between women's and men's talk have been criticised by feminist researchers for ignoring the unequal relations that obtain between women and men, and for adopting an essentialist view of women's and men's language – see e.g. Cameron (1995). See also LANGUAGE AND GENDER.

rational choice (model of language planning)   An approach to LANGUAGE PLANNING in which the planning process is regarded as a highly systematic and rationally driven activity: linguistic problems are identified, solutions are proposed, goals are formulated, costs and benefits are assessed; finally, the most practical solution is selected and implemented (e.g. Ray, 1963; see also some of the papers in Rubin and Jernudd, 1971). In reality, however, language planning is usually more *ad hoc* and 'messy' (see Cooper, 1989). Planners generally lack the necessary information to make informed decisions, for example for many countries there is no reliable information on speaker numbers, and the languages spoken are often not adequately described. Moreover, it is not clear how 'costs' and 'benefits' of language choices should be assessed (see COST–BENEFIT ANALYSIS).

reading passage   Used to elicit a relatively formal but fluent speaking style in sociolinguistic INTERVIEWS. Participants are asked to read a pre-selected passage from a text. In the reading part of the interview speakers still produce complete meaningful sentences but, because of the formality that is attached to the written language in many speech communities, tend to conform to prestige norms of pronunciation. Reading passages are usually designed by the investigator to include examples of words that contain pronunciation features relevant to the study. See STYLISTIC CONTINUUM.

real time An approach to the study of LANGUAGE CHANGE which compares linguistic data gathered at a certain point in time (T1) with data gathered at a later point in time (T2). For example, Joy Fowler studied POST-VOCALIC /r/ in New York in 1986 to see whether the CHANGE IN PROGRESS identified by LABOV in the 1960s did indeed continue across time. Her results confirmed Labov's analysis as she found that frequencies of /r/ had indeed increased between 1966 and 1986. Contrast APPARENT TIME.

realisation How abstract linguistic constructs are actually produced. For instance, the same PHONEME may be realised (pronounced) differently by different speakers or in different contexts etc. Other terms for this concept include **actualisation**.

reallocation Term coined by Peter Trudgill (1986) for a process that occurs when dialects of a language come into contact with each other, typically because of movements of their speakers. In such a situation alternative pronunciations, grammatical forms and words originally from different dialects may co-exist for a period of time. In the formation of a new dialect out of the older ones (a KOINÈ), several processes may occur. 'Reallocation' refers to the retention of what were once purely regional alternatives, with a realignment of functions – typically with one form serving as a formal and another as colloquial variant. Trudgill provides an example from Australian English in relation to the British dialect forms present at its formation. The vowel in *dance* demonstrates a broad distinction between northern and southern dialects of British English: it is represented as the phoneme /æ/ in northern dialects (like the vowel in *Pam*), but as /ɑː/ in southern dialects (like the vowel in *palm*). This regional contrast has been allocated new roles in varieties of Australian English. Whilst there is some regional differentiation within Australia, for many speakers the former vowel is associated with a local colloquial norm, while the latter vowel is associated with middle-class formal (or affected) styles.

Received Pronunciation (RP)   RP or Received Pronunciation (also popularly known as the Queen's English, Oxford English or BBC English) is the name used by linguists for the prestige ACCENT of the United Kingdom, typically used by the educated middle and aristocratic classes. Unlike other accents of English in the UK, RP is not restricted to a particular geographical region, and is particularly influential as the language associated with the British royalty, parliament, the Church of England, the High Courts and other national institutions. Within the study of English phonetics, RP was particularly important, as it was used as a model by Daniel Jones and others for the description of English, and continues to be an influential model, often used as a comparative norm in the description of other accents. The adjective 'received' is used in the sense of 'accepted, though not spoken, widely', though it has also been taken to mean 'the only accent received at the Royal court'. On variability and change within RP, see Wells (1982a, 1982b).

recreolisation   A process during which varieties on a CREOLE CONTINUUM start to become more, rather than less, CREOLE-like. A change in social circumstances may cause speakers to emphasise a Creole-based identity, rather than one which denotes an openness to the SUPERSTRATE (the dominant colonial language of a territory). It is argued that younger speakers of Caribbean Creole in Britain show a degree of recreolisation in response to social pressures.

reduplication   A grammatical term denoting the repetition of all or part of a word or MORPHEME with special semantic effect, typically to denote frequency, intensity or plurality. In Afrikaans the word/morpheme *plek* 'place' may be reduplicated as *plek-plek* to mean 'in several places'. A regular feature of SIGN LANGUAGES and of some PIDGIN and CREOLE languages.

referee design   See AUDIENCE DESIGN.

reference (referent, referential)
   1. Terms used in SEMANTICS to describe the way in which language refers to entities in the external world. **Referent** is the entity or phenomenon referred to by a particular use of language: for example, the referent of the word *book* is the object book. The **referential** nature of language describes that aspect of language

which is about something outside of language. This stands in contrast to **sense** relations, or the internal relationship between words in language: for example, in English, the meaning of any one of the three words *good, excellent, outstanding* is determined in part by the existence in the vocabulary system of the other two words.

2. Reference is also used to describe the different ways in which entities – things, people, events – are referred to within TEXTS. There are a range of linguistic features which enable speakers and writers to make such references: for example, pronouns (such as *he, she, it*) may refer to entities already mentioned or about to be mentioned (see ANAPHORIC and CATAPHORIC reference). Reference may be either ENDOPHORIC (referring to things mentioned in a text) or EXOPHORIC (referring to things outside the text). See also COHESION.

reflexivity

1. Refers to a fundamental aspect of human language, that is its capacity to facilitate explicit reflection on language itself, using language to talk about language (**reflexiveness** is also found in this sense). See LANGUAGE AWARENESS; CRITICAL LANGUAGE AWARENESS; METALANGUAGE)

2. Refers to the DISCOURSE PRACTICE of explicit commentary on the language and images being used in texts or the ways in which these are intended to be interpreted. This is common in advertising texts. Chouliaraki and Fairclough (1999) exemplify this in their analysis of a charity appeal where there is a picture of a young person alongside the word 'homeless'. One of the accompanying statements 'we could try to guilt trip you' is an explicit reference to the underlying aim of the text and an example of reflexivity in discourse. Chouliaraki and Fairclough see this **heightened reflexivity** as a feature of communication in late modernity (see MODERNITY).

3. An orientation to research and knowledge making which involves the researchers being critically self-aware of their own role in the research process. The importance of reflexivity is particularly emphasised in ethnographic research (see ETHNOGRAPHY).

regional language   A language which is spoken in a specific geographical region of a country but not across the entire political territory. Regional languages are rarely recognised in the national constitution of a country but are sometimes included in education policies. Examples of regional languages are Pushto in Pakistan or

Frisian in the Netherlands. The European Charter for Regional and Minority Languages, which came into force in 1998, sets out specific measures for the promotion of regional languages in Europe.

regional standard
1. A regionally marked version of the standard norm which has developed through STANDARD-dialect CONVERGENCE. See DESTANDARDISATION.
2. A regional NORM (or LANGUAGE STANDARD) which has developed through contact between dialects leading to dialect convergence. For example, the widely-used Bavarian regional standard developed not through standard-dialect convergence but through DIALECT LEVELLING (Auer, 1997).

regional variation   Linguistic differences that exist between speakers from different geographical areas, villages, towns or cities. This includes differences in ACCENT, vocabulary, morphology and sentence structure. For example, in the north-eastern part of North America the term *Dutch cheese* is used, in the American midland the same object is referred to as *cottage cheese*. Traditionally such regional varieties are called DIALECTS. DIALECTOLOGY is the systematic linguistic study of regional variation.

register   Used to refer to variation according to the context in which language is used. For example, most people speak differently in formal contexts (an academic lecture, job interview etc.) than in informal contexts (e.g. bantering with friends and family). Relatively well-defined registers include the language of the law, the language of science and also the language of Hip Hop or jazz. Registers typically differ from one another in terms of LEXIS and SEMANTICS (e.g. scientific terminology in scientific registers). 'Register' is distinguished from DIALECT, which describes variation according to the social characteristics of language users (e.g. speakers' regional or social background, gender, age, etc.).

In Halliday's SYSTEMIC FUNCTIONAL LINGUISTICS, register is analysed in terms of three key subcategories: FIELD, the activity or institutional setting, for example a child playing; TENOR, the roles and relationships between participants, for example small child and parent; MODE the communication channel used, for example spoken (see Halliday, 1978: Chapter 3).

relativity (linguistic) See LINGUISTIC DETERMINISM.

relexification A particular kind of large-scale BORROWING during which LEXICAL WORDS ('content' words – typically nouns, verbs, adjectives, many adverbs but not other parts of speech) in one language are replaced by those from another. This usually happens when speakers feel the pressure to acquire a new language without having full access to it. During relexification other systems of the original language (e.g. syntax and phonology) are relatively un-affected. Relexification results in a MIXED CODE, with the grammar and vocabulary emanating from originally different systems. PID-GINS are believed to be susceptible to relexification.

relic area A DIALECT region which has maintained older linguistic forms. Typically such areas are separated from other dialect regions by natural boundaries (e.g. rivers, swamps or mountain ranges), or by sociopolitical boundaries (e.g. political borders, religious or cultural differences). A **relic feature** is a language item that has been retained in a particular dialect, in contrast to other dialects where it is no longer used. For example, the velar fricative /x/ in Scottish English words such as *loch* and *nicht*.

religion Membership in religious groups can affect language use and language variation, and religion has therefore been included as a SOCIAL VARIABLE in some studies. In the case of Ireland, for example, Catholicism has been shown to be a central marker of group identity and a factor which shapes language behaviour (McCafferty, 2001).

religious language(s)
1. A language used in religious rituals. Religious languages are often special languages which differ from the language used in everyday communication, for example Classical Hebrew, Quranic Arabic, Church Slavonic. These languages are sometimes taught in special schools which are located outside of the normal education system. Emphasis is usually placed on the ability to read and recite sacred texts. In many cases, however, local languages are used in religious functions such as conversion and religious instruction (e.g. the use of local languages in missionary work – see MISSIONARIES); and public prayer and liturgy (e.g. Reform Judaisms which support the use of local languages, such as English in the USA, in public prayer; also the change from Latin to the national languages in the

Catholic mass after 1969 by Pope Paul VI). See Cooper, 1989, for discussion.

2. 'Religious language' also refers to the type of language use, or language practices, associated with religious ceremony or RITUAL.

relocation diffusion   See DIFFUSION (2).

re-nativisation   Used by Robert Cooper (1989) to describe the reintroduction of a language, which was at one point the native language of a SPEECH COMMUNITY and which has become restricted in use, or which is on the verge of disappearing from the community's REPERTOIRE. The terms **language revival** and **language re-genesis** are also found (see Paulston et al., 1993). Examples of re-nativisation include Hebrew, i.e. from a language which had been limited to religious rituals to its current status as national and official language of Israel; or Maori in New Zealand, which in the early 1980s was only spoken by older people and was considered to be endangered. In the case of Maori, so-called 'language nests' (*kohunga reo*) were established and older speakers began to teach Maori to children. The use of Maori is now on the increase. Other examples include Catalan, Welsh, Irish, as well as some Australian Aboriginal languages (see Kaplan and Baldauf (1997) for further references).

renovation   According to Robert Cooper (1989), an aspect of corpus planning (see CORPUS PLANNING, STATUS PLANNING). Renovation refers to LANGUAGE-PLANNING activities which aim at reforming or changing the linguistic structures of an already existing standard language or language norm. Examples include SCRIPT REFORMS; SPELLING REFORMS. The term is also used to describe the efforts of the PLAIN LANGUAGE MOVEMENT as well as feminist suggestions for gender-inclusive language usage (e.g. *chairperson* instead of *chairman*). Language renovation is often motivated by non-linguistic goals (e.g. decolonisation, liberation, national unity, equality). The terms **re-standardisation** and **language reform** are also found.

repair   Used in CONVERSATION ANALYSIS and some forms of DISCOURSE analysis to refer to a means for dealing with some sort of 'trouble' in conversation. 'Same turn repair' occurs when a speaker deals with trouble in his or her own speaking turn, but repairs may also be initiated by other speakers. Repairs include a wide range of strategies. Examples would include 'cut-offs': speakers cutting off what they are saying, perhaps to rephrase the utterance; or use of 'fillers' such as *mmh* or *uh* that allow a speaker time to search for a word or formulate a response to a question.

repertoire Refers to the set of language varieties that may be employed either within a SPEECH COMMUNITY as a whole, or by an individual speaker.

repetition A pervasive feature of language. Repetition may operate on any linguistic level – the repetition of speech sounds (e.g. rhyme – *slim Jim*; 'alliteration' or the repetition of initial consonants – *cold comfort*); prosodic features (rhythm in poetry); words ('It was a *long, long* time ago . . .'); phrases or clauses (*'he said* yes, *he said* no, *he said* anything that came into his head'). Repetition is often said to have a POETIC function, both in literature and everyday language use (e.g. LANGUAGE PLAY), and is also associated with RITUAL. In everyday conversation it is said to have a range of interactional functions – enabling speakers to produce more language fluently and with reduced effort, providing some redundancy and so aiding comprehension, contributing to interactional INVOLVEMENT.

'Repetition' also relates to the observation that language use or DISCOURSE is more or less 'pre-patterned'. Sometimes speakers repeat pre-patterned chunks of language, such as *the more the merrier* (see FORMULAIC LANGUAGE). Repetition is also the means by which new words and expressions diffuse through the language of a speech community and become established. More generally, it is argued that all (spoken or written) texts are made up of words and meanings from other texts (see INTERTEXTUALITY). In this sense, repetition is consistent with a view of language as inherently DIALOGIC, in which all utterances relate to prior utterances (see also BAKHTIN). See Tannen (1989) for a discussion of repetition in discourse.

report (talk) See RAPPORT.

representation Refers to the ways in which language and other systems of communication (e.g. non-verbal communication, visual imagery) represent objects, ideas, people and events etc. The term is often used critically, implying that language does not simply convey ideas etc. but represents these in particular ways (e.g. in accordance with certain sets of values). It is also used in a comparative sense, for example to discuss the ways in which verbal and visual elements in a text represent people or events. See also REPRESENTATIONAL RESOURCES.

representational resources   Term used to refer to the range of resources available for individuals to use in order to make meaning, engage in interaction with others and develop the self. Language is one such key resource but other resources include the visual, sound, touch (e.g. Kress, 1996; see MULTIMODALITY). Other terms used in a similar way are **semiotic resources**, **members' resources** (Fairclough, 1992a) and **symbolic capital** (see SYMBOLIC POWER). The term **affordance** is sometimes used to emphasise that different representational resources, for example speech, writing, visual images, enable or 'afford' different ways of communicating (see Kress, 2003).

re-standardisation   See RENOVATION.

restricted code   See ELABORATED, RESTRICTED (CODES).

retroflex   A term used in the description and classification of CONSONANTS, relating to their PLACE OF ARTICULATION. Retroflex sounds are produced when the tip of the tongue bends backwards behind the alveolar ridge. A retroflex /r/ occurs in some varieties of English (e.g. rural varieties in the south-west of England). Retroflex sounds also occur in many Indian languages and may be heard in Indian English. See also PHONETICS; INTERNATIONAL PHONETIC ALPHABET.

rheme   See THEME, RHEME.

Rhenish fan   A TRANSITION AREA in the northern Rhine region, Germany. The Rhenish fan shows a complex pattern of ISOGLOSSES, which represent a set of gradual phonological changes. The changes affected the voiceless PLOSIVES /p/, /t/ and /k/. These became FRICATIVES in the south German dialects, but were maintained in the dialects of northern Germany. Thus, in the north a dialect speaker would say *Dorp* ('village'), *wat* ('what') and *maken* ('to make'); in the south speakers would say *Dorf, was* and *machen*. In the transition area of middle Germany, however, speakers make variable use of plosives and fricatives: south of Cologne speakers would use the fricative *machen* instead of *maken* but would maintain the plosives in *dorp* and *wat*; near Mainz speakers would say *machen* as well as *dorf*, but maintain the plosive /t/ in words such *wat*. See also BORDER DIALECT; DIALECT CONTINUUM; LANGUAGE CHANGE.

rhetoric (-al)

1. Term used in classical approaches to language to refer to the effective art of persuasion in speaking and writing. In this sense, analysis of the rhetoric of a text is similar to that of ARGUMENT.
2. In the phrase CONTRASTIVE RHETORIC, used to compare ways of constructing meaning in writing in different languages.
3. In a general sense, refers to the rhetorical purposes of specific language use, for example, to engage in interaction, construct knowledge, enact IDENTITY (see also PERFORMATIVITY; SUBJECTIVITY).

rhotic   Varieties of English in which POST-VOCALIC /r/ is pronounced, i.e. speakers pronounce the /r/ in words such as *lark* and *car*. The term **r-full** is also found. Rhotic varieties of English are spoken in south-west England, Scotland and Ireland as well as in North America. Varieties where the /r/ is not pronounced in this position are called **non-rhotic** (or **r-less**). Non-rhotic varieties are spoken in most of England, Wales and in the Southern Hemisphere (Australia, New Zealand, South Africa). RECEIVED PRONUNCIATION (RP) is also non-rhotic. Both rhotic and non-rhotic varieties of English are found in the Caribbean.

rhyming slang   A type of language use associated with Cockney (London) speakers but also found elsewhere, for example in Australia (in this case derived from Cockney rhyming slang). In rhyming slang words are replaced by rhyming words or phrases: for example, to give *apples and pears* for 'stairs'. The rhyming word in phrases may also be deleted (to give *butchers* for 'look' – from *butcher's hook*). These are well-known, traditional examples, but the practice is productive, with more recent examples such as *Becks and Posh* for 'food' (nosh). Cockney rhyming slang probably originated in the nineteenth century, although its precise origins are uncertain (see Ayto, 2002). In contemporary use it often functions as a form of LANGUAGE PLAY.

rhythm   An aspect of PROSODY. A sense of rhythm in speech derives from a regular pattern of stressed and unstressed syllables (see also STRESS).

ritual   Refers to repetitive and highly formalised performances which are distinguished from everyday social practices. Well-known examples of ritual include religious ceremonies, parades and carnivals, rites of passage (i.e. coming-of-age ceremonies), memorial services, etc. The language used in ritual events is typically highly stylised, formulaic and often archaic (on the defining features of ritual language see, Du Bois, 1986).

The concept of 'ritual' was generalised to everyday interaction by Erving GOFFMAN (1967) in his work on **interaction rituals**, in which he included highly formalised practices (such as lifting one's hat as part of a greeting routine, shaking hands, etc., i.e. activities which are also referred to as **etiquette**). According to Goffman, these behaviours can be interpreted as small-scale ritual ceremonies which serve to reaffirm and reproduce the structures of social hierarchies in everyday encounters.

John Haiman (1994, 1997) has used the term **ritualisation** to refer to the repetitive and habitual aspects of speech which establish innovations across time and ultimately allow for the formation of new languages (see also REPETITION).

Ben Rampton (1995, 2002) also draws on aspects of ritual theory in his work on LANGUAGE CROSSING, relating this to the notion of LIMINALITY, or ambiguity/in-betweenness.

ritual insults   See VERBAL DUELLING.

role   Term taken from drama.
1. Broadly speaking, it refers to the different parts people play in their daily lives. Each person plays many roles: for example one person may be a daughter, a mother, a footballer, a teacher. Each role has a cluster of social conventions or norms which define and regulate the function of that role. The ways in which people take up and enact such roles is the focus of studies on IDENTITY, SUBJECTIVITY and AGENCY.
2. In studies of interaction the roles of different participants are variously defined: for example, as listener, speaker, overhearer (see ADDRESSEE).
3. In SYSTEMIC FUNCTIONAL LINGUISTICS 'role' is used to refer to a key element of the clause (see TRANSITIVITY).

rounding (rounded)   In the description and classification of VOWELS, a distinction may be made between **rounded** vowels (produced with lip **rounding**) and **unrounded** vowels (produced without lip rounding). For instance, [u] (the vowel in English *boot*) is rounded, whereas [i] (the vowel in English *beat*) is unrounded. See also INTERNATIONAL PHONETIC ALPHABET; PHONETICS.

rule   A formal specification about the workings of language or a linguistic process. For instance, in standard English, verbs in the present tense have no inflectional ending except in the third person singular, where they take an -*s* inflection (I, you, we and they *speak*, but he/she *speaks*). This may be formulated as a rule. In linguistics such rules are intended to describe and account for actual usage, not to prescribe usage (contrast PRESCRIPTIVISM). Of interest within sociolinguistics is the fact that certain rules may be applied variably (in different linguistic environments, by different speakers, in different social contexts): see VARIABLE RULE.

S

S-curve   Convergent findings from the study of linguistic change indicate that the temporal DIFFUSION (2) of new linguistic forms follows an 'S-curve' pattern: the change starts slowly, and initially only few speakers (or writers) make use of a new form (the so-called EARLY ADOPTERS); this is followed by a period of (rapid) acceleration in which the change catches hold and the majority of the speech community adopts the new form; finally the trajectory of the spread slows down as the new forms are adopted by the remaining members of the speech community. 'S-curve' refers to the shape of the line when such findings are plotted on a graph (see Figure 5). The horizontal axis indicates the time dimension, the vertical axis the number of speakers who use the new linguistic form. The vertical axis can also indicate the numbers of texts or genres in which the new form occurs, or the number of lexical words which have been affected by a SOUND CHANGE. See also LANGUAGE SPREAD.

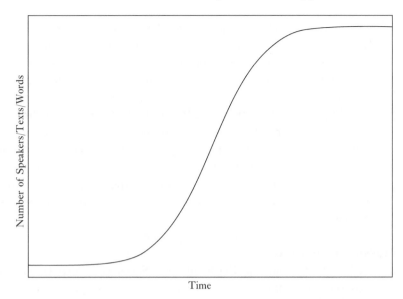

Figure 5 Schematic representation of an S-curve

sample Subsets of cases which are believed to be representative of the larger POPULATION that is of interest to a researcher. In sociolinguistic studies of language use the term sample could refer, for example, to a group of speakers which represent the wider speech community under study. Alternatively, researchers might collect a CORPUS of newspaper articles which are believed to be representative of newspaper writing. Sampling methods include: RANDOM SAMPLES, JUDGEMENT SAMPLES (constructed to include certain categories, e.g. members of specified social groups) and the FRIEND OF A FRIEND approach, in which a researcher begins with certain contacts in the community and is then referred on to others (also termed **snowball sampling**).

Sapir-Whorf hypothesis A claim that languages can differ so greatly in the way they encode semantic information (in LEXIS and GRAMMAR) that they can determine the way that speakers of a language think. For instance, natural phenomena (like climatic elements) are grouped or segmented in vastly different ways in different languages, and this will lead speakers of these languages to experience such phenomena differently. This theory of LINGUISTIC DETERMINISM, or linguistic relativity is attributed to Edward Sapir (an American anthropologist-cum-linguist) and his student, Benjamin Lee Whorf. Among their examples was the understanding of time as linear (e.g. past-present-future tense) in European and other languages as against some Native-American languages like Hopi, in which the tense system is only partly structured according to time in the Western sense, but also to space and the degree to which an event can be directly observed or learnt about by reporting (see Whorf, 1956: 63). The hypothesis has proved difficult to test, and more linguists today lean towards Chomsky's hypothesis of a universal grammar that stresses the single underlying capacity for language among all humans, and the limits to which languages vary. A weaker form of the Sapir–Whorf hypothesis specifies that language influences, rather than completely determines, thought. See also Whorfian.

Saussurean paradox

1. The Swiss linguist Ferdinand de Saussure (1857–1913), who described language as a social fact (that is, a communal or collective structure), nevertheless maintained that language can be studied adequately through the observation of any one individual speaker (typically the linguist herself/himself) who is a member of the SPEECH COMMUNITY. William Labov (1972a) called this the 'Saussurean Paradox', and argued that linguists interested in social aspects of language should instead study the language use of SOCIAL GROUPS (using representative SAMPLES of speakers).

2. In HISTORICAL LINGUISTICS (e.g. Trask, 2000) the term 'Saussurean paradox' is sometimes used to refer to a different problem, i.e. how does language as an ever-changing system function as a well-structured and stable medium of communication across generations? The problem was 'solved' by LABOVian variationist studies in the 1960s when it was shown that LANGUAGE CHANGE is a gradual and not abrupt process, and that old forms continue to exist next to new variants.

scaffolding   See ZONE OF PROXIMAL DEVELOPMENT.

schema   A term derived from work on artificial intelligence (AI) that has implications for how people understand language, or texts. A schema (pl. **schemata**) is a cognitive structure – a stereotypical representation of an object or an event, built up on the basis of people's cultural knowledge and experiences. People draw on familiar schemata in interpreting a text. For instance, if people talk about a visit to a doctor's surgery we can understand them partly because we know what doctors' surgeries are like and the kinds of activities that normally take place there. The notion of schema may also explain how people make different interpretations of the same text (i.e. if they draw on slightly different schemata); it may help explain cultural differences in communication, and misunderstandings or miscommunication (e.g. Roberts et al., 1992); and it has been used to explain the value of 'literary' texts (which, because they break conventions, have been said to challenge and 'refresh' familiar schemata; see Cook, 1994).

The term FRAME may be found with a similar meaning to schema. See also SCRIPT; WORLD KNOWLEDGE.

schizoglossia A medical metaphor used by Einar Haugen (1962) to describe situations where speakers are aware of the existence of two linguistic NORMS or VARIANTS (usually one 'STANDARD' and one 'NON-STANDARD'), but are unsure which is correct in a given context. See also HYPERCORRECTION; LINGUISTIC INSECURITY.

schwa See CENTRAL (vowel).

script
1. The form taken by the WRITING SYSTEM of a language. The Arabic, Cyrillic and Roman alphabets are examples of scripts. The same language may, in principle, be represented by different scripts, and SCRIPT REFORM is a common focus of LANGUAGE PLANNING.
2. Also, one of several terms sometimes used to explain how people understand language, or a text. A script is a stereotyped sequence of actions associated with a particular event or situation. People are said to draw on familiar scripts in interpreting a text. The notion of a script is therefore related to the notion of a SCHEMA, or FRAME. In interpreting an account of a visit to a doctor's surgery, for instance, a listener/reader might draw on a familiar schema (e.g. what the surgery would be expected to look like, the presence of certain things such as a desk, medical equipment, perhaps a curtained-off bed) and a familiar script (e.g. being invited in by the doctor or a receptionist, being asked to sit down, going through the routine of questions and answers, and perhaps an examination). Scripts, like schemata, may be useful in explaining listeners'/readers' differing interpretations of the same text, cultural differences in communication and MISCOMMUNICATION. Not all analysts make a strict distinction between 'script' and 'schema'

or 'frame', and the terms are sometimes used interchangeably. See also WORLD KNOWLEDGE.

script reform   An aspect of LANGUAGE PLANNING which concerns the adoption of a new SCRIPT. For example, in the 1930s Soviet language planners changed the local Arabic or Latin scripts which were used for many non-Slavic languages to the Cyrillic script in order to establish a uniform WRITING SYSTEM across the Soviet Union and to facilitate the acquisition of Russian as a second language (Lewis, 1983). After the disintegration of the Soviet Union many of these speech communities abandoned the Cyrillic script and returned to their former writing systems. The term **re-graphisation** is also found.

second-dialect acquisition (SDA)   The acquisition of a speech form which is considered to be a variety of the speaker's first language, e.g. the acquisition of the STANDARD by speakers of a NON-STANDARD variety, or the acquisition of the local dialect by speakers who have moved to a new dialect area. For most Australian Aboriginal children, for example, standard Australian English is a 'second dialect' which differs from their native variety, Australian Aboriginal English. Like SECOND LANGUAGE acquisition, successful second-dialect acquisition is restricted by the CRITICAL AGE of acquisition (see Chambers (2003) for a case study).

second language (acquisition) (SLA)   A second language (frequently abbreviated to **L2**) is the language of an individual or a community that is not acquired from birth, but at some stage subsequent to the first (or native) language. The term often refers to contexts in which the second language is available as a medium of communication (e.g. English learnt by Panjabi speakers in the UK, or Zulu by speakers of other languages in South Africa); contrast FOREIGN LANGUAGE. **Second-language acquisition** refers to the learning of a language under such conditions. The extent to which a second-language speaker acquires 'native-like' competence is affected partly by their age (see CRITICAL AGE). 'Second-language (acquisition)' may be used as a cover term for any language learnt subsequently to the first, since it has traditionally been argued that the principles of acquiring a second, third (etc.) language are similar. However, those who wish to emphasise the distinctiveness of different forms of acquistion tend to use separate terms (see THIRD LANGUAGE (ACQUISITION)).

Socially oriented studies of the acquisition of a second language have focused on a range of aspects, including the importance of context (van Lier, 2001); identity (Rampton, 1995); and power (Cummins, 1996). See also ENGLISH AS A SECOND LANGUAGE (X AS A SECOND LANGUAGE); LANGUAGE ACQUISITION.

secret language   Refers generally to a language variety used within a social group to maintain secrecy from outsiders. Secret languages usually consist of a set of vocabulary items, i.e. they are not actually languages in the conventional sense of the term. They may include invented words, or various transformations of words, designed to obscure meanings from outsiders (see ARGOT).

secular linguistics   See EMPIRICAL LINGUISTICS.

segmental (phonology)   See PHONOLOGY.

selection   The choice of a specific linguistic variety (usually a prestigious regional or social dialect) as the basis of a STANDARD language. For example, the Florentine dialect used by Dante and Petrach was selected in the sixteenth century as the linguistic basis of the early Italian standard language (see STANDARDISATION).

semantic derogation   See PEJORATION.

semantic field   Sometimes used in SEMANTICS to suggest that related words may be grouped into areas or fields. The meaning of a word would depend partly on its relationship to other items in the field. For instance, the meaning of *child* is related to that of *baby*, *youth*, *adult* and other terms that denote a particular stage of life. The composition and arrangement of semantic fields are likely to differ between languages and language varieties: languages may make different distinctions between recognised stages of life, family relations, colour terms, weather terms etc. and these may be analysed in terms of semantic fields. 'Semantic fields' is, however, a fuzzy concept and it is not always obvious how fields should be identified and differentiated.

semantics (semantic)   The study of linguistic meaning. Semantics is concerned with the meaning of words and sentences and with the relations between words (sometimes termed 'sense relations'). Word meanings may vary regionally and between social groups, giving rise to **semantic variation**. An example from English is the word *starved*, meaning 'cold' in some dialects spoken in northern England and 'hungry' in other dialects (including standard English). Some aspects of **semantic change** are also of interest within sociolinguistics; see AMELIORATION; PEJORATION). Semantic variation has, however, not been systematically studied within sociolinguistics. Many areas of sociolinguistics (e.g. INTERACTIONAL SOCIOLINGUISTICS, ETHNOGRAPHY of communication, various forms of DISCOURSE analysis) are concerned less with meaning as part of the linguistic system than with the use and interpretation of utterances in specific contexts.

semi-communication Introduced by Einar Haugen (1966a) to describe trans-national communication across the Scandinavian countries. Scandinavian semi-communication illustrates what Haugen has called the 'elasticity' of MUTUAL INTELLIGIBILITY. The national Scandinavian STANDARD languages show linguistic similarities (e.g. Danish and Norwegian share much of their lexical basis and Norwegian and Swedish are similar in pronunciation) as well as differences (e.g. the Danish pronunciation differs sharply from Swedish and Norwegian). Trans-national Scandinavian communication exploits the existing similarities in order to enable and facilitate communication between speakers from different language backgrounds. Generally, speakers continue to speak their native language (rather than a LINGUA FRANCA such as English), but modify it slightly in order to facilitate at least partial comprehension by the listener (i.e. they speak slowly, avoid grammatical constructions which are unfamiliar in the other languages, chose lexical variants which are common to all Scandinavian languages).

semi-Creole A term for a CREOLE-like language that arises out of language contact under conditions which are similar to those which produce a Creole. However, semi-Creoles do not involve a sharp break with the SUPERSTRATE (the dominant colonial language of a territory) in the way that Creoles (or BASILECTal Creoles) do. There is much disagreement whether the concept is a legitimate one, i.e. whether the dichotomy 'Creole – Non-Creole' permits any intermediaries (see Holm, 2000). Afrikaans and Reunion French are often cited as semi-Creoles – restructured

varieties of Dutch and French respectively, arising in a multilingual milieu that involved Europeans and slaves from many parts
of the world, but without ever becoming mutually unintelligible
with the European superstrates. See also CREOLOID.

semi-lingualism   Theory put forward by N.E. Hansegård (1968),
   and associated with Tove Skutnabb-Kangas, that in certain situations of SUBTRACTIVE BILINGUALISM individuals or groups may become bilingual without fully mastering the rules of either
   language. Such semi-linguals are held to lack 'full' competence
   in any language. The theory has been widely criticised on several
   grounds, especially since it compares the NORMS of two monolingual communities with a single bilingual one, whereas the latter
   is better thought of as a new SPEECH COMMUNITY with its own
   norms. It also sees the norms of speech communities as fixed and
   static and fails to draw a distinction between VERNACULAR (or
   everyday) contexts of language use and the very special, formal
   norms demanded in educational settings.

semiology   See SEMIOTICS.

semiotics (semiotic)   Semiotics is the scientific study of the properties of signalling systems, both artificial and natural – sometimes
   called 'the science of signs', associated with Charles Peirce (1834–
   1914). Semiotic systems include traffic lights, the use of flags in
   state institutions, and gestures in, say, animal communication.
   Above all, language is a semiotic system whose SIGNS are words
   (and morphemes) which stand in a particular relation to objects
   and concepts (see SYMBOL; INDEX; ICON). This approach was developed in the work of Ferdinand de Saussure, who identified two
   indivisible aspects of the sign – the SIGNIFIER and the signified.
   Semiology, Saussure's term for semiotics, has been further
   developed in Europe, especially in the work of Roland Barthes,
   who subjected different aspects of culture to semiotic/semiological
   analysis: music, eating, clothes, dance and literature.

semi-speaker   A term coined by Nancy Dorian (1981) for those
   speakers in a community undergoing LANGUAGE SHIFT, who start off
   with little or no speaking ability in the traditional community
   language, but who, through a rekindled LANGUAGE LOYALTY later on
   in life, begin to make an effort to speak it. The efforts of semi-
   speakers are often halting and reflect an imperfect command of

grammar and vocabulary. Yet, as Dorian argues, they are accepted by more fluent speakers as members of the same SPEECH COMMUNITY. See also PASSIVE BILINGUAL.

sequence (in conversation)   See SEQUENTIAL ORGANISATION.

sequential organisation   A major concern within CONVERSATION ANALYSIS. Rather than considering utterances in isolation, analysts pay attention to conversational sequences: for example, to how speakers open and close conversations, provide an account of an event and respond to the account, ask and answer questions. Close analysis of such sequences reveals how a SPEAKING TURN relates to a previous turn; and how it sets up, or prepares the way for certain following turns.

Within such sequences, conversation analysts have also focused on **preference** structure, distinguishing between 'preferred' and 'dispreferred' responses in conversation. For instance, an invitation may be followed by different responses, typically an acceptance or a rejection. These responses tend to have different 'shapes': whereas acceptances are fairly immediate, rejections may be preceded by a delay in the response, and may also include an explanation or justification. Rejections (and disagreements, refusals etc.) are referred to as 'dispreferred' and acceptances (and agreements etc.) as 'preferred'). This distinction is not meant to imply anything about speakers' feelings or motivations, but to characterise different response formats or shapes. The terms 'preferred turn shape' and 'dispreferred turn shape' are also sometimes used (see Pomerantz, 1984). See also ADJACENCY PAIR; CONVERSATION MANAGEMENT; TURN–TAKING.

setting   Part of a SPEECH EVENT, which may be associated with certain WAYS OF SPEAKING; setting refers to the time, place and physical environment in which a speech event takes place, for example a church, university tutorial room, office. See also CONTEXT; SPEAKING.

sex

1. Early sociolinguistic studies of women's and men's language tended to refer to **speaker sex** as a category that interacted with language, and to resultant **sex differences** in language use. For instance, sex was a SOCIAL VARIABLE in many VARIATIONIST studies

carried out in the 1960s and 1970s, along with other categories such as AGE and SOCIAL CLASS. Since the 1980s the term GENDER has become more frequent. This reflects a distinction commonly made in the social sciences between sex, as a biological attribute, and gender, as a social attribute. Differences in women's and men's language behaviour have usually been regarded as social and as requiring a social explanation. However, the idea of sex as a natural phenomenon (or a biological 'given'), and gender as a cultural reflection of this, is also challenged by some researchers who would regard both sex (the idea of a binary sexual difference) and gender as culturally constructed.

2. Sex is also found in the sense of sexual activity or sexual practice in literature on language and SEXUALITY. The relationship between sex (in both senses of the term), gender and sexuality is a matter of debate within research on LANGUAGE AND GENDER, and language and sexuality (see also LESBIAN AND GAY LANGUAGE; LESBIAN, GAY, BISEXUAL, TRANSGENDERED, QUEER (LGBTQ) LANGUAGE; QUEER LINGUISTICS.

sexism (in language)   Refers to discriminatory language practices, for example trivialising or demeaning references to women; or to sexist bias in the language system, for example GENERIC MASCULINE forms, LEXICAL GAPS (an absence of words referring to women's experiences), negative or sexual associations in words referring to women, historical PEJORATION in words referring to women. Studies of linguistic sexism have been motivated by a concern that inequalities in language reflect and contribute to the reproduction of broader social inequalities. These concerns have also led to feminist interventions designed to challenge sexism, ranging from guidelines to encourage **non-sexist** or **anti-sexist** language (e.g. the avoidance of 'generic *he*') to more radical attempts to subvert sexist practices. It has been argued that sexism results from male control of language – a contention that is disputed because it depends upon a homogeneous model of the language system; and it neglects actual language practices, including the role of female speakers. See Hellinger and Bussman (2001, 2002, 2003) on imbalances in the representation of gender across languages; and Cameron (1992) and Pauwels (1998) on feminist perceptions of language and feminist linguistic reforms.

sexuality   May refer to one or more of the following: a person's sexual orientation; their sexual identity (whether they identify themselves as 'gay', 'straight' etc.); their erotic desires. The relationship between language and sexuality is a matter of increasing interest in sociolinguistics and related disciplines/sub-disciplines (e.g. social anthropology). As an area of study, language and sexuality has been influenced by developments in several related and overlapping areas, for example LANGUAGE AND GENDER, FEMINISM and feminist linguistics and Queer theory/QUEER LINGUISTICS. See also DESIRE; LAVENDER LINGUISTICS, LANGUAGE(S); LESBIAN AND GAY LANGUAGE.

Many studies have interpreted sexuality as an aspect of a speaker's identity, focusing on language or language practices among people identified as lesbian, gay, transgendered etc. (traditionally there has been less research on language and heterosexual identities). Contemporary research tends to conceptualise sexuality, in this sense, as a discursive accomplishment rather than as an essential or fixed attribute of a speaker/writer, i.e. as something that may be realised differently, played up or played down, co-constructed or challenged in specific contexts (see also PERFORMATIVITY).

Deborah Cameron and Don Kulick (2003b) argue that an identity focus is over-narrow and that language and sexuality research should take a broader approach to include sexual/erotic desire: 'not only whom one desires but also what one desires to do' (p.8). See also Campbell-Kibler et al. (2002) and McIlvenny (2002) for examples of studies in language and sexuality.

shibboleth   A pronunciation regarded as distinctive of a particular group. Sometimes also used to refer to lexical or grammatical characteristics of language use which signal one's social background. Shibboleth is Hebrew for 'torrent' or 'stream' and its use as a linguistic term is based on a biblical story (Judges 12: 1–15): when the Gileadites, who were at war with the Ephraimites, had reached the Jordan, some of the Ephraimites tried to pass themselves off as Gileadites so that they would not be taken prisoner and could cross the river. However, since the Ephraimites could not pronounce the frictiave /ʃ/ (they pronounced the *sh* sound simply as *s*), the Gileadites simply asked all soldiers whom they encountered to pronounce the word *shibboleth* – those who weren't able to pronounce the fricative were thus identified as Ephraimites and killed.

short (speech sound)   See LONG, SHORT (SPEECH SOUNDS).

sign   In semiotics a sign is an element in a system that stands for an object, concept, state of affairs, etc. (e.g. a green traffic light stands for the command 'go'). The philosopher Charles Peirce (1940) distinguished three types of signs: SYMBOL, INDEX, ICON, each denoting a specific relationship between sign and object. In linguistics, the term **linguistic sign** is used for elements of the language system (words, morphemes, certain phrases) which stand for concepts, objects, states of affairs, etc. Ferdinand de Saussure ([1916] 1959) described two indivisible parts of the linguistic sign: SIGNIFIER (the linguistic form) and 'signified' (the concept it stood for or called into being). He stressed the (usually) arbitrary relationship between signifier and signified (a rose by any other name would still be a 'rose'). Some writers, especially the Soviet scholar V. S. Voloshinov, have stressed the ideological nature of the sign, claiming that different social groups, while speaking the same language, show fundamental disagreement over the meanings of key words and in matters of pronunciation.

sign language   A visual-gestural language used by DEAF people as their primary means of communication. Sign languages are rule-governed linguistic systems and are structured at different levels of analysis: semantics, syntax, morphology and phonology. Sign languages used in different countries are usually not mutually intelligible. Research into the structure of sign languages started in the 1970s and is a growing area of linguistic and sociolinguistic research. For a discussion of the sociolinguistic aspects of sign language, see Lucas (2001). See also FINGERSPELLING; SIGNED LANGUAGE.

signed language   Sometimes found with the same sense as SIGN LANGUAGE, but also used to describe artifically designed sign systems which represent the morpho-syntactic structure of a spoken language in a visual modality. Signs from the national sign language are borrowed, but arranged according to the word order of the spoken language (to give e.g. 'Signed English'); additional signs are also invented to represent inflections (such as a special sign for the third-person-singular inflection -*s* in English). Signed languages are not naturally used by Deaf people because they are slow and cumbersome. They are, however, quite commonly used in the education system by hearing teachers and support staff.

significance testing   Significance testing is used to calculate the probability or likelihood that the patterns of variation observed in a SAMPLE will also occur in the POPULATION from which the sample is drawn, i.e. they are not the result of a sampling error. The probability is represented by the so-called P-LEVEL. Results that yield $p < 0.05$ are generally considered **statistically significant**, i.e. in this case the patterns observed in the sample can be generalised to the population with a specifiable degree of confidence (the probability of error is smaller than 5 per cent). CHI-SQUARE, T-TEST and ANALYSIS OF VARIANCE (ANOVA) are frequently used for significance testing in sociolinguistic research.

signifier, signified   Terms associated with Ferdinand de Saussure's theory in which language is analysed as a system of SIGNs. Such signs (words or MORPHEMES) are made up of two indivisible parts: the **signified** is the concept or object referred to in language, while the **signifier** is the 'word for it'. Saussure stressed that the signified does not exist independently of the signifier – words do not just label objects or concepts, they call them into being. See also LANGUE, PAROLE.

signing   See FINGERSPELLING; SIGN LANGUAGE; SIGNED LANGUAGE.

silence   Silence is studied in sociolinguistics not simply as an absence of speech but as a potentially meaningful interactional device. Different levels and types of silence may be studied, for example the functions of pauses in conversation, silence as a strategy used by individual speakers, different cultural norms and meanings attached to silence. In POLITENESS theory, silence is sometimes associated with negative politeness, i.e. with not imposing on others or threatening their FACE. Silence has also been of interest within LANGUAGE AND GENDER, for example with the suggestion that, in many contexts, female speakers are effectively silenced, or at least have less opportunity to make themselves heard. Like other interactional features, silence may be used differently by different speakers and in different contexts: for example, in some contexts silence may be impolite (a refusal to acknowledge another speaker), or a threat. See also ETHNOGRAPHY; INTERACTIONAL SOCIOLINGUISTICS.

single-voice discourse   See DOUBLE-VOICE DISCOURSE.

situation Sometimes used to refer to aspects of the CONTEXT (e.g. SETTING, PARTICIPANTS) in which an interaction takes place, and which would be associated with language use. For example, relations between participants, and hence the way they use language, will differ in more, or less formal situations. See also CONTEXT OF SITUATION.

situational, metaphorical (code-switching) A distinction made by John GUMPERZ (e.g. Blom and Gumperz, 1972) and followed by some other researchers interested in the social motivations for CODE-SWITCHING. There is some lack of clarity in earlier definitions, but broadly: in situational code-switching a switch to a different language variety signals a change in the social situation to one in which different norms, interactional rights and relations between speakers obtain (e.g. a shift from a formal to a more informal context). Metaphorical code-switching involves the use of a variety not normally associated with the current social situation, and which brings with it the flavour of a different situation (e.g. the use of a formal or poetic expression in conversation between friends). In practice, such a clear-cut distinction is not always easy to maintain.

slang Variously defined but usually seen as a set of informal and colloquial words and phrases used within particular social groups and that are not part of the 'mainstream' language. Slang is often regarded as a counter-language, adopted in opposition to 'mainstream' values. It tends to date rapidly, but has been collected together in numerous dictionaries; see e.g. Green (1998); and the classic Partridge ([1961] 1974). Slang has a number of social functions: as an in-group variety it may be used to maintain group solidarity or increase social distance with outsiders; like other varieties, it may be used to redefine a context or relationship (e.g. as less serious); it may also be used as a form of humour, or language play. See also ARGOT; JARGON; RHYMING SLANG.

social class Historically the concept of social class goes back to Marxist sociology (see MARXISM). While classical Marxist analysis distinguishes only two classes (the bourgeoisie or owner class, and the 'exploited' proletariat or non-owner class), neo-Marxist approaches have identified an intermediate and ambiguous class, the middle class, which is both 'exploiter' and 'exploited' (see Poulantzas [1973] 1984). In sociolinguistics, class analysis has been used to show how language use clearly bifurcates along well-defined class lines (e.g. Rickford, 1986; see also Bernstein's (1971) account of ELABORATED and restricted codes). The existence of well-defined **class dialects** is typical for societies where one finds sharp STRATIFICATION between social groups.

Intuitive criteria are sometimes used to distinguish social classes. Most people find it fairly easy to judge whether an individual belongs to the working classes (also called 'blue-collar workers', i.e. people who are engaged in physical labour) or the middle classes (sometimes also called 'white-collar workers', i.e. people who work in offices and services). Sociolinguists have often worked with so-called SOCIO-ECONOMIC INDICES, which combine information about occupation, income, housing and education to determine 'social standing' (see STATUS). Socio-economic indices conceptualise social differentiation as gradual rather than dichotomous, and a greater number of (partially overlapping) groups are typically distinguished on the basis of such indices (e.g. lower working class, (middle) working class, upper working class etc.).

social construction (-ism) An approach to knowledge making and understanding which sees knowledge not as a body of facts but as constructed by communities of people in particular cultural and historical contexts (see Berger and Luckman, 1967). For example, sociologists of science argue that scientific knowledge is not a product of observation but the outcome of interactions between scientists working in a particular COMMUNITY OF PRACTICE (see Latour and Woolgar, 1986).

social constructivism An approach within psychology which emphasises that people actively construct meaning according to their current and past knowledge. Constructivism involves various approaches but these can be broadly characterised along two dimensions: those which emphasise cognition, that is the internal structures of the mind (e.g. Gregory, 1970) and those which emphasise social interaction (Vygotsky, 1986; Bruner, 1990). The latter in particular focus on the importance of language (see SOCIOCULTURAL). The term is sometimes used synonymously with SOCIAL CONSTRUCTIONISM.

social dialectology The study of language varieties and linguistic forms used by different SOCIAL GROUPS: see DIALECTOLOGY.

social distance   See SOLIDARITY.

social group   A network of people defined by regular interaction and shared values/norms. The term is also used more generally to describe sets of people who share certain social characteristics or attributes, but who do not necessarily interact regularly (e.g. women, men, teenagers, class groups). Often social groups within a given society or state are hierarchically organised and inequalities exist between groups. See also SOCIAL CLASS; SOCIAL NETWORK.

social history (of language)   See HISTORICAL LINGUISTICS; SOCIO-HISTORICAL LINGUISTICS.

social network   Individuals who interact regularly with each other are said to constitute a social network. **Social network analysis (SNA)** includes a range of tools and concepts which allow researchers to describe the structure of these interpersonal relationships. The units of analysis are the connections ('ties') between individuals, rather than the social attributes of these individuals (age, gender, ethnicity, etc.). Network analysts distinguish between **whole-network analysis** and **ego-network analysis**. Whole-network analysis describes all relations or ties between actors of a given group or subgroup (the guiding question is: 'Who knows whom?'); ego-network analysis focuses on the number and nature of ties reported by individuals, but does not aim to describe whole community networks (the guiding question is: 'Who does X know?'). In their work on language use in Philadelphia William LABOV and Wendell Harris (1986) made use of whole-network analysis; Lesley Milroy's (1987a) study of language variation in Belfast made use of ego-network analysis. Other sociolinguistic studies which have made use of social network analysis include Blom and Gumperz's (1972) study of language use in a Norwegian town; and Gal's (1979) study of LANGUAGE SHIFT in Austria.

Lesley Milroy's Belfast study has been particularly influential in developing a network model of LANGUAGE CHANGE and LANGUAGE MAINTENANCE (Lesley Milroy, 1987a; James and Lesley Milroy, 1985). Based on the results of fieldwork in Belfast, James and Lesley Milroy argue that a society's network structure can advance or obstruct the DIFFUSION (2) of linguistic changes. Frequency of contact in close-knit networks with STRONG TIES between community members has been shown to support the development of community NORMS and to promote the maintenance of established cultural practices (including language). Groups (or societies) with infrequently interacting group members, on the other hand, will exhibit more variable linguistic and social practices. Moreover, since loose-knit networks with WEAK TIES between members lack a linguistic norm of their own, the adoption of new linguistic forms or other types of behaviour by network members does not violate existing community norms and weak-tie networks are therefore generally more susceptible to innovation and change: see also EARLY ADOPTER; INNOVATOR.

See Wasserman and Faust (1994) for details regarding the application of SNA. Articles on SNA in general (i.e. not limited to its application in sociolinguistic research) are published in the journals *Social Network Analysis* and *Connections*.

social practice   See PRACTICE.

social psychology   Refers to a broad interdisciplinary field which draws on psychology and sociology to explore the relationship between the individual and the social world. Research within social psychology includes the study of attitudes, language use, meaning, social groups and institutions. The sociopsychological study of attitudes towards languages and language varieties (see EVALUATION); and of how speakers accommodate towards one another's speaking styles (see ACCOMMODATION) have been influential within sociolinguistics. DISCURSIVE PSYCHOLOGY is an area of social psychology that focuses on the analysis of DISCOURSE (see Potter and Wetherell, 1987), and thus has overlapping interests with sociolinguistics.

social semiotic(s)   M. A. K. HALLIDAY refers to language as social semiotic, that is a communication or sign system which is fundamentally social in nature (Halliday, 1978). Halliday argues that any **sociosemiotic** theory has to account for the relationship between the following different aspects of language: the TEXT (specific instances of language); the situation (see CONTEXT OF SITUATION); REGISTER; CODE (which he uses in Bernstein's sense); and SOCIAL STRUCTURE. More recent work referred to as social semiotics draws on SYSTEMIC FUNCTIONAL LINGUISTICS to analyse MULTIMODAL texts (see Kress and Van Leeuwen, 1996, 2001; Iedema, 2001).

social status   See STATUS.

social stratification   See STRATIFICATION.

social structure   Refers to the patterned relationships or structures that exist within society. The most prominent aspect of social structure to be studied in sociology is that of SOCIAL CLASS, and the relationship between social class and speaker variation has been a key focus in sociolinguistics (e.g. in VARIATIONIST studies; in early debates around the work of Basil BERNSTEIN – see ELABORATED, RESTRICTED (CODES)). Other aspects of social structure include ETHNICITY or 'RACE' and GENDER. A key focus in sociology and sociolinguistics is the extent to which social structures explain individual behaviour, including linguistic behaviour, or whether individuals through their actions and behaviour construct such social structures. This relationship is often understood as a tension or DIALECTIC. See also AGENCY.

social variable   Social variables are aspects of a speaker's social identity (e.g. SOCIAL CLASS, GENDER, AGE or ETHNICITY) which are correlated with language behaviour in QUANTITATIVE sociolinguistic research; contrast LINGUISTIC VARIABLE.

social variation   Refers to LANGUAGE VARIATION between social groups: how language varies according to SOCIAL CLASS, GENDER, AGE, ETHNICITY etc. Social variation therefore refers to INTERSPEAKER VARIATION, or variation between speakers, in contrast to INTRA-SPEAKER VARIATION, or variation within the speech of an individual speaker (STYLISTIC VARIATION). Sociolinguistic studies have demonstrated the systematic, patterned nature of social variation, and how this relates to LANGUAGE CHANGE; see VARIATIONIST (socio-linguistics).

socialisation   The process by which people learn the culture of their society, primarily via the family and peer group during childhood, and via school and the workplace later on. Language is a key part of this process, both as a medium for transmitting CULTURE as well as being a part of that culture.

sociocultural   Used to refer in broad terms to the ways in which language and communication are social and cultural phenomena. It is also used in a more specific way to refer to a particular approach within social psychology which focuses on the link between language and thought, and learning and teaching. Much work within this area has developed from the writings of Lev VYGOTSKY, who emphasised the important relationship between language, social interaction and learning. See also APPRENTICESHIP; ZONE OF PROXIMAL DEVELOPMENT.

socio-economic indices   Methodological tools for the description of social stratification, combining aspects of SOCIAL CLASS (economic position) and social STATUS (social prestige). This is frequently used in research in the LABOvian, VARIATIONIST tradition.

In his research on LANGUAGE VARIATION and LANGUAGE CHANGE in Philadelphia, William Labov assessed the social position of individual speakers by combining three six-category scales, reflecting occupational, educational and residential hierarchies; see Figure 6 below (Labov, 2001). Various combinations on the three separate scales are possible for individuals. The term **socio-economic status** may be used for a speaker's social position measured by such scales.

	Education	Occupation	Residence value
6	professional school	professional	$25,000 +
5	college graduate	white-collar (proprietor, manager)	$20,000–24,900
4	some college	white-collar (foreman, sales)	$15,000–19,900
3	high-school graduate	blue-collar (skilled)	$10,000–14,900
2	some high school	blue-collar (unskilled)	$5000–9,900
1	grade school	unemployed	$0–4,900

Figure 6   Socio-economic index scale (adapted from Labov, 2001: 61)

socio-historical linguistics   Introduced by Suzanne Romaine (1982) to describe studies which use sociolinguistic methods to reconstruct the social context of language use, variation and social differentiation for historical speech communities. Also called **historical sociolinguistics** and the **social history of language**. The latter is, however, often more macro-sociolinguistically orientated and is similar to Fishman's SOCIOLOGY OF LANGUAGE. See also HISTORICAL LINGUISTICS.

sociolect   See LECT.

sociolinguistic area   LINGUISTIC AREA denotes a territory in which unrelated or distantly-related languages have co-existed for such a long period (involving bilingualism) that they begin to resemble each other structurally (see CONVERGENCE). Prabodh Pandit (1972) introduced the broader concept of 'sociolinguistic area' to refer to a territory in which (a) an extended period of co-existence has produced structural similarities among originally disparate languages, and (b) speakers of these languages have begun to share a large number of sociolinguistic and sociocultural norms. Pandit described India as a sociolinguistic area in which there had been 'sociolinguistic convergence' between speakers of different language families in the expression of POLITENESS, in terms of ADDRESS, naming traditions, forms of greeting, onomatopoeic words, etc.

sociolinguistic interview   See INTERVIEW.

sociolinguistic variable   See LINGUISTIC VARIABLE.

sociolinguistic variation   See LANGUAGE VARIATION.

sociolinguistics (sociolinguistic)   An orientation to the study of language that stresses the inter-relationship between language and social life, rather than focusing narrowly on language structure. Whereas other branches of linguistics frequently play down the role of speakers in concentrating on grammar, phonetics or meaning, sociolinguistics highlights the COMMUNICATIVE COMPETENCE of speakers, the choices open to them and the ways in which they tailor language to different functions and interactional ends. Sociolinguistics stresses the variation inherent in a language, as speakers of different backgrounds use language not just for the communication of information but to express (and also to create) an individual and/or group identity. The field is characterised by a diversity of approaches according to the specific concerns of groups of scholars. Whilst uniting under the banner of sociolinguistics, different research traditions foreground the social context, speaker characteristics, the nature of the interaction, the choice of one language or variety over another, the study of marginalised languages, language in educational contexts, the ideology implicit in DISCOURSE etc. See also ETHNOGRAPHY (of speaking); INTERACTIONAL SOCIOLINGUISTICS; MACROSOCIOLINGUISTICS; MICROSOCIOLINGUISTICS; SOCIOLOGY OF LANGUAGE; VARIATIONIST (sociolinguistics).

sociology of language   Overlaps with the term SOCIOLINGUISTICS, while generally concerned more with MACROSOCIOLINGUISTICS rather than MICROSOCIOLINGUISTICS, and associated to a large extent with the work of Joshua FISHMAN (1968). Broadly speaking, whereas (micro) sociolinguistics takes language as its starting point and draws on society as a necessary background and analytic construct to understand language, the sociology of language takes society as its starting point and analyses language developments with a view to illuminating the nature of society. There are many instances, however, when the approaches seem to be two sides of the same coin, and several topics like LANGUAGE SHIFT, BILINGU-ALISM, CODE-SWITCHING, ACTS OF IDENTITY have been informed by both approaches.

sociophonetics Involves the application of PHONETICS to sociolinguistic study. For instance, research may draw on the acoustic measurement of speech sounds to investigate aspects of REGIONAL VARIATION, SOCIAL VARIATION, STYLISTIC VARIATION, or LANGUAGE CHANGE. For an illustration, see Docherty and Foulkes (1999).

sociopragmatics See PRAGMATICS.

solidarity The degree of closeness or **social distance** between people. Solidarity may be used as a general term referring to the close/distant dimension; it also refers more specifically to social closeness (as opposed to distance). The degree of solidarity that exists between speakers is a factor that may affect their language use. R. Brown and A. Gilman (1960) drew on the concept of solidarity in their analysis of T AND V PRONOUNS, arguing that in many European languages, the system of pronoun choice (i.e. whether speakers used T ('familiar') or V ('polite') pronouns to one another) had shifted from one based on POWER to one based on solidarity. Tannen (1993) argues that the relationship between power and solidarity is more complex than suggested by Brown and Gilman: for example, utterances in context are often ambiguous, and may contain elements of both power and solidarity.

sound change A LANGUAGE CHANGE which affects the phonological structure of a language, a phonological change. Changes in the pronunciation of vowels, for example, have been studied in considerable detail by sociolinguists (see e.g. CHAIN SHIFT).

sound law A statement which describes sound correspondences across related languages. These correspondences are the result of highly regular SOUND CHANGES and are believed to be exception-less. In other words, if a sound X changed to sound Y in one word, X would have changed to Y in comparable linguistic environments in every word in which it appeared. An example would be the regular correspondences which exist in the Indo-European language family, for example voiced plosives in Sanskrit such as /d/ (*dásá* 'ten') became unvoiced in the Germanic languages (Old English *ten(e)*, Dutch *tien*, Gothic *taíhun*). The German term *Lautgesetz* is also found.

source language
   1. In LANGUAGE CONTACT studies the language from which another language borrows a word or other linguistic item. For example, German is the source language for English *kindergarten*. See also BORROWING; contrast HOST LANGUAGE.
   2. In translation studies, the language from which a translation is made. For example, for a text translated from Finnish into Greek, Finnish is the source language. Contrast TARGET language.

Southern Hemisphere Shift   Term used to describe the CHAIN SHIFT in varieties of South African, Australian and New Zealand English, whose impetus lies in the influence of nineteenth-century working-class British settlers. The main characteristic shared by these varieties is the RAISING of FRONT vowels words such as in *bad* and *bed*, with concomitant changes to the vowel in *bid*. These 'Southern Hemisphere Englishes' share a number of similarities with English in the south of England, and the southern USA, hence William Labov's general term SOUTHERN SHIFT. However, they are a clearly demarcatable subset of the larger group in terms of their linguistic and sociolinguistic characteristics.

Southern Shift   A cover term used by William Labov for varieties of English that share a number of sound-shifts that differentiate them from RP, northern British English dialects and the northern cities of the USA. Somewhat fortuitously these varieties are spoken in the Southern Hemisphere territories (South Africa, New Zealand and Australia; see SOUTHERN HEMISPHERE SHIFT) and in the southern parts of England and the USA. These varieties share several characteristics of their vowel systems, including (a) turning the diphthong in *kite*, *time*, etc into a monophthong (see VOWEL) with some degree of BACKING and RAISING; and (b) raising FRONT vowels in words such as *bad* and *bed*, with concomitant changes to the vowel in *bid*. See also NORTHERN CITIES SHIFT.

speaker innovation   A novel linguistic form used by a speaker which has the potential to initiate a language change (Milroy, 1992). Speaker innovations can be accepted or resisted by the speech community. Changes which are accepted typically diffuse gradually through the community following the S-CURVE model. See also ACTUATION; INNOVATOR.

SPEAKING   An acronym coined by Dell HYMES (e.g. Hymes, 1972: 59ff.). The acronym incorporates what Hymes refers to as the 'components of speech': it is an attempt to specify relevant features of any SPEECH EVENT, such as an interview, conversation, lecture etc. It includes the following components:

SETTING and scene – 'setting' refers to time, place, physical circumstances; and 'scene' to the cultural definition of an occasion: within the same setting, the scene may be redefined (e.g. shifting from formal to informal).

PARTICIPANTS – all those involved in a speech interaction: speakers, those directly addressed, other listeners or audience members, etc.

Ends – the purposes, or goals and outcomes of an interaction: 'goals' are what speakers intend to achieve (termed 'ends in view' by Hymes), and 'outcomes' are what is actually accomplished (e.g. a decision, a settlement).

Act sequence – SPEECH ACTS are particular types of utterance (e.g. a greeting, a command); in the term 'act sequence', Hymes is referring both to the content, or topic of an utterance and its form (how it is said); he argues that both are central to the speech act and also that they are interdependent: '*how* something is said is part of *what* is said' (p. 59).

KEY – the tone, manner or spirit of a speech act; acts that are similar in other respects may differ in terms of key (e.g. between mock and serious, or painstaking and perfunctory).

Instrumentalities – refers both to the particular language variety/ies used and to the channel or mode of communication (e.g. oral, written).

NORMS (of interaction and interpretation) – 'norms of interaction' relate to certain rules of speaking (e.g. whether interruption is allowed or not, whether you can speak in a normal voice or need to whisper); 'norms of interpretation' refer to how such forms of speech may be interpreted (Hymes notes that norms of interpretation differ in different communities).

GENRES – categories that may be formally distinguished (e.g. poem, myth, tale, sermon, prayer). While these may coincide with speech events (see above) Hymes argues that they are analytically distinct, for example if a sermon (genre) were used for satirical effect, this would constitute a different speech event.

speaking pitch   See PITCH.

speaking style   See STYLE.

speaking turn   May be used by conversation analysts and interactional sociolinguists with its everyday meaning of a turn taken by a participant in a conversation. However, in practice the identification of distinct speaking turns is not straightforward (see also TURN-TAKING). Two or more speakers may jointly construct a turn (see DUETTING); in some analyses, certain utterances may not be seen as speaking turns at all (e.g. MINIMAL RESPONSES or BACK CHANNELS; 'off-record' talk or asides); and there is the possibility of silent turns (when SILENCE itself is meaningful) or non-verbal turns (e.g. a nod, eye-contact or gesture). See also CONVERSATION ANALYSIS; CONVERSATION MANAGEMENT.

Spearman Rank Order Correlation   See CORRELATION.

speech accommodation (theory)   See ACCOMMODATION.

speech act (theory)   Within a functional analysis of language, a speech act refers to the act performed by an utterance (e.g. a question, command or warning). This is distinct from the formal properties of the utterance: the same linguistic structure (*Is that your jacket on the bed?*) may, in different contexts, function as a question or a command (e.g. to hang the jacket up).

Speech act theory originated in the work of the philosopher J. L. Austin (see Austin's 1955 lectures, reproduced in Austin, 1962) and was further developed by J. R. Searle, a student of Austin's (e.g. 1969, 1975). Austin made an initial distinction between CONSTATIVE utterances, such as *The cat sat on the mat*, or *I went to Paris yesterday*, that were statements of fact and could be seen as either true or false; and performative utterances, which constituted an action simply by virtue of being uttered. For instance, *I promise to* *pay you back tomorrow* and *I warn you not to touch that* perform the acts of, respectively, promising and warning. Austin argued that while these utterances were in statement form, they were not statements of fact, and could not be regarded as true or false. They could, however, be what Austin termed 'happy' or 'unhappy'. To be happy, a performative needed to conform to certain conditions (termed FELICITY CONDITIONS). In the case of promising (above), for instance, the speaker would need to intend repaying what he or she had borrowed – to promise without the intention of repaying would constitute an abuse of the promise formula. Austin acknowledged that performatives did not necessarily require a performative verb such as *promise* or *warn* (*Don't touch that* may constitute a warning). He also came to recognise that the performative/constative distinction was itself problematical: all sorts of utterances, including those previously classified as constative, performed some sort of action (stating something could be regarded as an act). They also needed to satisfy conditions similar to felicity conditions. In the case of *The cat sat on the mat*, for instance, the speaker needs to believe there is a cat sitting on a mat, and this condition is similar to that of a speaker intending to fulfil a promise. The constative/performative distinction effectively collapsed, and speech-act theory became concerned more generally with the acts performed by a range of utterances.

Austin distinguished between three types of act: a **locutionary act**, which refers to the act of uttering itself (i.e. producing sounds that make up words that conform to a grammar and have a certain meaning); an **illocutionary act**, which is the act performed by the speaker by producing the utterance (as in the examples above – promising, warning etc.); and a **perlocutionary act**, which refers to the effect on a listener (e.g. persuading or convincing someone). The term 'force' is also used to indicate the way an utterance is to be taken (e.g. an utterance could have the illocutionary force of a promise.) It is illocutionary acts, or the illocutionary force of utterances, that have principally occupied subsequent research and the term speech act is often used in the sense of illocutionary act.

A number of problems have been identified with the notion of speech acts. For instance, these work best with 'made-up' sentences or highly ritualised occurrences: in naturally-occurring conversation it is hard to tie speech acts down to specific utterances (an utterance may perform several acts, or an act may be spread across several utterances); acts may also be ambiguous, or they may be identified on the basis of the response made to them rather than being evident (at least to the analyst) in the act itself; the number of speech acts is potentially vast and it is probably impossible to identify and categorise all of these. However, the idea of speech as a form of action has been widely influential across various forms of DISCOURSE analysis and CONVERSATION ANALYSIS.

speech community   A speech community comprises people who are in habitual contact with each other by means of language – either by a common language or by shared ways of interpreting linguistic behaviour where different languages are in use in an area. The concept is preferred to the grouping of people on the basis of nationhood (since many speech communities may exist within a state) or geographical borders (since a relatively unified speech community may be spread over 'soft' geographical borders; conversely speakers of the same language may not constitute a speech community if they are separated by rigid geographical barriers, as is the case of, say, British and American English).

Even within sociolinguistics, 'speech community' is used with different emphasis by scholars, to the extent that some question how useful the term is. Definitions have focused on the frequency of interaction by a group of people (Bloomfield, 1933); shared language use (Lyons, 1970); shared rules of speaking and inter-pretations of speech performance (Hymes, 1972); shared attitudes and values regarding language forms and language use (Labov, 1972a); and shared sociocultural understandings and presupposi-tions regarding speech events (Sherzer, 1977). Hymes' (1974: 51) summary combines these as '. . . a community sharing knowledge of rules for the conduct and interpretation of speech. Such sharing comprises knowledge of at least one form of speech, and know-ledge also of its patterns of use. Both conditions are necessary.' Other ways of conceptualising groups of speakers are becoming established in sociolinguistics, based on interests and goals (see DISCOURSE COMMUNITY) and joint activity (see COMMUNITY OF PRACTICE). These are arguably overlays upon the more general, if loosely defined, speech community that provides individuals with VERNACULAR speech early in life.

speech continuum   See DIALECT CONTINUUM.

speech evaluation   See EVALUATION

speech event   Associated particularly with ethnographically oriented sociolinguistics (see ETHNOGRAPHY), 'speech event' refers to a culturally recognised activity associated with particular rules or norms for the use of speech, for example a job interview, lecture, informal conversation (see e.g. Hymes, 1972). HYMES coined the acronym SPEAKING to specify the relevant components of any speech event.

speech island   From the German *Sprachinsel* (and also known as **language enclave**), referring to the existence of a language as a MINORITY LANGUAGE outside its original (or perceived) homeland. The speakers of such a language show an awareness of their linguistic, cultural and ethnic identity, and exhibit patterns of LANGUAGE MAINTENANCE well beyond the three to four generations commonly reported in studies of language shift in migrant communities (see e.g. Rayfield, 1970, for the USA). Within German sociolinguistics, a substantial area of comparative study has developed which focuses on German *Sprachinseln* varieties in Russia, the USA, Brazil, Namibia, etc. (see Mattheier, 1994). From a sociolinguistic point of view, not all linguistic minorities form speech islands – cases exist where such groups do not show awareness of links to other speech communities, like Breton in France, whose speakers do not claim wider links with other Celtic speakers. Speech islands form a subset of TRANSPLANTED languages, the difference being that some transplanted languages like Australian English are not minority languages and therefore do not form an 'enclave'.

speech level   See LEVEL (2).

speech style   See STYLE; LEVEL (2).

spelling pronunciation   Pronunciation of a word that has been influenced by its spelling, for exampe whereas *forehead* was once widely pronounced [fɒɹɪd] (as if it were *forrid*), the influence of its spelling has led many speakers to pronounce it [fɔːhɛd]. Similarly, *often* has developed two common pronunciations, without and with the *t*. The latter is a spelling pronunciation. These are isolated instances, since FIRST LANGUAGE speakers master the pronunciation NORMS of their dialect before they learn how to spell. Spelling pronunciation is thus more likely to occur with 'difficult' or 'foreign' words that one first encounters in print.

spelling reform   Changes in an established spelling system (e.g. the German spelling reform of 1996 (see Johnson, 2002), which changed, among other things, the traditional rules for capitalisation and punctuation, and replaced the German letter *ß* with *ss*); this is usually aimed at improving the relationship between 'sound' and 'letter', which is believed to facilitate literacy teaching. See also LITERACY PLANNING.

Sprachbund   See LINGUISTIC AREA.

spread   See LANGUAGE SPREAD.

stable bilingualism   A situation when two languages co-exist in a society over a long period of time in a relatively stable relationship, i.e. characterised by LANGUAGE MAINTENANCE rather than LANGUAGE SHIFT. Furthermore, the DOMAINS in which each language is used typically remain the same over time. See also BILINGUALISM.

stable pidgin   See PIDGIN.

stable variation   Patterns of VARIATION which persist across time, and which are thus not indicative of a CHANGE IN PROGRESS.

standard (language, variety)   A standard language is usually identified as a relatively uniform variety of a language which does not show regional variation, and which is used in a wide range of communicative functions (e.g. OFFICIAL LANGUAGE, MEDIUM OF INSTRUCTION, LITERARY LANGUAGE, scientific language, etc.). Standard varieties tend to observe prescriptive, written NORMs, which are codified in grammars and dictionaries. They are thus different from NON-STANDARD varieties, whose norms are generally uncodified and unwritten. Although standard languages are often regarded as discrete varieties, it is not usually possible to establish clear boundaries that distinguish them from other varieties. In many European countries, REGIONAL STANDARDS have developed which show varying degrees of influence from the local dialects. Standard languages may, therefore, be better regarded as idealised varieties.

See DESTANDARDISATION; LANGUAGE STANDARD; STANDARD LANGUAGE IDEOLOGY; STANDARDISATION.

standard language ideology   A concept introduced to sociolinguistics by James Milroy and Lesley Milroy (1999) in order to describe the prescriptive attitudes that accompany the emergence of STANDARD languages. Standard Language Ideologies (SLIs) are characterised by a metalinguistically articulated and culturally dominant belief that there is only one correct way of speaking (i.e. the standard language). The SLI leads to a general intolerance towards linguistic variation, and non-standard varieties in particular are regarded as 'undesirable' and 'deviant'. See also COMPLAINT; LANGUAGE IDEOLOGY; PRESCRIPTIVISM.

standardisation   The process by which STANDARD languages are developed. Following Einar Haugen (1966b), four stages are commonly distinguished in the standardisation process: the choice of a regional or social variety as the basis of the standard language (SELECTION of norm); the description of prescriptive (usually written) language norms in grammars, spelling manuals and dictionaries (CODIFICATION of form); the promotion and acceptance of these norms by the speech community (IMPLEMENTATION); and the ongoing development of the standard language which allows speakers to meet a wide range of communicative demands (ELABORATION of function). The aim of standardisation is to achieve 'minimal variation in form' and 'maximal variation in function' (Haugen, 1972). See also LANGUAGE PLANNING.

standardisation cycle   According to Greenberg (1986) and Ferguson (1988), a regular historical process by which an originally relatively uniform language splits into several DIALECTs; then at a later stage a common, uniform STANDARD is established on the basis of these dialects. Finally, this variety will again split into regional and social varieties and the cycle will start again. See also DESTANDARDISATION; DIALECTALISATION.

statistical significance   See P-LEVEL; SIGNIFICANCE TESTING.

stative   A subcategory of verbs, denoting a state or situation rather than an activity. In many languages stative verbs are treated differently from **non-stative** verbs. In standard English, non-stative verbs may take the PROGRESSIVE form in some forms of *be* + *-ing*; stative verbs may not. Thus *eat*, *play*, *wonder* are non-stative verbs, which allow *I'm eating, playing, wondering* while *know, love, belong* are statives, which disallow **I'm knowing, loving, belonging*.

The distinction is not always clear-cut in actual usage and many varieties of English in Africa and Asia do allow *be* + *-ing* with stative verbs.

status

1. The concept of status, or **social status**, was introduced by the sociologist Max Weber (1864–1920) to describe the non-economic, cultural aspects of social STRATIFICATION. Status differentiation is based on the social honour or prestige assigned to certain groups by others and is typically determined on the basis of education, vocation or achievements (i.e. **achieved status**), as well as on the basis of heredity (**ascribed status**), for example an aristocratic title. Social status thus differs from traditional CASTE systems, which are defined solely in terms of heredity. Status differentiation is independent of SOCIAL CLASS membership, which is economically motivated, and status groups can be formed across class lines. For example, the social status of immigrant workers is usually lower than the status of indigenous workers, although both may share the same class position. Status groups may evolve into a close caste and higher-status groups operate mechanisms of social closure to keep out those below (ELITE CLOSURE).
2. In sociolinguistics 'status' is not always used in the original sense of Weber but can also occur as a broad synonym for SOCIAL CLASS.

For **socio-economic status**, see SOCIO-ECONOMIC INDICES.

status planning   See CORPUS PLANNING, STATUS PLANNING.

stereotype

1. A particular type of LINGUISTIC VARIABLE containing a VARIANT that is recognised (or misrecognised) by some members of a speech community and used as a basis for negative comments on varieties that contain such a variant. H-DROPPING in Cockney and other English dialects is a variable that is subject to stereotyping. Likewise outsiders stereotype New York working-class speech on the basis of pronunciations like *thoidy-thoid* for *thirty-third (street)*. Linguists point to the inaccuracies of the stereotype since it misrepresents the actual pronunciation, which uses the diphthong [əɪ] rather than [ɔɪ]. Stereotypes contrast with INDICATORS (variables of which speakers are unaware); and MARKERS (variables of which speakers are aware, but which are not associated with stereotyping).
2. More generally, in the study of intergroup relations and language

attitudes, the usual sense of 'stereotype' prevails – i.e. an uninformed and frequently culturally-biased overgeneralisation about sub-groups (and their language or dialect) that may or may not be based on a small degree of truth. Stereotypes concerning language may involve assertions like 'women are excessively talkative', 'Italian is beautiful', etc. See also FOLK LINGUISTICS.

stop   See PLOSIVE.

stratification (stratified)   The existence of different SOCIAL GROUPS (characterised by different social and linguistic practices as well as differences in STATUS and SOCIAL CLASS) in a society. Sociolinguists distinguish between **sharp stratification** and **gradient stratification** in relation to LINGUISTIC VARIABLES. Sharply **stratified** variables show discontinuities across social groups, i.e. some groups use a given linguistic form or variety frequently, while other groups use the same form or variety only rarely. Situations of sharp stratification may give rise to the development of relatively well-defined **class dialects**. Gradient (or fine) stratification exists in those cases where the differences between social groups are relatively small, gradual and incremental.

stress   'Stress' refers to the prominence attached to certain syllables in a word or utterance (e.g. in the word 'habit' the first syllable is stressed, indicated by the symbol ', the INTERNATIONAL PHONETIC ALPHABET marker of stress). The pattern of stressed and unstressed syllables contributes to a sense of RHYTHM in speech. 'Stress' may also be used for the emphasis given to certain words in an utterance, as in 'I couldn't do *that*', with the emphasis on *that*.

The term **stress-timed** has sometimes been used of languages such as English, where the timing between stressed syllables is roughly equivalent, irrespective of how many unstressed syllables occur between these. This is said to contrast with **syllable-timed** languages such as French, where roughly equal time is given to each syllable. This distinction may also be made between different varieties of English: for instance the varieties of English spoken in the Caribbean and India have been characterised as syllable-timed.

strong ties   Frequently used, reciprocal and intimate interpersonal relationships in SOCIAL NETWORKS. The strength of ties is usually measured in terms of frequency of contact and the number of different capacities within which speakers interact with one another (see MULTIPLEX). Relationships between family members who are in frequent contact with one another, who are also neighbours and workmates and share leisure activities would be an example of strong-tie connections. Strong ties have been shown to support the formation as well as maintenance of social, cultural and linguistic NORMS. Contrast WEAK TIES.

structuralism Term strongly associated with the anthropologist Claude Lévi-Strauss and used to refer to an approach to human behaviour which emphasises patterns or structures: for example, social class structures, kinship structures. In specific relation to language, structuralism refers to an approach which focuses on language as a structure or system made of smaller structures or units at different LEVELS (e.g. sound, grammar, meaning). It is often associated with those linguists who are particularly interested in describing the form of language, and language as an AUTONOMOUS system, for example in the traditions associated with Ferdinand de Saussure and Noam Chomsky. Contrast POST-STRUCTURALISM.

structured variation Also **structured** or **orderly heterogeneity** (Weinreich et al., 1968). Refers to the observation that linguistic variation in a speech community is not random but linguistically as well as socially structured, i.e. the use of linguistic forms is determined by the speakers' social group membership. See also LANGUAGE VARIATION.

style In its most general sense, style refers to a distinctive way of speaking or writing. People adopt different styles in different CONTEXTS (e.g. in the case of **speaking style**, depending on whom they are talking to, the TOPIC of conversation, the physical SETTING etc.). Styles may differ on several linguistic LEVELS (e.g. in terms of words, grammatical structures, pronunciation). Stylistic choices are meaningful, partly in terms of contrasts (e.g. the choice of one word, pronunciation etc. rather than another that might have been used). See also REGISTER.

In VARIATIONIST sociolinguistics, style is found in a narrower sense to refer to the relative FORMALITY of a situation. In this case, speaking style may be analysed in terms of a STYLISTIC CONTINUUM running from more to less formal. However, it has been argued that this is too narrow a conception of style, and that STYLISTIC

VARIATION is better seen as operating along a range of dimensions.

In Allan Bell's theory of AUDIENCE DESIGN, style is seen as a speaker's response to an AUDIENCE (Bell, 1984). Other contextual factors (e.g. conversational topic) are subsumed within a categorisation of different types of audience that affect stylistic choices.

style axiom   In relation to STYLISTIC VARIATION, the style axiom states that: 'Variation on the style dimension within the speech of a single speaker derives from and echoes the variation which exists between speakers on the "social" dimension' (Bell, 1984: 151). The style axiom forms part of Allan Bell's theory of AUDIENCE DESIGN. The claim is that SOCIAL VARIATION is prior to stylistic variation (both historically and in terms of contemporary language use); and that speakers draw on language features associated with groups of speakers as a response to particular audiences and to convey certain social meanings.

style shifting   See STYLISTIC VARIATION.

stylistic continuum   William LABOV (1972a) conceptualised STYLISTIC VARIATION along a one-dimensional, monolingual continuum, which includes two conversational styles (CASUAL SPEECH and CAREFUL SPEECH) and three categories of reading: a READING PASSAGE of continuous prose, a simple WORD LIST and lists of MINIMAL PAIRS, in this case, words whose pronunciation differs in the STANDARD or PRESTIGE variety, but which are pronounced identically in the VERNACULAR (e.g. *guard* and *god* in New York – see POST-VOCALIC /r/). Labov argued that the different conversational and reading styles can be distinguished with regard to the amount of ATTENTION paid to speech. Conscious self-monitoring is least pronounced in casual speech and most marked when reading aloud from a list of minimal pairs. As a result, vernacular forms are more common in casual speech, while (overt) PRESTIGE forms occur most frequently in the reading styles. The research construct of a single stylistic continuum allowed Labov to document regular patterns in speakers' stylistic choices; however, this approach has also been criticised. In particular, the integration of conversational speech on a continuum with reading is seen as problematical, since literacy and attitudes towards reading cannot be taken as uniform across speech communities (see Milroy, 1987b). In Belfast, for example, Lesley Milroy found that conversational styles and reading styles were not located on a gradual continuum. Rather, there existed two sharply separated NORMS, one employed in conversation, and one used in reading styles. Speakers in Belfast deleted intervocalic /d/ (the middle consonant in *mother*) almost categorically in the conversational styles. In the reading passages, however, the same speakers showed near categorical realisation of intervocalic /d/. Bell (1984) furthermore criticised Labov's focus on the amount of attention paid to speech and suggested that speakers' awareness of their IN-TERLOCUTOR is stronger in determining the frequency of prestige or STANDARD forms than the 'attention factor' (see also AUDIENCE DESIGN). Researchers have also argued that style in general is a multidimensional phenomenon which cannot be modelled on a single unidimensional continuum.

stylistic variation   Refers to speakers' variable use of different speaking STYLES. Stylistic variation has been studied in VARIATION-IST research carried out in the Labovian tradition (see LABOV). In this case, studies have focused on the QUANTITATIVE distribution of linguistic features across different speaking styles or contexts (a common finding is that speaking styles range along a STYLISTIC CONTINUUM from more to less FORMAL, as in Labov's (1972a) account of variation in the speech of New York City). The term **style shifting** is also found for speakers' use of different speaking styles. 'Style shifting' is often used in qualitative studies of how speakers shift between styles during the course of an interaction, with a focus on the communicative effects of the use of different sets of linguistic features (for an example, see Coupland, 1985). Such monolingual style shifting may be seen as comparable to CODE-SWITCHING between languages/varieties. See also CONTEXTUAL VARIATION; INTRA-SPEAKER VARIATION; LANGUAGE VARIATION; STYLISTIC CONTINUUM.

stylistics   The study of STYLE in the sense of a distinctive way of speaking or writing. Stylistics has tended to focus on the analysis of literary language – for example, the language use of a particular author or type of author, TEXT (a novel or poem) or TEXT TYPE (narrative fiction) – but may also be drawn on to study a range of non-literary texts. Stylistics assumes that speakers or writers need to make choices (to choose certain types of language and not others) and that such choices are meaningful – at least by implication, that they are interpreted in a certain way by listeners or readers. Stylistics has been influenced by different linguistic approaches and also by other disciplines (e.g. by literary theory in the analysis of literary texts). As an academic area, therefore, it is characterised by diversity. Studies that take a critical approach (e.g. influenced by CRITICAL DISCOURSE ANALYSIS) and/or that have an interest in social or cultural issues come closest to the concerns of sociolinguistics.

subculture   The distinctive norms, values and practices that characterise a particular group, seen as being marginal in certain respects from the mainstream CULTURE of the wider society. 'Subculture' may also be used for the group itself. Sometimes the term suggests opposition to mainstream values; **counterculture** is also found for this latter usage. Sociolinguists have been interested in the distinctive forms of language and language practices associated with subcultures. Many studies have focused on the language of youth subcultures: for example, William LABOV's classic (1972b) study of language use in African American PEER GROUPS on the streets of New York; and Penelope Eckert's (1989, 2000) study of the language of so-called JOCKS AND BURNOUTS in a Detroit high school. See also ADOLESCENCE; ANTI-LANGUAGE; YOUTH LANGUAGE.

subject (in research)   See INFORMANT.

subject position   Used to emphasise the influence of IDEOLOGY and in particular DISCOURSE in individual behaviour and consciousness. Following Althusser's notion of INTERPELLATION and FOUCAULT's theorisation of discourse, individuals, rather than acting independently or freely, are said to take up different kinds of subject positions. For example, two obvious subject positions that the discourse of schooling makes available are those of 'teacher' and 'student', which involve very specific ways of being and interacting. There is considerable debate about the extent to which individuals are constrained or determined by the discourses available and the extent to which they can opt out of these. Norman FAIRCLOUGH argues that while discourses regulate what kinds of subject positions are available to individuals, they do not completely determine what individuals can do. Although the discourse of schooling makes available the positions of 'teacher' and 'student', the precise ways in which these are taken up varies. Fairclough refers to the 'felicitous ambiguity' of the term 'subject', which signals the individual as both the 'object' or effect of discourse (subject to) and also as the 'subject' or agent of discourse

(2001: 32). Individuals or subjects are thus understood as being both shaped by the discourses in which they move and shapers of those discourses. See also CRITICAL DISCOURSE ANALYSIS.

Subjective Vitality Questionnaire   See ETHNOLINGUISTIC VITALITY.

subjectivity   A key term in POSTSTRUCTURALIST approaches to language, often contrasted with the term IDENTITY as used in humanist or STRUCTURALIST approaches. For those drawing on poststructuralist writings on language, 'subjectivity' is often the preferred term for describing the individual's sense of who he or she is: ' "Subjectivity" is used to refer to the conscious and unconscious thoughts and emotions of the individual, her sense of herself and her ways of understanding her relation to the world' (Weedon, 1987: 32).

Whereas humanist approaches to the self presuppose an essence at the heart of the individual which is unique, coherent and stable, 'subjectivity' emphasises the constant making of the subject, or self. Language or DISCOURSE is central to subjectivity, for it is through language that subjectivity is formed. 'Subjectivity' is concerned with this process in relation to the individual and often stands in contrast to a related concept, SUBJECT POSITION, which emphasises the function and power of DISCOURSE.

Intersubjectivity refers to the relation between individuals or subjects and the shared meanings that they draw on in making sense of and in engaging in interactions. See also PERFORMATIVITY.

substrate (substratum)   In historical linguistics a language formerly spoken by a community which continues to exert an influence on its new language. This influence may persist for generations in areas like phonetics and grammar. French differs from other Romance languages derived from Latin and one reason for this was the influence of the substrate Celtic languages, whose speakers adopted and modified colloquial Latin. The requirement that the substrate be no longer spoken is sometimes relaxed in sociolinguistics, where the term describes the influence of the less dominant (and possibly receding) community language upon a socially dominant language in a bilingual community. In PIDGIN and CREOLE studies the substrates are believed to make a particularly important contribution to the grammars of the new varieties arising out of LANGUAGE CONTACT. Contrast SUPERSTRATE; ADSTRATE.

subtractive bilingualism   A process whereby introducing a second language into a community, often as a language of instruction in schools, leads to a decline in the use of the original community language. Contrast ADDITIVE BILINGUALISM. See also BILINGUALISM; LANGUAGE SHIFT; STABLE BILINGUALISM.

Summer Institute of Linguistics (SIL)   Also known as SIL International; a Christian language development organisation that began in 1934 as a summer school in the USA to teach young people indigenous languages. It has since grown into a major organisation that has come to be known for its work in translating the Bible into indigenous languages. Notwithstanding this proselytising function, the organisation has been involved in promoting literacy, raising cultural awareness, training teachers and developing field methods. Out of these concerns theories of linguistic description have arisen, notably in the work of Eugene Nida (1949) and Kenneth Pike (1947). One of the most widely used books published by SIL is the *ETHNOLOGUE*, a comprehensive listing of the languages of the world country by country, with detail concerning demography, dialects, extent of bilingualism and the state of Bible translation.

superstrate (superstratum)   The socially and/or politically dominant language in a multilingual society, which has an influence upon less dominant varieties. Frequently this influence takes the form of LOANWORDS, though it may also apply to BORROWING other aspects of language like grammar. In North Africa, Arabic exerts such a superstratal influence over other languages, while in many parts of the world indigenous languages have felt the similar influence of French and/or English. In PIDGIN and CREOLE formation the superstrates provide the vocabulary for the new varieties, while the grammar comes from other sources. Contrast SUBSTRATE; ADSTRATE.

suprasegmental (phonology)   See PHONOLOGY.

surreptitious recording   The recording of speech data without informing speakers that they are being recorded. While this has been used in sociolinguistic research, it is now generally regarded as unethical (see ETHICS).

survey   Dialect surveys have collected systematic information on the use of dialect forms across a particular region, often carrying out interviews with local speakers (e.g. see SURVEY OF ENGLISH DIALECTS). Surveys have also been used to collect large-scale QUANTITATIVE data on language use and/or language ATTITUDES, often for whole countries or cities. Large-scale surveys are typically based on RANDOM SAMPLES and use QUESTIONNAIRES rather than interviews. See also CENSUS; LANGUAGE DOCUMENTATION.

Survey of English Dialects (SED)   A survey initially proposed in 1946 (by Eugen Dieth and Harold Orton) and carried out between 1950 and 1961, with the aim of compiling a LINGUISTIC ATLAS of England. The SED was designed to document 'traditional' dialects which were feared to be dying out. It therefore focused mainly on stable rural communities and fieldworkers interviewed primarily elderly male informants living in the locality, who were felt to be the most likely users of local VERNACULAR forms (see NORM). Information was collected on the words, grammatical structures and pronunciations that characterised regional dialects across England. For examples see the linguistic atlas (Orton et al., 1978) and the dictionary and grammar (Upton et al., 1994). See also DIALECTOLOGY.

syllable-timed (languages)   See STRESS.

symbol, symbolic   A term from semiotics as developed by Charles Peirce for a SIGN which stands in an arbitrary relationship to the object or concept it denotes, and is understood by convention, for example a red light meaning 'stop' (contrast ICON, INDEX). In language, apart from cases of onomatopoeia and compound words, words are symbols, since there is no necessary relationship between a concept and 'the word for it'. Language is a symbolic system, in which words are associated with objects, ideas and actions by convention.

symbolic capital   See SYMBOLIC POWER.

symbolic domination   See SYMBOLIC POWER.

symbolic interactionism   A school of thought in sociology that studies societies in terms of small-scale encounters between individuals ('bottom up') rather than in terms of large-scale social systems ('top down'). Symbolic interactionism is principally associated with the work of the American sociologist George H. Mead, who focused on the development of the self (see Mead, 1934). Mead conceived the relationship between the individual and the self, and the self and society, as one of an exchange of symbols, gesture and communication being key forms or symbols used in interaction. It is through this symbolic interaction – with the self and others – that the individual comes into being. Interactionists argue that one's place within a social system is not fixed, but develops and is constantly modified by interactions with people in a variety of settings. The most important work of linguistic significance in this field has come from Erving GOFFMAN. Socio-linguists influenced by this approach (e.g. in INTERACTIONAL SOCIOLINGUISTICS) focus on face-to-face spoken encounters with particular attention to how meaning is built up within an unfolding context, and how language is used strategically in negotiations within that context.

symbolic marketplace   See LINGUISTIC MARKETPLACE; SYMBOLIC POWER.

symbolic power   Term associated with the work of BOURDIEU and used to refer to the way in which POWER, rather than being a physical force, may be exercised symbolically. Bourdieu (1991) refers to control of the **symbolic marketplace** (i.e. control over what counts as, and who gets access to e.g. appropriate dress, language use, leisure activities) as **symbolic domination**. The resources in the symbolic marketplace consist of four principal types of 'capital': economic capital (wealth in terms of money and property); CULTURAL CAPITAL (forms of knowledge, skill and education); social capital (resources made available though social networks and group membership); **symbolic capital** (prestige, honour). See also LINGUISTIC MARKETPLACE.

synchronic   An approach to the study of a language that focuses on it as a system at a given moment of time. Linguistics before Ferdinand de Saussure was largely DIACHRONIC, focusing on the history of languages and the SOUND CHANGES they underwent. Saussure argued that this approach failed to define what a language really was. Saussure's synchronic approach stressed language as an abstract system of elements which were characterised by their differences from each another. Thus the meaning of a word like *lion* lay not in its etymology, but its presence in a set of related terms like *tiger, leopard, cheetah,* etc., and – crucially – its difference from each member of the set. See also PANCHRONIC.

syntagmatic   A relation between linguistic elements that can be arranged in linear sequences often in some kind of 'co-occurrence' relationship. In PHONOLOGY the elements *s-t-r* have a syntagmatic relationship since they form a linear sequence in a word like *strong*. However, *p-t-r* do not have such a relationship. In SYNTAX, in a sentence like *The pelican saw a sailor,* there is a syntagmatic relationship between *a* and *sailor; the* and *pelican; saw* and *a,* etc. In Saussure's theory of language such syntagmatic relations, along with PARADIGMATIC relations, specified the 'value' of each linguistic element in the language system.

syntax (syntactic)   An aspect of GRAMMAR, referring to sentence or clause structure (i.e. how words combine to form sentences). Syntax may be contrasted with MORPHOLOGY, or word structure. Syntactic structures may vary between languages and language varieties, and also socially and stylistically. Sociolinguists have studied several aspects of **syntactic variation,** but this raises a number of methodological issues: specific syntactic structures occur less frequently and with less regularity in spoken discourse than do phonological features, and for this reason their study may be problematical. For examples, see Jenny Cheshire and James Milroy's (1993) discussion of syntactic variation in non-standard varieties of English; and Aidan Coveney's (1996) study of interrogatives (question forms) and negation (negative structures) in French.

system (vs use)   A distinction is sometimes made in linguistics between language as an abstract system, studied in areas such as PHONOLOGY, MORPHOLOGY, SYNTAX, SEMANTICS; and how language is actually used (produced and interpreted) in specific contexts, this latter being more properly the subject of PRAGMATICS and much of SOCIOLINGUISTICS. See also AUTONOMOUS (2).

Systemic Functional Linguistics (SFL)   An approach to the analysis of language most notably associated with the work of

M. A. K. HALLIDAY (1978, 1989). Systemic Functional Linguistics (SFL) is both a theory of language, that is, a way of thinking about why language is as it is, and a complex set of tools for analysing actual texts.

A basic premise of SFL is that language is *functional*, that is, it is a resource for meaning-making that has evolved, and continues to evolve, to meet human needs. Analysis of language therefore focuses on language as it is used in its social CONTEXT. Key analytic categories developed in order to acknowledge this contextual dimension are GENRE and REGISTER. Genre focuses on the activity being carried out and register on the different aspects of this activity as they impinge on language use: FIELD (topic), TENOR (relationship between language users, e.g. formal or informal), and MODE (written, spoken, visual). The linguistic analysis of texts focuses on the systems of choices available from the language, for example the choice of 'active' rather than 'passive' VOICE in a clause.

The complex set of analytic tools developed in SFL are not viewed simply as alternative labels for traditional grammatical terms. While traditional grammars tend to focus on language FORMS (e.g. noun, verb, other 'parts of speech'), the aim of SFL is to develop an analytical and labelling system that treats form as always bound up with function and meaning-making. Grammatical choices are therefore understood as choices not simply about form, but also about meaning and, indeed, about the representation of particular worldviews. See also META-FUNCTIONS.

T

T and V pronouns   A distinction made in languages such as French that have different second-person-singular PRONOUN forms that are sometimes identified as 'familiar' (*tu* in French) or 'polite' (*vous* in French). The terms T and V come from the Latin forms *tu* and *vos*. This distinction allows the expression of different relationships between speakers. In a classic study of T and V pronouns, R. Brown and A. Gilman (1960) characterise pronoun choice as having to do with POWER or SOLIDARITY. When power is a key factor, pronoun usage will be non-reciprocal between more and less powerful speakers: a more powerful speaker will use T to a less powerful speaker, but the less powerful speaker will use V in return. Speakers who are socially equal will use reciprocal T or V (Brown and Gilman point out that in medieval Europe high-status speakers used V and low-status speakers T). The solidarity dimension, by contrast, relates to the degree of closeness (solidarity) or social distance between participants. Speakers will use reciprocal T to express solidarity and reciprocal V to express social distance. Brown and Gilman argue that, in many European languages, there has been a shift from a system of pronoun choice based on power to one based on solidarity.

-t/-d deletion   Describes loss of word-final *-t/-d* in consonant clusters. Deletion of *-t/-d* is common in CASUAL SPEECH if the following word starts with a consonant (e.g. *firs' thing* or *las' month*). It is less frequent if the following word begins with a vowel (e.g. *firs' of all* or *las' October*). *-t/-d* deletion tends to be avoided in formal speech. In some varieties of American English one also finds variable deletion of the past tense marker (e.g. *kep'* instead of *kept*, see Labov, 1989). *-t/-d* deletion was one of the first linguistic variables to be described (see Labov et al., 1968); the sociolinguistic variability of *-t/-d* deletion has also been described from a historical perspective (Romaine, 1984). See also CONSONANT CLUSTER SIMPLIFICATION; VARIABLE RULE.

t-glottalling   See GLOTTAL.

t-test   A widely used statistical test which allows researchers to compare the mean scores of two groups in a SAMPLE; for example, one could compare features of language used by men and women, or differences between spoken and written discourse. See also ANALYSIS OF VARIANCE; SIGNIFICANCE TESTING

taboo   Taboo words are words that are avoided by certain speakers or in certain contexts. These might include swear-words, other words referring to sexual activity, profanity etc. Avoidance may be justified in a number of ways, including religious, moral or aesthetic principles. What is considered taboo will differ in different cultural contexts and therefore serves as an indicator of social or cultural values. Taboo is sometimes a feature of LANGUAGE CONTACT situations where speakers may avoid a word in one language because it bears a phonetic resemblance to a word considered vulgar or obscene in another language. For instance, Mary Haas ([1957] 1964) reports that speakers of Creek (a Native-American language) who were bilingual in English would avoid words such as *fákki* ('soil, earth, clay') and *apíssi* ('fat') in the presence of white American-English speakers, although these speakers would not have been able to perceive individual Creek words in the rapid flow of speech. In such contexts taboo has been a factor in language change. See also AVOIDANCE.

tag questions   A question attached to the end of a statement, of the form: 'It's hot in here, *isn't it?*' In standard English English, a positive statement is usually followed by a negative tag (as in the example above) and a negative statement by a positive tag ('You wouldn't go, *would you?*'). But the pattern positive statement + positive tag is also found ('You're going to eat that, *are you?*'), as well as, more rarely, negative statement + negative tag ('She can't see, *can't she?*'). Tag questions have been of interest in studies of the English language because their forms vary in different Englishes: for example, 'She can come, *can she not?*' is found in Tyneside English and the invariant tag *isn't it* ('You're going home now, *isn't it?*') is found in several varieties including West African and Indian English.

The functions of tag questions have also been of interest in studies of spoken interaction: for instance, in some early studies of LANGUAGE AND GENDER, tags were associated with uncertainty and hesitancy and there was debate over whether they were used more by female/less powerful speakers. More recent studies have acknowledged the diversity of functions that tag questions may fulfil (see, e.g., Holmes, 1995).

tagging   The process by which one assigns grammatical categories to words in a sentence or text. Tagging is a tool of corpus linguistics (i.e. the study of language structure and use based on systematically collected language data, see CORPUS). **Tagged corpora** include grammatical information for each word.

tap   See FLAP.

target (language)
   1. In LANGUAGE CONTACT studies and language teaching, the language that learners or groups of learners aim to acquire in addition to their own first language(s). The actual versions of the target

language that different learners display are termed INTER-LANGUAGES. Many scholars believe that PIDGINS and CREOLES differ from such interlanguages in that there was no prior target language: speakers who developed a pidgin or Creole were motivated by the needs of communication rather than a desire to master a particular language.

2. In translation studies, the language into which a translation is made (e.g. in entries in a BILINGUAL dictionary); contrast SOURCE LANGUAGE.

Teaching English to Speakers of Other Languages (TESOL)
North-American term, usually found as the acronym TESOL. TESOL is a general term for the teaching of English to speakers of other languages in a range of contexts. It is increasingly more widely used than UK equivalents, **Teaching English as a Foreign Language (TEFL)** and **Teaching English as a Second Language (TESL)**, which distinguish different teaching contexts and the approaches associated with these (see ENGLISH AS A FOREIGN LANGUAGE; ENGLISH AS A SECOND LANGUAGE); and **English Language Teaching (ELT)**, which, like TESOL, has more general reference. There is significant debate about which terms should be used because of the issues surrounding the status and role of English in different national contexts and globally (see CENTRE, PERIPHERY; LINGUISTIC IMPERIALISM; THREE CIRCLES OF ENGLISH). The teaching of English to speakers of other languages and the publication of relevant textbooks is a significant industry because of the global status of English and the demand for English teaching. It has given rise to substantial research, including second-language acquisition, the impact of different methods of teaching and learning, individual learner differences (see e.g. Ellis, 1997; Lightbrown and Spada, 1999.). There is also ongoing heated debate about the role and status of English globally, the relation between language and culture, the differential status between those teachers who are NATIVE and 'non-native' speakers of English (see Canagarajah, 1999; Pennycook, 1994).

telegraphic speech Language reminiscent of telegrams, used to describe, *inter alia*, the speech of young children at the stage when they string words together without grammatical elements like articles and prepositions, for example *Doggie gone*. Also applies to certain types of language ATTRITION among stroke victims and people suffering from related brain disorders.

tenor   Used in SYSTEMIC FUNCTIONAL LINGUISTICS to refer to one of the three aspects of REGISTER, the other two being FIELD and MODE. 'Tenor' refers to the relationships between participants in any interaction, which in turn influences the kind of language chosen. For example, the relationship between a doctor and a patient is likely to be more formal than a relationship between close friends, and the language they use to communicate will reflect that formality/informality.

tense   Verb category used to indicate the time of an event in relation to the time of speaking: this usually occurs as present, future, or past. However, the relation between tense and time is not straightforward. While *I go* is 'prototypically' present tense, it can also be used as a future (*I go to school tomorrow*). The present tense can also be used for 'timeless' statements (*Icebergs float on water*). Of particular interest to studies of NARRATIVES in everyday speech is the conversational HISTORIC PRESENT, the use of the present tense to dramatise a past event. See also ASPECT; TENSE–MODALITY–ASPECT.

tense–modality–aspect   Three overlapping categories associated with verb forms that are sometimes studied as one coherent system. In CREOLE languages these frequently appear as pre-verbal particles which cover a complex range of perspectives upon the action expressed by the verb. The **tense** particle typically denotes a change in focus upon the time of action (e.g. past to pluperfect or present to past). **Modality** typically refers to whether the action was realised/is realisable, or not (see IRREALIS). **Aspect** typically refers to whether the action was completed or not. See also TENSE; ASPECT; MOOD; PERFECT(IVE); PROGRESSIVE.

terms of address   See ADDRESS.

territorial principle   A principle of LANGUAGE LEGISLATION and LANGUAGE POLICY which divides multilingual states into distinct, largely monolingual language areas. For example, the Belgian western region of Wallonia is officially French-speaking (i.e. all public, official interactions take place using French), whereas Flanders to the north-east makes use of Flemish in official communications. Only the capital Brussels is bilingual. The territorial principle is also the basis of the Swiss and Canadian language policies. Contrast PERSONALITY PRINCIPLE.

text   Term widely used in sociolinguistics to refer to specific instances of language and communication. Thus all of the following can be referred to as 'texts': a letter; a transcription of a conversation between two people; a magazine article with both words and images. Texts can be written, spoken and MULTIMODAL.

text type   Refers to the range of different classes of language uses or TEXTS that exist. Texts are classified into text types according to their social function, such as interviews, essays, jokes and political speeches and/or according to their linguistic features (see discussion in Askehave and Swales, 2001). Sometimes used synonymously with GENRE. Text types can be identified at different levels. For example, an interview can be understood as a particular text type, and a political interview or a celebrity interview can be seen as different examples of this type.

textual   Adjective from TEXT. In SYSTEMIC FUNCTIONAL LINGUISTICS the term refers more specifically to one of three broad META-FUNCTIONS of language: the way language is organised into meaningful texts. See COHESION; also IDEATIONAL and INTERPERSONAL metafunctions.

texture   Sometimes referred to as **textuality,** used to refer to the overall sense of a TEXT being a text, rather than a collection of unconnected sentences or utterances. Analysing the texture of a text involves focusing on both COHESION, that is, the linguistic features which connect different elements of a text and serve to make the whole text 'cohesive'; and COHERENCE, that is the kind of extra-linguistic or background knowledge that readers/listeners use in order to perceive a particular text as coherent.

theme, rheme   In SYSTEMIC FUNCTIONAL LINGUISTICS these are labels used to refer to the organisation of a clause as a unit of meaning. M.A.K. HALLIDAY (1994) defines **theme** as 'the point of departure of the message'; what follows is referred to as **rheme**. Thus theme and rheme can be identified in the following clause as follows: *The woman* (theme) *sped past the finishing post* (rheme). In Systemic Functional Linguistics a distinction is made between theme/rheme and GIVEN/new. Broadly speaking, 'theme'/'rheme' refers to the internal elements of a clause from an organisational or structural perspective, whereas 'given'/'new' refers to the elements of a clause from an informational perspective, that is, as they relate to previous clauses, or to assumed knowledge. In other areas of linguists, the relationship between theme/rheme and given/new may be less distinct (see discussion in Francis, 1990; Thompson, 1999).

'they' code   See 'WE' AND 'THEY' CODES.

third language (acquisition)   Conventionally the term 'SECOND LANGUAGE acquisition' has been used to include the acquisition of 'third', 'fourth' and 'nth' languages. However, since learners of additional foreign languages typically draw on their previous foreign-language learning experiences and TRANSFER is therefore not limited to the first language or MOTHER TONGUE, a new field of research has emerged which focuses on the acquisition of such additional (nth) foreign languages by speakers who have already acquired one or more foreign languages.

third space   Drawn from Homi Bhaba (1994), this concept is used by researchers to refer to a relatively abstract notion of space which is defined in terms of culture and identity rather than primarily in terms of geographical or physical location. Bhaba uses this notion to define a space in which postcolonial peoples both find themselves and also are striving to create, emphasising HYBRIDITY in cultures and practices. It has been used in sociolinguistic studies to discuss how people work at transforming linguistic practices in particular contexts, for example bilingual students' and teachers' use of two languages in school classrooms where monolingualism is dominant (Gutierrez et al 1999); or prisoners' transformation of institutional prison literacy practices into those associated with everyday or home literacy practices (Wilson, 2000).

Three Circles of English   A model proposed by Braj KACHRU (1988) that conceptualises the spread of English (see LANGUAGE SPREAD). It comprises three circles:
- an **inner circle** made up of British, US, Australian, Canadian and similar FIRST LANGUAGE varieties, which are described as 'norm-providing';
- an **outer circle** made up of ENGLISH AS A SECOND LANGUAGE varieties developed under British (or American) colonialism, like Indian and Nigerian English, which are described as 'norm-developing' (i.e. developing independent norms); and

- an **expanding circle**, made up of ENGLISH AS A FOREIGN LANGUAGE areas, as in China and Sweden, which are described as 'norm-dependent'.

Traditionally, much of the research stemming from this model focused on the growing independence of outer circle varieties as they stabilise features that arose out of LANGUAGE CONTACT (between English and local languages). Increasing attention is now turning to the expanding circle in the context of globalisation, education and business, as evident in the journals *World Englishes* and *English Today*. See also NEW ENGLISH(ES); WORLD ENGLISH(ES).

three-language formula An aspect of India's multilingual LANGUAGE POLICY. In Indian secondary schools three languages are taught: the REGIONAL LANGUAGE, Hindi (the NATIONAL LANGUAGE) and English (the former colonial language which serves as a LINGUA FRANCA and OFFICIAL LANGUAGE). In Hindi-speaking areas an alternative Indian language should be taught in addition to Hindi and English.

tip A term coined by Nancy Dorian (1981) for a situation in which a language which has been demographically highly stable for several centuries may begin to undergo LANGUAGE SHIFT as speakers opt for some other language. This tip occurs at a relatively accelerated pace usually in response to socio-economic change.

tone Describes the PITCH level ('high', 'low', 'mid') of a syllable. Tone is an aspect of INTONATION and sequences of tones make up the characteristic intonation contour of different dialects and varieties. In some languages, tone is used to distinguish different words or grammatical forms. Many African and South-East Asian languages are **tone languages**. In Mandarin, for example, the sequence /ba/ can have different meanings depending on the pitch with which it is pronounced: /ba/ with a high pitch means 'hemp', /ba/ with a low pitch means 'to scold'.

top–down In relation to linguistic analysis, 'top–down' refers to approaches that begin with larger units (e.g. TEXTS) and work down to smaller units (e.g. words). In relation to LANGUAGE PLANNING, the term refers to decisions which are made by those with power and authority (high-ranking civil servants, politicians, members of social elites). Detailed and ongoing consultation with the majority of the population and community organisations is not part of the decision-making process. Contrast BOTTOM–UP.

topic   One factor said to influence a speaker's choice of a particular language, language variety or communicative strategy is the topic or subject matter being talked about. In bi- and multilingual communities, speakers may choose one of their languages to talk about a certain topic because they are more familiar with relevant words and expressions in that language, or because they regard the language as being more appropriate for the topic. Speakers' stylistic choices in monolingual contexts are also affected by conversational topic; this may be built into research design, as in William LABOV's use of DANGER OF DEATH stories to elicit VERNACULAR language from speakers in New York City. See also LANGUAGE CHOICE; STYLISTIC VARIATION.

transcript (transcription)   The systematic representation of speech in writing. Transcription reflects different levels of analysis, for example it may focus closely on the sounds of language or more broadly on conversation or interaction.
1. A wide range of systems has been developed to transcribe PROSODY, or INTONATION (e.g. to represent STRESS and PITCH movement visually). Systems tend to reflect different theoretical or research interests and no general standardised system exists.
2. PHONETIC and PHONEMIC transcription is rather better developed. Phonetic transcription attempts to represent speech sounds as these are articulated. The most widely-used system is the INTERNATIONAL PHONETIC ALPHABET (IPA) (for the full set of symbols, see the International Phonetic Association web site: http:// www.arts.gla.ac.uk/IPA/ipachart.html (accessed October 2003)). Some IPA symbols have been drawn from the Roman alphabet (e.g. [b], [d], [f]) but additional symbols are needed to represent the range of sounds that may be produced (e.g. [ʃ] to represent the 'sh' sound in English *ship*; [θ] and [ð] to represent the 'th' sounds in *thin* and *then* respectively). Phonetic transcription may be relatively **narrow** (reflecting considerable phonetic detail) or **broad** (less detailed). Phonetic transcription is conventionally enclosed within square brackets. Phonemic transcription is used to represent the phonemes in a given language. While it shares some symbols with phonetic transcription, it requires fewer of

these (e.g. 44 to represent the phonemes in Received Pronunciation (RP)). While phonemic transcriptions use many symbols that
reflect pronunciation (in the phonemic transcription of RP /b/
represents the 'b' sound in *book*, /d/ the 'd' sound in *dog*, etc.),
the transcriptions are actually concerned to represent abstract
linguistic units rather than to provide an accurate record of
pronunciation. Phonemic transcription is conventionally set
between slashes, as in the examples above. The terms phonetic
or phonemic **notation** or script are also found.

3. Conversational transcription is an attempt to represent the features of a conversation or interaction. The transcript produced
(what is actually transcribed) will depend on the focus of the
research and/or any theoretical underpinning, i.e. different transcripts may highlight different aspects of conversations. Conversational transcripts are often laid out like the dialogue in a play,
but other layouts are possible (e.g. **column transcripts** allocate a
separate vertical column to each speaker; **stave transcripts** are
set out like musical staves, with each speaker allocated a separate
line in the stave – for examples see Coates, 1996). Transcripts use
certain conventions to represent discourse features such as pauses
or overlaps; paralinguistic information such as loudness or speed
of delivery; vocalisations such as in-breaths; and visual information such as gestures or eye-contact. Transcripts may also attempt
to represent the pronunciation of speech sounds. Systematic
phonemic or phonetic notation is not usually thought appropriate,
however. Some transcripts have recourse to eye-dialect representations such as *doin* (vs *doing*), *ah mean, 'em* (vs *them*). There is
a danger here of highlighting features associated with certain types
of speaker (e.g. working-class speakers, children) and making
these appear deviant.

Elinor Ochs (1979) developed the notion of 'transcription as
theory': the idea that transcription is not a neutral representation
of speech but necessarily involves some degree of interpretation.
While Ochs considered this in relation to conversation, the point
would apply to any form of transcription.

transfer   The influence of a speaker's first language upon a subse-
quently-learnt language, a target language. This influence extends to
features of the language system, like the substitution of a sound from
the first language for a sound in the language being learnt. For
example speakers of French may substitute an [s] for the English
sound 'th' (i.e. [θ]). Transfer of grammatical patterns is also possible,

though scholars of second-language acquisition suggest that transfer is but one of several strategies open to the language learner, and not always the most important. A distinction is also drawn between **positive transfer**, when features of the first language and target language coincide; and **negative transfer**, when a first-language pattern or feature is mistakenly retained for a dissimilar target-language pattern. Negative transfer is also known as **interference**, though this older term is no longer widely used on account of its negative connotations. See also INTERLANGUAGE.

transition   The route by which LANGUAGE CHANGE spreads across speakers (SOCIAL GROUPS, generations) as well as across linguistic ENVIRONMENTS (see DIFFUSION (2)). For example, a new linguistic form might first be used by lower social groups and then gradually spread into higher social groups (or vice versa). Similarly, language changes do not affect all possible words and linguistic contexts simultaneously, but move gradually across the lexicon. See also EMBEDDING; S-CURVE.

transition area (transitional area)   A geographical area located near a linguistic border (see ISOGLOSS) which geographically separates two regional DIALECTS. The linguistic variety spoken in such transition areas typically combines features from the adjacent regions. See also BORDER DIALECT; RHENISH FAN.

transition relevance place (TRP)   Within research on CONVERSATION MANAGEMENT or TURN-TAKING (and initially in Sacks et al., 1974), this refers to a point when a SPEAKING TURN is potentially complete, although the speaker may not actually stop at this point. Transition-relevance places may be identified by cues such as grammatical structure (e.g. a clause boundary). It is likely that one way in which speakers are able to co-ordinate smooth turn-taking is by predicting such possible completion points. See also CONVERSATION ANALYSIS.

transitivity   One of the key systems within SYSTEMIC FUNCTIONAL LINGUISTICS, which refers to the representation of 'who is doing what to whom'. At clause level, transitivity involves meanings that are organised in terms of **participants** and **processes**, which can be further analysed in terms of **participant roles** and **process types**. This roughly corresponds in traditional grammar to the subject, verb and object of a sentence. Thus, in the clause *I kicked* *the ball* – *I* and *ball* are the participants and *kick* is the process. *I* and *ball* have different participant roles: in this example *I* is an **actor** and *ball* is the **goal**. *Kick* is a particular type of process, a **material process** relating to some form of action or 'doing' (see Halliday (1994b) for full description of processes and participants). The potential of transitivity to represent different types of participant and process has been of central interest in CRITICAL LINGUISTICS.

transplanted (dialect, language) A dialect or language which, as a result of migration, is spoken in a new, non-adjacent geographical area or country. Examples include the Eastern Hindi Diaspora (see Mesthrie, 1992); Pennsylvania *Deitsch* (based on the Palatinate dialect of German) spoken by the Amish in North America; Quebec French; as well as varieties of colonial English. In order to account for the linguistic structures of transplanted dialects, two hypotheses have been suggested: a **single-origin hypothesis** and a **multiple-origin hypothesis**. Hammerström's (1980) view that Australian English is based on nineteenth-century Cockney would be an example of a single-origin hypothesis. Many sociolinguists have, however, pointed out that in most extraterritorial settings there is extensive dialect CONVERGENCE and KOINÈISATION between different mainland dialects. This would support a multiple-origin hypothesis: i.e. convergence would lead to the development of new varieties which can be interpreted as an 'interdialectal compromise' (e.g. Trudgill, 1986). The terms **extraterritorial** and **transported (dialect, language)** (Hickey, 2003) are also found. See also FOUNDER (PRINCIPLE, POPULATION); SPEECH ISLAND.

transported (dialect) See TRANSPLANTED (DIALECT, LANGUAGE).

trill A term used in the description and classification of CONSONANTS, relating to their MANNER OF ARTICULATION. Trills are produced when one articulator vibrates against another. A trilled /r/ sound exists in several languages, such as Spanish, and in some varieties of English, including Scottish English. See also INTERNATIONAL PHONETIC ALPHABET; PHONETICS.

turn (in conversation) See SPEAKING TURN.

turn-taking The means by which participants in an interaction co-ordinate the exchange of SPEAKING TURNS. Conversation analysts have been interested in the cues used by participants to predict the end of a current speaker's turn (and so when someone else may legitimately begin speaking). Such predictability is necessary because gaps between turns are frequently very short: to be able to interact smoothly, therefore, participants need to anticipate the upcoming end of a turn. Of particular interest to sociolinguistics is the fact that turn-taking patterns are variable between contexts and groups of speakers. Early research (such as Sacks et al.'s (1974) classic account of turn-taking) assumed a 'one-person-at-a-time' model of conversation. But some recent work has looked at relatively complex patterns of turn-taking (e.g. how several speakers may hold the floor at once, or construct joint speaking turns) and at how turn-taking practices may indicate, and be a means of negotiating, relations between speakers (e.g. the expression of power relations through the use of features such as INTERRUPTION). See also CONVERSATION ANALYSIS; CONVERSATION MANAGEMENT; DUETTING; TRANSITION RELEVANCE PLACE.

U, Non-U   A popular shorthand for 'upper class' (**U**) and 'non-upper class' (**Non-U**) varieties. The expression originated in Britain and was used by Alan Ross in his early discussion of social variation (1959). U and Non-U are described rather impressionistically by Ross in terms of lexicon (e.g. *vegetables* is U, *greens* is Non-U) and pronunciation.

Überdachung   Literally 'roofing'. Used by Kloss (1978) to describe the hierarchical and overarching relationship between STANDARD and NON-STANDARD varieties. See also AUTONOMY, HETERONOMY.

underlexicalisation   See LEXICALISATION.

ungrammatical   See GRAMMATICAL.

uniformitarian principle   A fundamental principle of historical analysis which states that the forces governing LANGUAGE CHANGE are the same today as they were in the past. Linguists can thus study 'the past through the present'; that is, studies of CHANGE IN

PROGRESS in contemporary speech communities (for which linguistic data is more plentiful than for historical times) can contribute to a better understanding of language change in general. The uniformitarian principle was originally formulated by the nineteenth-century geologist Charles Lyell (1833, *Principles of Geology*) who argued that today's geological landscapes were created by slow and gradual processes which are still going on around us. The principle was introduced to linguistics by William Dwight Whitney (1867, *Language and the Study of Language*). It was popularised in sociolinguistics by William LABOV (1972a). See also HISTORICAL LINGUISTICS.

uniplex (-ity) See MULTIPLEX.

unmarked An 'unmarked' linguistic form or usage is one that is considered to have more general currency, to be more 'neutral' or expected than a corresponding **marked** form (see MARKEDNESS; MARKEDNESS MODEL).

unmitigated See MITIGATION.

unrounded (vowels) See ROUNDING.

utterance
1. Within PRAGMATICS, utterances have been distinguished from sentences, where sentences are abstract entities, part of the linguistic system, and utterances are realisations of sentences, or parts of sentences, produced by particular speakers/writers in particular contexts. In this sense, utterance meaning would be the subject of pragmatics and sentence meaning the subject of SEMANTICS. In practice, however, it is not possible to maintain such a straightforward distinction (for a discussion of this in relation to pragmatics, see Levinson, 1983). Emphasis on language as historically situated utterances is also a key notion in BAKHTIN's theory of language (see ADDRESSIVITY; DIALOGIC).
2. 'Utterance' may also refer loosely to a stretch of (usually spoken) language, making no assumptions about any linguistic properties or structure.
3. 'Utterance' has sometimes been used more specifically as the equivalent to a SPEAKING TURN in an interaction, but in this sense it shares the analytical shortcomings associated with speaking turn – it may include very different types of talk, and even its formal

identification may be problematical (i.e. particularly in multi-party talk it is not always obvious what to count as a discrete utterance).

uvular   A term used in the description and classification of CONSO-NANTS, relating to their PLACE OF ARTICULATION. Uvular sounds are produced when the back of the tongue comes into contact with the uvula. A 'uvular /r/' (transcribed phonetically as [ʀ]) exists in Northumberland, in the north-east of England. The /r/ sound in French is also uvular. See also INTERNATIONAL PHONETIC ALPHABET; PHONETICS.

Varbrul   See VARIABLE RULE.

variable   See LINGUISTIC VARIABLE; SOCIAL VARIABLE.

variable rule   The notion of variable rules was introduced by William LABOV to describe the probability that an optional rule (i.e. a rule that occurs variably and not categorically) will be applied by members of a SOCIAL GROUP. -T/-D DELETION is an example of a variable rule: word-final *-t* or *-d* may be deleted after a consonantal segment. Deletion is most frequent in those cases where the following word begins with a consonant (e.g. *firs' thing* but not *firs' of all*). It is less common in cases where there exists a morpheme boundary immediately before *-t/-d*; thus, reduced past tense forms such *he pass'* instead of *he pass-ed* occur only infrequently. The rule can be formally expressed as follows:

$$\text{-t/-d} \rightarrow \emptyset / \ [+\text{cons}] \ <\text{-} \ \#\ >^{\beta}\_\_\_\#\# \ <\text{-syll}>^{\alpha} \ (\text{optional})$$

In this notation the arrow (→) stands for 'becomes'; Ø stands for 'deleted'; the forward slash / for 'in the context of'; [+cons] signals the presence of a (preceding) consonant; # stands for 'morpheme boundary' and <- #> therefore means deletion is supported by the absence of a (preceding) morpheme boundary; ___ indicates the place where *-t/-d* deletion would usually occur: this is in word final position (the following ## stands for a word boundary); 'syll' means a vowel (and so < - syll > means deletion is supported by the absence of a (following) vowel); α describes the environment which favours deletion most strongly, and β the environment whose influence is less strong. Thus the rule states that -*t*/-*d* are optionally deleted in contexts where they are preceded by a consonant and followed by a word boundary. Deletion is supported by the absence of a morpheme boundary before -*t*/-*d* (and is therefore rare for past-tense forms such as *pass-ed*) as well as (and even more strongly) by the absence of a vowel following the word boundary.

Social factors can also be incorporated into variable rules, such as in New York, where the feature [+ working class] can be said to have a constraining effect on the realisation of post-vocalic /r/ (i.e. working-class speakers use this pronunciation less frequently). A computer program **Varbrul** has been developed for calculating such probabilistic rules from a set of linguistic data. Varbrul is available from the University of Pennsylvania. See also LINGUISTIC VARIABLE.

variant   In the study of LANGUAGE VARIATION, variants are alternative forms or realisations of a LINGUISTIC VARIABLE which vary according to social and/or stylistic factors. For example, in some varieties of English [t] and [ʔ] (a GLOTTAL stop) are variants of the variable (t): the second consonant in *butter*.

variation   See LANGUAGE VARIATION.

variationist (sociolinguistics)   Sociolinguistic work in the tradition inspired by William LABOV, which describes patterns and structures of LANGUAGE VARIATION. Variationist approaches commonly adopt a QUANTITATIVE methodology, focusing on the frequency with which linguistic forms (e.g. pronunciation or grammatical features) occur across speakers, groups of speakers or speaking styles: terms such as **quantitative sociolinguistics**, the **quantitative paradigm**, the **Labovian tradition** and EMPIRICAL LINGUISTICS are also found.

Labov's study of language variation in New York is a classic example of a quantitative variationist study (e.g. Labov, 1972a). For instance, Labov looked at the distribution of instances of the pronunciation of POST-VOCALIC /r/ in the speech of individuals belonging to different social groups, and was able to show that there were systematic differences in usage: post-vocalic /r/ was used most frequently by speakers belonging to the higher social groups (i.e. upper middle class), and less frequently by those belonging to lower social groups; it also occurred most frequently in formal speaking styles (see STYLISTIC CONTINUUM). Labov was therefore able to demonstrate systematic SOCIAL VARIATION and STYLISTIC VARIATION. Variationist studies in the tradition of Labov's work have also contributed significantly to our understanding of LANGUAGE CHANGE by carefully identifying groups whose members were the first to make use of new linguistic forms and also by showing how the new forms spread across social groups (see EMBEDDING and DIFFUSION (2)). See also Milroy and Gordon (2003) for discussion of relevant aspects of variationist methodology.

variety A linguistic system used by a certain group of speakers or in certain social contexts. 'Variety' is often used as an alternative to DIALECT and LANGUAGE, and can be a useful way of circumventing the difficulty of making a clear distinction between the two on linguistic grounds (see LANGUAGE). Terms such as **regional variety** and **social variety**, STANDARD variety and NON-STANDARD variety may be used to specify the dimension according to which varieties are being distinguished.

variety grammar From the German *Varietätengrammatik*. Introduced by Wolfgang Klein (1974) in his analysis of GASTAR-BEITERDEUTSCH ('Guest workers' German', i.e. the German of migrant workers). Klein developed a type of grammatical description which focuses on varieties (see VARIETY) rather than on the analysis of individual VARIABLES. Based on social aspects of language use (e.g. SOCIAL CLASS membership, situational CONTEXT, geographical area), a so-called 'variety space' (*Varietätenraum*) is established and the individual varieties which make up a language system are located within this multidimensional space. The grammatical description then identifies the likelihood with which the linguistic rules of the larger language system are applied to each of the different social varieties. See Dittmar (1997) for a summary.

variety imitation Used by Dennis Preston (1992) to describe linguistic performances in which members of a social group imitate the linguistic behaviour of another social group (e.g. their accent). Such variety imitations are an intrinsic part of folk culture (see FOLK LINGUISTICS) and POPULAR CULTURE. However, they are rarely faithful reflections of the actual linguistic characteristics; over-generalisation of otherwise rare (but perceptually salient) linguistic features is common. See also MOCK LANGUAGE, STEREOTYPE.

vector   Term used in the analysis of VISUAL images: 'vectors' are the 'lines which lead the eye' in an image (Kress and Van Leeuwen, 1996; Goodman, 1996). Vectors, or lines, are formed by the things in an image – objects, people etc. – and the relationship between them. For example, if in the left hand side of a photograph a soldier is holding a gun and in the right hand side a woman is lying on the ground, the reader's eye may be directed from the soldier and his gun to the woman. The story of the image here is something like 'the soldier has killed the woman' or 'the soldier has fired his gun at the woman'. Drawing on SYSTEMIC FUNCTIONAL LINGUISTICS, Kress and Van Leeuwen point to vectors as being part of a 'visual grammar', in particular the system of TRANSITIVITY, that is, who is doing what to whom.

velar   A term used in the description and classification of CONSO-NANTS, relating to their PLACE OF ARTICULATION. Velar sounds are produced when the back of the tongue comes close to or touches the velum, or soft palate. Examples from English include: [k], [g] and [ŋ] (the final sound in *ring*). See also INTERNATIONAL PHONETIC ALPHABET; PHONETICS.

ventriloquation   Term used by BAKHTIN to refer to the way in which all language use involves speaking through the VOICES – words, phrases, DISCOURSES – of others. A simple example of this is where a child repeats words or phases heard from a parent. Bakhtin states: 'the word does not exist in a neutral and impersonal language – but rather it exists in other people's concrete contexts, serving other people's intentions' ([1935] 1981: 293–4). The struggles surrounding individuals' control over meaning is a key focus in Bakhtin's work. See also DIALOGIC.

verb phrase (VP)
1. May be used for a verb or group of verbs: for example, in *Miriam will start a new business*, *will start* is a verb phrase consisting of an AUXILIARY verb, *will*, and a main verb, *start*. The term **verbal group** is found in some traditions (see GROUP). There has been considerable sociolinguistic interest in variation at the level of the

verb phrase: for example, variation in verb endings or inflections between different dialects, variation in the use of (MODAL) auxiliaries, variation in TENSE and ASPECT.

2. In generative grammar the term is used for a phrase whose head is a verb, essentially equivalent to the traditional term 'predicate'. In this sense, in *Miriam will start a new business* the verb phrase is *will start a new business*. In this framework, a verb phrase may still consist of a single verb (e.g. in the sentence *John died*, the verb phrase is the single item *died*). See also NOUN PHRASE.

verbal

1. The adjective from 'verb', found in phrases such as 'verbal GROUP'.
2. Having to do with language, in phrases such as VERBAL DUELLING and VERBAL HYGIENE. In this sense, 'verbal' forms of communication (conventional spoken or written language) may also be contrasted with 'non-verbal' forms (gesture, facial expression etc.); see NON-VERBAL COMMUNICATION. In the case of SIGN LANGUAGES, gesture used as a visual/spatial sign would have a verbal rather than a non-verbal function.
3. Verbal in the sense of 'spoken' (rather than written) is not conventionally used in sociolinguistic description.

verbal duelling   A form of competitive LANGUAGE PLAY found in many parts of the world, in which participants draw on their linguistic skills to put one over on an opponent. This can develop into elaborate contests in which opponents are cheered on by spectators. Verbal duelling often takes the form of a series of **ritual insults** between two speakers, in which taunts are capped by appropriate retorts. The ritual nature of the insults is important – they are distinct from personal insults in that they are acknowledged by participants not to be true. Many studies have investigated such forms of behaviour among boys and young men, where duelling is often of a highly sexual nature. Verbal duelling is bound by conventions known to participants. As an example see Labov (1972c) for a classic study of the rules of 'ritual insults' among African American boys/young men. Guy Cook (2000) extends the notion of verbal duelling to examples that might be seen as more 'serious', for example exchanges between politicians in the British House of Commons.

verbal hygiene   A term coined by Deborah Cameron (1995) for attempts by people to 'improve' or 'clean up' language, where it is deemed to be in need of it. Such practices typically involve judgements about 'good' and 'bad' language. They may entail attempts at STANDARDISATION of grammar and writing, PLAIN LANGUAGE movements, SPELLING REFORM, and the inculcation of non-sexist language (see SEXISM). Whereas linguists have traditionally condemned PRESCRIPTIVISM as irrelevant to their field, the study of verbal hygiene suggests that the role of prescriptivists, reformers and planners has a significant impact on language use and the history of languages. Cameron argues that since language is always an abstraction or idealisation from the interactions of speakers, rule writing by linguists involves making decisions about what is 'in the language' or not. Linguists are also called upon to make judgements about language if they are involved in dictionary making, LANGUAGE PLANNING, etc. In practice, therefore, Cameron argues, there are overlaps between the prescriptivism of grammarians and schoolteachers and the DESCRIPTIVISM of linguists, even though linguists argue that their subject is a descriptive, not a prescriptive one. See also CORRECTNESS.

verbal play   See LANGUAGE PLAY.

vernacular
1. Refers to relatively homogeneous and well-defined NON-STANDARD varieties which are used regularly by particular geographical, ethnic or SOCIAL GROUPS and which exist in opposition to a dominant (not necessarily related) STANDARD variety (such as, for example, AFRICAN AMERICAN VERNACULAR ENGLISH in the United States).
2. According to William LABOV, the most CASUAL SPEECH style in the linguistic REPERTOIRE of a speaker. The vernacular is used when talking to friends and family in informal contexts. It is acquired in childhood and is believed to be linguistically more regular than more formal, CAREFUL SPEECH styles, which typically show varying degrees of influence from STANDARD varieties or other local high-PRESTIGE varieties.

visual   The visual nature of communication is of interest in sociolinguistics in relation to, for example, studies of NON-VERBAL COMMUNICATION; and the description and analysis of visual-gestural SIGN LANGUAGES used by Deaf people. There is also increasing interest in sociolinguistic studies in other forms of visual communication, such as photographs and film images, as well as specific aspects of the visual, such as colour, size and shape.

The need to develop ways of analysing the visual as a key element of MULTIMODALITY is said to be particularly important given that information technologies are providing opportunities for new ways of communicating that include visual and other dimensions (see Kress and Van Leeuwen, 1996, 2001). See also VECTOR.

voice (-ed, -ing)
1. In the description and classification of speech sounds, sounds may be categorised as **voiced** – i.e. produced with vocal-cord vibration; or **voiceless/unvoiced** – produced without vocal cord vibration. **Voicing** is commonly used to distinguish pairs of CONSONANTS. For example, the [g] sound in English *gap* is voiced, whereas the [k] sound in *cap* is unvoiced. Consonants are categorised more fully in terms of their PLACE OF ARTICULATION, MANNER OF ARTICULATION and whether or not they are voiced. In this sense, see also PHONETICS; INTERNATIONAL PHONETIC ALPHABET.
2. 'Voice' also distinguishes between types of clause structure where the **active voice**, for example, *The girl kicked the ball* is distinguished from the **passive voice**, for example *The ball was kicked by the girl*.
3. 'Voice' has a central place in BAKHTIN's theory of language. Language is seen as 'polyphonic', that is, multi-voiced, and any specific use of language – whether as single words, phrases or DISCOURSES – carries the voices, that is intentions and interests and values, of previous users of language. In this sense, see DOUBLE-VOICING; HETEROGLOSSIA; POLYPHONY; VENTRILOQUATION.
4. Drawing on traditions in anthropology, 'voice' is also used to refer to people's lived experiences, and, in a more broadly political sense, to mean taking control or claiming authority over naming experience. For example, in feminist writings 'finding a voice' involves a focus on how people claim the right to speak of their experience in their own terms. Voice often involves a focus on IDENTITY and AGENCY.

voice quality   Refers to the overall 'shape' of a speaker's voice: whether a voice sounds 'harsh', 'soft', 'nasal', 'metallic' etc. Voice quality is said to derive from ARTICULATORY SETTING, or habitual configurations of the vocal tract. It corresponds to a combination of phonetic features but is often identified impressionistically. Voice quality may represent permanent or at least long-term characteristics of a particular speaker's voice; it may also represent changing characteristics (e.g. a speaker's voice may change according to his or her emotional state); and it may characterise a group of speakers or a particular accent: Gerry Knowles (1978) has discussed the voice quality of the Liverpool accent of English, sometimes referred to as 'adenoidal'; see also discussions of voice quality as a 'marker' of social identity in Scherer and Giles (1979). As a feature of accent, however, voice quality has not been as well studied as other characteristics.

Voloshinov, Valentin Nikolaevich (1895–1936)   A Russian academic who is best known for his books *Marxism and the Philosophy of Language* ([1929] 1973) and *Freudianism: A Marxist Critique* ([1927] 1976). The former is a systematic critique of Ferdinand de Saussure's ([1916] 1959) *Course in General Linguistics*. Whereas Saussure focused on the structural nature of the SIGN (including linguistic signs such as words and phrases), Voloshinov emphasised its ideological nature: in a famous dictum he argued that the 'sign becomes an arena of the class struggle' (1973: 23). The sign is open to different orientations and evaluations in the social world. Voloshinov's ideas are compatible with those of his contemporary Mikhail BAKHTIN, who enjoys an important place in literary theory and several branches of linguistics including CRITICAL DISCOURSE ANALYSIS. Claims have been made that in the oppressive political climate of the times Bakhtin used Voloshinov's name for publication. However, such claims remain highly controversial. Alternative transliterations are found for Voloshinov's name, for example Volósinov.

vowel (vocalic)   Speech sounds are often categorised as vowels or CONSONANTS: when vowels are articulated the air-stream is allowed to flow freely (i.e. it is not blocked, or constricted to create friction). Vowels are usually produced with vocal-cord vibration. Vowels are often classified or distinguished from one another in articulatory terms, depending on the position of the highest part of the tongue: whether this is CLOSE (or high) or OPEN (low), and whether it is towards the FRONT or BACK of the mouth; various intermediate positions also occur. Another factor taken into account is lip ROUNDING. For instance, the sound [i] in the English word *peat* is a close front vowel produced without lip rounding (or 'unrounded'). Vowels are sometimes distinguished in terms of length (LONG vs short vowels). 'Pure' vowels or **monophthongs** may also be distinguished from **diphthongs**, where there is a change in articulatory position. The transcription of diphthongs may reflect their initial and final vowel qualities, as in [eɪ] to represent the vowel sound in *pail* in many varieties of English.

Vowels are used as LINGUISTIC VARIABLES in many VARIATIONIST studies of LANGUAGE VARIATION and LANGUAGE CHANGE. In this case, they are usually regarded as continuous variables (where there is a continuum of pronunciations ranging from, e.g., more to less close). To produce a manageable and quantifiable set of VARIANTS, however, the continuum is usually segmented to give (say) three or four variant pronunciations. Language change may be described in terms of a shift in vowel position (e.g. vowels may be 'raised' (see RAISE) or 'fronted' – for examples of shifts, see the GREAT VOWEL SHIFT; NORTHERN CITIES SHIFT; SOUTHERN HEMISPHERE SHIFT). While different vowel qualities are usually identified by ear, acoustic measurement may also be used, in which case vowels would be identified in terms of FORMANT frequencies reflecting the size and shape of the vocal tract; see Milroy and Gordon (2003) for discussion of relevant aspects of methodology.

vowel merger   See MERGER.

Vygotsky, Lev (1896–1934)   A Russian psychologist whose work on the relationship between language and learning has become increasingly influential over the past twenty years in many parts of the world. Vygotsky starts from the premise that language is a cultural tool for meaning-making and argues that this has profound implications for how we conceptualise the relationship between thought and language, and teaching and learning. Core Vygotskian notions, such as ZONE OF PROXIMAL DEVELOPMENT form the basis of much work in what is often referred to as a SOCIO-CULTURAL approach to teaching and learning.

wave model   A model of language DIFFUSION (2) which was originally developed in the nineteenth century by the German linguist Johannes Schmidt. In English-language linguistics it is commonly associated with the work of C.-J. N. Bailey (1973; see also DEVELOPMENTAL LINGUISTICS (2)) According to the wave model, LANGUAGE CHANGE begins at some geographical point and then spreads gradually across a wider territory over time. The effect of the spread will be strongest near the centre, where the new form emerged. Areas further away from the centre will not adopt the change in its entirety (limiting it, for example, to specific linguistic environments). The terms **wave theory** or *Wellentheorie* are also found. See also GRAVITY MODEL.

ways of speaking A term associated particularly with Dell HYMES, and proposed as part of Hymes' project to identify and characterise systematicity in the inherent diversity of human communication. 'Ways of speaking' is a highly general term that encompasses the range of speaking styles available within a community; the norms of interaction that govern the use of these; and the attitudes and beliefs associated with speaking styles and norms of interaction – see e.g. Hymes (1972, 1974). For Hymes, ways of speaking were best investigated within an ethnographic approach (see also ETHNOGRAPHY).

'we' and 'they' codes These terms derive from the work of John GUMPERZ on CODE-SWITCHING (e.g. Gumperz, 1982). In BILINGUAL or BIDIALECTAL communities, 'we' codes are language varieties associated with in-group usage (often with local, informal activity) and 'they' codes with out-group usage (often with more formal, public interactions). The danger of this distinction is that it may suggest more consistent and stable patterns of use than actually occur, and Gumperz himself noted that the distinction was to be regarded as symbolic and was not intended to predict actual usage.

weak ties Irregularly used, non-reciprocal and non-intimate interpersonal relationships between individuals in a SOCIAL NETWORK. The strength of ties is usually measured in terms of frequency of contact and the different capacities or relationships in which speakers interact with each other (see MULTIPLEX). Interactions between lecturers and students, shop assistants and customers, doctors and patients are typical examples of weak-tie connections: their contacts are irregular and they generally interact with each other in only one capacity. In the study of LANGUAGE CHANGE weak-tie networks have been shown to facilitate the spread of new linguistic forms across social groups. Weak-tie networks, which are common for modern, industrialised societies, do not usually support language maintenance. Contrast STRONG TIES.

Whinnom formula   Keith Whinnom (1971) hypothesised that PID-
GINS arise in situations of contact between three or more languages,
whose speakers do not have a common language. His general
formula was:

$$\text{Pidgin} = \frac{\text{Target language}}{\text{substrate languages A x B (x C . . .)}}$$

In this formulation a pidgin does not arise out of BILINGUAL
situations. Rather, it involves a TARGET language and at least
two SUBSTRATE languages. The pidgin arises as a compromise
between speakers of language A's version of the target language
(usually a socially or politically dominant language) with speakers
of language B's version of it (and so forth). While this has
remained a useful way of conceptualising PIDGINISATION, critics
argue that (a) there have been pidgins like Russenorsk arising out
of two-way contacts (between Russian and Norwegian fishermen)
and (b) that in some situations pidgins had no 'target language' –
speakers were concerned with forming a means of communication,
rather than learning a pre-existing language.

Whorfian   An adjective derived from Benjamin Lee Whorf, whose
studies of American-Indian languages in the early twentieth
century led him (and his teacher, Edward Sapir) to propose that
languages could differ so greatly in the expression of externally
similar phenomena as to influence the way speakers habitually
observed and evaluated these phenomena. Language thus determines thought rather than the other way round (Whorf, 1956); see
LINGUISTIC DETERMINISM. The **Whorfian hypothesis** (or SAPIR–
WHORF HYPOTHESIS) suggests that accurate translation between
widely different languages is not possible, since the worldviews
embodied in such languages clash. Meaning is relative to the
language system, rather than absolute or independent of language.
'Whorfian' as an adjective alludes to such a relativist view of
language. It has acquired a slightly derogatory nuance with the
dominance of universalist accounts of language associated with
Noam Chomsky since the 1950s, as many modern linguists hold
that the Whorfian hypothesis is untestable and hence unscientific.

women's language   Attempts to characterise discrete forms of
'women's language' have been evident both within linguistics and
within folklinguistic traditions (see FOLK LINGUISTICS). Motivations

for these vary – they include sexist accounts of women's linguistic 'inadequacies', feminist accounts of women's linguistic powerlessness and feminist attempts to revalue women's language (for discussion, see Cameron, 1992). Despite their different motivations, such attempts share an assumption that women's language is a distinctive, unitary phenomenon, and that this requires scrutiny and explanation. This is at odds with the current tendency in LANGUAGE AND GENDER studies to emphasise diversity within social groups, and recent research would be unlikely to refer to 'women's language' as a unitary category. Traditionally, there has been less focus on 'men's language' as an object of study. Recent research on language and MASCULINITY attempts to redress the balance, but, in line with current thinking, this tends to emphasise differences between men rather than trying to provide a general characterisation of men's linguistic behaviour.

word list   Used to elicit a formal speaking style in sociolinguistic INTERVIEWS. Word lists include words that contain pronunciation features particularly relevant to the sociolinguistic study. For example, they might include words such as *three* and *nothing* if the study were interested in the variable (th): whether this was pronounced [f] or [θ]: see (STYLISTIC CONTINUUM).

wording   See LEXICOGRAMMAR.

working class   A social group engaged in blue-collar work and often located towards the lower end of the social hierarchy (in terms of e.g. income, housing and social STATUS). The presence of a working class is typical for industrial societies and mostly concentrated in cities and larger manufacturing towns. Marxist class analysis emphasises the exploitation and manipulation of the working class by those who own the means of production (the bourgeoisie or owner class) – e.g. see FALSE CONSCIOUSNESS. Some sociolinguistic studies operate with a binary distinction between working class and MIDDLE CLASS; others make further distinctions within the social hierarchy (e.g. between upper and lower working class) (see SOCIAL CLASS).

World English (-es)   A cover term coined by Braj KACHRU for varieties of English that have developed outside England. **World Englishes** is often used interchangeably with NEW ENGLISHES. However, whereas ENGLISH AS A FOREIGN LANGUAGE is excluded in many formulations of 'New Englishes', they are included in most formulations of 'World Englishes'. Generally speaking, PIDGINS and CREOLES are excluded from definitions of World Englishes, as they are separate systems, though this disciplinary boundary is less firm than it once was.

In the singular, **World English** may have a similar sense, but is also used by some to refer to the development of one variety of (standard) English to be used across the world – in this latter sense, it is not a descriptive sociolinguistic concept. See also THREE CIRCLES OF ENGLISH.

world knowledge People's knowledge of the world and how it works, sometimes contrasted with 'linguistic knowledge' or knowledge of the language system. It is argued (e.g. in PRAGMATICS) that, in order to produce and interpret utterances, speakers need to draw on world knowledge as well as linguistic knowledge, and that this needs to be taken into account in the analysis of meaning. This idea is prevalent within sociolinguistics: for example, concepts such as FRAME, SCHEMA and SCRIPT, drawn on in some sociolinguistic analyses, incorporate world knowledge (though the term itself may not necessarily be used). In practice, it is difficult to make a strict division between linguistic and world knowledge, for example in considering the meaning of any word or expression it is hard to determine where 'linguistic meaning' stops and world knowledge begins; for discussion, see Graddol et al. (1994: Chapter 4).

writing system A system for representing a language in writing, often defined more formally as a given set of written marks along with a set of conventions for their use (after Sampson, 1985). The term **orthography** is also found in this general sense (i.e. not restricted to spelling as it sometimes is in more everyday uses). Writing systems may take different forms: a distinction is commonly made between alphabetic systems (in which written symbols represent sounds or PHONEMES, as in the Roman and Cyrillic alphabets); syllabic systems (in which symbols represent syllables, as in the Hiragana and Katakana scripts used for writing Japanese); and logographic systems (in which symbols represent words or morphemes, as in Chinese). Mixed systems are also possible (e.g. Japanese also uses Chinese characters and some Roman characters).

Writing systems are sociolinguistically interesting because, like speech, writing is part of the culture of a community and carries important cultural meanings. Certain forms of writing may be associated with identity at national, group and individual levels. For instance, a single SCRIPT may be selected to express a common identity across different language communities; alternatively, different scripts may be preferred to express distinct community identities (see SCRIPT REFORM). At a more local level, there has been sociolinguistic interest in forms of writing, spelling conventions etc. used in graffiti, computer-mediated communication and other contemporary language practices. On writing systems in general, see Coulmas (2003); on the sociolinguistics of orthography/writing, see Sebba (2001).

youth language   The specific linguistic styles or practices used within adolescent PEER GROUPS. Early scholarly as well as folk-linguistic descriptions (see FOLK LINGUISTICS) of such age-related practices have described youth language as a relatively unitary phenomenon, characterised most prominently by a specific lexicon and the extensive use of certain pragmatic markers (e.g. *eh*, *like*). Sociolinguists (e.g. Schlobinski et al., 1993) have criticised this undifferentiated and often stereotypical view of youth language as a well-defined phenomenon, and have argued that the study of **youth languages** (in the plural) should aim at describing the diversity and ambiguity of adolescent speech styles from an ethnographic perspective. See also AGE-GRADING; JOCKS AND BURNOUTS.

zone of proximal development (ZPD)   A term coined by VYGOTSKY to describe 'the distance between the actual developmental level [of a child] as determined by independent problem solving and the level of potential development as determined through problem solving under adult guidance or in collaboration with more capable peers'. (Vygotsky, 1978: 86). Vygotsky used the notion of ZPD to question the widespread assessment practice of focusing on children's individual performance and to emphasise the importance of looking at what a child can do with the help of an adult – a parent or teacher. Jerome Bruner famously refers to the guidance or support that adults and more capable peers can offer as **scaffolding** (see Wood et al., 1976). Much SOCIOCULTURAL research uses the notions of the ZPD and 'scaffolding' to explore the talk between teachers and students. See also APPROPRIATION; VYGOTSKY.

Bibliography

Alba, R. (1990) *Ethnic Identity: The Transformation of White America.* New Haven: Yale University Press.

Alexander, R. (2000) *Culture and Pedagogy: International Comparisons in Primary Education.* Oxford: Blackwell.

Althusser, L. (1971) *Lenin and Philosophy and Other Essays.* London: New Left Books.

Antaki, C. and Widdicombe, S. (eds) (1998) *Identities in Talk.* London: Sage.

Ardener, S. (1978) 'Introduction: the nature of women in society', in S. Ardener (ed.) *Defining Females: The Nature of Women in Society.* London: Croom Helm.

Arends, J., Muysken, P. and Smith, N. (1995) *Pidgins and Creoles: An Introduction.* Amsterdam: John Benjamins.

Askehave, I. and Swales, J. (2001) 'Genre identification and communicative purpose: a problem and a possible solution', *Applied Linguistics*, 22: 195–212.

Auer, P. (1984) *Bilingual Conversation.* Amsterdam: John Benjamins.

Auer, P. (1997) 'Führt Dialektabbau zur Stärkung oder Schwächung der Standardvarietät? Zwei phonologische Fallstudien', in K. J. Mattheier and E. Radtke (eds) *Standardisierung und Destandardisierung europäischer Nationalsprachen.* Frankfurt: Peter Lang.

Auer, P. (1998) 'Introduction: *Bilingual Conversation* revisited', in P. Auer (ed.) *Code-Switching in Conversation: Language, Interaction and Identity.* London and New York: Routledge.

Austin, J. L. (1962) *How To Do Things With Words.* Oxford: Oxford University Press.

Ayto, J. (2002) *The Oxford Dictionary of Rhyming Slang.* Oxford: Oxford University Press.

Bailey, C.-J. N. (1973) *Variation and Linguistic Theory.* Arlington, VA: Center for Applied Linguistics.

Bailey, C.-J. N. (1996) *Essays on Time-Based Linguistic Analysis.* Oxford: Clarendon Press.

Baker, P. (1994) 'Creativity in Creole Genesis', in D. Adone and I. Plag (eds) *Creolization and Language Change*. Tübingen: Niemeyer.

Baker, P. (1995) 'Motivation in Creole Genesis', in P. Baker (ed.) *From Contact to Creole and Beyond*. London: University of Westminster Press.

Baker, P. (2002) *Polari – The Lost Language of Gay Men*. London: Routledge.

Baker, P. and Eversley, J. (2000) *Multilingual Capital: The Languages of London's School Children and the Economic and Social Implications*. London: Battlebridge Press.

Bakhtin, M. M. ([1929] 1984a) *Problems of Dostoevsky's Poetics*, ed. and trans. by C. Emerson. Minneapolis: University of Minnnesota Press.

Bakhtin, M. M. ([1935] 1981) *The Dialogic Imagination: Four essays by M. M. Bakhtin*, ed. M. Holquist, trans. C. Emerson and M. Holquist. Austin, TX: University of Texas Press.

Bakhtin, M. M. ([1953] 1986) 'The problem of speech genres', in C. Emerson and M. Holquist (eds) *Speech Genres and Other Late Essays*, trans. V. W. McGee. Austin, TX: University of Texas Press.

Bakhtin, M. M. ([1965] 1984b) *Rabelais and His World*, trans. H. Iswolsky. Bloomington, IN: Indiana University Press.

Bakker, P. and Muysken, P. (1995) 'Mixed languages and language intertwining', in J. Arends, P. Muysken and N. Smith (eds) *Pidgins and Creoles: An Introduction*. Amsterdam: John Benjamins.

Barrett, R. (1997) 'The homo-genius speech community', in A. Livia and K. Hall (eds) *Queerly Phrased: Language, Gender and Sexuality*. New York: Oxford University Press.

Barthes, R. (1977) *Image, Music, Text*. London: Fontana.

Barton, D. and Hamilton, M. (1998) *Local Literacies: Reading and Writing in One Community*. London: Routledge.

Barton, M. E. and Tomasello, M. (1994) 'The rest of the family: the role of fathers and siblings in early language development', in C. Gallaway and B. J. Richards (eds) *Input and Interaction in Language Acquisition*. Cambridge: Cambridge University Press.

Bateson, G. (1972) *Steps to an Ecology of Mind*. New York: Ballantine.

Baugh, J. (1980) 'A Re-examination of the Black English Copula', in W. Labov (ed.) *Locating Language in Time and Space*. New York: Academic Press.

Baugh, J. (2000) *Beyond Ebonics: Linguistic Pride and Racial Prejudice*. New York: Oxford University Press.

Bauman, R. and Sherzer, J. ([1974] 1989) (eds) *Explorations in the*

Ethnography of Speaking, 2nd edn. Cambridge: Cambridge University Press.

Beal, J. (1993) 'The grammar of Tyneside and Northumbrian English', in J. Milroy and L. Milroy (eds) *Real English: The Grammar of English Dialects in the British Isles*. London: Longman.

Bell, A. (1984) 'Language style as audience design', *Language in Society*, 13: 145–204.

Bell, A. (1991) *The Language of News Media*. Oxford: Blackwell.

Bell, A. (2002) 'Back in style: reworking audience design', in P. Eckert and J. R. Rickford (eds) *Style and Sociolinguistic Variation*. Cambridge: Cambridge University Press.

Bennett, T. (1979) *Formalism and Marxism*. London: Methuen.

Bereiter, C. and Englemann, S. (1966) 'An academically oriented pre-school for culturally deprived children', in F. M. Hechinger (ed.) *Pre-School Education Today*. New York: Doubleday.

Berger, P. L. and Luckman, T. (1967) *The Social Construction of Reality*. New York: Doubleday.

Bernstein, B. (1971) *Class, Codes and Control*, vol. 1. London: Routledge and Kegan Paul.

Bernstein, B. (1977) *Class, Codes and Control*, vol. 3. London: Routledge and Kegan Paul.

Bernstein, B. (1996) *Pedagogy, Symbolic Control and Identity: Theory, Research, Critique*. London: Taylor and Francis.

Bhaba, H. K. (1994) *The Location of Culture*. London: Routledge.

Bhaskar, R. (1979) *The Possibility of Naturalism*. Hemel Hempstead: Harvester Wheatsheaf.

Bhatia, V. K. (1993) *Analysing Genre: Language Use in Professional Settings*. London: Longman.

Biber, D., Conrad, S. and Reppen, R. (1998) *Corpus Linguistics: Investigating Language Structure and Use*. Cambridge: Cambridge University Press.

Bickerton, D. (1972) 'The structure of polylectal grammars', in R. Shuy (ed.) *Sociolinguistics*. Washington, DC: Georgetown University Press.

Bickerton, D. (1981) *Roots of Language*. Ann Arbor: Karoma.

Blom, J.-P. and Gumperz, J. J. (1972) 'Social meaning in linguistic structures: code-switching in Norway', in J. J. Gumperz and D. Hymes (eds) *Directions in Sociolinguistics*. Oxford: Basil Blackwell.

Blommaert, J. (2001) 'The Asmara Declaration as a sociolinguistic problem: reflections on scholarship and linguistic rights', *Journal of Sociolinguistics*, 5: 131–42.

Blommaert, J. (ed.) (1999) *Language Ideological Debates*. Berlin and New York: Mouton de Gruyter.

Bloomfield, L. (1964) 'Literate and Illiterate Speech', in D. Hymes (ed.) *Language in Culture and Society*. New York: Harper and Row.

Bloomfield, L. W. (1933) *Language*. New York: Holt, Rhinehart and Winston.

Boden, D. (1994) *The Business of Talk: Organizations in Action*. Cambridge: Polity Press.

Bourdieu, P. (1977) *Outline of a Theory of Practice*. Cambridge: Cambridge University Press.

Bourdieu, P. (1984) *Distinction: A Social Critique of the Judgement of Taste*. London: Routledge and Kegan Paul.

Bourdieu, P. (1991) *Language and Symbolic Power*. Cambridge: Polity Press

Bourhis, R., Giles, H. and Rosenthal, D. (1981) 'Notes on the construction of a subjective vitality questionnaire', *Journal of Multicultural and Multilingual Development*, 2: 145–55.

Bright, W. and Ramanujan, A. K. (1964) 'Sociolinguistic variation and linguistic change', in H.G. Lunt (ed.) *Proceedings of the Ninth International Congress of Linguists (1962)*. The Hague: Mouton.

Brisk, M. E. (1998) *Bilingual Education: From Contemporary to Quality Schooling*. Mahwah, NJ: Lawrence Erlbaum.

Brown, P. (1980) 'How and why are women more polite: some evidence from a Mayan community', in S. McConnell-Ginet, R. Borker and N. Furman (eds) *Women and Language in Literature and Society*. New York: Praeger.

Brown, P. (1990) 'Gender, politeness, and confrontation in Tenejapa', *Discourse Processes*, 13: 123–41.

Brown, P. and Levinson, S. (1987) *Politeness: Some Universals in Language Usage*. Cambridge: Cambridge University Press.

Brown, R. (1973) *A First Language: The Early Stages*. London: George Allen and Unwin.

Brown, R. and Gilman, A. (1960) 'The pronouns of power and solidarity', in J. Hutchinson and S. Laver (eds) (1972) *Communication in Face to Face Interaction*. Harmondsworth: Penguin.

Bruner, J. (1990) *Acts of meaning*. Cambridge, MA: Harvard University Press.

Burke, P., and Porter, R. (eds) (1995). *Languages and Jargons: Contributions to a Social History of Language*. Cambridge: Polity Press.

Burke, S. (1995) *Authorship: from Plato to the Postmodern; a Reader*. Edinburgh: Edinburgh University Press.

Butler, J. ([1990] 1999) *Gender Trouble: Feminism and the Subversion of Identity*, 2nd edn. New York and London: Routledge.

Button, G. (ed.) (1991) *Ethnomethodology and the Human Sciences*. Cambridge: Cambridge University Press.

Byrne, F. (1987) *Grammatical Relations in a Radical Creole*. Amsterdam: John Benjamins.

Caldas-Coulthard, R. (1996) 'Women who pay for sex. And enjoy it: transgression versus morality in women's magazines', in C. Caldas-Coulthard and M. Coulthard (eds) *Texts and Practices: Readings in Critical Discourse Analysis*. London: Routledge.

Cameron, D. (1992) *Feminism and Linguistic Theory*, 2nd edn. Basingstoke and London: Macmillan.

Cameron, D. (1995) *Verbal Hygiene*. London: Routledge.

Cameron, D. (1997) 'Performing gender identity: young men's talk and the construction of heterosexual masculinity', in S. Johnson and U. H. Meinhof (eds) *Language and Masculinity*. Oxford: Blackwell Publishers.

Cameron, D. (2000) *Good to Talk*. London: Sage.

Cameron, D. and Kulick, D. (2003a) 'Introduction: language and desire in theory and practice', *Language and Communication*, 23: 93–105.

Cameron, D. and Kulick, D. (2003b) *Language and Sexuality*. Cambridge: Cambridge University Press.

Cameron, D., Frazer, E., Harvey, P., Rampton, M. B. H. and Richardson, K. (1992) *Researching Language: Issues of Power and Method*. London: Routledge.

Campell, L. (1997) *American Indian Languages: The Historical Linguistics of Native America*. Oxford: Oxford University Press.

Campbell-Kibler, K., Podesva, R., Roberts, S. J. and Wong, A. (eds) (2002) *Language and Sexuality: Contesting Meaning in Theory and Practice*. Stanford, California: CSLI Publications.

Canagarajah, A. S. (1999) *Resisting Linguistic Imperialism in English Teaching*. Oxford: Oxford University Press.

Canagarajah, A. S. (2002) *A Geopolitics of Academic Writing*. Pittsburgh: University of Pittsburgh Press.

Carter, R. (2004) *Language and Creativity: The Art of Common Talk*. London: Routledge.

Carter, R. (ed.) (1990) *Knowledge about Language and the Curriculum: The LINC Reader*. London: Hodder and Stoughton.

Castells, M. (2000) *The Rise of the Network Society*, 2nd edn. Oxford: Blackwell.

Chambers, J. K. (2003) *Sociolinguistic Theory*, 3rd edn. Oxford: Basil Blackwell.

Chambers, J. K. and Trudgill, P. (1998) *Dialectology*, 2nd edn. Cambridge: Cambridge University Press.

Chen, M. Y. (1977) 'The time dimension contribution toward a theory of sound change', in W. S-Y. Wang (ed.) *The Lexicon in Phonological Change*. The Hague: Mouton.

Chesebro, J. W. (1981) *Gayspeak: Gay Male and Lesbian Communication*. New York: Pilgrim Press.

Chesire, J. (1982) *Variation in an English Dialect: A Sociolinguistic Study*. Cambridge: Cambridge University Press.

Cheshire, J. (ed.) (1991) *English around the World*. Cambridge: Cambridge University Press.

Cheshire, J. and Milroy, J. (1993) 'Syntactic variation in nonstandard dialects', in J. Milroy and L. Milroy (eds) *Real English: The Grammar of English Dialects in the British Isles*. London: Longman.

Childs, P. (2000) *Modernism*. London and New York: Routledge.

Chomsky, N. (1957) *Syntactic Structures*. The Hague: Mouton.

Chomsky, N. (1965) *Aspects of the Theory of Syntax*. Cambridge, MA: MIT Press.

Chouliaraki, L. and Fairclough, N. (1999) *Discourse in Late Modernity: Rethinking Critical Discourse Analysis*. Edinburgh: Edinburgh University Press.

Clark, R. and Ivanic, R. (1997) *The Politics of Writing*. London: Routledge.

Clark, R. and Ivanic, R. (eds) (1999) 'Raising awareness of language: a curriculum aim for the new millenium', *Language Awareness* (Special issue) (8): 63–70.

Clark, R., Fairclough, N., Ivanic, R. and Martin-Jones, M. (1991) 'Critical language awareness, part II: towards critical alternatives', *Language and Education*, 5: 41–54.

Clyne, M. (1968) 'Zum Pidgin-Deutsch der Gastarbeiter', *Zeitschrift für Mundartforschung*, 35: 130–35.

Clyne, M. (1991) *Community Languages: The Australian Experience*. Cambridge: Cambridge University Press.

Coates, J. (1996) *Women Talk: Conversation between Women Friends*. Oxford: Blackwell Publishers.

Coates, J. (2003) *Men Talk*. Oxford: Blackwell Publishing.

Coates, J. (ed.) (1998) *Language and Gender: A Reader*. Oxford: Blackwell Publishers.

Cobarrubias J. (1983) 'Ethical issues in status planning', in J. Cobarrubias and J. A. Fishman (eds) *Progress in Language Planning*. Berlin: Mouton.

Cohen, S. (1987) *Folk Devils and Moral Panics: The Creation of Mods and Rockers*. Oxford: Basil Blackwell.

Collins, R. (1975) *Conflict Theory: Toward an Explanatory Science*. New York: Academic Press.

Connell, R. W. (1995) *Masculinities*. Cambridge: Polity Press.

Cook, G. (1994) *Discourse and Literature: The Interplay of Form and Mind*. Oxford: Oxford University Press.

Cook, G. (2000) *Language Play, Language Learning*. Oxford: Oxford University Press.

Cooper, R. (1982) *Language Spread*. Bloomington: Indiana University Press.

Cooper, R. L. (1989) *Language Planning and Social Change*. Cambridge: Cambridge University Press.

Corbett, G. (1991) *Gender*. Cambridge: Cambridge University Press.

Coulmas, F. (1985) *Sprache und Staat: Studien über Sprachplanung und Sprachpolitik*. Berlin: De Gruyter.

Coulmas, F. (2003) *Writing Systems: An Introduction to their Linguistic Analysis*. Cambridge: Cambridge University Press.

Coupland, N. (1985) ' "Hark, hark the lark": social motivations for phonological style-shifting', *Language and Communication*, 5 (3): 153–71.

Coveney, A. (1996) *Variability in Spoken French: A Sociolinguistic Study of Interrogation and Negation*. Exeter, England: Elm Bank Publications.

Crawford, J. (2000) *At War with Diversity: US Language Policy in an Age of Anxiety*. Clevedon: Multilingual Matters.

Crystal, D. (1997) *English as a Global Language*. Cambridge: Cambridge University Press.

Crystal, D. (1998) *Language Play*. London: Penguin Books.

Crystal, D. (2001) *Language and the Internet*. Cambridge: Cambridge University Press.

Crystal, D. (2002) *A Dictionary of Linguistics and Phonetics*. Oxford: Blackwell.

Cummins, J. (1996) *Negotiating Identities: Education for Empowerment in a Diverse Society*. Ontario, CA: California Association for Bilingual Education.

Curtiss, S. (1977) *Genie: A Psycholinguistic Study of a Modern Day Wild Child*. New York: Academic Press.

DeCamp, D. (1971) 'Toward the generative analysis of a post-creole speech continuum', in D. Hymes (ed.) *Pidginization and Creolization of Languages*. Cambridge: Cambridge University Press.

Department of Education and Science (1950) *A Language for Life* [The Bullock Report]. London: HMSO.

Department of Education and Science (1989) *English for Ages 5 to 16* [The Cox Report]. London: HMSO.

Derrida, J. (1978) *Writing and Difference*. London: Routledge.

Deumert, A. and Vandenbussche, W. (eds) (2003) *Germanic Standardizations – Past to Present*. Amsterdam: John Benjamins.

Dillard, J. L. (1970) 'Principles in the history of American English: paradox, virginity, and cafeteria', *Florida Foreign Language Reporter*, 8: 32–3.

Dittmar, N. (1997) *Grundlagen der Soziolinguistik: Ein Arbeitsbuch mit Aufgaben*. Tübingen: Niemeyer.

Docherty, G. J. and Foulkes, P. (1999) 'Derby and Newcastle: instrumental phonetics and variationist studies', in P. Foulkes and G. J. Docherty (eds) *Urban Voices*. London: Arnold.

Dorcey, M. (1991) *Moving into the Space Cleared by Other Mothers*. Dublin: Salmon Publishing.

Dorian, N. (1981) *Language Death: The Life Cycle of a Scottish Gaelic Dialect*. Philadelphia: University of Pennsylvania Press.

Drew, P. and Heritage, J. (1992) (eds) *Talk at Work: Interaction in Institutional Settings*. Cambridge: Cambridge University Press.

Du Bois, J. W. (1986) 'Self-Evidence and Ritual Speech', in W. Chafe and J. Nichols (eds) *Evidentiality: The Linguistic Coding of Epistemology*. Norwood, NJ: Ablex.

Duranti, A. (1992) 'Language in context and language as context: the Samoan respect vocabulary', in A. Duranti and C. Goodwin (eds) *Rethinking Context: Language as an Interactive Phenomenon*. Cambridge: Cambridge University Press.

Duranti, A. (1997) *Linguistic Anthropology*. Cambridge: Cambridge University Press.

Duranti, A. and Brenneis, D. (1986) 'The audience as co-author', *Text* (Special edition) 6: 239–347.

Eades, D. (1992). *Aboriginal English and the Law: Communicating with Aboriginal English Speaking Clients: A Handbook for Legal Practitioners*. Brisbane: Queensland Law Society.

Eades, D. (1995) 'Aboriginal English on trial: the case for Stuart and Condren', in D. Eades (ed.) *Language in Evidence: Issues Confronting Aboriginal and multicultural Australia*. Sydney: University of New South Wales Press.

Eckert, P. (1989) *Jocks and Burnouts: Social Categories and Identity in the High School*. New York: Teachers College Press.

Eckert, P. (1997) 'Age as a Sociolinguistic Variable', in F. Coulmas (ed.) *The Handbook of Sociolinguistics*. Oxford: Basil Blackwell.

Eckert, P. (2000) *Language Variation as Social Practice*. Oxford: Blackwell.

Eckert, P. and McConnell-Ginet, S. (1992) 'Communities of practice: where language, gender, and power all live', in K. Hall, M. Bucholtz and B. Moonwomon (eds) *Locating Power: proceedings of the Second Berkeley Women and Language Conference*. Berkeley, CA: Berkeley Women and Language Group.

Eckert, P. and McConnell-Ginet, S. (2003) *Language and Gender*. Cambridge: Cambridge University Press.

Eco, U. (1995) *The Search for the Perfect Language*. Oxford: Blackwell.

Edelsky, C. (1981) 'Who's got the floor?', *Language in Society*, 10: 383–421.

Edwards, V. (1986) *Language in a Black Community*. Clevedon: Multilingual Matters.

Eliot, T. S. (1972) *The Wasteland and Other Poems*. London: Faber and Faber.

Ellis, R. (1997) *SLA Research and Language Teaching*. Oxford: Oxford University Press.

Errington, J. J. (1988) *Structure and Style in Javanese: A Semiotic View of Linguistic Etiquette*. Philadelphia: University of Pennsylvania Press.

Esling, J. H. (1998) 'Everyone has an accent except me', in L. Bauer and P. Trudgill (eds) *Language Myths*. Harmondsworth: Penguin Books.

Fairclough, N. (1992a) *Discourse and Social Change*. Cambridge: Polity Press.

Fairclough, N. (1992c) 'The appropriacy of "appropriateness"', in N. Fairclough (ed.) *Critical Language Awareness*. London: Longman.

Fairclough, N. (1995) *Critical Discourse Analysis: The Critical Study of Language*. London: Longman.

Fairclough, N. (1996) 'Border crossings: discourse and social change in contemporary societies', in H. Coleman and L. Cameron (eds) *Change and Language*. Papers from the annual meeting of the British Association of Applied linguistics. Leeds: BAAL/Multilingual Matters.

Fairclough, N. (2000) *New Labour, New Language?* London: Routledge.

Fairclough, N. (2001) *Language and Power*, 2nd edn. London: Longman.

Fairclough, N. (ed.) (1992b) *Critical Language Awareness*. London: Longman.

Faraclas, N. (1996) *Nigerian Pidgin*. London: Routledge.

Fasold, R. (1984) *The Sociolinguistics of Society*. Oxford: Blackwell.

Ferguson, C. A. (1959) 'Diglossia', *Word*, 15: 325–40.

Ferguson, C. A. (1968) 'Language development', in J. A. Fishman, C. A. Ferguson and J. Das Gupta (eds) *Language Problems of Developing Nations*. New York: John Wiley and Sons.

Ferguson, C. A. (1971) 'Absence of copula and the notion of simplicity: a study of normal speech, baby talk and pidgins', in D. Hymes (ed.) *Pidginization and Creolization of Language*. Cambridge: Cambridge University Press.

Ferguson, C. A. (1988) 'Standardization as a form of language spread', in P. Lowenberg (ed.) *Language Spread and Language Policy: Issues, Implications, and Case Studies*. Georgetown University Round Table on Languages and Linguistics, 1987. Washington, DC: Georgetown University Press.

Finnegan, R. (2002) *Communicating: The Multiple Modes of Human Interconnection*. London and New York: Routledge.

Fischer, J. A. (1958) 'Social influences on the choice of a linguistic variant', *Word*, 14: 47–56.

Fishman, J. A. (1964) 'Language maintenance and shift as fields of inquiry', *Linguistics*, 9: 32–70.

Fishman, J. A. (1966) *Language Loyalty in the United States*. The Hague: Mouton.

Fishman, J. A. (1967) 'Bilingualism with and without diglossia, diglossia with and without bilingualism', *Journal of Social Issues*, 23: 29–38.

Fishman, J. A. (1972) *Language and Nationalism: Two Integrative Essays*. Rowley, MA: Newbury House.

Fishman, J. A. (1991) *Reversing Language Shift*. Clevedon, UK: Multilingual Matters.

Fishman, J. A. (ed.) (1968) *Readings in the Sociology of Language*. The Hague: Mouton.

Fishman, J. A., Cooper, R. and Ma, R. (1971) *Bilingualism in the Barrio*: *Language Sciences* (Special edition) 5.

Fishman, J. A., Gertner, M. H., Lowy, E. G. and Milán, W. G. (1985) *The Rise and Fall of the Ethnic Revival: Perspectives on Language and Ethnicity*. Berlin: Mouton.

Fludernik, M. (1993) *The Fictions of Language and the Languages of Fiction*. London: Routledge.

Foulkes, P. and Docherty, G. J. (1999) *Urban Voices*. London: Arnold.

Fowler, J. (1986) *The Social Stratification of (r) in New York City Department Stores, 24 Years after Labov*. New York University, MS.

Fowler, R. (1977) *Linguistics and the Novel*. London: Methuen.

Fowler, R. (1986) *Linguistic Criticism*, 2nd edn. Oxford: Oxford University Press.

Fowler, R. (1991) *Language in the News: Discourse and Ideology in the Press*. London: Routledge.

Fowler, R., Hodge, B., Kress, G. and Trew, T. (1979) *Language and Control*. London: Routledge.

Francis, G. (1990) 'Theme in the daily press', *Occasional Papers in Systemic Linguistics*, 4: 51–87.

Freccero, J. (1986) 'Autobiography and narrative', in T. C. Heller, M. Sosna and D. E. Wellbery, with A. I. Davidson, A. Swidler and I. Watt (eds) *Reconstructing Individualism: Autonomy, Individuality and the Self in Western Thought*. Stanford: Stanford University Press.

Freire, P. (1972) *Pedagogy of the Oppressed*. London: Penguin.

Freire, P. and Macedo, D. (1987) *Literacy: Reading the Word and the World*. London: Routledge and Kegan Paul.

Fries, P. H. and Francis, G. (1992) 'Exploring theme: problems for research', *Occasional Papers in Systemic Linguistics*, 6: 45–60.

Gal, S. (1978) 'Peasant men can't get wives: language change and sex roles in a bilingual community', *Language in Society*, 7: 1–16.

Gal, S. (1979) *Language Shift: Social Determinants of Linguistic Change in Bilingual Communities*. New York: Academic Press.

Garfinkel, H. (1963) 'A conception of, and experiments with, "trust" as a condition of stable concerted actions', in O. J. Harvey (ed.) *Motivation and Social Interaction*. New York: Ronald Press Company.

Garfinkel, H. ([1967] 1984) *Studies in Ethnomethodology*. Cambridge: Polity Press.

Gee, J. (1996) *Social Linguistics and Literacies: Ideologies in Discourses*, 2nd edn. Basingstoke: Falmer Press.

Gee, J. (1999) *An Introduction to Discourse Analysis, Theory and Method*. London: Routledge.

Gibbons, J. P. (1983) 'Attitudes towards languages and code-mixing in Hong Kong', *Journal of Multilingual and Multicultural Development*, 4: 129–47.

Giddens, A. (1979) *Central Problems in Social Theory: Action, Structure and Contradiction in Social Analysis*. Berkeley: University of California Press.

Giddens, A. (1990) *The Consequences of Modernity*. Cambridge: Polity Press.

Giddens, A. (1991) *Modernity and self-identity*. Cambridge: Polity Press.

Gilbert, N. G. and Mulkay, M. (1984) *Opening Pandora's Box: A Sociological Analysis of Scientists' Discourse*. Cambridge: Cambridge University Press.

Giles, H. and Powesland, R. (1975) *Speech Style and Social Evaluation*. London: Academic Press.

Giles, H., Bourhis, R. Y. and Taylor, D. M. (1977) 'Towards a theory of language in ethnic group relations', in H. Giles (ed.) *Language, Ethnicity and Intergroup Relations*. London: Academic Press.

Giles, H., Coupland, N. and Coupland, J. (1991) 'Accommodation theory: communication, context and consequence', in H. Giles, J. Coupland and N. Coupland (eds) *Contexts of Accommodation: Developments in Applied Sociolinguistics*. Cambridge: Cambridge University Press.

Gloy, K. (1975) *Sprachnormen I. Linguistische und soziologische Analysen*. Stuttgart/Bad Cannstatt: Fromann-Holzboog.

Goffman, E. (1955) 'On face-work: an analysis of ritual element in social interaction', *Psychiatry*, 18: 213–31. Reproduced in Hutchinson, J. and Laver, S. (eds) (1972) *Communication in Face to Face Interaction*. Harmondsworth: Penguin Books.

Goffman, E. (1959) *The Presentation of Self in Everyday Life*. Anchor Books. (Published in 1971 in Pelican Books.)

Goffman, E. (1967) *Interaction ritual*. Garden City, NY: Anchor.

Goffman, E. (1974) *Frame Analysis: An Essay on the Organization of Experience*. Harmondsworth: Penguin.

Gogolin, I. (2001) 'Linguistic habitus', in R. Mesthrie (ed.) *Concise Encyclopedia of Sociolinguistics*. Amsterdam: Elsevier.

Goodman, S. (1996) 'Visual English', in S. Goodman and D. Graddol (eds) *Redesigning English: New Texts, New Identities*. London: Routledge.

Görlach, M. (1987) 'Colonial Lag?: the alleged conservative character of American English and other colonial varieties', *English Worldwide*, 8: 41–60.

Görlach, M. (1991) 'Colonial Lag?', in M. Görlach *Englishes: Studies in Varieties of English, 1984–1988*. Amsterdam: John Benjamins.

Graddol, D. (1997) *The Future of English?* London: The British Council.

Graddol, D. and Swann, J. (1989) *Gender Voices*. Oxford: Blackwell.

Graddol, D., Cheshire, J. and Swann, J. (1994) *Describing Language*, 2nd edn. Buckingham: Open University Press.

Graff, H. (1987) *The Labyrinths of Literacy: Reflections on Literacy Past and Present*. New York: Falmer Press.

Gramsci, A. (1971) *Selections from the Prison Notebooks*, ed. and trans. by Q. Hoare and G. Nowell. London: Lawrence and Wishart.

Green, J. (1998) *The Cassell Dictionary of Slang*. London: Cassell.

Greenberg, J. H. (1986) 'Were there Egyptian koines?', in A. Fishman, A. Tabouret-Keller, M. Clyne, B. Krishnamurti and M. Abdulaziz (eds) *The Fergusonian Impact*, vol. I. Berlin and New York: Mouton de Gruyter.

Gregory, R. L. (1970) *The Intelligent Eye*. New York: McGraw-Hill.

Grice, H. P. (1975) 'Logic and conversation', in P. Cole and J. Morgan (eds) *Syntax and Semantics, 3: Speech Acts*. New York: Academic Press.

Grobler, E., Prinsloo, K. P. and van der Merwe, I. J. (1990) *Language Atlas of South Africa: Language and Literacy Patterns*. Pretoria, Republic of South Africa: Human Sciences Research Council.

Gumperz, J. J. (1982) *Discourse Strategies*. Cambridge: Cambridge University Press.

Gumperz, J. J. and Hymes, D. (eds) ([1972] 1986) *Directions in Sociolinguistics: The Ethnography of Communication*. Oxford: Basil Blackwell.

Gutierrez, K. D., Baquedano-Lopez, P. and Tejeda, C. (1999) 'Rethinking diversity: hybridity and hybrid language practices in the third space', *Mind Culture and Activity*, 6: 286–303.

Guttman, L. (1944) 'A basis for scaling quantitative data', *American Sociological Review*, 9: 139–50.

Guy, G., Horvath, B., Vonwiller, J., Daisley, E. and Rogers, I. (1986) 'An intonational change in progress in Australian English', *Language in Society*, 15: 22–52.

Haarmann, H. (1990) 'Language planning in the light of a general theory of language: a methodological framework', *International Journal of the Sociology of Language*, 86: 103–26.

Haas ([1957] 1964) 'Interlingual word taboo', in D. Hymes (ed.) *Language in Culture and Society: A Reader in Linguistics and Anthropology*. New York: Harper and Row.

Haiman, J. (1994) 'Ritualization and the development of language', in W. Pagliuca (ed.) *Perspectives on Grammaticalization*. Amsterdam: John Benjamins.

Haiman, J. (1997) 'Repetition and identity', *Lingua*, 100: 57–70.

Hall, R. A. (Jnr) (1966) *Pidgin and Creole Languages*. Ithaca: Cornell University Press.

Halliday, M. A. K. (1978) *Language as Social Semiotic: The Social Interpretation of Language and Meaning*. Sydney: Edward Arnold.

Halliday, M. A. K. (1989) *Spoken and Written Language*. Oxford: Oxford University Press.

Halliday, M. A. K. (1993) *Writing Science: Literacy and Discursive Power*. Bristol, PA: Falmer Press.

Halliday, M. A. K. (1994a) 'Spoken and written modes of meaning', in D. Graddol and O. Boyd-Barrett (eds) *Media Texts: Authors and Readers*. Clevedon: Multilingual Matters/Open University Press.

Halliday, M. A. K. (1994b) *An Introduction to Functional Grammar*, 2nd edn. London: Edward Arnold.

Halliday, M. A. K. and Hasan, R. (1976) *Cohesion in English*. London: Longman.

Halliday, M. A. K. and Hasan, R. (1985) *Language, Context and Text: Aspects of Language in a Social-Semiotic Perspective*. Victoria, Australia: Deakin University Press.

Hammersley, M. (1996) 'On the foundations of critical discourse analysis', *Occasional Papers 42*. Centre for Language and Education, University of Southampton.

Hammerström, G. (1980) *Australian English: Its Origin and Status*. Hamburg: Buske.

Hansegård, N. E. (1968) *Tvåspråkighet eller halvspråkighet?* Stockholm: Aldus/Banniers.

Hansen, M. L. (1938) 'The problem of the third generation immigrant'. Reprinted in W. Sollors. H. B. Cabot and A. M. Cabot (eds) (1996) *Theories of Ethnicity: A Classical Reader*. Basingstoke: Macmillan.

Harré, R. and Stearns, P. (eds) (1995) *Discursive Psychology in Practice*. London: Sage.

Harris, J. (1993) 'The grammar of Irish English', in J. Milroy and L. Milroy (eds) *Real English: The Grammar of English Dialects in the British Isles*. London: Longman.

Harries, P. (1995) 'Discovering languages: the historical origins of standard Tsonga in southern Africa', in R. Mesthrie (ed.) *Language and Social History. Studies in South African Sociolinguistics*. Cape Town/Johannesburg: David Phillips.

Harris, R. (1981) *The Language Myth*. London: Duckworth.

Harrison, G. A., Tanner, J. M., Pillbeam, D. R. and Baker, P. T. (1988) *Human Biology: An Introduction to Human Evolution, Variation, Growth and Adaptability*. Oxford: Oxford University Press.

Harvey, K. and Shalom, C. (eds) (1997) *Language and Desire: Encoding Sex, Romance and Intimacy*. London: Routledge.

Haugen, E. (1962) 'Schizoglossia and the linguistic norm', in *Thirteenth Annual Round Table Meeting* (Georgetown University Monograph Series on Language and Linguistics, no. 15). Washington, DC: Georgetown University Press.

Haugen, E. (1966a) 'Semicommunication: the language gap in Scandinavia', *Sociological Enquiry*, 36: 280–97.

Haugen, E. (1966b) 'Linguistics and language planning', in J. A. Fishman (ed.) *Readings in the Sociology of Language*. The Hague: Mouton.

Haugen, E. (1972) *The Ecology of Language*. Selected and introduced by A. S. Dil. Stanford, CA: Stanford University Press.

Hawkins, E. (1984) *Awareness of Language: An Introduction*. Cambridge: Cambridge University Press.

Headland, T. N. (1996) 'Missionaries and social justice: are they part of the problem or part of the solution?', *Missiology*, 24: 167–78.

Heath, S. B. (1982) 'What no bedtime story means: narrative skills at home and school', *Language and Society*, 11: 49–76.

Heath, S. B. (1983) *Ways with Words: Language, Life and Work in Communities and Classrooms*. Cambridge: Cambridge University Press.

Hechter, M. and Opp, K-D. (eds) (2001) *Social Norms*. New York: Sage.

Hegel, G. W. F. (1974) *Hegel: The Essential Writings*. London: Harper and Row.

Hellinger, M. and Bussmann, H. (eds) (2001) *Gender across Languages: The Linguistic Representation of Women and Men*, vol. I. Amsterdam: John Benjamins.

Hellinger, M. and Bussman, H. (eds) (2002) *Gender across Languages*, vol. II. Amsterdam: John Benjamins.

Hellinger, M. and Bussman, H. (eds) (2003) *Gender across Languages: The Linguistic Representation of Women and Men*, vol. III. Amsterdam: John Benjamins.

Heritage, J. C. (1984) *Garfinkel and Ethnomethodology*. Cambridge: Polity.

Herring, S. C. (ed.) (1996) *Computer-mediated Communication: Linguistic, Social and Cross-cultural Perspectives*. Amsterdam: John Benjamins.

Hickey, R. (ed.) (2003) *Legacies of Colonial English: The Study of Transported Dialects*. Cambridge: Cambridge University Press.

Hill, J. (1993) '*Hasta la vista baby* – Anglo Spanish in the American Southwest', *Critique of Anthropology*, 13: 145–76.

Hill, J. (1995) 'The voices of Don Gabriel: responsibility and self in modern Mexican narrative', in D. Tedlock and B. Mannheim (eds) *The Dialogic Emergence of Culture*. Urbana: University of Illinois Press.

Hirsch, Jr, E. D. (1987) *Cultural Literacy: What Every American Needs to Know*. Boston, MA: Houghton Mifflin.

Hockey, S. (1998) 'Textual databases', in J. Lawler and H. Arister Dry (eds) *Using Computers in Linguistics: A Practical Guide*. London: Routledge.

Hodge, R. and Kress, G. (1993) *Language as Ideology*, 2nd edn. London: Routledge and Kegan Paul.

Holm, J. (2000) *An Introduction to Pidgins and Creoles*. Cambridge: Cambridge University Press.

Holmes, J. (1995) *Women, Men and Politeness*. New York: Longman.

Holmes, J. (1996) 'Women's role in language change: a place for quantification', in N. Warner, J. Ahlers, L. Bilmes, M. Oliver, S. Wertheim and M. Chen (eds) *Gender and Belief Systems: Proceedings of the Fourth Berkeley Women and Language Conference*, 19–21 April 1996. Berkeley, CA: Berkeley Women and Language Group.

Holmes, J. and Meyerhoff, M. (eds) (2003) *The Handbook of Language and Gender*. Oxford: Blackwell Publishing.

Hopper, P. J. and Traugott, E. C. (1993) *Grammaticalization*. Cambridge: Cambridge University Press.

Horvath, B. (1985) *Variation in Australian English: The Sociolects of Sydney*. Cambridge: Cambridge University Press.

Hudson, R. A. (1996) *Sociolinguistics*. Cambridge: Cambridge University Press.

Hutton, C. (1998) *Linguistics and the Third Reich: Mother Tongue Fascism, Race and the Science of Language*. London: Routledge.

Hymes, D. (1972) 'Models of the interaction of language and social life', in J. J. Gumperz and D. Hymes (eds) *Directions in Sociolinguistics*. Oxford: Basil Blackwell.

Hymes, D. (1974) *Foundations in Sociolinguistics: An Ethnographic Approach*. Philadelphia: University of Pennsylvania Press.

Hymes, D. (1981) *In Vain I Tried To Tell You: Essays in Native American Ethnopoetics*. Philadelphia: University of Pennsylvania Press.

Hymes, D. (2003) *Now I Know Only So Far: Essays in Ethnopoetics*. Lincoln: University of Nebraska Press

Iedema, R. (2001) 'Analysing film and television: a social semiotic account of Hospital, an Unhealthy Business', in G. E. Hawisher and C. L. Selfe (eds) *Global Literacies and the World Wide Web*. London: Routledge.

Isaacs, M. (1999) 'Haredi, haymish and frim: Yiddish vitality and language choice in a transnational, multilingual community', *International Journal of the Sociology of Language*, 138: 9–30.

Jakobson, R. (1960) 'Closing statement: linguistics and poetics', in T. A. Sebeok (ed.) *Style and Language*. Cambridge, MA: MIT Press.

James, C. and Garrett, P. (eds) (1991) *Language Awareness in the Classroom*. London: Longman.

Janda, R. D. and Auger, J. (1992) 'Quantitative evidence, qualitative hypercorrection, sociolinguistic variables – and French speakers', *Language and Communication*, 12: 195–236.

Janks, H. (2000) 'Domination, access, diversity and design: a synthesis for critical literacy education', *Educational Review*, 52 (2): 175–86.

Janks, H. (ed.) (1993) *Critical Language Awareness Series*. Johannesburg: Hodder and Stoughton and Witwatersrand University Press.

Jernudd, B. H. (1973) 'Language planning as a type of language treatment', in J. Rubin and R. Shuy (eds) *Language Planning: Current Issues*. Washington, DC: Georgetown University Press.

Johnson, S. (2002) 'On the origin of linguistic norms: orthography, ideology and the first constitutional challenge to the 1996 reform of German', *Language in Society*, 31: 549–76.

Johnson, S. and Meinhof, U. H. (eds) (1997) *Language and Masculinity*. Oxford: Blackwell Publishers.

Jones, C., Turner, J. and Street, B. (eds) (1999) *Students Writing in the University: Cultural and Epistemological Issues*. Amsterdam: John Benjamins.

Joseph, J. E. (1987) *Eloquence and Power: The Rise of Language Standards and Standard Languages*. Oxford: Basil Blackwell.

Jourdan, A. C. (1991) 'Pidgins and creoles: the blurring of categories', *Annual Review of Anthropology*, 20: 187–209.

Kachru, B. (ed.) (1992) *The Other Tongue: English across Cultures*, 2nd edn. Urbana Champaign: University of Illinois Press.

Kachru, B. B. (1986) *The Alchemy of English*. Oxford: Pergamon.

Kachru, B. B. (1988) 'The sacred cows of English', *English Today*, 4(4): 3–8.

Kaplan, R. B. and Baldauf, R. B. (1997) *Language Planning: From Practice to Theory*. Clevedon: Multilingual Matters.

Kempson, R. (2001) 'Pragmatics: language and communication', in M. Aronoff and J. Rees-Miller (eds) *The Handbook of Linguistics*. Oxford: Blackwell Publishers.

Kerswill, P. (1996) 'Children, adolescents, and language change', *Language Variation and Change*, 8: 177–202.

Kerswill, P. and Williams, A. (2000) 'Creating a new town koinè: children and language change in Milton Keynes', *Language in Society*, 29: 65–115.

Kiesling, S. (2002) 'Playing the straight man: displaying and maintaining heterosexuality in discourse', in K. Campbell-Kibler, R. Podesva, S. J. Roberts and A. Wong (eds) (2001) *Language and Sexuality: Contesting Meaning in Theory and Practice*. Stanford, CA: CSLI Publications.

Klein, W. (1974) *Variation in der Sprache: Ein Verfahren zu ihrer Beschreibung*. Kronberg, Ts: Scriptor.

Klein, W. and Dittmar, N. (1979) *Developing Grammars: The Acquisition of German by Foreign Workers*. Heidelberg and New York: Springer.

Klima, E. and Bellugi, U. (1979) *The Signs of Language*. Cambridge, MA: Harvard University Press.

Kloss, H. (1967) 'Abstand languages and Ausbau languages', *Anthropological Linguistics*, 9: 29–41.

Kloss, H. (1969) *Research Possibilities on Group Bilingualism: A Report*. Quebec: International Center for Research on Bilingualism.

Kloss, H. (1978) *Die Entwicklung neuer germanischer Kultursprachen seit 1800*. Düsseldorf: Pädagogischer Verlag Schwann.

Knowles, G. O. (1978) 'The nature of phonological variables in Scouse', in P. Trudgill (ed.) *Sociolinguistic Patterns in British English*. London: Edward Arnold.

Kramsch, C. (1993) *Context and Culture in Language Teaching*. Oxford: Oxford University Press.

Krashen, S. D. (1987) *Principles and Practice in Second Language Acquisition*. London: Prentice-Hall International.

Krauss, M. (1992) 'The world's languages in crisis', *Language*, 68: 4–10.

Kress, G. (1996) 'Representational resources and the production of subjectivity: questions for the theoretical development of critical discourse analysis in a multicultural society', in C. Caldas-Coulthard and M. Coulthard (eds) *Texts and Practices*. London: Routledge.

Kress, G. (1998) 'Visual and verbal modes of representation in electronically mediated communication: the potentials of new forms of text', in I. Snyder (ed.) *Page to Screen*. London: Routledge.

Kress, G. (2000) 'Multimodality', in B. Cope and M. Kalantzis (eds) *Multiliteracies: Literacy Learning and the Design of Social Futures*. London: Routledge.

Kress, G. (2001) 'Critical sociolinguistics', in R. Mesthrie (ed.) *Concise Encyclopaedia of Sociolinguistics*. Amsterdam: Elsevier.

Kress, G. (2003) *Literacy in the New Media Age*. London: Routledge.

Kress, G. and Hodge, R. (1979) *Language as Ideology*. London: Routledge.

Kress, G. and Van Leeuwen, T. (1996) *Reading Images: The Grammar of Visual Design*. London: Routledge.

Kress, G. and Van Leeuwen, T. (2001) *Multimodal Discourse: The Modes and Media of Contemporary Communication*. London: Hodder.

Krishnamurthy, R. (1996) 'Ethnic, racial and tribal: the language of racism?', in C. Caldas-Coulthard and M. Coulthard (eds) *Texts and Practices: Readings in Critical Discourse Analysis*. London: Routledge.

Kristeva, J. (1986) 'Word, dialogue and the novel', in T. Moi (ed.) *The Kristeva Reader*. Oxford: Basil Blackwell.

Kroch, A. (1996) 'Dialect and style in the speech of upper class Philadelphia', in G. Guy et al. (eds) *Towards a Social Science of Language: Papers in Honor of William Labov, Vol. 1: Variation and Change in Language and Society*. Amsterdam: John Benjamins.

Kulick, D. (2000) 'Gay and lesbian language', *Annual Review of Anthropology*, 29: 243–85.

Labov, W. (1963) 'The social motivation of a sound change', *Word*, 19: 273–309.

Labov, W. (1965) 'On the mechanism of linguistic change', *Georgetown Monographs on Language and Linguistics*, 18: 91–114.

Labov, W. (1966) *The Social Stratification of English in New York City*. Washington, DC: Center for Applied Linguistics.

Labov, W. (1972a) *Sociolinguistic Patterns*. Philadelphia: University of Pennsylvania Press.

Labov, W. (1972b) 'Some principles of linguistic methodology', *Language in Society*, 1: 97–120.

Labov, W. (1972c) *Language in the Inner City: Studies in Black English Vernacular*. Philadelphia: University of Philadelphia Press.

Labov, W. (1975) 'On the use of the present to explain the past', in L. Heilmann (ed.) *Proceedings of the 11th International Congress of Linguists*. Bologna: Il Mulino.

Labov, W. (1982) 'Objectivity and commitment in linguistic science: the case of the Black English trial in Ann Arbor', *Language in Society*, 11: 165–201.

Labov, W. (1989) 'The child as linguistic historian', *Language Variation and Change*, 1: 85–7.

Labov, W. (1994) *Principles of Linguistic Change. Volume 1: External Factors*. Oxford: Basil Blackwell.

Labov, W. (2001) *Principles of Linguistic Change. Volume II: Social Factors*. Oxford: Basil Blackwell.

Labov, W. and Fanshel, D. (1977) *Therapeutic Discourse: Psychotherapy as Conversation*. New York: Academic Press.

Labov, W. and Harris, W. A. (1986) 'De facto segregation of black and white vernaculars', in D. Sankoff (ed.) *Diversity and Diachrony*. Amsterdam: John Benjamins.

Labov, W., Cohen, P., Robins, C. and Lewis, J. (1968) *A Study of the Non-Standard English of Negro and Puerto Rican Speakers in New York City. Cooperative Research Project 3288*, 2 vols. Philadelphia: US Regional Survey (Linguistics Laboratory, University of Pennsylvania).

Ladefoged, P. (2001) *A Course in Phonetics*, 4th edn. New York. Harcourt Brace.

Lakoff, R. (1975) *Language and Woman's Place*. New York: Harper and Row.

Lakoff, R. (2000) *The Language War*. New York: Columbia University Press.

Lambert, W. E., Hodgson, R., Gardner, C. and Fillenbaum, S. (1960) 'Evaluational reactions to spoken languages', *Journal of Abnormal and Social Psychology*, 60: 44–51.

Lass, R. and Wright, S. (1986) 'Endogeny versus contact: "Afrikaans influence" on South African English', *English World Wide*, 7: 201–24.

Latour, B. and Woolgar, S. (1986) *The Social Construction of Scientific Facts*, 2nd edn. Princeton: Princeton University Press.

Lave, J. and Wenger, E. (1991) *Situated Learning: Legitimate Peripheral Participation*. Cambridge: Cambridge University Press.

Le Page, R. B. and Tabouret-Keller, A. (1985) *Acts of Identity: Creole-based Approaches to Language and Ethnicity*. Cambridge: Cambridge University Press.

Lea, M. and Street, B. (1998) 'Student writing in higher education: an academic literacies approach', *Studies in Higher Education*, 11: 182–99.

Leap, W. L. (1983) 'Linguistics and written discourse in particular languages: contrastive studies: English and American Indian Languages', *Annual Review of Applied Linguistics*, 3: 24–37.

Leap, W. L. (1996) *Word's Out: Gay Men's English*. Minneapolis: University of Minnesota Press.

Leap, W. L. (ed.) (1995) *Beyond the Lavender Lexicon: Authenticity, Imagination and Appropriation in Gay and Lesbian Languages*. Newark: Gordon and Breach.

Leech, G. (1983) *Principles of Pragmatics*. London: Longman.

Leith, D. (1997) *A Social History of English*, 2nd edn. London and New York: Routledge.

Lemke, (1989) 'Semantics and social values', *Word*, 40: 37–50.

Leonard, S. A. ([1929] 1962) *The Doctrine of Correctness in English Usage, 1700–1800*. New York: Russell and Russell.

Leont'ev, A. N. (1981) *Problems of the Development of Mind*. Moscow: Progress.

Lepper, G. (2000) *Categories in Text and Talk*. London: Sage.

Levinson, S. (1983) *Pragmatics*. Cambridge: Cambridge University Press.

Lewis, E. G. (1983) 'Implementation of language planning in the Soviet Union', in J. Cobarrubias and J. A. Fishman (eds) *Progress in Language Planning*. Berlin: Mouton.

Lieven, E. V. M. (1994) 'Crosslinguistic and crosscultural aspects of language addressed to children', in C. Galloway and B. J. Richards (eds) *Input and Interaction in Language Acquisition*. Cambridge: Cambridge University Press.

Lightbrown, P. and Spada, N. (1999) *How Languages are Learned*, 2nd edn. Oxford: Oxford University Press.

Livia, A. and Hall, K. (eds) (1997) *Queerly Phrased: Language, Gender and Sexuality*. New York: Oxford University Press.

Lucas, C. (ed.) (2001) *The Sociolinguistics of Sign Language*. Cambridge: Cambridge University Press.

Luke, A. and Walton, C. (1994) 'Critical reading: teaching and assessing', in T. Husen and T. N. Postlethwaite *International Encyclopaedia of education*, 2nd edn. Oxford: Pergamon.

Lynch, M. (1993) *Scientific Practice and Ordinary Action: Ethnomethodology and Social Studies of Science*. Cambridge: Cambridge University Press.

Lyons, J. (1970) *New Horizons in Linguistics*. Harmondsworth: Penguin.

Lyotard, J. F. (1984) *The Postmodern Condition: A Report on Knowledge*. Manchester: Manchester University Press.

MacArthur, T. (1998) *The English Languages*. Cambridge: Cambridge University Press.

McCafferty, K. (2001) *Ethnicity in Language Change: English in (London) Derry Northern Ireland*. Amsterdam: John Benjamins.

McIlvenny, P. (ed.) (2002) *Talking Gender and Sexuality*. Amsterdam: John Benjamins.

Maclure, M. (1993) 'Talking in class: four rationales for the rise of oracy in the UK', in B. Stierer and J. Maybin (eds) *Language, Literacy and Learning in Educational Practice*. Clevedon: Multilingual Matters/ Open University Press.

Maclure, M., Phillips, T. and Wilkinson, A. M. (1988) *Oracy Matters*. Milton Keynes: Open University Press.

Macnamara, J. (1966) *Bilingualism and Primary Education: A Study of Irish Experience*. Edinburgh: Edinburgh University Press.

Malik, B. (1972) *Language of the Underworld of West Bengal*. Research Series 76, Calcutta, India: Sanskrit College.

Malinowski, B. (1923) 'The problem of meaning in primitive languages'. Supplement to C. K. Ogden and I. A. Richards *The Meaning of Meaning*. London: Routledge and Kegan Paul.

Malinowski, B. (1935) *Coral Gardens and their Magic*, vol. 2. London: Allen and Unwin.

Maltz, D. N. and Borker, R. A. (1982) 'A cultural approach to male-female miscommunication', in J. J. Gumperz (ed.) *Language and Social Identity*. Cambridge: Cambridge University Press.

Martin, J. R. (2001) 'Language, register and genre', in A. Burns and C. Coffin (eds) *Analysing English in a Global Context*. London: Routledge.

Master, P., Schumann, J. and Sokolik, M. E. (1989) 'The experimental creation of a pidgin language', *Journal of Pidgin and Creole Linguistics*, 4: 37–63.

Mattheier, K. J. (1994) 'Theorie der Sprachinsel: Voraussetzungen und Strukturierungen', in N. Berend and K. J. Mattheier (eds) *Sprachinselforschung*. Frankfurt: Peter Lang.

Maybin. J. (1997) 'Story voices: the use of reported speech in 10–12 year olds' spontaneous narratives', in L. Thompson (ed.) *Children Talking: The Development of Pragmatic Confidence*. Clevedon: Multilingual Matters.

Maybin, J. (2003) 'Voices, intertextuality and induction into schooling', in S. Goodman, T. Lillis, J. Maybin and N. Mercer (eds) *Language, Literacy and Education: A Reader*. Stoke-on-Trent: Trentham.

Mead, G. H. (1934) *Mind, Self and Society*. Chicago: University of Chicago Press.

Mehan, H. (1979) *Learning Lessons: Social Organization in the Classroom.* Cambridge: Cambridge University Press.

Meillet, A. (1912) *Linguistique Historique et Linguistique Générale.* Paris: Champion.

Menezes de Souza, L. M. T. (2003) 'Literacy and dreamspace: multimodal texts in a Brazilian indigenous community', in S. Goodman, T. Lillis, J. Maybin and N. Mercer (eds) *Language, Literacy and Education: a Reader.* Stoke on Trent: Trentham Books.

Mesthrie, R. (1992) *English in Language Shift: The History, Structure and Sociolinguistics of South African Indian English.* Cambridge: Cambridge University Press.

Mesthrie, R., Swann, J., Deumert, A. and Leap, W. (2000) *Introducing Sociolinguistics.* Edinburgh: Edinburgh University Press.

Mesthrie, R. (ed.) (2001) *Concise Encyclopedia of Sociolinguistics.* Amsterdam: Elsevier.

Miller, C. R. (1984) 'Genre as social action', *Quarterly Journal of Speech,* 70: 157–78.

Miller, J. (1993) 'The grammar of Scottish English', in J. Milroy and L. Milroy (eds) *Real English: The Grammar of English Dialects in the British Isles.* London: Longman.

Milroy, J. (1992) *Linguistic Variation and Change. On the Historical Sociolinguistics of Language.* Oxford: Basil Blackwell.

Milroy, J. and Milroy, L. (1985) 'Linguistic change: social network and speaker innovation', *Journal of Linguistics,* 21: 339–84.

Milroy, J. and Milroy, L. (1992) 'Social network and social class: towards an integrated sociolinguistic model', *Language in Society,* 21: 1–26.

Milroy, J. and Milroy, L. (1999) *Authority in Language: Investigating Standard English,* 3rd edn. London: Routledge.

Milroy, J., Milroy, L. and Hartley, S. (1994) 'Local and supra-local change in British English: the case of glottalisation', *English Worldwide,* 15: 1–33.

Milroy, L. (1987a) *Language and Social Networks,* 2nd edn. Oxford: Basil Blackwell.

Milroy, L. (1987b) *Observing and Analysing Natural Language. A Critical Account of Sociolinguistic Method.* Oxford: Blackwell.

Milroy, L. and Gordon, M. (2003) *Sociolinguistics: Method and Interpretation.* Oxford: Blackwell Publishing.

Mitchell, A. G. and Delbridge, A. (1965) *The Pronunciation of English in Australia.* Sydney: Angus and Robertson.

Morrish, L. and Leap, W. (2003) 'Sex talk: language, desire, identity and beyond'. Paper presented at the 10th Annual Lavender Languages and Linguistics Conference, American University, Washington, DC. Available at: http://www.american.edu/cas/anthro/lavenderlanguages/Liz&BillFINAL.html.

Mufwene, S. (1996) 'The Founder Principle in Creole genesis', *Diachronica*, 13: 83–134.

Mufwene, S. (2001) *The Ecology of Language Evolution*. Cambridge: Cambridge University Press.

Mühlhäusler, P. (1996) *Linguistic Ecology: Language Change and Linguistic Imperialism in the Pacific Region*. London: Routledge.

Mühlhäusler, P. and Harré, R. (1990) *Pronouns and People: The Linguistic Construction of Social and Personal Identity*. Oxford: Blackwell.

Mumby, D. K. and Clair, R. P. (1997) 'Organizational discourse', in T. van Dijk (ed.) *Discourse as Social Interaction*. London: Sage.

Myers-Scotton, C. (1993a) *Duelling Languages: Grammatical Structure in Codeswitching*. Oxford: Clarendon.

Myers-Scotton, C. (1993b) *Social Motivations for Codeswitching: Evidence from Africa*. Oxford: Clarendon.

Neustupný, J. V. (1983) 'Towards a paradigm for language planning', *Language Planning Newsletter*, 9: 1–4.

New London Group (2000) 'A pedagogy of multiliteracies: designing social futures', in B. Cope and M. Kalantzis (eds) *Multiliteracies: Literacy, Learning and the Design of Social Futures*. London: Routledge.

Newman, D., Griffin, P. and Cole, M. (1989) *The Construction Zone: Working for Cognitive Change in School*. Cambridge: Cambridge University Press.

Newman, P. and Ratliff, M. (eds) (2001) *Linguistic Fieldwork*. Cambridge: Cambridge University Press.

Newton, M. (2003) *Savage Girls and Wild Boys: A History of Feral Children*. London: Faber and Faber.

Nida, E. (1949) *Morphology*. Ann Arbor: University of Michigan Press.

Niedzielski, N. A. and Preston, D. R. (2000) *Folk Linguistics*. Berlin and New York: Mouton de Gruyter.

Norton, B. (2000) *Identity and Language Learning: Gender, Ethnicity and Educational Change*. London: Longman.

Ochs, E. (1979) 'Transcription as theory', in E. Ochs and B. B. Schieffelin (eds) *Developmental Pragmatics*. New York: Academic Press.

Ochs, E. (1997) 'Narrative', in T. Van Dijk (ed.) *Discourse as Structure and Process: Discourse Studies: A Multidisciplinary Introduction*, vol. 1. London: Sage.

Odgen, C. K. (1938) *Basic English*. London: Kegan Paul.

Omi, M. and Winant, H. (1994) 'On the theoretical status of the concept of race', in C. McCarthy and W. Crichlow (eds) *Race Identity and Representation in Education*. New York and London: Routledge.

Ong, W. (1982) *Orality and Literacy: The Technologizing of the Word*. London: Routledge.

Orton, H., Sanderson, S. and Widdowson, J. (1978) *The Linguistic Atlas of England*. London: Croom Helm.

Pandit, P. (1972) *India as a Sociolinguistic Area*. Poona: University of Poona.

Partridge, E. ([1961] 1974) *A Dictionary of Slang and Unconventional English: Colloquialisms and Catch-phrases, Solecisms and Catachreses, Nicknames, Vulgarisms and such Americanisms as have been Naturalized*. London: Routledge and Kegan Paul.

Paulston, C. B., Pow, C. C. and Connerty, M. C. (1993) 'Language regenesis: a conceptual overview of language revival, revitalisation and reversal', *Journal of Multilingual and Multicultural Development*, 14: 275–86.

Pauwels, A. (1998) *Women Changing Language*. London: Longman.

Peirce, C. S. (ed.) (1940) 'Logic as semiotic: the theory of signs', in J. Buchler (ed.) *Philosophical Writings of Peirce: Selected Writings*. London: Routledge and Kegan Paul.

Pennycook, A. (1994) *The Cultural Politics of English as an International Language*. London: Longman.

Pennycook, A. (2002) 'Mother tongues, governmentality and protectionism', *International Journal of the Sociology of Language*, 154: 11–28.

Phillipson, R. (1992) *Linguistic Imperialism*. Oxford: Oxford University Press.

Piaget, J. (1935) *The Language and Thought of the Child*, trans. M. Gabin. New York: Harcourt Brace.

Pike, K. (1947) *Phonemics: A Technique for Reducing Languages to Writing*. Ann Arbor: University of Michigan Press.

Pike, K. (1967) *Language in Relation to the Unified Theory of the Structure of Human Behaviour*, 2nd edn. The Hague: Mouton.

Pillai, S. (1968) 'Tamil Dialect Notes – Fishermen of Kanyakumari', *Anthropological Linguistics*, 10: 1–10.

Platt, J. T. (1975) 'The Singapore English Speech continuum and its basilect "Singlish" as a creoloid', *Anthropological Linguistics*, 17: 313–74.

Platt, J. T. (1977) 'A mode for polyglossia and multilingualism (with special reference to Singapore and Malaysia)', *Language in Society*, 6: 361–79.

Platt, J. T., Weber, H. and Ho, M. L. (1984) *The New Englishes*. London: Routledge.

Pomerantz, A. (1984) 'Agreeing and disagreeing with assessments: some features of preferred/dispreferred turn shapes', in J. M. Atkinson and J. Heritage (eds) *Structures of Social Action: Studies in Conversation Analysis*. Cambridge: Cambridge University Press.

Poplack, S. (1980) 'Sometimes I'll start a sentence in English y termino en español: towards a typology of code-switching', *Linguistics*, 18: 581–618.

Poplack, S., Sankoff, D. and Miller, C. (1988) 'The social correlates and linguistic processes of lexical borrowing and assimilation', *Linguistics*, 26: 47–104.

Potter, J. and Wetherell, M. (1987) *Discourse and Social Psychology: Beyond Attitudes and Behaviour*. London: Sage.

Poulantzas, T. M. ([1973] 1984) 'On Social Classes', in A. Giddens and D. Held (eds) *Classes, Power and Conflict: Classical and Contemporary Debates*. London: Macmillian.

Preston, D. R. (1989) *Perceptual Dialectology: Nonlinguists' Views of Areal Linguistics*. Dordrecht: Foris Publications.

Preston, D. R. (1992) 'Talking black and talking white: a study in variety imitation', in J. H. Hall, N. Doane and D. Ringler (eds) *Old English and New: Studies in the Honor of Frederic G. Cassidy*. New York: Garland Publishing.

Propp, V. ([1928] 1968) *Morphology of the Folktale*. Austin: University of Texas Press.

Quirk, R., Geenbaum, S., Leech, G. and Svartik, J. (1985) *A Comprehensive Grammar of the English Language*. London: Longman.

Rampton, B. (1995) *Crossing: Language and Ethnicity among Adolescents*. London: Longman.

Rampton, B. (2002) 'Ritual and foreign language practices at school', *Language in Society*, 31: 491–525.

Ray P. S. (1963) *Language Standardization*. The Hague: Mouton.

Rayfield, J. R. (1970) *The Languages of a Bilingual Community*. The Hague: Mouton.

Reid, S. (1987) *Working with Statistics*. Cambridge: Polity Press.

Reisgl, M. and Wodak, R. (2000) *The Semiotics of Racism: Approaches in Critical Discourse Analysis*. Vienna: Passagen.

Rickford, J. R. (1986) 'The need for new approaches to social class analysis in sociolinguistics', *Language and Communication*, 6: 215–21.

Rickford, J. R. (1987) *Dimensions of a Creole Continuum: History, Texts and Linguistic Analysis of Guyanese Creole*. Stanford: Stanford University Press.

Robb, T., Ross, S., and Shortreed, I. (1986) 'Salience of feedback on error and its effect on EFL writing quality', *TESOL Quarterly*, 20: 83–93.

Roberts, C., Davies, E. And Jupp, T. (1992) *Language and Discrimination*. London: Longman

Rogers, E. M. (1978) *Diffusion of Innovations*. New York: Free Press.

Romaine, S. (1982) *Socio-historical Linguistics: Its Status and Methodology*. Cambridge: Cambridge University Press.

Romaine, S. (1984) 'The sociolinguistic history of t/d deletion', *Folia Linguistica Historica*, 2: 221–5.

Romaine. S. (1998) *Communicating Gender*. Mahwah, NJ: Lawrence Erlbaum.

Ronkin, M. and Karn, H. E. (1999) 'Mock Ebonics: linguistic racism in parodies of Ebonics on the Internet', *Journal of Sociolinguistics*, 3: 360–80.

Rosewarne, D. (1994) 'Estuary English: tomorrow's RP?', *English Today*, 10: 3–8.

Ross, A. (1959) 'U and non-U: an essay in sociological linguistics', in N. Mitford (ed.) *Noblesse Oblige*. Harmondsworth: Penguin.

Rubin, J. (1977) 'New insights into the nature of language change offered by language planning', in B. G. Blount and M. Sabches, *Sociocultural Dimensions of Language Change*. New York: Academic Press.

Rubin, J. and Jernudd, B. H. (ed.) (1971) *Can Language Be Planned? Sociolinguistic Theory and Practice for Developing Nations*. Honolulu: University Press of Hawaii.

Russell, D. (1997) 'Rethinking genre in school and society: an activity theory analysis', *Written Communication*, 14: 504–54.

Sacks, H. (1972) 'On the analyzability of stories by children', in J. J. Gumperz and D. Hymes (eds) ([1972] 1986) *Directions in Sociolinguistics: The Ethnography of Communication*. Oxford: Basil Blackwell.

Sacks, H., Schegloff, E. A. and Jefferson, G. (1974) 'A simplest systematics for the oganisation of turn-taking for conversation', *Language*, 50: 696–735.

Sampson, G. (1985) *Writing Systems*. London: Hutchinson.

Sapir, E. (1921) *Language*. New York: Harcourt, Brace, World.

Sarangi, S. and Roberts, C. (1999) *Talk Work and Institutional Order: Discourse in Medical Mediation and Management Settings*. Berlin: Mouton de Gruyter.

Saussure, F. de ([1916] 1959) *Course in General Linguistics*, ed. C. Bally and A. Sechehaye, trans. W. Baskin. New York: McGraw Hill.

Saville-Troike, M. (2003) *The Ethnography of Communication: An Introduction*, 2nd edn. Oxford: Blackwell Publishing.

Schegloff, E. A. (1997) 'Whose text, whose context?', *Discourse and Society*, 8: 165–87.

Schegloff, E. A. and Sacks, H. (1973) 'Opening up closings', *Semiotica*, 8: 289–327.

Schegloff, E. A., Jefferson, G. and Sacks, H. (1977) 'The preference for self-correction in the organization of repair in conversation', *Language*, 53: 361–82.

Scherer, K. R. and Giles, H. (eds) (1979) *Social Markers in Speech*. Cambridge: Cambridge University Press.

Schieffelin, B. B., Woolard, K. A. and Kroskrity, P. V. (eds) (1998) *Language Ideologies: Practice and Theory*. Oxford: Oxford University Press.

Schiffman, H. (1996) *Linguistic Culture and Language Policy*. London: Routledge.

Schiffrin, D. (2001) 'Language, experience and history: 'What happened' in World War II', *Journal of Sociolinguistics*, 5: 323–52.

Schlobinski, P., Kohn, G. and Ludewigt, I. (1993) *Jugendsprache – Fiktion und Wirklichkeit*. Opladen: Westdeutscher Verlag.

Schumann, J. (1974) 'Implication of pidginisation and creolisation for the study of adult second language acquisition', in R. C. Gringas (ed.) *Second Language Acquisition and Foreign Language Teaching*. Arlington, VA: Center for Applied Linguistics.

Scollon, R. and Scollon, S. W. (1981) *Narrative, Literacy and Face in Interethnic Communication*. Norword, NJ: Ablex.

Scollon, R. and Scollon, S. W. (1995) *Intercultural Communication: A Discourse Approach*. Oxford: Blackwell.

Scribner, S. and Cole, M. (1981) *The Psychology of Literacy*. Cambridge, MA: Harvard University Press.

Searle, J. R. (1969) *Speech Acts: An Essay in the Philosophy of Language*. Cambridge: Cambridge University Press.

Searle, J. R. (1975) 'Indirect speech acts', in P. Cole and J. Morgan (eds) *Syntax and Semantics, 3: Speech Acts*. New York: Academic Press.

Sebba, M. (1993) *London Jamaican: Language Systems in Interaction*. London: Longman.

Sebba, M. (2001) 'Orthography', in R. Mesthrie (ed.) *Concise Encyclopedia of Sociolinguistics*. Amsterdam: Elsevier.

Selinker, L. (1972) 'Interlanguage', *International Review of Applied Linguistics*, 10: 209–30.

Sheldon, A. (1997) 'Talking power: girls, gender enculturation and discourse', in R. Wodak (ed.) *Gender and Discourse*. London: Sage.

Sherzer, J. (1977) 'The ethnography of speaking: a critical appraisal', in M. Saville-Troike (ed.) *Linguistics and Anthropology*. Washington, DC: Georgetown University Press.

Simpson, P. (1993) *Language, Ideology and Point of View*. London: Routledge.

Sinclair, J. (ed.) (1987) *Collins Cobuild English Language Dictionary*. London: Collins.

Sinclair, J. (ed.) (1991) *Corpus, Concordance, Collocation*. Oxford: Oxford University Press.

Sinclair, J. and Coulthard, M. (1975) *Towards an Analysis of Discourse: The English used by Teachers and Pupils*. Oxford: Oxford University Press.

Singh, R. (ed.) (1998) *The Native Speaker: Multilingual Perspectives*. New Delhi: Sage.

Skutnabb-Kangas, T. (1986) 'Multilingualism and the education of minority children', in R. Phillipson and T. Skutnabb-Kangas (eds) *Linguicism Rules in Education*. Roskilde, Denmark: Roskilde University Centre, Institute IV.

Skutnabb-Kangas, T. (ed.) (1995) *Multilingualism For All: European Studies on Multilingualism*. The Netherlands: Swets and Zeitlinger.

Skutnabb-Kangas, T. (2000) *Linguistic Genocide in Education or World-wide Diversity and Human Rights?* Mahwah, NJ: Erlbaum.

Smith, B. (1998) *Modernism's History: A Study in Twentieth-century Art and Ideas*. New Haven: Yale University Press.

Smith, P. M. (1985) *Language, the Sexes and Society*. Oxford: Basil Blackwell.

Smitherman, G. (2000) *Talkin' that Talk: Language Culture and Education in African America*. London: Routledge.

Smolicz, J. J. (1981) 'Core values and cultural identity', *Ethnic and Racial Studies*, 4: 75–90.

Spencer, A. (1996) *Phonology: Theory and Description*. Oxford: Blackwell.

Stewart, W. A. (1965) 'Urban negro speech: sociolinguistic factors affecting English teaching', in R. Shuy (ed.) *Social Dialects and Language Learning*. Champaign, IL: National Council for Teachers of English.

Street, B. (1984) *Literacy in Theory and Practice*. Cambridge: Cambridge University Press.

Street, B. (ed.) (1993) *Journal of Research in Reading* (Special edition) 16 (2).

Street, B. (ed.) (2001) *Literacy and Development*. London: Routledge.

Stubbs, M. (1986) *Educational Linguistics*. Oxford: Basil Blackwell.

Stubbs, M. (1996) *Texts and Corpus Analysis*. Oxford: Basil Blackwell.

Stubbs, M. (1997) 'Whorf's children: critical comments on Critical Discourse Analysis (CDA)', in A. Ryan and A. Wray (eds) *Evolving Models of Language*. Clevedon: British Association for Applied Linguistics and Multilingual Matters.

Swales, J. M. (1981) *Aspects of Article Introductions*. Birmingham, UK: University of Aston, Language Studies Unit.

Swales, J. M. (1990) *Genre Analysis: English in Academic and Research Settings*. Cambridge: Cambridge University Press.

Swales, J. M. (1998) *Other Floors Other Voices: A Textography of a Small University Building*. New Jersey: Lawrence Erlbaum.

Swann, J. (1998) 'Towards consensus? English in the national curriculum', in Kibee, D. (ed.) *Language Legislation and Linguistic Rights*. Amsterdam: John Benjamins.

Talbot, M. M. (1998) *Language and Gender: An Introduction*. Cambridge: Polity Press.

Tannen, D. (1984) *Conversational Style: Analysing Talk among Friends*. Norwood, NJ: Ablex.

Tannen, D. (1989) *Talking Voices: Repetition, Dialogue and Imagery in Conversational Discourse*. Cambridge: Cambridge University Press.

Tannen, D. (1990) *You Just Don't Understand: Women and Men in Conversation*. New York: William Morrow.

Tannen, D. (1993) 'The relativity of discourse strategies', in D. Tannen (ed.) *Gender and Conversational Interaction*. Oxford: Oxford University Press.

Tannen, D. and Wallat, C. (1993) 'Interactive frames and knowledge schemas in interaction: examples from a medical examination/interview', in D. Tannen (ed.) *Framing in Discourse*. New York: Oxford University Press.

Tauli, V. (1968) *Introduction to a Theory of Language Planning*. Uppsala: Almqvist and Wiksell.

Thomas, L. (1996) 'Variation in English Grammar', in D. Graddol, D. Leith and J. Swann (eds) *English: History, Diversity and Change*. London: Routledge.

Thomason, S. G. (2001) *Language Contact: An Introduction*. Edinburgh: Edinburgh University Press.

Thomason, S. G. and Kaufman, T. (1988) *Language Contact, Creolization and Genetic Linguistics*. Berkeley, CA: University of California Press.

Thompson, G. (1996) *Introducing Functional Grammar*. London: Arnold.

Thornburn, T. (1971) 'Cost-benefit analysis in language planning', in J. Rubin and B. H. Jernudd. (eds) *Can Language Be Planned? Sociolinguistic Theory and Practice for Developing Nations*. Honolulu: University Press of Hawaii.

Toulmin, S. (1958) *The Uses of Argument*. Cambridge: Cambridge University Press.

Toulmin, S., Rieke, R. and Janik, A. (1984) *An Introduction to Reasoning*, 2nd edn. London: Collier Macmillan.

Trask, R. L. (2000) *The Dictionary of Historical and Comparative Linguistics*. Edinburgh: Edinburgh University Press.

Troemel Ploetz, S. (1991) 'Selling the apolitical', *Discourse and Society*, 2: 489–502.

Trudgill, P. (1974a) 'Linguistic change and diffusion: description and explanation in sociolinguistic dialect geography', *Language in Society*, 3: 215–46.

Trudgill, P. (1974b) *The Social Differentiation of English in Norwich*. Cambridge: Cambridge University Press.

Trudgill, P. (1983) *On Dialect*. Oxford: Blackwell.

Trudgill, P. (1986) *Dialects in Contact*. Oxford: Blackwell.

Trudgill, P. (2000) *Sociolinguistics: An Introduction to Language and Society*, 4th edn. London: Penguin.

Trudgill, P. and Chambers, J. K. (1980) *Dialectology*. Cambridge: Cambridge University Press.

Turner, V. (1969) *The Ritual Process: Structure and Anti-structure*. Chicago: Aldine Publishing Co.

Upton, C., Parry, D. and Widdowson, J. D. A. (1994) *Survey of English Dialects: The Dictionary and Grammar*. London: Routledge.

van Dijk, T. (1993) *Discourse and Elite Racism*. London: Sage.

van Lier, L. (1996) *Interaction in the Language Curriculum: Awareness, Autonomy and Authenticity*. London: Longman.

van Lier, L. (2001) 'Constraints and resources in classroom talk: issues of equality and symmetry', in C. Candlin and N. Mercer (eds) *English Language Teaching in its Social Context: A Reader*. London: Routledge.

Varenes, F. (1996) *Language, Minorities and Human Rights*. The Hague: Nijhoff.

Voloshinov, V. N. ([1927] 1976) *Freudianism: A Marxist Critique*. New York: Academic Press.

Voloshinov, V. N. ([1929] 1973) *Marxism and the Philosophy of Language*. New York: Seminar Press.

Vygotsky, L. (1978) *Mind in Society: Development of Higher Psychological Processes*. Cambridge, MA: Harvard University Press.

Vygotsky, L. (1986) *Thought and Language*. Cambridge, MA: MIT Press.

Wales, K. (2001) *A Dictionary of Stylistics*, 2nd edn. London: Longman.

Wallerstein, I. (1974) *The Modern World-system, 1: Capitalist Agriculture and the Origins of the European world Economy in the Sixteenth Century*. New York: Academic Press.

Wallerstein, I. (1991) *Geopolitics and Geoculture*. Cambridge: Cambridge University Press.

Wasserman, S. and Faust, K. (1994) *Social Network Analysis: Methods and Applications*. Cambridge: Cambridge University Press.

Waters, M. (1991) 'Collapse and convergence in class theory: the return of the social in the analysis of stratification arrangements', *Theory and Society*, 20: 141–72.

Weedon, C. (1987) *Feminist Practice and Poststructuralist Theory*. Oxford: Basil Blackwell.

Weinreich, U. ([1953] 1968) *Languages in Contact*. The Hague: Mouton.

Weinreich, U. (1954) 'Is a structural dialectology possible?', *Word*, 10: 388–400.

Weinreich, U., Labov, W. and Herzog, M. (1968) 'Empirical foundations for a theory of language change', in W.P. Lehmann and Y. Makiel (eds) *Directions in Historical Linguistics*. Austin: University of Texas Press.

Weinstein, B. (1979) 'Language strategists: redefining political frontiers on the basis of linguistic choices', *World Politics*, 31: 345–64.

Wells, J. C. (1982a) *Accents of English 1: An Introduction*. Cambridge: Cambridge University Press.

Wells, J. C. (1982b) *Accents of English 2: The British Isles*. Cambridge: Cambridge University Press.

Wenger, E. (1998) *Communities of Practice: Learning, Meaning and Identity*. Cambridge: Cambridge University Press.

Wetherell, M. (1998) 'Positioning and interpretative repertoires: conversation analysis and post-structuralism in dialogue', *Discourse and Society*, 9: 387–412.

Wetherell, M., Taylor, S. and Yates, S. (2001) *Discourse, Theory and Practice*. London: Sage.

Whinnom, K. (1971) 'Linguistic hybridisation and the "special case" of pidgins and creoles', in D. Hymes (ed.) *Pidginisation and Creolisation of Languages*. Cambridge: Cambridge University Press.

Whorf, B. L. (1956) *Language, Thought and Reality: Selected Writings*. Cambridge, MA: MIT Press.

Widdowson, H. (1996) 'Discourse analysis: a critical view', *Language and Literature*, 4: 157–72.

Wiggershaus, R. (1994) *The Frankfurt School: Its History, Theories and Political Significance*. Cambridge: Polity Press.

Wilkinson, A. M. with Davies, A. and Atkinson, D. (1965) 'Spoken English', *Educational Review Occasional Publications, No. 2*. Birmingham: Birmingham University.

Wilkinson, A. M., Stratta, L. and Dudley, P. (1974) *The Quality of Listening*. Basingstoke: Macmillan.

Williams, R. (1975) *Ebonics: The True Language of Black folks*. St Louis, MO: Robert Louis and Associates.

Wilson, A. (2000) 'There's no escape from third-space theory', in D. Barton, M. Hamilton and R. Ivanic (eds) *Situated Literacies*. London: Routledge.

Wodak, R. (1996) *Disorders of Discourse*. London: Longman.

Wodak, R. (ed.) (1989) *Language, Power and Ideology: Studies in Political Discourse*. Amsterdam: John Benjamins.

Wodak, R. (ed.) (1992) *Language, Power and Ideology*. Oxford: Blackwell.

Wolfram W., Christian, D. and Adger, C. (1999) *Dialects in Schools and Communities*. Mahwah, NJ: Lawrence Erlbaum.

Wolfson, N. (1976) 'Speech events and natural speech: some implications for sociolinguistic methodology', *Language in Society*, 5: 189–209.

Wolfson, N. (1982) *CHP: The Conversational Historic Present in American English Narrative*. Dordrecht: Foris.

Wood, D., Bruner, J. and Ross, G. (1976) 'The role of tutoring in problem-solving', *Journal of Child Psychology and Psychiatry*, 17: 89–100.

Yates, S. J. (2001) 'Researching internet interaction: sociolinguistics and corpus analysis', in M. Wetherell, S. Taylor and S. J. Yates (eds) *Discourse as Data: A Guide for Analysis*. London: Sage Publications in association with The Open University.